A HODDER

CATHERINE MARSHALL CLASSICS

Adventures in Prayer
Light in My Darkest Night
Something More

Catherine Marshall Classics

ADVENTURES IN PRAYER
LIGHT IN MY DARKEST NIGHT
SOMETHING MORE

Hodder & Stoughton
LONDON SYDNEY AUCKLAND

British Library Cataloguing in Publication Data
A record for this book is available from the British Library

ISBN 0 340 72153 7

Printed and bound in Great Britain by
Mackays of Chatham PLC, Chatham, Kent

Hodder and Stoughton
A division of Hodder Headline PLC
338 Euston Road
London NW1 3BH

ADVENTURES IN PRAYER

Adventures in Prayer

Catherine Marshall

Hodder & Stoughton
LONDON SYDNEY AUCKLAND

CONTENTS

PROLOGUE

Admittance to the School of Prayer is by an entrance test with only two questions. The first one is: Are you in real need? The second is: Do you admit that you are helpless to handle that need?

Whatever I have learned about prayer has come as the result of times when I could answer a resounding *yes* to both questions. Looking back over my life, those times of need stand out like mountain peaks rather than, as one might suppose, valleys of despond. Peaks — because each time I learned something important about God — how real He is and how gloriously able to answer prayer.

In childhood one of those times of learning came through my desperate fear of the dark. In my teens, there was the dire need of funds for college. What I learned then I share in 'The Prayer That Helps Your Dreams Come True'.

At twenty-seven the need was a serious illness. There the mountain-peak learning was 'The Prayer of Relinquishment'.

The peak in my thirties was the gigantic one of my husband Peter Marshall's sudden death, along with lesser hills of need: how to rear a son without his father, how to find a career for myself at this point in life and without any specialised training. During that era I was taught 'The Claiming Prayer'.

Years later, after my marriage to Leonard Le-Sourd and the taking on of three young children, it was back to the School of Prayer again. As usual, there was no problem about passing the entrance test; my need was great, my inadequacy obvious. Out of these years came 'The Prayer of Helplessness'.

More often, of course, the situation that drove me to my knees was not so intensely personal. The need might be a friend's — or one I had only read about somewhere in our war-torn and hungry world. But always the criteria held: great needs and insufficient resources of my own with which to meet them.

In time I shared many of my prayer discoveries in the pages of *Guideposts* magazine. Eventually, a booklet of six prayer articles was put together. There has been a continuous demand for it ever since. Recently, I was asked to edit this material for a more permanent small book. Editing was necessary because each article had been condensed and shortened to fit *Guideposts*' necessarily limited space. Thus in the pages that follow, there appears for the first time the complete original text of the six prayer articles. This material falls into the category of a 'classic' only in the sense that it has already been time-tested in print.

In addition, since new times are already bringing new lessons in prayer, I have added two new chapters, 'Prayer Is Asking' and 'The Waiting Prayer'.

I have also written for this book a special prayer to follow each chapter. All of us have days when prayer seems to flow effortlessly, spontaneously. At other times the burden of our hearts needs help in finding its way to our lips, and it is for such moments that these prayers are offered — not as a substitute for our individual petitions, but as a launching pad for them.

Of course, no lifetime and no book, even one many times the length of this one, can do more than skim the surface of a subject as vast and all-encompassing as prayer. In this volume I have nowhere mentioned even the little I know about prayer as adoration — thanksgiving — praise — contemplation — meditation — or simply the lifting of the human heart in silent communion with the Lover of our souls. This is not because I consider such dimensions of prayer unimportant — quite the contrary — but because down through the centuries writers far more qualified than I have left us classics of instruction in their use.

What I have found strangely lacking in my

own times of need are guidelines to prayer at its humblest and most basic: prayer as *asking*. The prayer of a child quite simply running to its father for help. This is what we would rediscover in an age of perplexity — how do we run to the Father?

In the seventies, the halls and classrooms of the School of Prayer are crowded as never before because our needs press upon us with new urgency: worldwide economic crises, marriage problems on the rise, a widening generation gap, drug addiction, alcoholism, cancer of almost epidemic frequency. No wonder we rush to school! Our thirst is deep, our eagerness to learn is enormous.

What good news it is that our very inadequacy is the master key swinging wide the door to His adequacy. Forever and forever our thirst and hunger drive us to 'taste and see that the Lord is good'. Who but Jesus could ever have thought of a plan like that!

CATHERINE MARSHALL
March 1975

CHAPTER ONE

PRAYER IS ASKING

Recently a friend told me this incident ... Her daughter Elizabeth had taken a summer job wrapping meat in a supermarket to earn money for college. Just before time to leave for work one morning, Elizabeth missed one of her contact lenses. Though her mother joined in the search, the lens was nowhere to be found.

After Elizabeth had left for work wearing her regular glasses, her mother sat sipping a cup of coffee, thinking about their little crisis. There were a thousand and one places that tiny teardrop of plastic could have lodged. Then she wondered: should she pray about this? Was it too trivial? This friend, Tib Sherrill, had always had a special horror of prayers which treated the Lord of the Universe like a bellhop or a celestial Santa Claus.

Yet Tib knew that to replace the lens would cost Elizabeth a week's salary — money she was counting on for school needs. There would also be a week of sniffles from the refrigerated room where she worked, and of burnt fingers from the hot sealing wire.

Into my friend's mind came the remembrance of the parable which Jesus had told about a woman searching for one lost silver coin — a valuable one.[1] 'The story shows,' she mused, 'that Jesus cared about such things, not because they are important in themselves, but because they are important to us.'

'Yes, Lord,' she concluded, 'we do need help with this. Will You lead me to the missing lens?'

For no reason she was aware of, she got up and walked to the bathroom. Stooping, she ran her hands carefully through the thick pile of the bathroom rug. No, nothing.

She stood up and glanced at the basin. 'Why,' she thought, 'it could have fallen out here and been washed right down the drain.' She lifted out the chrome plunger to peer into the pipe. And there, at the very bottom of the metal plunger tube, was the missing lens, clinging like a tiny droplet of water. The first person to turn on the tap would have washed it away.

'It had been less than a minute since I made that prayer in the kitchen,' Tib told me. 'And of all possible places I might have thought to look, it would never in a million years have occurred to me to lift out that plunger.'

This mother had experienced answered prayer at its most basic level — asking. We are in need or trouble: a major crisis or a minor one. Taking Jesus at His word that God really is our Father, we come as His child, telling Him our need in the most simple direct way, asking His help.

If any of us has not yet experienced the glory of such a definite answer to prayer, then, as the Apostle James tells us — it's our own fault: '. . . you miss what you want because you do not *ask* God for it.'[2]

James had learned the necessity of asking from Jesus Himself. As the band of twelve men travelled from village to village with the Master, how often they had watched Him compel a supplicant to state his request straight out in plain terms. The Master would tolerate no generalities, no fuzziness. Like the day in Jericho when two blind men kept calling after Jesus, repeating over and over, 'O Lord, Son of David, have pity on us!'[3]

The beggars' blindness was as obvious to Jesus as to the disciples. Yet the Master had silenced the men's singsong chant with the blunt question, 'What do you want me to do for you?'

The directness of the question shocked the beggars out of their self-pitying, pious stance. 'Lord,' they told Him with a new directness, 'we want our eyes opened.'

Instantly, Jesus responded. At such moments, it was the look of love and compassion on their Master's face that James and the others would remember afterwards. How poignantly He cared about people! So Jesus had touched the eyes of each beggar in turn, and immediately their eyes received sight.

After watching a procession of such incidents, gradually the disciples came to know this as Jesus' way ... 'Tell Me exactly what you want,' He was always saying. 'Talk to Me. *Ask* Me.'

The importance of expressing our needs to our heavenly Father was a point He came back to over and over in His teaching:

> ... how much more will your Father in heaven give good gifts to those who *ask* him?[4]

> *Ask* and the gift will be yours ... for everyone who *asks* receives ...[5]

> ... *ask* and you will receive, that your joy may be full.[6]

He went on to teach that when we ask for bread, we won't get a stone. If we ask for an egg, God won't give us a scorpion any more than an earthly father would.[7] When we knock on the door, the door will swing open before us. Thus daringly, Jesus insisted that the answer to prayer is receiving what we ask for.

As the disciples listened to such statements, did blunt Peter or sceptical Thomas ever blurt out to their Master the question we often wonder about, 'But Lord, since the Father in heaven knows everything about us and our needs anyway, what's the point of having to ask?'

Jesus' answer to this is implicit in much of His teaching about prayer. He had a great deal to say about the connection between prayer and child-likeness:

> ... anyone who refuses to come to God as a little child will never be allowed into his Kingdom.[8]

How often Jesus prefaced some teaching to His big, burly disciples with an affectionate: 'Little children, I tell you ...' And of course, the characteristic position of childhood is that of simple asking.

A little child who has no shyness or hesitation about asking his parents for what he needs is unselfconsciously revealing his helplessness — along with a normal, right relationship with his father and mother. In the same way, asking immediately puts us into a right relationship to God. It is acting out the fact that He is the Creator with the riches and resources we need; we are the creatures who need help. It's a cap-in-hand stance which we resist because it diminishes us — a certain amount of pride and self has to go for us to ask for help — whether of God or of another human being.

Simple happenings uncover our pride and stubbornness about asking — like the motorist who loses his way. Often we will go miles off our route, waste time trying one road after another, rather than stop to ask for the help we need.

God insists that we ask, not because *He* needs to know our situation, but because *we* need the spiritual discipline of asking. Similarly, making our requests specific forces us to take a step forward in faith. The reason many of us retreat into vague generalities when we pray is not because we think too highly of God, but because we think too little. If we pray for something definite and our request is not granted, we fear to lose the little faith we had. So we fall back on the safe route of highly 'spiritual' prayers — the kind that Jesus brushed aside as not true prayer at all, just self-deceptive 'talking to ourselves'.[9]

In commenting on such non-prayers in his famous book *The Screwtape Letters*, C. S. Lewis has the devil, Screwtape, give this advice to his understudy, Wormwood:

It is, no doubt, impossible to prevent his praying for his mother, but we have means of rendering the prayers innocuous. Make sure that they are very 'spiritual', that he is always concerned with the state of her soul and never with her rheumatism . . .[10]

Oddly, we who are afraid to ask that the pain of rheumatism be removed or a lost contact lens found, often do not hesitate to pray for world peace or the salvation of souls or a revival to change the face of our time. It never occurs to us that if God's power is lacking for these everyday prayers, His power to handle big, all-inclusive petititons will be lacking too.

In order to make sure that we are not retreating from the tension of faith, it is helpful to ask ourselves as we pray, 'Do I really expect anything to happen?' This will prevent us from going window-shopping in prayer. At times window-shopping can be enjoyable — but there it ends. It costs nothing. We are just looking, have no intention of buying anything; so we bring nothing home to show for the hours of browsing. Too many of our prayers — private and public — are just browsing amongst possible petitions, not down to cases at all. We expect nothing from our prayers except perhaps an euphoric feeling.

As for our losing faith in God if our request is not granted in the precise form we wish, can any of us possibly be as concerned about the state of our faith as God is? That we should trust Him is not only His will, but the passion of His Father-heart. Surely then, we can turn over to His keeping any worry about our losing faith.

Beyond that, are we afraid that a *no* answer will back us up against our own deficiencies, our failure to meet God's conditions? And if so, again, are we not really questioning God's ability to supply *everything* we lack — faith or perseverance or inner tensile strength to meet His conditions?

Jesus spoke often of heaven's 'rewards'. If that offends us by seeming too materialistic, perhaps we should be wary of being more 'spiritual' than our Lord.

One veteran prayer warrior, John R. Rice, has expressed it bluntly in *Asking and Receiving*: 'Prayer is not a lovely sedan for a sightseeing trip around the city. Prayer is a truck that goes straight to the warehouse, backs up, loads, and comes home with the goods . . .'[11]

If we think we'll never be able to summon the faith for such prayer, we're right. However, those saints who have had the most experience here tell us that God uses our most stumbling, faltering faith-step as the open door to His doing for us 'more than we ask or think'. We decide to ask His help with some small immediate need. Our asking is like stepping into a tiny anteroom. Taking a hesitant step forward, we discover that the anteroom leads into the King's spacious reception hall. To our astonishment, the King Himself comes forward to meet us, offering a gift so momentous as to be worthy only of the King: a lifetime gift of a friendship with the Lord of Glory.

'You asked Me for money for this month's rent,' He smiles. 'Sit here at My feet and we'll talk about the rent, but also of other matters too. I have much to say to you. If you accept My friendship, you and I have years of joyous interchange ahead. I've so much to teach you. It's going to take eternity to handle all of it.'

Our situation reminds us of that nameless woman long ago, of whom the Master asked a drink of water from Jacob's Well at Sychar. Under the Stranger's penetrating gaze and His incisive questions, she found that the thirst that necessitated her daily trip to the well was but her surface problem. The Rabbi knew all about her, all the rotten things she'd ever done. Yet there was no condemnation, just a tender, healing love pointing her to the answers she had sought so long.[12]

Even so, our entering into a one-to-One relationship with Jesus enables Him to handle not only our immediate material and physical needs, but also deeper needs, the hidden ones involving right attitudes and healthy emotions, proper motivation, and how to solve our relationship problems.

Soon we discern that asking involves more than verbalisation. Our lips do not always communicate accurately the heart's true cry. In some instances, that's because we are so out of touch with our own emotions that our prayers deal in unrealities. Sometimes we are divided within ourselves about what we actually want, so that we cannot ask wholeheartedly. Or perhaps we do not even know enough about our hopes and dreams to make our asking specific.

Then, we conclude, there must be different levels of asking. There's so much I want to learn about that: 'Lord, teach me to pray.'

I DO ASK

Lord Jesus, You who were born in a stable and laid in the straw, You who walked dusty roads and were thirsty, and relished the feel of cool water sliding down Your throat, and laughed, and sometimes cried salty tears — You are the One summoning me back to reality. I see it now — what I have considered lofty spirituality is sham and humbug in Your eyes. Worse than that, often it has been a cloak to hide my fear of not receiving what I ask You for.

You who are so much more alive than I am, now want to go with me down the city street and help me find a parking place, and remind me where I misplaced that slip of paper with the telephone number. You want to give my wife a good night's sleep, to heal my neighbour's arthritis, to help John find a job. Happiness floods my heart at the knowledge of Your being *Man* as well as God; the essence of any difficulty I ever encounter, You have experienced before me.

So You are bidding me tell You my every need and promising that joy and good gifts await my asking. Lord, I sorely need _____. I would also ask You for _____.

Would You give me Your thoughts about these requests? Is it, without my suspecting it, a petition for harm and not for good? Is there some step of growth, forgiveness, obedience that I must take before You can grant my request? And Lord, if I need patience to wait

out Your perfect timing, then I also ask You to supply
the patience.

In joyful anticipation, I await Your answer. Thank
You, Lord Jesus. *Amen.*

CHAPTER TWO

THE PRAYER OF HELPLESSNESS

When I lived in the nation's capital, I used to notice how often the Washington papers reported suicide leaps from the Calvert Street Bridge. In fact, this happens so repeatedly that the site is often called 'suicide bridge'.

Sensing the human drama behind these brief notices — like the plunge of the Air Corps major's thirty-one-year-old wife with inoperable cancer, or that of the elderly man whose wife had just died — I often thought that there was probably a common denominator in all of these tragedies. Each person must have felt helpless, And I have thought, 'If I could speak with such persons at the zero hour, I would try to stop them with the thought that helplessness is one of the greatest assets a human being can have.'

For I believe that the old cliché, 'God helps those who help themselves,' is not only misleading but often dead wrong. My most spectacular answers to prayers have come when I was so helpless, so out of control as to be able to do nothing at all for myself.

The Psalmist says: *When I was hemmed in, thou hast freed me often.*[1] Gradually I have learned to recognise this hemming-in as one of God's most loving devices for teaching us that He is real and gloriously adequate for our problems.

One such experience occurred during the writing of my first book. As the young widow of Peter Marshall, Scottish Presbyterian pastor and Chaplain of the United States Senate, I was attempting what many felt was the rather audacious project of writing his biography. About midway in the manuscript, I received devastating criticism from one whose judgment I trusted. He told me bluntly, 'You haven't even begun to get inside the man Peter Marshall.' And he was right, that was the sting of it. The realisation of my inadequacy as a writer was not only an intellectual one. It was also emotional; there were plenty of tears. But out of the crisis came a major realisation.

In my helplessness, there was no alternative but to put the project into God's hands. I prayed that *A Man Called Peter* be His book, and that the results be all His too.

And they were. I still regard as incredible the several million copies of *A Man Called Peter* circulating around the world. But that and the successful 20th Century-Fox motion picture were of little importance compared to what I hear from time to time of lives changed through this book — of men entering the ministry through the inspiration of Peter Marshall's life.

Years later I saw the Prayer of Helplessness work in an everyday situation — the matter of household help. Before my marriage to Leonard LeSourd in the fall of 1959, I was full of trepidation at the thought of taking on the care of his three young children. My son, Peter John, had been away at school for over three years, and I had involved myself with a writing career. In his efforts to reassure me, Len was blithe with promises of household help.

But the help situation in Chappaqua, New York proved unbelievably tight. Months passed. One woman stayed a few weeks, then left. We tried the classified columns without success; persistent prayer brought us no nearer a solution. I finally decided I would have to do it all myself, but soon found it was more than a full-time job running a lively household: week after week I did not get near my desk.

So — once again the old familiar pattern — the Prayer of Helplessness — the admission that I could not do everything myself — then the insight that my main responsibility was to our home. If God wanted me to resume my writing, He would show me the way.

After that admission of helplessness, Lucy Arsenault was sent to us. Lucy — steady, reliable, loyal, a marvellous cook, a great person.

Why would God insist on helplessness as a prerequisite to answered prayer? One obvious reason is because our human helplessness is bedrock fact. God is a realist and insists that we be realists too. So long as we are deluding ourselves that human resources can supply our heart's desires, we are believing a lie. And it is impossible for prayers to be answered out of a foundation of self-deception and untruth.

Then what is the truth about our human condition? None of us had anything to do with our being born; no control over whether we are male or female, Japanese or Russian or American, white or yellow or black. Nor can we influence our ancestry, nor our basic mental or physical equipment.

After we are born, an automatic nervous system controls every vital function that sustains life. A power that no one really understands keeps our heart beating, our lungs breathing, our blood circulating, our body temperature at 98·6 degrees fahrenheit.

A surgeon can cut tissues, but he is helpless to force the body to bind the severed tissue together again.

We grow old relentlessly and automatically.

Self-sufficient? Scarcely!

Even the planet on which we live . . . we had nothing to do with its creation either. The little planet Earth is exactly the right distance — some ninety-three million miles — from the source of its heat and light. Any nearer and we would be consumed by solar radiation; any farther and we would be frozen to death. The balance of oxygen and nitrogen in the air is exactly right for the support of life, the elements in our soil, and the creation of rare rock deposits — all of this goes on quite apart from man — little man who struts and fumes upon the earth.

Did Jesus have any comment to make about all this? Yes, as always, He put His finger on the very heart of the matter: '. . . without me ye can do nothing,' He said.[2]

Nothing? That seems a trifle sweeping. After all, we men have made great progress. We've almost eliminated diseases like smallpox, bubonic plague, tuberculosis, polio, and most of the communicable diseases of childhood. We have learned to control our environment to quite an extent. We have put men on the moon. How can all that be helplessness? Most of us do not enjoy that idea. The cult of humanism in our day has trained us to believe that we are quite adequate to be masters of our own destiny.

Yet not only did Jesus insist on the truth of our helplessness; He underscored it by telling us that this same helplessness applied equally to Him while He wore human flesh: 'I can of mine own self do nothing: [He told His apostles,] The Father in me doeth the works.'[3] In this as in everything else, He was setting the pattern of perfect humanity.

The Scriptures spell out for us point by point how helpless we are in relation to our spiritual lives as well as our physical ones . . .

We feel an impulse towards God. *We* think that *we* are reaching out for Him. Not so, Jesus told us, 'No one is able to come to me unless he is drawn by the Father . . .'[4]

We want salvation from our sins, and eternal life. We think that we can earn this salvation. No. The truth is '. . . it is the gift of God: Not of works, lest any man should boast.'[5]

So far as the virtues and graces we need for victory in our lives — faith, joy, patience, peace of mind, the ability to love the wretched and the unlovely — there is no way we can work up such qualities. Paul tells us in Galatians 5: 22, 23, that these are gifts of the Holy Spirit. They can be had in no other way. '. . . A man can receive nothing, except it be given him from heaven.'[6]

This emphasis on our helplessness is found over and over in the writings of Christians in other eras. For instance, in that little jewel of a seventeenth-century book, Brother Lawrence's *The Practice of the Presence of God*, helplessness was the hinge upon which turned the Carmelite lay brother's relationship with God:

That when an occasion of practising some

virtue offered, he addressed himself to God, saying, LORD, *I cannot do this unless Thou enablest me*; and that then he received strength more than sufficient.

That when he had failed in his duty, he only confessed his fault, saying to GOD, *I shall never do otherwise if You leave me to myself; it is You who must hinder my falling, and mend what is amiss.* That after this he gave himself no further uneasiness about it.[7]

Though few of us have Brother Lawrence's maturity, nevertheless, sometime in life every one of us finds himself out of control, caught in circumstances that he is helpless to change. When this happens, welcome such times! Often it is only then that we lesser spirits enter into the truth of Jesus' statement from the fifteenth chapter of John: 'Apart from Me ye can do nothing.'

Dr. Arthur Gossip, who wrote the exposition on John for the *Interpreter's Bible*, has this interesting comment: 'These are surely the most hopeful words in Scripture . . . *Apart from Me ye can do nothing*. For it is on the basis of that frank recognition of our utter fecklessness apart from Him, that Christ . . . gives us His great promises . . .'

Great promises, like that glorious one, sweeping enough to make up a thousand times over for our helplessness: '. . . with God all things are possible.' He is telling us that an omnipotent, transcendent,

and immanent God is above all and through all
far more completely than we realise.

With helplessness alone, one would be like a
bird trying to fly with one wing. But when the
other wing of God's adequacy is added to our
helplessness, then the bird can soar triumphantly
above and through problems that hitherto have
defeated us.

I have always been impressed by the story of
Dr. A. B. Simpson, a famous New York preacher.[9]
Poor health had haunted this man. Two nervous
breakdowns plus a heart condition led a well-
known New York physician to tell him when he
was only thirty-eight that he would never live to
be forty.

The physician's diagnosis only underscored the
physical helplessness that the minister knew only
too well. Preaching was an agonising effort.
Climbing even a slight elevation brought on a
suffocating agony of breathlessness.

In desperation, sick in body and despairing in
spirit, at last Dr. Simpson went to his Bible to find
out exactly what Jesus had to say about disease.
He became convinced that He had always meant
healing to be a part of His Gospel for the redemption of man's total being.

One Friday afternoon soon after this revelation,
Dr. Simpson took a walk in the country. He was
forced to walk painfully, slowly, for he was always
out of breath. Coming to a pine-wood, he sat

down on a log to rest. Soon he found himself praying, telling God of his complete helplessness with regard to his physical condition. But to this helplessness he added his belief that God was 'for health' all the way. It was that majestically powerful combination again, 'My total inadequacy — Your perfect adequacy.' He then asked Christ to enter him and to become his physical life for all the needs of his body until his lifework was done.

'There in the woods, I made a connection with God,' he said later. 'Every fibre in me was tingling with the sense of God's presence.'

A few days after that, Simpson climbed a mountain three thousand feet high. 'When I reached the top,' he related joyfully, 'the world of weakness and fear was lying at my feet. From that time on I had literally a new heart in my breast.'

And so he did. During the first three years after this healing he preached more than a thousand sermons; sometimes as many as twenty meetings in one week. His testimony was that never once did he feel exhausted. For the rest of his life, he was noted for the amazing volume of his sermonic, pastoral, and literary work. He lived to be seventy-six.

Moreover, Simpson's work has lived after him. The Christian and Missionary Alliance which he founded is still a potent spiritual force today; his books are still being published and have blessed millions.

Why is prayer so startlingly effective when we admit our helplessness? First, as we have seen, because God insists upon our facing up to the true facts of our human situation. Thus we lay under our prayer-structure the firm foundation of truth rather than self-delusion or wishful thinking.

This recognition and acknowledgment of our helplessness is also the quickest way to that right attitude which God recognises as essential to prayer. It deals a mortal blow to the most serious sin of all — man's independence that ignores God.

Another reason is that we cannot learn first-hand about God — what He is like, His love for us as individuals, and His real power — so long as we are relying on ourselves and other people. And fellowship with Jesus is the true purpose of life and the only foundation for eternity. It is real, this daily fellowship He offers us.

So if your every human plan and calculation has miscarried, if, one by one, human props have been knocked out, and doors have shut in your face, take heart. God is trying to get a message through to you, and the message is: 'Stop depending on inadequate human resources. Let Me handle the matter.'

Here are three suggestions for presenting to Him the Prayer of Helplessness.

First, be honest with God. Tell Him that you

are aware of the fact that in His eyes you are helpless. Give God permission to make you feel your helplessness *at the emotional level*, if that's what He wants. And recognise that this may be painful. There is good psychological reason why this first step is necessary. Unless the power of our emotions is touched, it is as if a fuse remains unlit.

Second, take your heart's desire to God. You have accepted your helplessness. Now grip with equal strength of will your belief that God can do through you what you cannot. It may seem to you for a time that you are relying on emptiness, dangling over a chasm. Disregard these feelings, and quietly thank God that He is working things out.

Third, watch now for opening doors. When the right door opens, you will have a quiet inner assurance that God's hand is on the knob. That is the time of action for you, an opportunity for creativity.

One sunny day in the future, you will look back and your heart will overflow with praise to God that He cared about you enough to shut you up to Him alone. Without that stringently kind providence you could never have learned first-hand the amazing power of the Prayer of Helplessness.

WHERE ARE YOU, LORD?

Lord, I have been so defeated by circumstances. I have felt like an animal trapped in a corner with nowhere to flee. Where are *You* in all this, Lord? The night is dark. I cannot feel Your presence.

Help me to know that the darkness is really 'Shade of Your hand, outstretched caressingly';[10] that the 'hemming in' is Your doing. Perhaps there was no other way You could get my full attention, no other way I would allow You to demonstrate what You can do in my life.

I see now that the emptier my cup is, the more space there is to receive Your love and supply. Lord, I hand to You this situation: _____, asking You to fill it from Your bountiful reservoirs in Your own time and Your own way.

How I thank You, Father in heaven, that Your riches are available to me, not on the basis of my deserving, but of Jesus and His worthiness. Therefore, in the strength of His name, I pray. *Amen.*

CHAPTER THREE

THE PRAYER THAT HELPS
YOUR DREAMS COME TRUE

One of the most provocative facts I know is that every man-made object, as well as most activity in your life and mine, starts with an idea or a picture in the mind. My mother first taught me this, and at the same time she vividly demonstrated to me the prayer that helps dreams come true.

In my teens I long had the dream of going to college. But this was a depression time and the West Virginia church my father served was suffering financially too. I was accepted at Agnes Scott College in Decatur, Georgia, had saved some money from debating prizes, had the promise of a work scholarship — yet we were still several hundred dollars short.

One evening Mother found me lying across my bed, face-down, sobbing. She sat down beside me. 'You and I are going to pray about this,' she said quietly. We went into the guest room and knelt beside the old-fashioned, golden oak bed, the one that Mother and Father had bought for their first home. 'I know it's right for you to go to college,'

Mother said. 'I believe God planted this dream in you; let's ask Him to tell us how to bring it to reality.'

During those quiet moments in the bedroom, confidence and fresh determination flowed in. Mother's faith was contagious. The answer would come. How, we did not know.

I went ahead and made preparations for Agnes Scott. A short time later, Mother received an offer from the Federal Writers' Project to write the history of the county. Her salary was enough to pay for the major part of my college expenses.

An even more dramatic example of Mother's use of this Dreaming Prayer involved a young man from 'Radical Hill', a run-down section of our West Virginia town. Raymond Thomas, who lived with foster parents, had no idea who his real parents were.

Dressed in working clothes and knee-high clodhoppers, Ray used to come to talk with my mother. He was always clean, but he didn't even own a suit of clothes. Of a summer's day he would settle himself on the top step of our vine-shaded front porch talking . . . talking . . . while Mother sat in a wooden rocker shelling peas or stringing beans or darning socks. Mother soon saw his boundless energy and fine mind.

On one particular afternoon there emerged for Ray the same inner longing which I had had —

college. Once his dream was out in the open, standing there shimmering, poised in the air, Mother was delighted to see the wistfulness in Ray's brown eyes replaced by kindling hope.

'But how can I manage it?' the boy asked. 'I've no money saved. Nor any prospects.'

Mother sensed that with Ray, however, the Dreaming Prayer should involve, more than just college, a completely new approach to life. 'Raymond, whatever you need, God has the supply ready for you, provided you're ready to receive it. And ours is still a land of opportunity, Raymond. The sky is the limit! The money will be there for every dream that's right for you, every dream for which you're willing to work.'

For a preacher's wife who had little enough herself, this was a doughty philosophy. But Mother believed it and had often proved it so. And these truths took root in Ray.

There came the day when Ray accepted Mother's philosophy so completely that she could lead him in the prayer that releases dreams to make them come true. After having heard her pray it for me, I can easily imagine how it was for Ray . . .

'Father, You've given Raymond a fine mind. We believe You want that mind to be developed, that You want Raymond's potential to be used to help You lift and lighten some portion of Your world. Since all the wealth of the world is Yours, please help Raymond find everything he needs for an education.

'And, Father, we also believe you have even bigger plans for Raymond. Plant in his mind and heart the vivid pictures, the specific dreams that reflect Your plans for him after college. And oh, give him joy in dreaming — great joy.'

With a flat pocketbook but faith in his dream, Raymond Thomas got on a bus and went off to college. How he made it is much too long to chronicle here. It involved Mother's finding a woman to start him off with a loan — writing him encouraging letters — praying. And Ray himself accepting responsibility, developing initiative. In four years he had twelve jobs, budgeting time as well as money: so many hours for classes, study, church work, recreation. It was a proud day for Mother when Ray received his Bachelor of Science degree, *cum laude*.

During World War II and afterwards I lost touch with Ray, though I knew he had settled in Vienna. Then in the summer of 1958, I wrote Ray that I was coming to Europe.

In Rome I found a letter from him waiting for me . . .

I have a surprise for you. You will hear from the office of the Reveranda Fabrica di San Pietro whom I've contacted on your behalf. The point is that only with their permission can you see the most wonderful sight in Rome, the excavated street of tombs sixteen centuries old beneath the nave of the High Altar in St. Peter's. I explored every bit of it two years ago . . .

Then when I checked into the hotel in Florence, the mail clerk handed me another letter from Ray . . .

When you see the high dome of the Duomo, remember that it took Brunelleschi fourteen years to build it. Last winter I climbed to the highest balcony right at the top of the dome and crawled all around it . . .

By now I was consumed with curiosity about Ray. This man seemed to bear no resemblance to the boy from Radical Hill. Obviously he knew Europe as few Americans do. And the drive and indefatigable zest apparent in his letters intrigued me.

The letters kept coming . . . Venice:

I've written to my friend at the Salviati Glass Works and asked him to send a gondola for you. You must see the master glassblowers at work . .

Bad Gastein:

You'll find it rugged. I've skied near there . . .

Ray met me at the Vienna airport, a bouquet of flowers in hand. 'Flowers and music are a part of Vienna,' he explained. 'Here we always take flowers to our hostess even for a dinner party.' Later, over *Sacher torte* and coffee, he began answering my questions. 'The fact that I could sit on your front steps and — with no money at all — dream of going to college and achieve it, proved something to me. Very simply, what your mother had said, was true — any right dream can be realised. Material resources *are* at the beck and call of the dreamer. And prayer helps you know if it is right and gives you the power to stay with it.'

He described his war experience — one of the few survivors of a torpedoed destroyer — and how during convalescence he dreamed of the plan for the rest of his life.

'I wanted to be the kind of world citizen who could serve my country in peacetime, to travel and master several languages, to get a Ph.D. degree.'

'It interests me that your dreams were that specific,' I interposed.

Ray sipped his coffee, seeming lost in thought as he stared out of the window. 'This dreaming process won't work unless we *are* specific. That's because a big part of the power to make the dream come true arises from a mental picture. And you sure do have to have specifics to form a mental picture.'

Then Ray went on to sum up how much of his dream had been realised: travel in sixty countries, his Ph.D. in physics from the University of Vienna, which meant mastering German. He also speaks Spanish, passable French, some Italian, Dutch and Swedish — and a little Russian. He serves his country through a job with the U.S. Atomic Energy Programme in Europe.

A story like Ray's reveals the connection between constructive dreaming and prayer. For, in a sense all such dreaming is praying. It is certainly the Creator's will that the desires and talents that He Himself has planted in us be realised. God is supremely concerned about the fulfilment of the great person He envisions each of us. He wants us to catch from Him some of His vision for us. After all, this is what prayer is, men co-operating with God in bringing from heaven to earth His wondrously good plans for us.

Sadly, sometimes we fail to catch His vision for us because our capacity to dream has been atrophied by some condition which has given us a poverty-complex. My first glimpse of this was in a former college friend who had suffered a poverty-stricken childhood. Dot, as I'll call her, was unable to visualise what she wanted in the vocational field.

Yet she had come to Washington with idealistic ideas about a government job. 'I don't want just any job,' Dot had explained to me soon after she arrived. 'I go along with the idea that God has a plan for my life. Only I haven't yet found it, so how do I pray about this job situation?'

'What job would give you the most joy?' I asked her. 'Usually that's a key to what one *should* do.'

My friend merely looked puzzled and shook her head.

'Do you ever daydream?' I persisted. 'Is there anything you've always longed to do?'

'No — o. Nothing.'

The reason that this particular girl could not dream constructively was that during financially difficult years her widowed mother had taught her that those who hope for little or nothing will never suffer disappointment. Actually this had been nothing less than excellent training in poverty expectation. Sadly, I watched my friend fall into a routine government filing job that used but a fraction of her abilities.

I know now that there is healing for such a situation. When we become aware of such damaged areas in the unconscious, we can call on the power of the Holy Spirit. He can walk back with us into the past and drain out all poison, make the rough places smooth, and create a highway for our God to come marching triumphantly into the present with His long-forgotten, oft-delayed plan for our lives.

In fact, there is no limit to what this combination of dreams and prayer can achieve. I have seen amazing results in many areas: like finding the right mate or the right job, or locating the ideal house, or in rearing children, or in building a business.

The story of the Olivettis came to my attention some years ago when I visited their beautiful typewriter-and-office-equipment plant in Ivrea, northwest Italy in the Alps-ringed Canavese region. There I saw fifty-four carefully landscaped acres; nearby an infirmary for the workers; an employees' library; rows of pastel-coloured apartments. The factory is as noted for its workers' benefits and enlightened welfare programme as for its international success. And I was entranced to find that all of it is the result of a dream . . .

One autumn day years ago a young Italian visitor stood in the yard of the Underwood factory in Hartford, Connecticut, staring at the red brick buildings. A passer-by, seeing the young man, would have marvelled at his total absorption, for there was nothing unusual about the rambling red brick buildings on which he was so intent: they looked like thousands of other New England factories.

Yet to Adriano Olivetti the old buildings represented a lifetime dream. At that time UNDERWOOD was the greatest name in typewriters. Someday, he vowed, he would own a company like that, and the name OLIVETTI would carry the same implication of quality. By fixing the actual physical buildings in his mind and heart, he was creating a mental image on which he could focus his prayers.

Thirty-four years later, Adriano returned to the United States as president of Ing. C. Olivetti & Co. At that time he telephoned a colleague in Italy to tell him the good news. 'I have just bought something . . .' Here his voice broke with emotion. 'I've just bought the Underwood Company.'

Eight million, seven hundred thousand dollars had just exchanged hands. With his acquisition of the control of the old American company, Adriano Olivetti had seen the fulfilment of his thirty-four-year-old dream.

There are those who are wary of this Prayer That Helps Your Dreams Come True because they are dubious about praying for material needs such as bread, clothing, a catch of fish, or to put it in modern terms, a parking place for a car. Rightly, they also ask, 'Isn't there danger of trying to use God and spiritual principles for selfish ends?'

Each is a valid question that needs to be answered. As for whether God means for us to include material needs in our petitions, certainly Christ was interested in men's bodies as well as their souls. He was concerned about their diseases, their physical hunger. Christianity, almost alone among world religions, acknowledges material things as real and important — real enough that Christ had to die in a real body on a real Cross.

And as for the danger that our dreams may spring from our selfish human will rather than God's will, there are tests for this. Only when a dream has passed such a series of tests — so that we are certain that our heart's desire is also God's dream *before* we pray — can we pray the Dreaming Prayer with faith and thus with power.

Let's begin by acknowledging that God's laws are in operation in our universe — whether we recognise them or not. We have to co-operate with these laws, not defy them. For example, ask yourself questions like these:

- Will my dream fulfil the talents, the temperament, and emotional needs which God has planted in my being? This is not easy to answer. It involves knowing oneself, the real person, as few of us do.

- Does my dream involve taking anything or any person belonging to someone else? Would its fulfilment hurt any other human being? If so, you can be fairly sure that this particular dream is not God's will for you.

- Am I willing to make all my relationships with other people right? If I hold resentments, grudges, bitterness — no matter how justified — these wrong emotions will cut me off from God, the source of creativity. Furthermore, no dream can be achieved in a vacuum of human relationships. Even one such wrong relationship can cut the channel of power.

- Do I want this dream with my whole heart? Dreams are not usually brought to fruition in divided personalities; only the whole heart will be willing to do its part towards implementing the dream.

- Am I willing to wait patiently for God's timing?

- Am I dreaming big? The bigger the dream and the more persons it will benefit, the more apt it is to stem from the infinite designs of God.

If your heart's desire can pass a series of tests like this, then you are ready for the final necessary step in the Dreaming Prayer! Hand your dream over to God, and then leave it in His keeping. There seem to be periods when the dream is like a seed that must be planted in the dark earth and left there to germinate. This is not a time of passiveness on our part. There are things we can and must do — fertilising, watering, weeding — hard work and self-discipline.

But the growth of that seed, the mysterious and irresistible burgeoning of life in dark and in secret, *that* is God's part of the process. We must not keep digging up our dream, examining and measuring it to see how it is coming along. I will have more to say about the power of trustful and prayerful waiting in the following chapter.

But in the meantime, long before we see the fruition of our hopes, in fact the very moment a God-given dream is planted in our hearts, a strange happiness flows into us. I have come to think that at that moment all the resources of the universe are released to help us. Our praying is then at one with the will of God, a channel for the Creator's always joyous, triumphant purposes for us and our world.

GIVE ME A DREAM

Father, once — it seems long ago now — I had such big dreams, so much anticipation of the future. Now no shimmering horizon beckons me; my days are lacklustre. I see so little of lasting value in the daily round. Where is Your plan for my life, Father?

You have told us that without vision, we men perish.[1] So Father in heaven, knowing that I can ask in confidence for what is Your expressed will to give me,[2] I ask You to deposit in my mind and heart the particular dream, the special vision You have for my life.

And along with the dream, will You give me whatever graces, patience, and stamina it takes to see the dream through to fruition? I sense that this may involve adventures I have not bargained for. But I want to trust You enough to follow even if You lead along new paths. I admit to liking some of my ruts. But I know that habit patterns that seem like cosy nests from the inside, from Your vantage point may be prison cells. Lord, if You have to break down any prisons of mine before I can see the stars and catch the vision, then Lord, begin the process now. In joyous expectation. *Amen.*

CHAPTER FOUR

THE WAITING PRAYER

One day not long ago I was flipping through a beloved, dog-eared old Bible that I had not used for a while when I came across a series of little egg-shaped slips of paper. I smiled, remembering what they were all about.

When my son Peter John was small and I was in a typical motherly mood of worrying about him, I came across a seemingly almost childlike piece of 'how to' writing by Dr. Glenn Clark. Part of our problem in praying for our children, he suggested, is the time lag, the necessary slow maturation of our prayers. But that's the way of God's rhythm in nature. For instance, the hen must patiently sit on her eggs to incubate them before the baby chicks hatch.

With this picture in mind, Dr. Clark suggested that we parents spend some time each day for at least a week thinking through our hearts' deepest desires for our children. After listing them on paper, ask for Jesus' mind on them, sifting out everything superficial or selfish until we have reached the kernel of the Spirit's hopes and dreams for this particular person.

Then, said Dr. Clark, copy these hopes in the form of prayers on to slips of paper cut roughly into the shape of eggs. And then give these petitions to our Father to fulfil in His own time and His own way. To help dramatise the recognition that visible answers may be slow in coming, insert the slips of paper between the pages of some favourite Bible — signifying leaving them in God's keeping.

At the time I followed these suggestions, I did not mention to anyone what I had done for fear of seeming naïve. Yet, today I think just the opposite. I feel that those little paper eggs represent a very profound principle indeed. For when I came across them in my Bible, I found to my astonishment that a loving Father had fulfilled every single request.

Why? What was there about that form of prayer that He honoured so dramatically? Certainly it wasn't that I had cut out pieces of paper in a particular shape, or that there was any power in the physical presence of the Bible. As I pondered this, it occurred to me that part of the secret lay in the waiting. Waiting itself, if practised according to Biblical patterns, seems to be a strange but dynamic kind of communication between man and God.

Waiting certainly plays an enormous role in the unfolding story of God's relationship to man. It is

God's oft-repeated way of teaching us that His power is real and that He can answer our prayers without interference and manipulation from us.

But we have such trouble getting *our* will, *our* time schedules out of the way. Much of the time we act like a child who brings a broken toy to his father to be mended.[1] The father gladly takes the toy and begins work. Then after a while, childlike impatience takes over. Why is it taking so long?

The child stands by, getting his hands in the father's way, offering a lot of meaningless advice and some rather silly criticism. Finally in desperation, he snatches the toy from the father's hands and walks off with it, saying rather bitterly that he hadn't really thought his father could fix it anyway. Perhaps it isn't even 'his will' to mend toys.

On the other hand, whenever we are trustful enough to leave our 'broken toy' with the Father, not only do we eventually get it back gloriously restored, but are also handed a surprising plus. We find for ourselves what the saints and mystics affirm, that during the dark waiting period when self-effort had ceased, a spurt of astonishing spiritual growth took place in us. Afterwards we have qualities like more patience, more love for the Lord and those around us, more ability to hear His voice, greater willingness to obey.

The divine Husbandman has been teaching us the lesson of the Life in the Vine. During that waiting period (what seemed like a dark night of the soul) we were learning the great secret of *abiding*. Abiding is the key to unlock heaven's treasures.[2]

Our human hang-up is thinking that spirituality is something we *do*. 'Not so,' says Jesus. 'Rather it is My life in you.' The branch does not have to stretch and strain to grow and produce fruit. The branch's part is simply to remain connected to the Vine, to abide there so that the life-giving sap can flow. Then only do we 'bear much fruit'.

Jesus also had a great deal to say about His Father's timing, the principle that there is a God-given sequence and rate of growth for everything in His Creation:

> ... first the blade, then the ear, after that the full corn in the ear.[3]

'The time is fulfilled, and the kingdom of God is at hand,'[4] Jesus might say. Or when certain disciples were trying to get Him to act prematurely. 'My time is not yet come . . .'[5] Later as the shadows deepened around the Cross, 'My time is at hand.'[6] Always *His* timing. We force and try to hurry the divine schedule at our peril.

God does have His 'fullness of time' for the answer to each prayer. It follows then that He alone knows the magnitude of the changes that have to be wrought in us before we can receive our hearts' desires. He alone knows the changes and interplay of external events that must take place before our prayer can be answered. That's why Jesus told us, 'It is not for you to know the times or the seasons, which the Father hath put in his own power.'[7]

Thus the Lord seems constantly to use waiting as a tool for bringing us the very best of His gifts. He made the children of Israel wait generations for their freedom from slavery in Egypt. Because of their stubborn disobedience, they had to wait forty years before they were ready to enter the Promised Land. Waiting was the keynote of the exile. The whole story of the Old Testament is the patient waiting for 'the fullness of time' of the Saviour's birth. And after Jesus' Ascension, those gathered in the upper room had to wait a full ten days for the coming of the Holy Spirit.

No wonder some of God's promises are predicated upon our waiting trustingly for His timing:

The Lord is good unto them that wait for him ... [8]

Those that wait on the Lord shall possess the land.[9]

But they that wait upon the Lord shall renew their strength; they shall mount up with wings as eagles; they shall run, and not be weary; and they shall walk, and not faint.[10]

For since the world began no one has seen or heard of such a God as ours, who works for those who wait for him![11]

And let us not be weary in well doing: for in due season we shall reap, if we faint not.[12]

Waiting seems to be a kind of acted-out prayer that is required more often and honoured more often than I could understand until I saw what remarkable faith-muscles this act develops. For isn't it true that waiting demands patience, persistence, trust, expectancy — all the qualities we are continually beseeching God to give us?

I remember once being in a situation where the Lord told me to wait, to stand silently by, saying nothing, even though I thought I knew the answer to a problem. Even within this smaller scope, I was to wait on His timing, His invisible action in another human heart. It was an astounding experience in poised expectancy.

I had not seen Helen in nearly two years. Her telephone call was a shocker because she told me that her husband, Steve, was leaving her for a younger woman. She wanted to talk. 'Please, Catherine, may I come and see you?'

'Helen, I have no qualifications as a marriage counsellor,' I said.

'But you will pray with me, won't you?'

Yes, that I could certainly do and said so, little

realising what a strange form that prayer was to take.

Now, as Helen stood in the doorway of our home in Boynton Beach, Florida, I looked at her with a sinking heart. She was carelessly dressed, her eyes dull and bloodshot from weeping. She was overweight and her blonde-red hair needed attention.

As we settled down on the sofa in our living-room Helen launched into a story that had one recurring theme — throughout, she was con-stantly putting herself down. They had three children, but Steve had wanted more. Steve spent most of his home hours in front of TV, but then — she had never been much of a conversationalist. He hadn't taken her out in years, but she didn't mind much. Helen wasn't sure who the other woman was, but doubtless it was someone more stimulating — and so on and on.

As Helen talked on, I suddenly realised that I knew what the problem was. Not that it took much insight: Helen had been screaming the news to me from the moment she walked in. This woman couldn't stand herself. And the minute this became clear, I knew something else. I was to say nothing. The Lord spoke to my heart crisply. I was to wait. I was to sit on this piece of insight until the Lord gave it to Helen Himself, in His own time and in His own way. The self-control required of me was incredible, as for two

hours Helen spelled out in a score of different
ways what I already knew. But incredible also
was the sense of expectancy as I watched the Lord
at work. He had brought Helen here for the
specific purpose of giving her time — time to
think coherently and connectedly about her problem. I was there only to keep her thoughts on the
track. Helen needed to reach her understanding
on her own, and He was giving me supernatural
supplies of patience (for me) while He led her
there ever so gently.

With this gift of grace, the two hours sped by
as I found myself almost leaning forward in
anticipation. The time was a blend of talking,
reading Scriptures, silence, and listening. At last
Helen asked me if she might go out into the garden to be alone for a while.

When she returned, her words came tumbling
out, 'That Bible verse, Catherine, about Jesus
loving us before we loved Him — recently it's
been hard to believe that *anyone* loves me. But out
there in your garden I got to thinking. When you
really believe that God loves you as a person,
well then you've got to love yourself, too.'

I nodded, not daring to speak, and she went on:
'Well, it just occurred to me that I've dis-
honoured Him, in a sense, by the way I let myself
and the house get run-down. I mean my weight,
TV dinners all the time, beds never made . . .'

As I listened, I marvelled at God's ways. If I

had tried to say these things to Helen as a friend giving advice, chances are she would have taken offence, or at best accepted my suggestions reluctantly. Needless to say, this did not solve the problems in Helen's marriage overnight; there were many rough months to follow. But eventually, as Helen cleaned up her house and her person, swept out resentments and smothered angers, and came to see herself for the cherished person she was in God's eyes, the marriage too was healed. As I know from the amazing long-distance phone call that came from her over a year later. 'I just thought you'd like to know, Catherine, that Steve and I are back together. We're off on a sort of second honeymoon now. We're spending hours just talking . . .'

So the Bible extols waiting, partly because it requires qualities which the Lord wants to encourage in us, like patience, which I need so badly. But there is another reason too. Waiting works. It is a joining of man and God to achieve an end, and the end is always a form of the Easter story.

An incident I've never forgotten is related by Patt Barnes of Milwaukee, who tells of an aged flower vendor he once met who taught him the secret of the 'three days'. Patt Barnes was so impressed by the old woman's visible radiant joy that he commented that her life must be remarkably trouble free. Oh no, she said, she had as many troubles as the next one, but she knew that problems held a resurrection hidden within them. When Jesus died, all looked black, but then three days later came Easter. 'So that's why I'm happy,' she said. 'I know the secret. When trouble comes, give God a chance — wait three days.'

We can allow an apparent defeat to turn into victory through trusting in the principle of resurrection. The time may not be a literal three days, but the principle is always the same. Nor, as the Bible prototype (Easter) was not a passive event, neither is this kind of waiting. Here too, something must be put to death, usually worry or trying to 'do it yourself'.

Some years ago a friend of mine in Washington confided to me a kind of prayer she was saying for her son, then a boy of ten. 'Already I've begun praying for that just-right marriage partner for Bobby. I pray for this future wife's protection from evil, for her proper growth, both physical and spiritual,' she told me.

That was a new idea to me. But it struck me as so right that I acted on it. Each morning for some days, I worked on that creative type of prayer which, I had learned from experience, God delights to honour. I asked myself, 'What would be the characteristics of spirit and mind and heart of that just-right girl for my son?' I was not so much concerned with whether she would be a blonde or a brunette; surely, the inner beauty would indicate the outer.

Item by item — quite specifically — the lineaments of my dream girl were put on paper. Most importantly, she would have met Jesus Christ for herself and would have fallen in love with Him. She would have a good mind, enough education for mutual intellectual stimulation. She would have a lot of the joy of life in her, a sense of humour, a certain zing — and so on.

Then when the portrait seemed complete, one morning I gave it to the Lord, asking Him to correct any flaws in it and bring it to fruition in Peter's life in His own time and His own way. I buried it, as it were, as a farmer buries his seed, by placing the notes about my dream girl between the pages of the same favourite Bible.

In the years that followed it was difficult not to dig the seed up again and examine it as in time, a procession of girls passed through Peter's life. Many were attractive; some would have been hard to accept. But the time of creative waiting came to an end when Peter John was in his middle year at Princeton Seminary. The girl's name was Edith.

Sometime after Edith and Peter were engaged I came across those written notes and reread them with amazement. There — detail by detail — was Edith. Of course, as always, God had thrown in a few extra goodies for dividends. She was tall, like

Peter; blonde, like Peter; a wonderful cook — what man wouldn't like that? She was strong physically, with joyous vitality. And she was interested in gardening and handicrafts and other hobbies which Peter enjoys. I loved her immediately and have never stopped thanking God for such a marvellous answer to the mysterious, triumphant Waiting Prayer.

WHILE I WAIT

Lord Jesus, You want honest words on my lips: no thought of mine is hidden from You anyway ... I am puzzled about the Father's timing. You know how long I have been praying about _____ _____, and I have tried to be patient about the answer. But Lord, why does Your providence have to move so slowly?

I know that the seasons come and go in majestic sequence. The earth rotates on its axis in a predetermined rhythm. No prayers of mine could change any of this. I know that Your ways are not my ways; Your timing is not my timing. But Lord, how do I, so earthbound, come to terms with the pace of eternity?

I want to be teachable, Lord. Is there something You want to show me, some block You want removed, some change You want in me or my attitudes before You can answer my prayer? Give me the gift of eyes that see, of ears that hear what You are saying to me.

Come Lord Jesus, and abide in my heart. How grateful I am to realise that the answer to my prayer does not depend on me at all. As I quietly abide in You and let Your life flow into me, what freedom it is to know that the Father does not see my threadbare patience or insufficient trust, rather only Your patience, Lord, and Your confidence that the Father has everything in hand.

In Your faith I thank You right now for a more glorious answer to my prayer than I can imagine. *Amen.*

CHAPTER FIVE

THE PRAYER OF
RELINQUISHMENT

Like most people, when I first began active experimentation with prayer, I was full of questions, such as: Why are some agonisingly sincere prayers granted, while others are not?

Today I still have questions. Mysteries about prayer are always ahead of knowledge — luring, beckoning on to further experimentation.

But one thing I do know; I learned it through hard experience. It is a way of prayer that has resulted consistently in a glorious answer, glorious because each time power beyond human reckoning has been released. This is the Prayer of Relinquishment.

I got my first glimpse of it in the fall of 1943. I had then been ill for six months with a widespread lung infection, and a bevy of specialists seemed unable to help. Persistent prayer, using all the faith I could muster, had resulted in — nothing. I was still in bed full time.

One afternoon a pamphlet was put in my hands. It was the story of a missionary who had been an invalid for eight years. Constantly she had prayed that God would make her well, so that she might do His work. Finally, worn out with futile petition, she prayed, 'All right. I give up. If You want me to be an invalid, that's Your business. Anyway, I want You even more than I want health. You decide.' In two weeks the woman was out of bed, completely well.

This made no sense to me, yet I could not forget the story. On the morning of September 14 — how can I ever forget the date? — I came to the same point of abject acceptance. 'I'm tired of asking,' was the burden of my prayer. 'I'm beaten, finished. God, You decide what You want for me.'

Tears flowed. I felt no faith as I understood faith, expected nothing. The gift of my sick self was made with no trace of graciousness.

And the result? It was as if I had touched a button that opened windows in heaven; as if some dynamo of heavenly power began flowing, flowing. Within a few hours I had experienced the presence of the Living Christ in a way that wiped away all doubt and revolutionised my life. From that moment my recovery began.

Through this incident and others that followed, God was trying to teach me something important about prayer. Gradually, I saw that a demanding spirit, with self-will as its rudder, blocks prayer. I understood that the reason for this is that God absolutely refuses to violate our free will; that therefore, unless self-will is voluntarily given up, even God cannot move to answer prayer.

In time, I gained more understanding about the Prayer of Relinquishment through the experiences of others, both in contemporary life and through books. Jesus' prayer in the Garden of Gethsemane, I came to see, is the pattern for us. Christ could have avoided the Cross. He did not have to go up to Jerusalem the last time. He could have compromised with the priests, bargained with Caiaphas. He could have capitalised on His following and appeased Judas by setting up the beginning of an earthly Kingdom. Pilate wanted to release Him, all but begged Him to say the right words that would let him do so. Even in the Garden on the night of the betrayal, He had plenty of time and opportunity to flee. Instead Christ used His free will to turn the decision over to His Father.

The Phillips translation of the Gospels brings Jesus' prayer into special focus: 'Dear Father . . . all things are possible to you. Let me not have to drink this cup! Yet it is not what I want but what you want.'[1]

The prayer was not answered as the human Jesus wished. Yet power has been flowing from His Cross ever since.

Even at the moment when Christ was bowing to the possibility of an awful death by crucifixion,

He never forgot either the presence or the power of God. There is a crucial difference here between acceptance and resignation. There is no resignation in the Prayer of Relinquishment. Resignation says, 'This is my situation, and I resign myself and settle down to it.' Resignation lies down in the dust of a godless universe and steels itself for the worst.

Acceptance says, 'True, this is my situation at the moment. I'll look unblinkingly at the reality of it. But I'll also open my hands to accept willingly whatever a loving Father sends.' Thus acceptance never slams the door on hope.

Yet even while it hopes, our relinquishment must be the real thing — and this giving up of self-will is the hardest thing we human beings are ever called on to do.

I remember the agony of one attractive young girl, Sara B., who shared with me her doubts about her engagement. 'I love Jeb,' she said, 'and Jeb loves me. But the problem is, he drinks. Not that he's an alcoholic or anything. But the drinking is a sort of symbol of a lot of ideas he has. It keeps bothering me — enough that I wonder if God is trying to tell me to give up Jeb.'

As we talked, Sara came to her own conclusion. It was that she would lose something infinitely precious if she did not follow the highest and the best that she knew. Tears glistened in her eyes as she said, 'I'm going to break the engagement.

If God wants me to marry Jeb, He will see that things change — about the drinking and all.'

Right then, simply and poignantly, she told God of her decision. She was putting her broken dreams and her now unknown future into God's hands.

Jeb's ideas and ideals did not change, and Sara did not marry him. A year later Sara wrote me an ecstatic letter. 'It nearly killed me to give up Jeb. Yet God knew that he wasn't the one for me. Recently I've met *the* man and we're to be married. Today I *really* have something to say about the wisdom and the joy of trusting God . . .'

It's good to remember that not even the Master Shepherd can lead if the sheep do not follow Him but insist on running ahead of Him or taking side paths. That's the *why* of Christ's insistence on a very practical obedience: *And why call ye me, Lord, Lord, and do not the things which I say?*[2] Obey . . . obedience . . . trust . . . is all over the Gospels. The pliability of an obedient heart must be complete from the set of our wills right on through to our actions.

When we come right down to it, how can we make obedience real except as we give over our self-will in reference to each of life's episodes as it unfolds — whether we understand it or not, and even if evil appears to have initiated the episode in question? That's why it should not surprise us that at the heart of the secret of answered prayer lies the Law of Relinquishment.

So Mrs. Nathaniel Hawthorne, wife of the famous American author, found as she wrestled in prayer in the city of Rome one February day in 1860. Una, the Hawthorne's eldest daughter, was dying of a virulent form of malaria. The attending physician, Dr. Franco, had warned that afternoon that unless the young girl's fever abated before morning, she would die.

As Mrs. Hawthorne sat by Una's bed, her thoughts went to her husband in the adjoining room and what he had said earlier that day, 'I cannot endure the alternations of hope and fear; therefore I have settled with myself not to hope at all.'

But the mother could not share Nathaniel's hopelessness. Una could not, must not die. This daughter strongly resembled her father, had the finest mind, the most complex character of all the Hawthorne children. Why should some capricious Providence demand that they give her up?

Moreover, Una had been delirious for several days, had recognised no one. Were she to die this night, there could not even be the solace of farewells.

As the night deepened, the girl lay so still that she seemed to be in the anteroom of death. The mother went to the window and looked out on the piazza. There was no moonlight; a dark and silent sky was heavy with clouds.

'I cannot bear this loss — cannot — cannot ...' Then suddenly, unaccountably, another thought took over. 'Why should I doubt the goodness of God? Let Him take Una, if He sees best. More than that: I can *give* her to Him! I do give her to You, Lord, I won't fight against You any more.'

Then an even stranger thing happened. Having made this great sacrifice, Mrs. Hawthorne expected to feel sadder. Instead she felt lighter, happier than at any time since Una's long illness had begun.

Some minutes later she walked back to the girl's bedside, felt her daughter's forehead. It was moist and cool. Her pulse was slow and regular. Una was sleeping naturally. And the mother rushed into the next room to tell her husband that a miracle had happened.

In the realm of answered prayer the progression of events in Una's recovery was not unique. For in the years since I first read the Hawthornes' story, I keep hearing of strikingly similar experiences. This one was given me by a friend in a letter:

... Three years ago our son was born. At first he seemed a normal, healthy baby. But when he was not quite twelve hours old, while I was holding him in my arms for the first time, he had a convulsion. More convulsions followed in the next few days.

The only explanation the doctors had was that he must have suffered a brain injury of some kind at birth. This only added to my terror. If he lived, perhaps he would be blind, deaf, dumb, or a cripple, or with his mind affected. I've never felt so alone during the time that followed. I prayed, but I couldn't feel that God cared about me anymore. Why had this had to happen to *my* baby?

I know now that my prayers were not prayers at all, but accusations. I was demanding that God heal my child.

Then out of sheer exhaustion of body and soul, I stopped commanding God and gave in to Him completely. I just said, 'Take him if that's what You want. *Anything* You decide will be all right with me. Even if You want him to be crippled or retarded , then I will just have to learn to accept it and live with it.' I put myself entirely in His hands.

From that instant, not only did Larry begin to improve, but suddenly my tears left, and my fears went with them. An inexplicable peace filled my heart, and I knew, just knew that Larry would not only live but would have a normal, useful life . . .

Well, the end of the story is that Larry is now a normal and healthy little boy. He's very, very intelligent, and if he were any more active, well, I'd be the one to be a cripple . . .

It is obvious that Larry's story and Una's have several points in common. In each case, the mother wanted something desperately — life and health for her child. Each mother virtually commanded God to answer her prayer. While this demanding spirit had the upper hand, God seemed remote, unapproachable. Then through a combination of the obvious futility of the demanding prayer, plus weariness of body and spirit, the one praying surrendered to the possibility of what she feared most. At that instant, there came a turning point. Suddenly and unaccountably, fear left. Peace crept into the heart. There followed a feeling of lightness and joy that had nothing to do with outer circumstances. That was the turning point. From that moment, the prayer began to be answered.

Now the intriguing question is: What is the secret or spiritual law implicit in this Prayer of Relinquishment?

Here is part of it . . . We know that fear is like a screen erected between us and God so that His power cannot get through to us. So, how does one get rid of fear?

This is not easy when the life of someone dear

hangs in the balance, or when what we want most in all the world is involved. At such times, every emotion, every passion, is tied up in the dread of what may happen. Obviously only drastic measures can deal with such a gigantic fear and the demanding spirit that usually goes along with it. My experience has been that trying to deal with it by repeating faith affirmations is not drastic enough.

So then we are squarely up against the Law of Relinquishment. Was Jesus showing us how to use this law when He said, 'Resist not evil'?[3] Stop fleeing from and denying this terrible prospect. Look squarely at the possibility of what you fear most.

At the time, it seems to us that this is the opposite of trust. 'Lord,' we are inclined to protest, 'didn't You tell us to pray with faith? I'm confused. Does relinquishment mean that we can never be sure about praying for any definite thing? If it does, Lord, then how can that be faith?'

To all such pleas to understand, Jesus always patiently gives the same answer, 'Obey Me. Then — after that — you will know and begin to understand.'

So we take the first hard steps of obedience. And lo, as we stop hiding our eyes, force ourselves to walk up to the fear and look it full in the face — never forgetting that God and His power are still the supreme reality — the fear evaporates. Drastic? Yes. But it is one sure way of releasing prayer power into human affairs.

Sometimes the miracle of prayer gloriously answered takes place at that point. With other situations the Good Shepherd leads us from relinquishment on into *knowing*. Such knowing is different from trying to think positively or making affirmations. It is not our doing at all; it is the gift of God.[4]

Sometimes the gift of faith is given to us through a verse of Scripture which leaps from the printed page or out of our remembrance and sets the heart afire. Or the knowing may come after a self-authenticating, interior Word from the Lord Himself about what is going to happen in our situation. Upon occasion, God may tell us that He cannot grant us what we have asked for, as in the case of Sara B. Obviously, we have not really meant business about the Prayer of Relinquishment until we have faced that eventuality too.

Whenever a loving Father grants our wish, the Word appears in exterior circumstances and the miracle happens — we understand that relinquishment and faith are not contradictory. The Prayer of Relinquishment is the child dropping his rebellion against being a child, placing his hand in the big, protective hand of the Father, and trusting Him to lead us even in the dark.

In the Prayer of Faith our hand is still in His.

Our heart is still obedient. But now He has led us out of the frightening darkness, with only the pressure of His hand to reassure us, into the sunlight. We look into the Face beside us with a thrill of recognition — the hand of the Father is Jesus' hand!

All along, our heart told us it was so. Relinquishment? Faith? Just daring to trust Jesus.

I RELINQUISH THIS TO YOU

Father, for such a long time I have pleaded before You this, the deep desire of my heart: _____ _____. Yet the more I've clamoured for Your help with this, the more remote You have seemed.

I confess my demanding spirit in this matter. I've tried suggesting to You ways my prayer could be answered. To my shame, I've even bargained with You. Yet I know that trying to manipulate the Lord of the Universe is utter foolishness. No wonder my spirit is so sore and weary!

I want to trust You, Father. My spirit knows that these verities are forever trustworthy even when I *feel* nothing . . .

> That You are there.
> (You said, 'Lo, I am with you alway.')[5]
> That You love me.
> (You said, 'I have loved thee with an everlasting love.')[6]
> That You alone know what is best for me.
> (For in You, Lord, 'are hid all the treasures of wisdom and knowledge.')[7]

Perhaps all along, You have been waiting for me to give up self-effort. At last I want You in my life even more than I want _____. So now, by an act of my will I relinquish this to You. I will accept Your will, whatever that may be. Thank You for counting this act of my will as the decision of the real person even when my emotions protest. I ask You to hold me true to this decision. To You, Lord God, who alone are worthy of worship, I bend the knee with thanksgiving that this too will 'work together for good'.[8] Amen.

CHAPTER SIX

THE PRAYER IN SECRET

In the summer of 1960 — when I saw for the first time the Sistine Chapel in Rome — I was intrigued to learn something of the working habits of Michelangelo Buonarroti. The four years that it took the great Florentine to paint the vault of the chapel were largely spent in isolation behind locked doors. While very young, Michelangelo had found that for him, work of integrity was impossible without secrecy.

Learning this reminded me again of the power that lies in secrecy. It was in connection with my first book, *A Man Called Peter*,[1] that I experienced its validity. After a rough outline had been approved by the publishers, some instinct told me that until the book was completed, the work should be kept as secret as possible.

Looking back now, I can see at least two reasons why this secrecy was right. I knew that the creativity necessary for the writing was a delicate plant indeed. It could easily wither and die under discouragement or non-constructive criticism.

I also knew that the ideas of others might cloud my own, could dull and confuse those deepest inner convictions that had to be followed for writing integrity.

Many another writer has found that when he shares an idea for an article or a book too soon, his ability to get the idea on paper sharply deteriorates.

Ernest Hemingway, for instance, has described the trouble he plunged himself into while working on the manuscript of *The Sun Also Rises*. The setting was the village of Schruns in the Austrian Alps. Around the fireside of a winter's evening, Hemingway made the mistake of reading aloud portions of his novel. The danger to him was not negative criticism, rather damage to his own critical judgment through too much unthinking praise, as he describes in *A Moveable Feast*:

> When they said, 'It's great, Ernest. Truly, it's great,' I wagged my tail in pleasure . . . instead of thinking, 'If they . . . like it, what is wrong with it?' That was what I would think if I had been functioning as a professional — although if I had been functioning as a professional, I would never have read it to them.[2]

It was after I had discovered the power of secrecy in the arts that I realised its strength in the equally creative realm of prayer.

In the Sermon on the Mount, Jesus reveals the mysterious spiritual power in secrecy: 'But when thou doest alms, let not thy left hand know what thy right hand doeth: That thine alms may be in secret: and thy Father which seeth in secret himself shall reward thee openly.'[3]

In addition to charitable giving and good deeds, Jesus applied the principle specifically to two other areas — prayer[4] and spiritual disciplines such as fasting.[5]

One man who took these words literally was George Müller. The result was a story of prayer power that amazed the world. Müller, a German with a practical businessman's mind, was seized with the conviction that he should establish orphanages in nineteenth-century England where there were few provisions for homeless children.

Especially astounding in view of his business background, was the way in which Müller determined to raise the money for this project — by secret prayer. His associates were appalled when he spelled out some of the details:

- No funds would be solicited directly. The method for obtaining contributions would be by prayer *alone*. No worker could give out information about specific needs.

- Names of contributors would also be kept secret. They would be thanked privately.

Nor would prominent names ever be used to advertise the institution.

* In spite of these seemingly unpromising pre-conditions, no debts were to be incurred — all transactions were strictly cash.

George Müller then set aside one hour each day for prayer. As punctually as a Swiss watch, George would retire to his room at the allotted time. On his knees he could concentrate on meeting his Lord, pouring out to God his wishes and hopes and dreams for his work and the needs of his orphans. Once every week, he met with all his associates in a session of prayer — also behind closed doors.

There was something so irresistibly challenging about Müller's formula that despite his aversion to publicity, the news travelled and purses were eagerly opened. Starting with one rented house, two workers, and forty-three children, in time there were five new buildings and 110 workers for 2,050 orphans. In all, during his lifetime, 121,000 orphans were sheltered, fed, educated — a million and a half pounds sterling administered. (Müller kept careful records of every transaction.) The work is still going on as a monument to faith. And at its heart was the Prayer in Secret.

As we walk with Jesus through the Gospel narratives, we find Him acting on this principle Himself. On one occasion when He had just healed a leper, we are told that 'Jesus sent him away . . . with the strict injunction, "Mind you say nothing at all to anybody".'[6] At another time, when Jesus had raised Jairus's twelve-year-old daughter, we read that her restoration sent her parents almost 'out of their minds with joy. But Jesus gave them strict instructions not to let anyone know what had happened . . .'[7]

The Prayer in Secret need not conflict with praying two-by-two or with small-group prayer. When Jesus raised Jairus's daughter, there were seven persons in the room — the girl, the child's parents, Peter, James, and John, and Christ. Yet following such a group experience, Jesus seems to say that additional power is released if there is no gossip about it outside the prayer room.

When I first read these accounts of Christ's ministry, I assumed that He wanted certain miracles kept secret lest He be not able to cope with the eager crowds or because this might speed Him on His way to the Cross prematurely. But I believe that a more significant reason is involved — that answers to prayer can be diminished, even nullified, by exposing the experience to the comments of the unbelieving. When Jesus returned to His hometown, Nazareth, where the townspeople thought of Him merely as the local carpenter's son, we are told: 'And he did not many mighty works there because of their unbelief.'[8]

Since this happened to Christ Himself, then

how much more easily it could happen to any of us!

How Jesus loved to pray in secret Himself! He had a habit of 'rising up a great while before day' and going outdoors — to a mountainside or some other deserted place — to pray. Perhaps because of the small, crowded Palestinian houses, that was the only way He could find privacy and solitude.

Before major decisions — such as His choosing of the twelve apostles — He would pray alone an entire night. And going back to the beginning of His public ministry, we find Jesus going off into the desert for forty days and forty nights of seclusion and concentrated prayer. He knew that power was needed; in secret He would find it.

There are other reasons why Jesus instructs us to pray in secret. Real power in prayer flows only when man's spirit touches God's Spirit. As in worship, so in prayer: 'God is a Spirit: and they that worship him must worship him in spirit and in truth.'[9] Secrecy helps us get rid of hindrances to praying with our spirit. For instance, in our room with the door shut, we are not so likely to strut and pose and pretend as we are when another human being is present. We know that we cannot deceive God. Transparent honesty before Him is easier for us in isolation.

Then too, there is the necessity of shutting out distractions — the doorbell, the telephone, the laundryman, the children. God asks that we worship Him with concentrated minds as well as allowing the Spirit to direct our wills and emotions. A divided and scattered mind is not at its most receptive.

There is also the matter of our spiritual balance sheets. When we perform a good deed, we are usually quick to advertise it, display it, collect the credit — use it up. Unworthy or bad deeds we hide. The 'credit' (i.e. debit) of the bad acts stays with us, accumulates. Thus our personalities are always on the debit side. Spiritually we remain chronically bankrupt.

Jesus told us that if we want to become fulfilled and productive persons, we must reverse the process. That is, we are to divest ourselves of weaknesses, faults, and sins by confessing them openly, while kindnesses and good deeds are to be kept secret. The result is an inner reservoir of power.

As the reservoir begins to fill, we experience the Father's 'reward' as promised by Jesus: God's presence in our life and affairs with all the attendant blessings.

What these blessings turn out to be can be shared with others only long after our Prayer in Secret has been answered. That is why I can now tell about our prayer for the Stowe family. (Of course, this is not their real name.)

It happened one autumn when our children were small. We knew Mr. Stowe because he was a schoolteacher in our son's school, a man who gave all of himself to his profession. As such, he symbolised to us all those unsung citizens who serve selflessly but often with small pay. The Stowes had five children, lived in a house too small for such a large family, and were having a hard time making it financially. Yet they could always be counted on for community projects. But we knew that they themselves had too few of the necessities and none of those extras of the good life that some of us take for granted.

Our concern took the form of dinner-table conversations followed later on by some prayer for the Stowes during one of our Family Times. Then we asked the question, 'Lord, is there anything You would like *us* to do for the Stowes?'

The answer was not long in coming. We were directed back to an old novel we had all but forgotten, Lloyd C. Douglas's *The Magnificent Obsession*. As we refreshed our minds about the story, we remembered that Randolph, a sculptor, found that when he gave money away as Jesus instructed in the Sermon on the Mount, without letting anyone discover his generous action, power flowed into his life through new energy in his work, fresh sureness and poise in relationships with people, and answered prayers. The sculptor's petition was not for money or fame, but rather for his work: '. . . the capacity to do just one credible work of statuary.'

Randolph's prayer was abundantly answered — he became a gifted sculptor. Eventually in fact, fame and material benefits followed as well.

In Douglas's book the 'secret of keeping a secret' was then passed on to others — including a brain surgeon — with equally startling results.

All of this led to our deciding to make the Stowes' Christmas a family project, and to keep this a secret from the Stowes as from everyone else.

Other ground rules were laid down: We were to make as many of the presents as possible — like cakes and cookies from cherished old recipes, sequined and beribboned Christmas ornaments; a tiny Christmas tree for the birds, decorated with eatable goodies for them. In addition, our children were to save or earn the money for at least one gift for each of the Stowes.

By Christmas Eve a large carton was filled to the brim with gifts. Attached was a note explaining to our friends that these gifts were to try to say to them how much their continual unselfish giving had meant to many in the community; that since this gift was from the Christ Child Himself, other names were not needed. With each gift went a prayer for God's abundant blessing on their family. The box was then left on the Stowes' doorstep.

And the giving and Prayer in Secret was marvellously answered. Word came to us that the Stowes had one of the greatest Christmases of their lives. Not long after that, Mr. Stowe was offered a better position with a larger salary. Suddenly, the whole community began to show more appreciation for the Stowes' selfless service. The children found various ways to go to college. Blessings for all of us came out of the experience.

Because the prime condition of this prayer *is* secrecy, illustrations beyond one's personal experience with it are not easily come by.

It was only after Janet Ritter's death (not her real name, since we cannot violate her secret either) that members of her family and close friends discovered what a powerful factor the Prayer in Secret had been in her life.

Janet was married to a successful New York journalist. In her forties she became an alcoholic. The best professional care could not cure her. Her defeat and self-loathing took a curious form. Often her husband would come home to their Park Avenue apartment to find his wife unconscious on the floor of her closet. Obsessed by a feeling of guilt during her drinking, Janet would often decide to clean out her closet. She would work at it desperately until she passed out. In the end, the closet held the clue to Janet's release. From the little that Janet told us, we have been able to piece the story together . . .

On a particular day, she lay across her bed

fighting a desperate inner battle. Thanks to
Alcoholics Anonymous, she had been dry for two
months. That morning she had an overwhelming
urge for just one drink. She well knew that once
she had one, a hundred more would never be
enough. 'God help me,' she cried. 'I can't let my
husband and children down again.'

On the nightstand beside her was a Bible
bound in white leather — little used. That day,
however, she opened the Bible by chance to the
Sermon on the Mount. Her eyes fell on the word
closet ... Instantly her attention was arrested.
Closet! Her closet had become a symbol to her, a
hated symbol.

> But thou, when thou prayest, enter into thy
> closet, and when thou hast shut thy door, pray
> to thy Father which is in secret; and thy Father
> which seeth in secret shall reward thee openly.[10]

Pray in the closet? Why? Janet had no idea
why. But that closet drew her as a magnet. Once
again she found herself huddling in among her
belongings. Only this time, she was praying,
praying for release from her bondage.

The open reward that Jesus promised was given
to Janet Ritter. She overcame her temptation for
alcohol. In addition, her personality took on such
magnetism that, five years after her death, I have
seen the faces of friends glow when they speak of
her.

Many of the details of her story we shall never uncover. We do know that after that morning, Jesus' formula for power became Janet's guide. She found that giving part of herself or her possessions, in secret, formed the base for rejuvenating her life.

Here are two incidents that came out inadvertently. A private school in New York was instructed to select a worthy girl from a slum district. She would be sent to school, all expenses paid. She must never know her benefactor.

A New York bachelor friend, ill with bronchitis, had a tureen of delicious soup and a tray of delicacies delivered to his door each day. The messenger gave no name; there was no name on the tray. In this case, the bachelor guessed and finally made Janet admit it.

Undoubtedly there was a long series of kindnesses — large and small — all kept secret. The rewards were so open that Janet Ritter's influence for good will go on and on. In addition, to an amazing degree, her personality took on that indefinable feminine charm and magnetism for which every woman longs.

If you feel that your prayers are ineffective, as we all do at times, I suggest you explore the formula for prayer that Jesus bequeathed to us. The world desperately needs the concentrated power that comes from praying in secret.

OUR SECRET

Father, I begin to see that You have decreed the Law of Secrecy all through Your Creation. Seeds secreted in the warm earth are invisible to all eyes but Yours during the long days of germination. Baby chicks hidden in the eggs do not cackle or crow during the weeks of incubation beneath the patient mother-hen. Our creation too requires the months of seclusion in the dark of the womb. So I see that prayer, the highest form of creation, must also for a time be hidden with You for Your work to be accomplished.

Lord, here is a request dear to my heart: _____ _____. It strengthens my faith to know that You want this petition to be our secret; that as I hide my request in You, I have touched the creative heart of the universe.

So I leave this prayer with You, Father. As day follows day with no results visible to me, give me the gift of knowing that since You care for me more tenderly than for any seeds or eggs, Your work of Creation on my behalf is going on just as surely. How I thank You! In the beauty and strength of Jesus' name I pray. *Amen.*

A suggestion: for most of us a bit of dramatisation helps. You could write out your Prayer in Secret, date it, and insert it between the pages of a little-used Bible close to a promise that speaks to you, such as Matthew 6: 3, 4. Then leave it there until your prayer is answered. C.M.

CHAPTER SEVEN

THE PRAYER OF
JOYOUS BLESSING

Some years ago, I knew of a home in Washington, D.C., which was full of tension because of an aunt's nagging faultfinding with the children. Ellen R——, the mother of the family, did much praying about this situation, mostly that God would take away the aunt's hypercritical attitude. Nothing at all seemed to happen as a result, and Ellen became increasingly resentful of the aunt's attitude and presence in her home.

One afternoon, Ellen — whom I had known for many years — dropped by our home to return a borrowed book.

'I know I must look a wreck,' she apologised. 'I feel like a ball knocked back and forth between the children and Auntie.'

In the midst of discussing her problem, I had a sudden inspiration. 'You've been asking God to change your aunt's disposition, and you say she's more fault-finding than ever. So why not forget about trying to change your aunt and just ask God to bless her — in anything and everything?'

Ellen looked astonished. 'You mean I should ask God to bless Auntie whether she deserves it or not?'

Before I could answer, my friend had a counter thought. 'I see it,' Ellen said thoughtfully. 'I guess none of us *deserves* anything from God, do we?'

'That's exactly my thought,' I told Ellen. 'Nothing we could ever do would be good enough to earn a scrap or a rag from His hands.'

'Then, Catherine, let's try your idea. But will you pray with me about it right now?'

'Of course. But remember, Ellen, when you ask God to bless someone, what you're really saying is, "Make him or her happy." That's the literal meaning of *blessing* in the Bible — happiness.'

As I recall, Ellen's prayer went something like this: 'Lord, I know it's Your will that we be happier in our house than we have been. And I know that can't happen while any one of us is unhappy. Bless Auntie now in whatever ways she needs. Give her the gift of happiness. Help the children to love and respect her — and show me how I can be kinder to her. *Amen.*'

A week later my friend telephoned. Ellen said that day by day her prayer was being abundantly answered. 'The atmosphere here at home is completely different. You know this blessing business is dynamite! But I still don't understand why that prayer was answered when none of the others were. Why would there be such power in wishing joy for someone?'

Perhaps one reason we are surprised when God moves to bless someone when we ask it, is that we have thought of Jesus Christ as primarily 'a man of sorrows, and acquainted with grief'.[1] No man with an attitude of gloom could ever have drawn little children to Him. Only an enthusiastic man who went out to meet life with unflagging zest could have attracted rugged fishermen as His disciples. Sadness couldn't last long when a man delightedly threw away his crutches or a leper went off leaping and singing on his way to show his clean new flesh to the priest. And don't forget that the Gospels record Jesus as breaking up every funeral He attended!

Certainly, Jesus was unblinkingly aware of life's problems and disappointments: 'In the world ye shall have tribulation,' He promised His disciples. 'But,' He added, 'be of good cheer; I have overcome the world.'[2] Or in other words, 'Cheer up! The worst that the world can do is no match for Me.'

The real source of Jesus' joy is given us in unforgettable words first spoken by the Psalmist[3] and centuries later by the author of Hebrews:

Thou [Christ] hast loved righteousness, and hated iniquity; therefore God, even thy God, hath anointed thee with the oil of gladness above thy fellows.[4]

He who knew no sin and *is* righteousness, had a personality sparkling and overflowing with a degree of gladness which none of us can match. How could it be otherwise!

That's why the Prayer of Joyous Blessing does not depend on our merit or lack of it. Jesus is the *only* righteous One, therefore the only finally joyous One. But this joy He longs to share with all who will receive it.

Now we begin to see why my friend Ellen was on firm ground in not making her aunt's 'worthiness' a condition for her Prayer of Joyous Blessing. She knew that Jesus has told us: 'Love your enemies . . . Bless them that curse you.'[5]

As soon as we begin to obey Him, we find that blessing those with whom we are having difficulties and the *answer* to these difficulties, go hand in hand.

I had this connection between the Prayer of Joyous Blessing and God's power to transform situations dramatised for me some years ago when a woman came to see me, asking my advice about her marriage. Over a cup of tea she told me her problem. She had just had the hardest blow the feminine ego can sustain — her husband had announced that he no longer loved her and was going to leave her.

Mrs. B____ felt that their marital problems were her husband's fault and she was full of harsh criticism of him — he never went to church; he spent little time with their children; he was unfaithful. 'Only God can save him,' Mrs. B____ intoned gloomily.

'Here's an idea how to pray for your husband,' I suggested. 'Ask God to rain His blessings — spiritual, physical, and material — on him, and leave the rest to God.'

My visitor sipped her tea, and her lips pursed into a firmer line. 'My husband has prospered too much already,' she said. 'That's the trouble with him. The only thing that will ever bring him to his senses and back to God is trouble, and more trouble.'

She left, saying that she was going to pray that God would change her husband, make him good, then bring him back to her and the children. And her prayers fell to the ground. The husband eventually got a divorce and married someone else.

In one of His parables, Jesus left us His comments about Mrs. B____'s kind of prayer for her husband. One day Jesus had watched two men praying in the Temple — an important, well-educated Pharisee and a lowly publican. 'Don't do as the Pharisee,' the Master later told His disciples. 'His prayer was, "I thank thee that I am not as other men are — extortioners, unjust, adulterers, or even as this publican".'[6]

Then Jesus threw in the wry suggestion that the Pharisee was not 'praying' at all, he was talking to himself. Of course he did not go down to his house 'justified',[7] that is, his prayer was not answered.

Why not? Because God hears not what our lips say, but what we really mean behind the facade of words. So what did the Pharisee mean? Something like this: 'Lord, I thank Thee that I'm not like Mr. _____. I am good; this other person is bad. He does not deserve Your blessings. I suggest that You send this sinner a lot of trouble. That ought to bring him to his senses. It won't do, Lord, to have the wicked prosper.'

If you and I were running the world, probably we would not allow the wicked to prosper. But the simple truth is that often they do prosper. All through the centuries, this fact has bothered men. In what may be the oldest book in the Bible, Job wrestles with the problem. It is mentioned in Psalm after Psalm. But Jesus was and always is the Realist. He simply took it for granted that because God is all love, the wicked *will* often prosper: '. . . for he maketh his sun to rise on the evil and on the good, and sendeth rain on the just and on the unjust.'[8]

'Therefore,' said Jesus, 'if you are going to be true sons of your Father in heaven, then you'll have to pray for the very best to happen to everyone you know — no matter how you personally may have been mistreated or hurt by them.'[9]

Is Jesus saying then, that goodness or wickedness are of no consequence to God? Not at all!
Sin is a serious matter, serious enough to have
sent Christ to His Cross, and our world closer and
closer to the brink of disaster. But the point is that
self-righteous prayers or accusing prayers do not
change men from bad to good. Only joyous love
redeems.

Our Dutch friend, Corrie ten Boom, was trying
hard to obey Jesus by loving her enemies one
night in a Munich church. She had just finished
her talk when she spied him — a former German
S.S. guard especially loathed by the prisoners in
the concentration camp at Ravensbruck. This
man had been one of many who had 'despitefully
used' Corrie and her sister Betsie during their
imprisonment there. Betsie had died in this camp.
After Corrie was released in late 1945, she went
about the former enemy country of Germany
speaking out to all who would listen, the message
that God had laid on her heart like a live coal —
forgiveness.

And now here he was, the first of her actual
jailers whom Corrie had seen since her release.
This was the man with the leering face and the
mocking voice who had stood guard at the shower-
room door in Ravensbruck. Corrie's heart sank
as she saw the man coming towards her.

'Fraulein,' he said ingratiatingly, extending his

hand, 'thank you for your message. To think that He has washed our sins away!'

Corrie felt her right arm go stiff, ramrod straight against her side. Even as a storm of angry, vengeful thoughts boiled up inside her, she knew how wrong they were. She who had just finished talking about loving our enemies, was being asked to make good her words.

She tried to smile, struggled to raise her arm, but she could not. Her heart felt no trace of warmth for the man standing there with his hand extended.

'Jesus, I cannot forgive him,' went her quick inward prayer. 'Give me *Your* forgiveness.' Then Corrie's arm reached out and as her fingers touched the man's, incredibly, she felt something like an electric current begin at her shoulder, race along her arm and pass into the German. Simultaneously, into her heart sprang such a joyful love for the former guard as she would not have believed possible.[10] Thereafter, Corrie found that she *could* pray with ease that God would rain abundant blessings on the former guard.

That's the way Corrie ten Boom discovered what all of us have to come to sooner or later: We can love our 'enemy' enough to ask gladness for him, only if He who was anointed with so much gladness, does it for us.

Long before Jesus' day, the ancient Israelites had stumbled on the truth that gladness is a key to God's presence: *The joy of the Lord is your strength . . . In thy presence is fullness of joy . . . Serve the Lord with gladness: come before His presence with singing.*[11]

As he wrote his Psalms, perhaps David was remembering the day he had literally come into God's presence with singing — and dancing. Israel's standing enemies, the Philistines, had finally been defeated. The sacred ark could now safely be brought to Jerusalem. So David had brought it: 'With gladness . . . he danced before the Lord with all his might . . . with shouting and the sound of the trumpet.'[12]

And Michal, his wife, watching his joyous abandon, had been embarrassed. Her husband was making a fool of himself! So she 'despised him in her heart'. The writer of the old story then adds a curious footnote to the story. Michal was never to have the most fervent desire of her heart granted: she was to remain childless until the day of her death.[13]

Scripture does not explain this further. We can guess that Michal's inability to enter into David's joyousness was merely a symptom of deeper trouble. The queen despised her husband. Like Mrs. B____, she was probably habitually nursing grudges and resentments — prime blockages to answered prayer.

Had Michal been able to forgive, joy could have joined hands with love, perhaps to grant her fervent desire for children along with many another answered prayer.

Agnes Sanford, the Episcopal rector's widow, has told about how she first met the power of joy when her baby had been ill for six weeks with abscessed ears. Her prayers for healing, she said later, had been negated by the fear and desperation in her heart. Then one day a young minister called. 'I'll go upstairs and have a prayer with the baby,' he offered.

The mother was sceptical about his prayer achieving anything that hers had not, but showed him the way to the baby's room. The young rector tenderly held the baby's head in his big hands. Mrs. Sanford said later, remembering the incident, 'Light shone in the minister's eyes. I looked at him and saw his loving joyfulness, and I believed. For joy is the heavenly 'okay' of the inner life of power . . .'[14]

The baby promptly went to sleep. When he awoke, he was well.

Queen Elizabeth's standard flying over Buckingham Palace in London is the sign that the queen is in residence. Joy looking out of the Christian's eyes is the sign that the King is in residence within. Similarly, in prayer, joy is a sure sign of the King's approval.

It is possible to find the way to pray with joy even in a very serious and seemingly tragic situation. Do we need healing? One way is to ask ourselves why we want health. Then make a series of happy pictures in the mind of the creative ways that we would use health.

Or do we need financial help? How would we use adequate financial resources? One way of joyous prayer is to create a series of pictures in the mind of the way we would use money, not just for ourselves, but to extend His joy to others.

Having so often seen the Prayer of Joyous Blessing gloriously answered, I've begun to wonder recently if here we don't have a key to the problem of world peace. Even for those who take prayer seriously, it isn't easy to know how to pray for other nations. It is especially hard when their ideals are not ours, and when they consider themselves our enemies.

Perhaps Christ would say to us, 'The people of all nations are My children, too. The more violent greedy men ignore Me and prey on My innocents, the more they need to be released to My all-encompassing love.'

Now obviously, we cannot bless and pray for people who despitefully use others or with whom we are at odds, unless we recognise that no self-effort can manage this and let Christ — living in us — love others for us.

But it may be that if even a handful of citizens could pray with that kind of joy for the people of 'enemy' nations, with the expectation of good, asking for God's all-abundant blessings on them in every sphere — tremendous results would be forthcoming.

Our first reaction to that suggestion may be exactly what Mrs. B____'s was. Too risky! Which of us wants other nations to pull out ahead of our nation in the sciences, in the exploration of outer space, in military know-how, or in the economic sphere?

But it is not a risky way to pray, once we see that God's way is to make 'his sun to rise on the just and on the unjust', and that His sun of joy is the only power in the universe capable of transforming the hearts of men — no matter what their problems, their politics, or their nationality.

BLESS US, FATHER

Father, I cringe to see myself in that Pharisee in the Temple,[15] for I have been believing a lie:

> That since I have tried to serve You, I have a right to ask for Your blessings.

> But that _____, so unbelieving and uncaring about You, deserves the difficulties he has.

Now I understand, Father, that You must manifest love and joy to us, Your creatures, because You *are* love and joy; that You, as the Sun of Righteousness in whom no darkness dwells,[16] shine upon us because it is Your nature to shine — not because a one of us is deserving of it.

I now release _____ from my judgment and I ask You to bless him abundantly in any and every way that seems good to You.

So live Your life in me, Lord, that from henceforward I shall desire as much good for others as I ask for myself that I shall never again plead largess for myself and ir my heart begrudge Your blessings for others.

Cleanse me of all selfishness and ungenerosity. And O Father, fill me up with the joy of Him who was anointed with the oil of gladness[17] above us all. In His name, I pray. *Amen.*

CHAPTER EIGHT

THE CLAIMING PRAYER

I first became aware of the Claiming Prayer back in 1947 when I noticed a strange sentence written on the flyleaf of Peter Marshall's Bible . . .

It's the word of a Gentleman of the most sacred and strictest honour, and there's an end on it!

DAVID LIVINGSTONE

Underneath Livingstone's name, Peter had signed his own.

When I asked Peter for an explanation of the words, he thumped the cover of his Bible and said, 'In these pages are the living words of the living God. These words include a lot of promises, many of them with conditions attached. All we have to do is to meet the conditions, then step up and claim them.'

He was silent for a moment. Then . . . 'Remember how I promised Peter John to take him down to the train store this Saturday?'

I nodded.

'Well, I'd be a poor father if I failed to keep

promises like that to my son. And if I'm conscientious enough to want to keep my word, how much more so is God!'

'But that quote in the front of your Bible,' I reminded him, 'is there a story behind it?'

There was, and Peter referred me to the missionary's journals. It was 1856. Livingstone faced one of the gravest perils of his sixteen years in Africa. He was passing through the wild country of the native chief, Mburuma, who was hostile and had been seeking to rouse the countryside against the white man's expedition. Reports had been coming in that natives were creeping towards the camp.

Alone in his tent, Livingstone opened his Bible to the promise on which he had staked his life so often. Then he wrote in his journal:

January 14th, 1856. Evening. Felt much turmoil of spirit in view of having all my plans for the welfare of this great region and teeming population knocked on the head by savages tomorrow. But I read that Jesus came and said: *All power is given unto Me in heaven and in earth. Go ye therefore, and teach all nations . . . and lo, I am with you alway, even unto the end of the world.* It's the word of a Gentleman of the most sacred and strictest honour, so there's an end on it! I will not cross furtively by night as intended.[1]

Thus Livingstone claimed the promise of Jesus' presence.

During the hours of darkness nothing happened. The next morning Livingstone, still calm, superintended the crossing of the river for his company of 114 men and their riding oxen while Mburuma and his tribesmen watched from the jungle's edge.

The missionary reserved for himself the last place in the last canoe. One native bearer, fearful of treachery, pleaded with Livingstone not to give the chief a chance to shoot him in the back.

'Tell him to observe that I am not afraid,' Livingstone replied. Then with dignity he approached the astonished natives, thanked them, wished them God's peace, and walked slowly to the canoe. The crossing was made safely. During those moments the missionary-explorer must have been vividly aware of the One who walked beside him. 'Lo, I am with you alway,' he had penned the night before. And now faith had become fact: *He*, the Lord, was there beside him.

For the Risen One this was a re-enactment of an incident during His days on earth in the flesh. There had been the same kind of seething mob bent on treachery:

> . . . they mobbed him and took him to the edge of the hill on which the city was built to push him over the cliff.[2]

But he passing through the midst of them went his way.[3]

The Kingly Presence beside Livingstone gave the missionary such nobility of bearing that even native warriors felt it. Not a hand was raised to molest him.

Livingstone had prayed the Claiming Prayer. For himself and his company, he had claimed Jesus' promise, *Lo, I am with you alway.* And He of the sacred honour had fulfilled His word.

David Livingstone's experience made such an impression on me that those words in Peter's Bible have been associated with the Claiming Prayer ever since.

Yet I had no base on which to use this way of praying until my attitude towards the Bible changed. I began by considering Bible reading a dull chore. College courses in which we studied the Scriptures as literature or in Comparative Religion as simply one of many world religions, had not changed the tedium I felt.

Nor had such courses given me an answer about how I was to regard the Bible. Was it a collection of myths and folklore 'inspired' only in the sense that the plays of Shakespeare or the poetry of John Keats were inspired? Or was Scripture the authoritative Word of God Himself, somehow channelled through the minds and pens of certain picked men? I did not know.

But after I made an act of committing my life to God, gradually, for me, the Bible underwent a transformation. I wanted to read the Bible because it told me so much about the character and ways of God. I found myself eager to know how He dealt with men and women in every imaginable circumstance, so that I could have some idea how He would deal with me. And the more I read in this remarkable book, the more surely I knew that in its pages God Himself was speaking to me.

'But *how* do you know that?' I've been asked sometimes. 'How can you be certain?'

My answer came out of the dawning realisation that we human beings arrive at surety by one of two routes. With questions pertaining to our bodies or material matters, we are convinced by intellectual, scientific, or evidential proof. With questions pertaining to man's spirit, we are convinced only by personal revelation. For instance, a question like, 'How do I know He loves me?' can never be proved by reasoning or in the laboratory. For love is in the area of spirit from whose door the scientific kind of proof is turned away every time. Yet the flooding inner revelation: 'He *does* love me! He loved *me*!' is valid, bringing such surety that I am willing to commit my life to my love.

When we realise the range of important

questions which will always elude the net of final
intellectual or scientific proof, then we begin to
appreciate the significance of revelation. Surely,
here is a most important gift we should ask for
more often.

One of my friends, who like me arrived at this
place of surety via personal revelation, likes to
think of the Bible this way:

> The Scriptures *are* letters — personal letters
> from God to each one of us. If you want to open
> your mail, just read through any of the passages
> that begin with the word *whosoever* — and
> substitute the words 'that means me' for *who-*
> *soever*. These are the promises God has made to
> each one of us . . . And we can take God at His
> Word![4]

'We can take God at His Word,' says Colleen
Townsend Evans in *Love Is an Everyday Thing*. 'The
word of a Gentleman of the most sacred and
strictest honour,' David Livingstone wrote. Once
we too *know* like that, then we understand something else — that God means that all lives be lived
in co-operation with Him. His friendship, His
plans for us, His riches are awaiting each of us,
provided we want Him in our lives and tell Him
so.

And then the point of the Claiming Prayer
becomes clear — the riches of grace must be

claimed. '. . . *ye have not, because ye ask not,*' the
Apostle James cried.[5]

The process goes like this:

- God has made a promise.

- If there are conditions attached to it, we do
  our best to meet them.

- We make an act of claiming this promise at
  a specific time and place.

- God fulfils the promise in His own time and
  His own way.

How practical the Claiming Prayer can be was
illustrated by a series of incidents told me some
years ago by my long-time friend Colleen, the
wife of Louis Evans, the pastor of the National
Presbyterian Church in the nation's capital.

Colleen had been a rising movie star. For years,
tutors, studio cars, the services of makeup men,
and glamorous clothes had been at her disposal.

Before marrying Louis, Colleen made the
decision to give up her movie career. In the years
since, despite some tempting offers, she has never
compromised with that decision. But little did
Colleen know how difficult the transition would b e .

Four years after their marriage, Louis was
asked to start a new church in the Los Angeles
suburb of Bel Air. He accepted the challenge. His
salary was quite inadequate for a wife and by

then, three young children, the needs of a manse, money for the constant entertaining necessary, and ministerial books. Thus no paid household help was possible.

At the end of the first year in the new parish, Coke — as her friends call her — felt herself at the end of all physical and spiritual resources. Always tired, she could never see over the top of a mountain of home chores (since with no building, their home was the church) and church work. Nor could she even find time for a few minutes of quietness and prayer. She felt utterly exhausted and knew that she needed help.

Coke's first opportunity to think through the situation came during the family's summer vacation. Away from the parish and the tyranny of the telephone, with the children playing outdoors most of the days, she determined to pray her way through to some answers. She placed before God three acute problems:

- There was simply too much work. She felt like a servant in her own home. How could one woman be maid, cook, laundress, mother, wife, as well as church janitor?

- Constant interruptions from parishioners and friends through visits and telephone calls.

- The need for a daily Quiet Time. How could she manage that?

'That summer God gave me insight into every problem,' Coke told me. 'He answered me with words from Scripture that were manna to my spirit. He didn't pamper me or take away my difficulties, but He showed me how to make a new beginning in handling each situation by claiming His strength.'

These are the answers Coke received:

For feeling like a servant in her own home: 'I mean for My children to minister, to be servants in every way.[6] Accept your role. The important thing is your willingness to pick it up. Then I will do the rest. Above all, do not feel sorry for yourself.' Jesus also counted Himself servant of all.[7]

For too much work: No one has ever had a nervous breakdown just from overwork; it is the worrying about tomorrow and next week that is making your load unbearable. Claim My strength one day at a time with the promise: *And as thy days, so shall thy strength be.*[8] Also learn to say *no* sometimes. Ask yourself, 'Is this what people want, or what my Father wants?'

When interruptions come: Treat them as Jesus did. There were many times when He yearned to be left alone too. Yet He reacted to interruptions not by resisting or resenting them, but by accepting and using them as opportunities to teach and help people.[9] He understands your situation because He had it much worse. Claim His help in treating your interruptions His way.

Finding a Quiet Time: With young children in the home there will be few uninterrupted stretches of time. So watch for free minutes, chinks of time throughout the day to pray. The question really is, how much do you *want* to pray? Claim this promise for the quiet heart: *For God is not the author of confusion, but of peace* . . .[10]

Now, years later, there is abundant evidence how bountifully Colleen Evans' Claiming Prayers were answered. Though the children are older, there are still interruptions. Yet the old desperation and threat of a breakdown have long since given way to a quiet effectiveness. Rarely have I seen a more successful wife, mother, and minister's helpmate. To crown it all, Coke is still a glamorously beautiful woman. By now the author of two books, she even finds time to serve on the board of trustees of two outstanding educational institutions.

I believe the Claiming Prayer to be the crown of all ways of prayer because it inscribes a completed circle between earth and heaven, thus meeting the conditions of prayer power. For the purpose of all prayer is to find God's will and to make that will our prayer, so that as Jesus bade us pray in the Lord's Prayer, the Father's will may be done as perfectly on earth as it is in heaven.

Thus we go to God with a problem, seeking light on it. We give God a chance to speak to us either through Scripture or through His quiet voice in our hearts. This part makes half of the circle as our need sweeps up to God.

Then God points out to us one of His promises which applies to our situation. Our claiming of this promise will complete the circle — from heaven to earth.

This promise is the handle of faith that we can grasp in prayer. The Apostle John has expressed it in words of pure gold:

And this is the confidence that we have in him, that, if we ask anything according to his will, he heareth us: And if we know that he hear us, whatsoever we ask, we know that we have the petitions that we desired of him.[11]

Strange, how one's mind and spirit leap in joyful response to John's words. 'Yes, John, you're right. I see it! Of course God is going to grant me what has been His will for me all along.' So in that faith we make a specific act of claiming the promise that God Himself has given us.

If there are any conditions attached to this promise, we do our best to meet them, for he who will not let us down also will not let us off. To illustrate: the condition of having our sins cleansed is our forgiveness of others;[12] the condition of material blessing is that we give priority to the Kingdom of God;[13] one condition for guidance is acknowledging God in every area of our lives;[14] and the condition for world peace is high: humbling ourselves as a nation, praying, and turning from evil.[15]

After that, we wait for the fulfilment of the promise, secure in the knowledge of a God who cannot lie,[16] and that he who believes in Him will never be disappointed.[17]

The Claiming Prayer is the most incisive way of prayer that I know, resting its case as it does on that 'word of a Gentleman of the most sacred and strictest honour'.

Try it. He will never fail you.

I CLAIM YOUR PROMISE

Father, with my mind I have tried to understand You and Your ways. But the confusion and uncertainty in my life dramatise how limited my capacity for understanding is. I see now why You have provided us, Your creatures, with an added dimension beyond intelligence: an inner spirit to be a receiving set for Your Spirit. Father, if ever anyone needed the revelation of Spirit, I do. I ask now for the illumination that is the Spirit's gift of revelation about . . .

the Bible and how I should read it. (Is it really Your Word in a special sense?)

the particular promise from Scripture You want to give me today.

Father, I see how this promise relates to this situation:

_____

_____. In faith, I copy these 'words of a Gentleman' on a slip of paper.[18]

And now, Father, I claim them for myself and my situation by endorsing it on the back. How grateful I am that this cheque is signed by Him whose integrity is impeccable. I rest on the sure knowledge that behind this cheque stands final security — all the resources and reserves of heaven. Thank You, Father. *Amen.*

NOTES

Chapter 1 Prayer Is Asking

1. Luke 15: 8–10.
2. James 4: 2 MOFFATT.
3. Matthew 20: 29–34 MOFFATT.
4. Matthew 7: 11 MOFFATT (*italics* added).
5. Matthew 7: 7, 8 MOFFATT (*italics* added).
6. John 16: 24 MOFFATT (*italics* added).
7. Luke 11: 11, 12.
8. Mark 10: 15 LB.
9. Luke 18: 9–14 RSV.
10. C. S. Lewis, *The Screwtape Letters*.
11. John R. Rice, *Asking and Receiving*.
12. John 4: 5–30.

Chapter 2 The Prayer of Helplessness

1. Psalms 4: 1 MOFFATT.
2. John 15: 5.
3. John 5: 30, 36.
4. John 6: 44 MOFFATT.
5. Ephesians 2: 8, 9.
6. John 3: 27.
7. Brother Lawrence, *Conversations: The Practice of the Presence of God*.
8. Matthew 19: 26.
9. A. B. Simpson, *The Gospel of Healing*.
10. Adapted from 'The Hound of Heaven', from *Complete Poetical Works of Francis Thompson*. The poem reads: 'Is my gloom, after all, Shade of His hand, outstretched caressingly?'

Chapter 3 The Prayer That Helps Your Dreams Come True

1. Proverbs 29: 18.
2. 1 John 5: 14, 15.

Chapter 4 The Waiting Prayer

1. A favourite illustration of Peter Marshall's. He used it to help answer the question, 'How much should I do to help God answer my prayers, and how much should I leave with Him?' Catherine Marshall, *A Man Called Peter*.
2. John 15: 1–8.
3. Mark 4: 28.
4. Mark 1: 15.
5. John 7: 6.
6. Matthew 26: 18.
7. Acts 1: 7.
8. Lamentations 3: 25.
9. Psalms 37: 9.
10. Isaiah 40: 31.
11. Isaiah 64: 4 LB
12. Galatians 6: 9.

Chapter 5 The Prayer of Relinquishment

1. Mark 14: 36 PHILLIPS.
2. Luke 6: 46.
3. Matthew 5: 39.
4. Ephesians 2: 8; 1 Corinthians 12: 9.
5. Matthew 28: 20.
6. Jeremiah 31: 3.
7. Colossians 2: 3.
8. Romans 8: 28.

Chapter 6 The Prayer in Secret

1. Catherine Marshall, *A Man Called Peter*.
2. Ernest Hemingway, *A Moveable Feast*.
3. Matthew 6: 3, 4.
4. Matthew 6: 5, 6.
5. Matthew 6: 16–18.
6. Mark 1: 43, 44 PHILLIPS.
7. Mark 5: 42, 43 PHILLIPS.
8. Matthew 13: 58.
9. John 4: 24.
10. Matthew 6: 6.

Chapter 7 The Prayer of Joyous Blessing

1. Isaiah 53: 3.
2. John 16: 33.
3. Psalms 45: 7.
4. Hebrews 1: 9.
5. Luke 6: 27, 28.
6. Luke 18: 11.
7. Luke 18: 14.
8. Matthew 5: 45.
9. Matthew 5: 44; Luke 6: 28 (paraphrased).
10. Corrie ten Boom, *The Hiding Place.*
11. Nehemiah 8: 10; Psalms 16: 11; 100: 2.
12. 2 Samuel 6: 14–16.
13. 2 Samuel 6: 20–23.
14. Agnes Sanford, *The Healing Light.*
15. Luke 18: 11.
16. 1 John 1: 5.
17. Hebrews 1: 9.

Chapter 8 The Claiming Prayer

1. Isaac Schapera, ed., *Livingstone's African Journal 1853–1856,* 2 vols.
2. Luke 4: 29 LB
3. Luke 4: 30.
4. Colleen Townsend Evans, *Love Is an Everyday Thing.*
5. James 4: 2.
6. Mark 10: 44.
7. Mark 10: 45.
8. Deuteronomy 33: 25.
9. Mark 6: 31–46.
10. 1 Corinthians 14: 33.
11. 1 John 5: 14, 15.
12. Matthew 6: 14, 15.
13. Matthew 6: 33.
14. Proverbs 3: 6.
15. 2 Chronicles 7: 14.
16. Titus 1: 2.
17. 1 Peter 2: 6 MOFFATT.
18. It might be helpful to write out on a slip of paper the promise given to you.

LIGHT IN MY
DARKEST NIGHT

Light in my Darkest Night

Catherine Marshall

Hodder & Stoughton
LONDON SYDNEY AUCKLAND

To Amy Catherine Marshall
whose time on earth touched many lives

With Gratitude _____

Deepest appreciation goes to Theresa Mulligan, whose computer expertise and research skills solved countless problems; to Elaine Brink for invaluable typing and secretarial help; to Steven Payne, O.C.D., the editor of the Catholic quarterly *Spiritual Life* magazine, for reading the manuscript and making helpful suggestions.

Once again I pay special tribute to Elizabeth (Tib) Sherrill, who has provided priceless editorial help on Marshall-LeSourd books now for ·28 years. Because of her love for Catherine, Catherine's family, and the LeSourds, Tib worked on this book as if it were her own.

Finally, gratitude to the sixteen prayer warriors who gathered at Cape Cod in the summer of 1971, all of whom have been supportive and cooperative—and especially to all those family members who not only helped guide this project, but also contributed their written observations and experiences of that memorable period.

Contents

Editor's Foreword _____

Catherine Marshall LeSourd's *Light in My Darkest Night* has been waiting to be written for the past seventeen years. Catherine always intended to do it herself, but somehow the time never seemed right. As the years passed, I wondered whether the events of a profoundly significant phase of her life—and mine—would ever be told.

Yet as time went by, the story not only did not die, it kept arising in conversations with friends and family: "Remember the summer of 1971? . . . So many lives were touched. . . . How long did it take Catherine to get over it? . . . Where has Catherine written about it?"

The answer to that last question is—nowhere.

Except for tantalizing fragments in *Something More* and

Meeting God at Every Turn, this central crisis of her life remained concealed, segments of it known to family and close friends, portions of it poured out in her journals, the basic pain and frustration of it known by me chiefly through the dialogues the two of us had together.

There are two reasons why I'm convinced that Catherine would have wanted this book published. First, Catherine had a deep sense of mission about her life. She felt that God had called her to write, that she was to be fearless and selfless about revealing her spiritual valleys—as well as the mountaintops—to her readers. Early in her career she realized that God used her weaknesses more than her strengths as teaching points. Not many Christian writers have bared their souls with such transparent honesty as Catherine did in her books. This book especially reflects this sense of personal candor.

And second, the subject has a special urgency today. Christians today are going through periods of darkness, where even the certainty of the Light's existence is lost. There is tremendous need for teaching on how to survive these dark nights. Now is God's moment for this message, I believe. Perhaps this is why He did not give Catherine a "go" on this book before.

To tell the full story it is necessary to go back to some pre-1971 episodes, to pick up roots of conflicts that came to a head that year. In every dark night of the soul there are contributing factors that go back many years, sometimes many generations. My hope is that readers of this book who are going through dark times themselves will be encouraged to trace similar threads in their own lives. To some, the circumstances that contributed to Catherine's crisis of faith may not seem as dire or tragic as their own; others may find their troubles pale in comparison to Catherine's. Whatever the landscape of your particular valley, the truths that Catherine learned as she traveled hers are valid for all.

The structure of this book follows the pattern set by *A Closer Walk*: Most of the material comes from Catherine's own writings and journals, with background information and comments by me. In addition, I have drawn on twenty hours of tapes that Catherine and I made together in the fall of 1971, recording our recollections of, and reactions to, the tumultuous events of the preceding summer. Also important are reflections from other leading characters in the story: Peter and Edith Marshall, my daughter Linda LeSourd Lader, John and Elizabeth Sherrill, Virginia Lively, Jamie Buckingham.

Doing this book has been painful for me, yet also richly rewarding. I have had to go back in time to read, as Catherine read, accounts of the dark nights that earlier Christians went through. I've had to probe my memory and our files for missing pieces of the story. Out of it all has come a better understanding of Catherine that has made me cherish her memory more than ever. Also have come insights about myself. What a mixture of strengths and weaknesses we all are! Catherine's central message: *If we will let Him, the Lord will help us grow strong precisely in the weak places themselves.*

Catherine let Him. She went through a dark night experience that shook her faith and tested all her resources. It involved all-out spiritual warfare, not only for Catherine but for family members and friends.

My prayer is that the discoveries in this book will be a shaft of light into the minds and hearts of hurting people who do not understand why God seems to have abandoned them. Everywhere one turns today, there is a cry of pain, an anguished word of despair. Many are wandering in a personal darkness that renders them helpless and defeated. They desperately need to know there is a way toward the light.

For the good news that Catherine discovered was that God had not abandoned her; He had only withdrawn for a season . . . *in order to bring her into a still closer relation-ship with Himself.*

If you identify with Catherine's dark night of the soul, you can also look forward with confidence to the sunlit heights of a new and stronger faith. That's the bright promise of this book.

Leonard E. LeSourd
Evergreen Farm
Lincoln, Virginia

Light
in My
Darkest
Night

Section I
Gathering Shadows

The Winter of '49 _____

*C*atherine . . . Peter Marshall's death from a heart attack at age 46 was a devastating blow. "Why?" I asked the Lord. "Why take a man who loves You so much, who is in the prime time of life, whose impact on people for You is so great?" In the midst of grief, I had a million "whys."

Not one of them was answered. Instead, into my anguished emotions there crept one morning a strange, all-pervading peace. Through and around me flowed love as I had never before experienced it. It was as if Someone who loved me very much were wrapping me 'round and 'round with His infinite care and protection.

I knelt there marveling at what was happening. I had done nothing, said nothing, to bring it about. I understood no more than before the reason for my young husband's death. I only knew that in some way that transcended reason, it was deeply and eternally all right. Into my mind came a verse from the Bible, "Underneath are the everlasting arms." That described what I was feeling.

I opened my New Testament and found these strength-imparting words:

> So, up with your listless hands! Strengthen your weak knees! And make straight paths for your feet to walk in. . . .

> Hebrews 12:11–12, MOFFATT

Soon afterward I was led to begin writing my husband's biography, *A Man Called Peter.*

I had asked God to tell me *Why?* He gave me no answer to this question. Instead, He gave me

. . . infinite Love for my present need,

. . . step-by-step guidance for my future walk.

How much anguish I might have saved myself twenty years later if I had remembered this! If I'd thought back to the time of this first great bereavement, when instead of explanations, He gave me Himself.

The Decision _____

*C*atherine ... With the success of *A Man Called Peter* a new world opened up for me. My goal now was to communicate to others the excitement I felt for the living Lord.

The decade of the 1950s was one of much creativity—and much loneliness. I was not prepared at age 34, when widowhood began for me, to be a single parent to our son, Peter John, to manage my finances, and to handle a strenuous career of speaking and writing. There had been no training for any of this. At the time of Peter's death, I had been driving an automobile for only three months.

Yet in my weakness I discovered His strength. I needed Jesus every day, seeking Him in my morning time before all else.

And then after ten years of widowhood, I met Leonard LeSourd, the forty-year-old editor of *Guideposts* magazine. I liked Len's creative approach to publishing, his strong commitment to Jesus Christ, and the resourceful way he pursued me. In fact, for the first time since meeting Peter I was flushed with the joy of romance.

With a succession of housekeepers, Len had been struggling to rear three small children from a previous marriage. With Peter John now "out of the nest" and attending college, I had to decide if I was ready to take on full-time mothering again.

In my morning times that still, small Voice in my inner spirit asked me some searching questions:

Have you counted the cost? Have you really looked at the readjustments necessary for another marriage?

Are there not certain areas of your life where rigidity is creeping in? The rough and tumble of family life is My antidote to rigidity. But are you willing to be cured?

And do you not realize that My way would be to send you a man not just to satisfy your own needs, but because he has gigantic needs himself?

The issue was whether I was ready for that much commitment, not just to a man, but to three children too. Part of me was excited and stirred; the other part wanted to flee.

Both Len and I were agreed on the need to put Jesus at the center of any remarriage. Still I hung back. . . .

I thought with longing of the new house being built for me in Washington. It was almost finished. Adjoining my bedroom, cut off from the rest of the house, would be a step-down room where I could write. It would be my sanctuary. I was most reluctant to give up that prospect. Still, I would live in that house alone except for those brief holiday times when Peter John would be home from college.

Two roads stretched ahead, and I was at the parting of the

ways. In that house being built I might produce many articles and books. There I would have a cushioned, sheltered life—yes, and probably a lonely one.

And, if I chose the other road, I would plunge directly back into turbulent life. It would mean being a mother to Jeffrey, a mischievous imp of three; to Chester, six, with enormous brown eyes full of questions; to Linda, ten, approaching the challenging years of adolescence—and I had had no experience in rearing a daughter.

"Lord," I prayed one September morning in 1959, "I don't understand at all. Are You in this?"

I took a deep breath, for there was a sudden luminosity about this moment that I recognized. It had happened before when I asked Him for understanding. Once again, no illumination came to my mind. Instead, there was the overwhelming sense of His presence.

A bracing presence! No harp strings and angel choruses—this was no rosy-cloud vision. It was more like being slapped in the face with a wet washcloth. Or like being brought to earth with a thud and bidden to stand on one's feet.

Suddenly, the choice God was presenting to me was clear. To say yes to this man I loved, taking his children into my heart and life, meant a difficult adjustment. Yet I saw that if I said no and chose the other road, I would be turning away from the mainstream of life. The "no" way would be comfortable, but it would take me farther and farther from contact with people—and, ultimately, from God who shapes us through the people He places in our path.

At that moment His command seemed clear—"Say yes to life."

The Shadow _____

*L*en . . . I understood Catherine's struggle over whether to wed again, especially when three young children came with the package. Yet I confidently expected her to receive a "go" from the Lord to marry me. Why would He tell me one thing and Catherine another?

Six months before, I had been in a period of deep discouragement, trying to fill the role of single parent while commuting 75 miles from Carmel, New York, to my Manhattan job as executive editor of *Guideposts* magazine. My prayer was a most simple and direct one—"Lord, would You guide me to the woman You have selected to share my life?"

The first name dropped into my mind after this prayer

was Catherine's. I couldn't have been more surprised. I had met Catherine Marshall several years before when I had asked her to write an article for Guideposts. She did—coincidentally on the subject of "How to Find God's Guidance."

"Lord, can You be telling me that Catherine is Your choice as my wife?"

Silence. Nothing about it seemed to make sense, and I was far from experienced in asking for and receiving guidance from God. Still I figured I had nothing to lose by going to Washington, D.C., to see her. So we set up a date for a Saturday in August.

Catherine and I have described our courtship in previous books.[1] My main surprise was not only how we meshed together with our ideas and convictions, but the degree of physical attraction we had as well.

On that August Saturday we took a picnic lunch up to Skyline Drive in western Virginia and talked for ten straight hours, discovering what a lot we had in common. We were both PK's (preachers' kids), her father Presbyterian, mine Methodist. We came from strong, close-knit families. (Both sets of parents had marriages that were to last more than fifty years.) God had gifted us both with a love of words, Catherine as a writer, me as an editor. At that time we were both single parents.

One place where Catherine and I differed was in the timing of our Christian commitment. She met the Lord as a teenager, where I had resisted Him, seeking adventure in sports and as an Air Corps pilot during World War II. Like so many men of my time I had considered Jesus "loving but weak"—prejudiced, I think, by Sunday school pictures portraying Him as effeminate and unaggressive.

As a boy of twelve I had once cried in a sad movie and was so embarrassed by this show of emotion before my

---

[1] Catherine in *Meeting God at Every Turn*, I in *A Closer Walk*.

peers that I gave myself an order: "You will never cry again." In essence, I was telling myself not to feel strongly about anything or anyone. I didn't, either, until I was 29, becoming along the way shallow, self-centered, dead of spirit—a frozen man.

The thaw began in May 1948 at a weekend retreat for a group of young adults from the Marble Collegiate Church in New York City. I had gone to this group originally looking for a date. Somewhat against my will I went to the retreat, was annoyed to discover that my emotions were being touched at a deep level. Late Saturday night I found myself kneeling at the chapel altar below a virile picture of Jesus, where I surrendered my life to Him. The tears, dammed up for so many years, flowed.

It was at this same church that I met beautiful, talented Eve. Though I realized even as we were dating that she had a problem with alcohol, I felt naively that we could work this out once we were married. For I was ready now to settle down. Eve was not only a believer but a leader in our young adult group. Surely the love of God and our love for each other would see us over any rough places.

Eve and I were married at Marble Collegiate, had three children in seven years. The alcohol problem was kept in check as long as we lived in New York City close to our Christian friends. When we moved 75 miles to the country, the internal pressures on Eve seemed to explode.

Eve had counsel from psychiatrists and pastors, therapy at a treatment center. As her condition worsened, she was hospitalized for seven months. Later, her father, a physician in the Midwest, committed her temporarily to a state institution. Nothing seemed to help. After ten years of marriage, "for the sake of the children" we divorced.

For me it was a complete and senseless tragedy. In helpless frustration over a five-year period I watched the life of the woman I loved deteriorate. Never had I even imagined such pain, such grief. It precipitated a crisis of faith. "Why,

Lord, would You let this happen to me? I've tried to be a good husband, a good Christian," was my self-righteous, rebellious plea.

God was silent. I've learned since that He has a way of giving those who belong to Him a long leash. So I turned my back on Him, tried to rediscover life in the fast lane. It didn't take much time for me to fall on my face. The attempt to resume my old lifestyle was a disaster for me and bad for the children.

When I came back to Him on my knees, repentant, He was merciful. That was when, in response to my prayer for a new life partner, the name *Catherine Marshall* popped into my mind.

Catherine shared with her readers on several occasions the problems she faced adjusting to the idea of mothering my three young children. She confronted another, graver concern, however, one which, out of respect for Eve and me, she wrote about only in her journals: marrying a divorced man.

Hadn't Jesus Himself expressly forbidden it?

> But I say to you that whoever divorces his wife for any reason except sexual immorality causes her to commit adultery; and whoever marries a woman who is divorced commits adultery.
>
> Matthew 5:32, NKJ

Catherine and I discussed the situation in depth, talked with Christian counselors and pastors ... receiving a bewildering variety of opinions. Catherine agonized over this, praying about it for weeks.

Finally she shared with me the word she believed she had received: *The Lord is in the business of restoring broken homes and healing damaged families. He hates divorce, as He hates all sin, for the harm it does in every life it touches. But He does not lock us into our sins; He is the God of redemption and new beginnings.*

At that time Catherine was serving as woman's editor for a Christian magazine. When our engagement was announced, the publisher flew to Washington and met with Catherine to express his concern. "Your Christian readers will be greatly upset if you marry a divorced man," he told her.

More anguish for Catherine, as she weighed not only her own possible flouting of God's law, but the harm it might do to others. In the end, though, she placed her trust in her understanding of the Lord as the One who ever wills to bind up what is broken.

Catherine and I were married on November 14, 1959, with both our pastor-fathers officiating, along with our mutual friend Dr. Norman Vincent Peale.

With the wedding, however, the divorce issue did not go away.

A New Life _____

*C*atherine, February 1960 ... Lord, I find myself surprised to be where I am this morning, looking out over a snow-covered backyard, hearing new noises in a strange house. Soon I will be busy getting two children off to school on the bus, driving a third to nursery school.

I am adjusting once again to a man's schedule. He catches an eight o'clock train to the city and his office at *Guideposts*. Love has come a second time, only this time I'm being asked to love three children as well. Loving Len comes naturally—he's warm, open, patient, giving. With the children—I'm making progress.

Home for us all is a sprawling white house with red shutters set in the rocky, tree-shaded countryside of Westchester County. Our town of Chappaqua is about forty miles north of New York City.

Two Guideposts editors, John and Elizabeth Sherrill, are neighbors. They also have three young children, close to the ages of our three; I can already see that our lives and those of the Sherrills will become closely entwined.

Daily Len and I are making new discoveries—new to us, at least—about You in relation to marriage and family life. That's why when the automatic coffeepot attached to our clock starts percolating each morning, we're beginning to anticipate rather than dread this early rising. We read Your Word, share our discoveries, then pray together.

This morning, we identified three very definite ways that You lift love and romance to a higher level:

The first is that You are able and eager to guide us into a satisfying emotional life, *if we will rid ourselves of the falsehood that You want to take away our fun.* Only You can reach deep enough to touch our emotions and bring them fully alive, balancing seriousness with a sense of humor, keeping play and passion in juxtaposition.

Secondly, love is a gift and You can give this gift only to those who are willing to keep their hearts open. To keep the heart open means running the risk of getting hurt; thus, we must trust You before we can truly experience love.

Finally, there is a joyous surprise in discovering You as the One who steps up the voltage of physical attraction. When You said, "I am come that they might have life," You didn't mean just spiritual life, but all of life. We sense that when the edge is gone off any part of living, then the spirit in us is growing dim.

So we have concluded that You are far more concerned with human love than we had realized. And learning day by day about love—both human and divine—absorbs us.

Lord, my prayer this morning is that I stay constantly in Your will. Guide me, protect me, sustain me, Lord, in all that I do and particularly now with my new family.

Spring 1960 . . . Len and I together have just prayed for our neighbor, John Sherrill, Lord. John received bad news yesterday from his doctor. A growth in his neck requires immediate surgery: two years ago an operation in the same area disclosed malignant melanoma.

Since Len and I are editorial associates with John and his wife, Tib, we have gotten to know them very well. They're intelligent, highly educated, endlessly curious about the world around them, and I think that's their problem. The diversity of religious experience is what fascinates them. They roam the length and breadth of this country seeking stories for Guideposts, interviewing people, ghost-writing their experiences . . . always other people's experiences. I think their oh-so-professional "objectivity" is a defense against letting faith get too personal.

This morning I'm sensing that our prayers for John's healing are not the end of my involvement. Suddenly John's crisis seems to be my crisis—part of my "bundle" of responsibility, as the Quakers express it. So, what is my next step since Len is already on his way to work?

A series of thoughts keep pounding at me: healing is not an end in itself; it is a dividend of the Gospel. Physical health is but one part of total wholeness. Then this—has John ever made an act of turning his whole being over to You, Lord?

Who am I to ask John a question like that? He's written about total commitment—other people's commitment—over and over. I'm sure the usual religious clichés would be repugnant to him. Considering all this, would not any question about his relationship to God be gross presumption on my part and anathema to him?

Yet, time is running out. Only 24 hours remain until John enters New York's Memorial Hospital for surgery. What he thinks of me does not matter at a time like this. The fact that a life is at stake prods me to telephone John and tell him that I have to see him.

The Leap

John Sherrill . . . Tib and I were having coffee in bed this morning after a sleepless night when the telephone rang. It was our neighbor, Catherine LeSourd, asking Tib and me to come over right away. Catherine met us at the door dressed in a housecoat, wearing neither makeup nor smile, which said more than words about the concern she was feeling. She led us into the family room, shut the door, and without polite talk, began.

"First of all I want to say that I know this is presumptuous of me. I'm going to talk to you about your religious life, and I have no right to assume that it lacks anything. After all, you've been writing for *Guideposts* for almost ten years; you respect religion, you've studied it from many angles. But there is so much more to it than that.

"John," Catherine pressed on, "do you believe Jesus was God?"

It was the last question in the world I'd expected. I'd supposed she'd have something to say about God being able to heal, or prayer being the antidote to fear—something to do with tomorrow's surgery.

But she'd put the question to me, so I considered it. Tib and I were Christian, certainly, in the sense that we wrote "Protestant" on application blanks, attended church with some regularity, sent our three children to Sunday school. Still, I knew that these were habits; the fact was, I had never come to grips with this very question. Was Jesus of Nazareth, in fact, God? And now, when I tried, there were mountains of logic that halted me. I started to map them for Catherine, but she stopped me.

"You're trying to approach Christianity through your mind, John," she said. "It simply can't be done that way.

"It's one of the peculiarities of Christianity," she went on, "that you cannot come to it through intellect. You have to be willing to experience it first, to do something you don't understand—and then, oddly enough, understanding often follows. And it's just that which I'm hoping for you today, that without understanding, without even knowing why, you say yes to Christ."

There was silence in the room. I had an eternity of reservations—and less than a day before going to the operating table. The biggest reservation of all was precisely that: it just didn't seem right to shy away from wholehearted commitment all these years and then come running when I had cancer and was scared and had my back to the wall.

"I'd feel like a hypocrite," I said.

"John," said Catherine almost in a whisper, "that's pride. You want to come to God in your way. When you will. As you will. Strong and healthy. Maybe God wants you now, without a shred to recommend you."

We talked for perhaps half an hour more, and when we

left I still had not brought myself to make that step that was apparently all-crucial. In the car a few moments later, however, I turned to Tib. "What do they call it, 'a leap of faith'?" I said. "All right, I'm going to make the leap: I believe that Jesus was God."

It was a cold-blooded laying down of my sense of what was logical, quite without emotional conviction. And with it went something that was essentially "me." All the bundle of self-consciousness that we call our ego seemed somehow involved in this decision. It was amazing how much it hurt, how desperately this thing fought for life, so that there was a real kind of death involved. But when it was dead and quiet finally, and I blurted out my simple statement of belief, there was room in me for something new and altogether mysterious.

Len . . . At the time of his second cancer crisis, John and Tib were working on a book about modern-day manifestations of the Holy Spirit. They'd completed a first draft—very objective, very much a compilation of "other people's experiences"—when Catherine made that telephone call. In the intensely personal book the Sherrills ultimately produced, *They Speak with Other Tongues*, they describe what followed: a miraculous healing, a personal encounter with Jesus, eventually John's baptism in the Holy Spirit.

Our relationship with the Sherrills took on new dimensions, too, as the four of us began meeting weekly to share both family and work concerns. In Tib, Catherine found the sensitive editor she had long been seeking; soon her manuscript *Beyond Our Selves* was taking shape.

Catherine, fall 1961 . . . I'm full of joy and gratitude this morning, Lord. So much good is happening in our lives. A letter from Billy Graham yesterday is full of praise for my new book *Beyond Our Selves*. This praise belongs to You.

You give me the words, Lord. And the book is bringing people to You.

The editorial meetings at Guideposts are stimulating times. Yesterday we went over the two-part series John Sherrill is doing on David Wilkerson, who's done such amazing work with teenage gangs in New York City. I've never seen John so excited about a story.

John's recovery from his cancer operation is complete . . . his gratitude to You beautiful to behold.

To me the most remarkable event of 1961 is what has happened to Peter. Len and I have been praying so faithfully for Peter every morning—for almost two years now. And You have answered our prayers in the most spectacular way.

Last spring I was so discouraged. One evening Peter looked me straight in the eye and told me that when he graduated from college in June, he intended to be "a beach boy at Virginia Beach." I didn't believe him, of course, but he seemed so hostile to the Christian faith. It was Len who persuaded him to go to the conference at Estes Park, Colorado, put on by the Fellowship of Christian Athletes. You know the rest, Lord.

No More Running Away

Peter John Marshall, fall 1961 ... If there was ever a lost soul, wandering about without purpose or direction, it was me in the summer of 1961. Having graduated from Yale University, I had come home to the red-shuttered house in Chappaqua with all my belongings—and no idea what to do next. I had no career plans (what does one do with a history degree if one doesn't want to teach?) and, to put it bluntly, no remote idea why I was living.

Up to this point, my life had been one of almost total self-centeredness, for I had withdrawn after my father's death into a world of lonely independence from everybody, including God. During my college years at Old Eli I had tried to fill the emptiness with the proverbial "wine, women, and song"; now in Chappaqua daily tennis matches were all that got me out of bed in the morning.

My stepfather, Len LeSourd, was on the board of the Fellowship of Christian Athletes, and he and my mother had to go to an FCA conference at Estes Park, Colorado, in July. Having nothing better to do, I went along for the fun of the athletics, but God had something else in mind.

The main speaker that week was Donn Moomaw, a huge former All-American center at UCLA. He was now a Presbyterian minister, and when he spoke to us young athletes about Jesus Christ being a man's man and the only man worth giving your life to, we listened.

Finally, toward the end of the conference, I waited until everyone else had left the large wooden auditorium, then went up to speak with Moomaw. I told him I had some questions about dating, but the Spirit of God enabled Donn to see through this smokescreen. "That's not what's the matter with you," he said. "Your problem is that you've been running away from God all your life. When are you going to be ready to give your life to Jesus Christ?"

Suddenly I had the strange sensation of standing about twenty feet away from myself, hearing myself say something I had no intention of saying. To my astonishment, what came out of me was: "Well, I guess I'm ready as I'll ever be."

Donn said, "That's the truth! Why don't you do it right now? Sit down and let's pray right here."

And we did. I knew what I was doing; my mother had always made it clear that giving your life to Christ meant giving up control, coming under His authority to live the rest of your life for His plans, not your own.

My prayer was short, even crude: "Lord, my life is a

mess. I have fouled it all up, and I'm sick of running it my way. You can have the whole stinking pile of garbage, and if You can do anything with it, it's all Yours."

During the next few days the sun of God's favor and love burned away the fog within like the hot Colorado sun dissolving the mountain mists. Now that I was seeking His will for my life, God moved with a speed that took my breath away.

After the conference, Mother, Len, and I flew to Los Angeles to visit Presbyterian minister Louis Evans and his wife, Colleen, whose house guest just happened to be the director of admissions at Princeton Theological Seminary. Praying for God's guidance about my future, I decided to talk to this man, and within days the Lord began opening doors. In August I was accepted for the September entering class at Princeton Seminary. Amazing—in that only a few weeks before all this, becoming a Christian, let alone a Christian minister, was the farthest thing from my mind!

And so now after years of avoiding God, I was following in my father's footsteps. What Jesus will do with my life, how He will lead me, remains to be seen. But at last I know that I am finally tracking with His loving plan for my life.

Explosion
of the Spirit _____

*C*atherine, spring 1962 ... This morning, Lord, Your power and Your joy and Your love seem to be trembling in the very air about me. First, the beautiful experience that happened to Len last night needs to be recorded here. He came to our prayer group last evening full of resentment against one of his associates. Several of us laid hands on him and prayed for a healing—specifically that he would be filled with the Holy Spirit. Nothing seemed to happen until....

We'd gone to bed and I was dropping off when Len whispered, "Catherine, are you asleep?

"I have the strangest feeling," he went on. "There's this rushing, headlong joy inside me! It started in the pit of my stomach after I got in bed and now it's bubbling up right into my head. I can't control it. Catherine, I feel like praising God—on my knees!"

Both of us got up and knelt beside the bed.

Len's prayer began quietly enough. First he expressed gratitude for the friends who had prayed for him. Next he thanked God for our life together. After that he expressed love for each member of our family near and far. In between he kept telling the Lord how much he loved Him. Then heartfelt love rose from the depths of his being for the very individual who had been such a thorn in his side. Finally, he began God-blessing everyone he could think of, as if this love were so great it had to encompass the whole universe.

I was astonished. Always before Len's prayers had been short, even abrupt, well thought out, words carefully chosen, but quite unemotional. In contrast, words last night poured from him lavishly, exuberantly repetitious, a geyser of deep emotion unabashedly expressed. Like a bird uncaged, his emotions were darting, wheeling, soaring, wanting nothing so much as to keep flying forever.

Len's experience of the Spirit follows Peter's of last winter. Peter also was in a group—a small gathering of classmates at Princeton Seminary who prayed that Peter would receive the infilling. As with Len, Your coming, Lord, was precisely tailored to his need.

Peter, as a boy, suffered a lot of sadness—sadness that had been crammed deep down inside him. There was his bewilderment and loss as a small child when I was bedridden for almost three years, his enormous grief over the loss of his father at age nine. So when the Holy Spirit came into Peter, You produced laughter ... laughter that welled up from the depths of his soul—up and up and up, never stopping for thirty minutes—a cleansing, healing flow washing the buried sorrow away. . . .

And still earlier came John Sherrill's remarkable experience. John's healing from cancer started a revolution in his life. What he discovered of the power of the Spirit in David Wilkerson intrigued John so much that this son of a liberal theologian decided to attend a convention on the Holy Spirit in Atlantic City.

What then took place in a hotel room was a kind of modern Damascus Road experience. First, Tib left the hotel to walk for miles along the seashore, deliberately taking with her the habitual reportorial onlooker's viewpoint. A group of half a dozen men then prayed for John to receive the Spirit. He told us later that the roof seemed to open up and light pour down on him. He found himself on the floor with his glasses spun off to one side, his notebook and pen to the other, and no idea how much time had gone by.

John phoned us in Chappaqua from Atlantic City an hour after he "came to." He was almost incoherent with excitement, saying over and over, "You've got to come down here. You've just got to come. Terrific things are going on."

We couldn't go down to Atlantic City then, but when John returned to Chappaqua several days later, he radiated the joy of the Spirit. Tib, too, although she had not had a personal experience, came back utterly persuaded of the reality of the things they had witnessed. A detective's daughter, Tib is suspicious of outward appearances. "Some of the excitement in the big meetings seemed worked-up," she told us. "And of course there were one or two exhibitionists. But I sat there in Atlantic City watching people experience God's love in a profound and life-transforming way."

With Len, Peter, and John—three of the most important people in my life—having such vivid encounters with You,

Lord, I have asked myself, "Am I missing something?" Going back through my life I realize that for a long time the term *Holy Spirit* was for me just a sort of religious garnish, a sprig of parsley on the ecclesiastical platter.

Then in the summer of 1944 as I lay bedridden from my lung ailment, a desire arose inside me to know more about this vague-seeming subject. This led me to months of topical Bible study on the Holy Spirit in both Old and New Testaments. What I discovered astonished me. My inescapable conclusion was that since Your resurrection, ascension, and glorification, and until You return again, we are living in the era of the Holy Spirit.

Without the Spirit we are without any vivid sense of Your presence. We are without guidance or wisdom or peace or joy or any effective witness to other people. And so very simply and very quietly, with no one else present, I asked for the gift of the Holy Spirit, accepted His coming into my life by faith, and began to live that out day by day.

Nothing overtly exciting happened. My experience was a completely solitary one. I didn't know anyone back then in the '40s who was walking this particular road. There was nothing being written about the Holy Spirit that I could find.

However, during the years that followed there have been many manifestations in my life. A new awareness of Your guidance, for example—the kind that cautions or confirms. Wisdom was available for small daily decisions. I didn't have to muddle through many situations as I had before, trying to figure out everything for myself. The Helper was right there.

The question I have this morning is, "Is there something more?" This love everyone speaks of—You know, Lord, how badly I need that right now! After two and a half years of being mother to this family, the home situation is no easier. Harder, in fact, as the children get older. Len and I can't seem to agree on discipline, bedtimes, homework hours—anything. With Linda, especially, we're constantly at loggerheads. Linda flouts my rules, and I display my insecurity by losing my temper.

A Christian home should be a haven of peace, Lord; ours is too often a battlefield. How I need the love that flows from You!

Conflict _____

*L*inda . . . So many emotions were churning around inside me when Dad remarried. At ten I thought I was pretty adult. But looking back, I realize I was in great need of someone who understood my confused thoughts and emotions and could have helped me sort them out.

Eve ("Mommy," as I called her then) had been a wonderful mother to me in my very early years. We had done everything together and she treated me as her chief confidante. In fact, that became a problem. The burden of sometimes buying her liquor and secretly helping her dispose of the bottles in brown paper bags weighed heavily on me.

During my mother's long absences I missed her terribly and desperately, prayed she'd get better so we could be a normal, happy family again. Did some well-meaning but misguided adult suggest I must look after my younger brothers? Certainly I felt I should. I remember myself at nine, playing the little mother, preparing orange juice and doughnuts to serve with Saturday morning cartoons. Poor caretaker that I was, I was better than some of the house-keepers. One beat me with a belt when Dad went away on a trip. (She was fired.) And it seemed we were always being shuttled around to grandparents' or friends' houses.

When Dad married Catherine ("Mom," as I soon called her), I was excited. It signaled a return to normalcy. And a best-selling author seemed so glamorous to me! I'd even have an older brother, her son, Peter, a tall, handsome, worldly-wise college sophomore.

Yet I often thought of my "real mommy." Once years before she had awakened me at night, desperate for reassurance.

"Promise me one thing, Linda?"

"Sure, Mommy."

Her voice caught. "If you ever have another mother, promise me you won't call her 'Mommy.' Promise me I'll always be your 'Mommy.'"

I didn't know what she was talking about. "But Mommy, I don't *want* any other Mommy. I only want you. I want you to get well."

"Promise me, Linda?"

"I promise."

Thus began my difficulties with my stepmother, before I ever had one.

When Dad returned from his honeymoon with our new "Mom," they moved into a new house in a new community. Soon my brothers and I joined them—and right away I could see that things were not going to be as great as I had thought. As the new girl in my fifth-grade class I guess I tried too hard to show my classmates how great our family was: my dad an important editor ... my new mother a

famous writer . . . my big brother at Yale. It was too heady
for a ten-year-old to handle very well.

My stepmother and I soon began to clash over all sorts of
things: clothes, food, bedtime, money, duties around the
house. For someone who had had very little discipline up
to then, this super-structured new home life came as a
blow. To make things worse, I felt I had lost my father. When
he wasn't working in Manhattan, he and Mom were going
places, doing things, often without me and the boys. It
seemed that we saw more of the live-in housekeeper than
our parents.

Eventually I made it into the "in" crowd at school. That
entailed "hanging out" at local restaurants, weekend parties, trying out alcohol and cigarettes. All of these things
were forbidden to me, and I chafed at being the most re-
stricted of the group. Occasionally I would sneak out of the
house to join my friends, or lock myself into the bathroom
to smoke. When Mom caught me at these things, there were
some pretty bad scenes. Even Dad was upset with me at
times, but usually he'd just leave the room and later I could
hear raised voices behind my parents' door.

My schoolwork was another battleground. Though I had
always been a straight A student, my grades now seesawed
wildly. Sadly, I think it was my way of "getting back" at my
parents; no doubt it was also a cry for help. And help I got—
a teacher from school was hired as my tutor. But I spent
more energy trying to outsmart him than in doing my assignments.

Mom was warm and nice to me when I followed the rules
at home and performed well in school. But I didn't feel she
understood me—or wanted to try. I knew Dad loved me, but
most of his time seemed to be spent smoothing over conflicts between Mom and me. I'd been his "Number One girl"
for so long—now I felt I'd lost him.

As I entered my teens I was a very unhappy girl.

Family Crisis _____

*L*en ... The early '60s were exciting times ... high creativity and productivity ... exploring the Holy Spirit phenomenon ... stimulating travel. Challenging times, too, as the strong personalities in our combined families frequently clashed. I was often the man-in-the-middle, trying to balance the legitimate demands, for example, of both my wife and my daughter. Trying to keep peace in the family.

In 1965 there was a wonderful new addition to that family. For years Catherine had been praying for her son's future mate. She had even written down a description of her: "Strong Christian, tall because Peter's so tall, probably blonde, fun to be with. . . ." Peter met Edith Wallis, a fellow student, at Princeton Theological Seminary during his final year there. Peter knew nothing about his mother's prayer and would probably have called it "spiritual manipulation" if he had. In any case he fell in love with Edith: tall, blonde, and definitely "fun to be with." They were married in 1965 and settled in West Hartford, Connecticut, where Peter became assistant pastor at a Presbyterian church.

On a trip to the Holy Land in the summer of 1963 Catherine had contracted a bad case of bronchitis. When it lingered on throughout the following winter, threatening a return of her dreaded lung ailment, doctors urged a move to a warmer climate. We bought a house in Florida in the spring of 1964 and moved to Boynton Beach that fall. Catherine's mother, Leonora Wood, joined us there in the cold months. For me it meant long-distance commuting to my job at Guideposts, alternating one week in New York and one week in Florida. I did this for ten years.

The close relationship with the Sherrills continued, with Tib making frequent trips to Boynton Beach as work progressed on Catherine's novel, Christy. Linda was now at Emma Willard School in Troy, New York, while Chet and Jeff attended Florida schools. Physical separation eased the tension between Catherine and Linda, but I sensed that basic issues remained unresolved.

Meanwhile the relationship between Catherine and me was suffering. From comments she let drop almost without being aware of them, I could tell that she had never really come to terms with the fact of my divorce. The grinding back-and-forth commute I had from Florida to New York did not make for family closeness either. And then came a family emergency.

Catherine, November 27, 1966 ... Lord, because I know You sometimes communicate with us in dreams, I cannot stop thinking about the terrifying one Mother had last week. It was about the baby Edith is carrying, due any day now. Mother dreamed that the baby was in a basket on a little boat in a rushing stream. One end of a fragile cord was attached to the boat. The other end was in Mother's hands and she was struggling to bring the boat onto shore.

Then the stream disappeared out of the dream, and Mother was standing in front of a stoop behind which was a narrow door, holding the basket in her hands. As she laid the basket down to open the door, all at once the baby disappeared from the basket.

Mother woke, shaking.

Lord, was this just an ordinary nightmare—or was it from You? And if so, what does this mean?

December 3, 1966 . . . Two weeks after Mother's dream Edith had her baby. Peter called to say it was a boy, but his voice was not as excited as a man's should be over his first child. Then it came. "Something's wrong, Mom. 'Poor muscle tone,' the doctors call it."

Lung congestion followed, the threat of pneumonia. On Sunday Peter crawled in under the oxygen tent to christen the baby Peter Christopher—"Christ-bearer."

All who saw Peter Christopher sensed something unusual within the perfectly formed little body, the round head covered with just a hint of blonde fuzz. People used the word *gentle* when they spoke of him—"a beautiful gentle spirit."

A torrent of prayer went up for Peter Christopher Marshall.

Edith . . . Mom arrived at the Hartford Hospital from Florida on December 17. She had wanted very much to come earlier, but had felt restrained by the Holy Spirit—for what reason she did not know. I remember it was a very cold day and she was bundled up in a heavy coat. Entering Peter Christopher's room in the pediatric ward, she first hugged Peter and me, then headed to the little crib where the baby was sleeping underneath an oxygen tent.

She caressed his little body, touched his head, and commented on how beautiful he was. Then, after a few preliminary words to Peter and me, explaining that the Holy Spirit had given her this directive, she reached under the tent, and laying both hands on little Peter, she said a prayer which I recognized as essentially one of relinquishment. She concluded with these words:

"Peter Christopher, you are His little prince, and as such I am authorized and directed to crown you with thanksgiving." I sensed in her voice that with this prayer she had fulfilled some kind of responsibility.

Shortly thereafter a nurse, checking underneath the oxygen tent, noticed that the baby was in distress. The three of us (Peter, Mom, and I) were asked to leave the room while a red-headed intern did an examination. A few minutes later, the doctor came out and told us in the hallway that Peter Christopher had died.

For a while we were all too stricken to speak. What Mom said at last was: "I got here in time to do what I was commissioned to do."

Peter ... Edith and I decided that the funeral service for Peter Christopher had to express victory. As I stood in the pulpit, looking down at the tiny white casket, only 36 inches long, I spelled out the truth from Scripture as I believed it:

> For I am persuaded that neither death nor life ... shall be able to separate us from the love of God.
>
> Romans 8:38–39, NKJ

> In all these things we are more than conquerors through him who loved us.
>
> Romans 8:37, NKJ

> Glory in this ... that I am the Lord, exercising lovingkindness, judgment, and righteousness in the earth.
>
> Jeremiah 9:24, NKJ

Then I explained that Edith and I were comforted by the knowledge that even though we couldn't understand why the Lord had allowed such a thing to happen to our first-born, nevertheless He was still a God who could be trusted.

"A deeper understanding of the meaning of life is ours because of our experience with Peter Christopher," I went on, speaking for us both. "For life is not to be measured in length of days, but rather in how well we fulfill our destiny. We believe that in two short weeks Peter Christopher has perfectly fulfilled his destiny and his purpose."

Len ... The loss of her grandson was a severe blow to Catherine, but her grief was normal and not prolonged. The deaths of both her first husband (in 1949) and her father (in 1961) had prepared her to face and accept sudden loss. Moreover, the special commission to Peter Christopher given her by the Holy Spirit reassured her, and Peter and Edith, that the baby's future was truly in God's hands. For this, our whole family gave thanksgiving.

Furthermore, Peter and Edith would be having more children.

Taking Correction _____

*C*atherine, spring 1967 ... Lord, I come to You each morning for a time of fellowship together ... to share my concerns, to feel Your love, to receive Your guidance and, yes, even Your reproof.

Len and I had a heated session the other night during which he spoke words of correction to me about my tendency to be critical, my aloofness from people, my inability to demonstrate love even to certain members of my own family. I knew there was truth in what he said and he did it lovingly, but I was resistant.

After that session with Len, it was obvious to me that

revelations that come from the inside, from You, Lord, I can "take" with ease—no matter how negative they may be.

Whereas if the same insights come from another human being, they are immediately suspect and get me wrought up. I confess this as stubbornness on my part and I see it as building a barrier between Len and me.

Jesus, I hear You speak even as I write these words on paper. Len, as my husband, is the spiritual head of our home. He has the right, even the responsibility, to correct the members of his family. I need to see You in Len and trust that You are working in him.

But I confess something else here, Lord. I continue to be troubled in my spirit about Len's divorce. I thought I heard Your will on this before I married him. There has been no problem with his first wife. Not only is there no bitterness between them, there is gratitude on her part for Len's financial support. And she hasn't asked for visitation rights to the children during the seven-plus years Len and I have been married.

Perhaps the real reason for my uneasiness is the question I keep asking myself: "Did I have a right to remarry? Was that in any way a betrayal of Peter?"

Perhaps I only kidded and rationalized myself into thinking that I *did* have Your approval to remarry. Could the truth have been for me that I was meant to be content in the state in which I found myself after Peter's death?

After You Yourself had opened the door into the writing world for me, and authored my books and blessed them immeasurably, did You not mean for me to be grateful and to leave it there?

In marrying Len, was I not manipulating? Was it man-made, not God-given? Was it the result of my rebelling against the single condition to which You had called me, thereby violating a law of the Spirit?

So now—I open myself to Your mercy, Lord. You alone can help me through this situation.

Summer 1967 ... During the years of my widowhood I dreamed periodically that Peter Marshall was not dead, but was waiting somewhere for me. Last night I had this same dream.

Peter appeared to be in some sort of institution where there were lots of people and where he had some sort of position. With a thrill of recognition I spotted him: he was dancing! At last his eyes met mine. He seemed greatly surprised (I had already noted that there was no ring on his left hand).

He stopped dancing, came over to me, and began talking. Here I cannot recapture all the dream, only that Peter shook my hand rather than kissing me. He was friendly and open, but not a lover. In the dream both he and I knew that I had married again.

The dream might have been prompted by a counseling session I had a few days ago with a woman separated from her husband. I was pretty blunt in warning her about the price both husband and wife pay if they divorce, all the while resurrecting, I fear, the guilt I feel in marrying a divorced man.

Fall 1967 ... A Bible verse is alive for me this morning, Lord. "Come out from among them and be ye separate" (2 Corinthians 6:17, KJV).

You call for a "peculiar people." Nudged by this word I did a quick personal inventory. Yes, I'm certainly one of those peculiar ones who never went along with "the crowd." In fact, if "the crowd" was for something, then I was usually against it.

There was that weekend at college when the gang wanted to stay up all night. I thought this was silly, so was the only one who went to bed. In a sense this was rebellion—and rebellion is seldom right.

I was so resistant to peer pressure that I never won an elective school office in my life. I told myself that I didn't care, but of course, I did care.

This determination to be "different" undoubtedly came from my parents who cherished me so intensely that they convinced me that I was of finer clay than ordinary humanity, destined for great things.

I see on reflection this morning that this "finer clay" philosophy can be a highly dangerous one. What can it lead to except pride, self-centeredness, even arrogance? Scripture instructs us not to think of ourselves more highly than we ought. Is "being different" not a denial of my common humanity?

I do not want to displease You, Lord. I want to be different, peculiar, for You.

Summer 1968 ... How can I show my gratitude, Lord, for the success of my novel, Christy? It has been up to number two on the New York Times bestseller list, been picked up by the Reader's Digest book club, and a motion picture sale is in the works. It was over nine years ago when I started work on Christy, wondering if I could write a novel. Thank You, Lord, for giving me the ideas, the persistence, and the editorial help to bring it off.

Edith Marshall, March 1, 1969 ... As I lay in the delivery room at Goddard Memorial Hospital in Stoughton, Massachusetts, I had no thought but that we were going to have a bouncing, healthy baby. The doctors had given us no reason to suspect otherwise. Having done our grief work, the pain of Peter Christopher's death had been put behind us, and we were filled with the anticipation of child-rearing.

Peter was pastoring his own church now on Cape Cod, the East Dennis Community Church.

We had traveled seventy miles from our home on Cape Cod to find a doctor who was supportive of our desire to be active participants in the birth process through "natural childbirth." Goddard Hospital where he worked welcomed prepared fathers into the labor room—though not yet, in those days, into the actual delivery room. We wanted to give our baby the best possible start in life: a birth free from the effects of anesthesia and two eager and attuned parents ready to welcome and bond with their baby immediately after birth. We were excited.

And we were not disappointed. Mary Elizabeth was born amidst jubilant whoops. My exhilaration was overwhelming. She couldn't have been healthier, more beautiful, more loved. The joy of motherhood was mine at last.

Peter Marshall . . . As I helped Edith through her labor, I was the typical anxious father. After they wheeled her into delivery the waiting seemed eternal, while I paced around the little area for fathers out in the hospital corridor. Finally, the delivery room nurse came out to tell me that we had a baby girl. My heart leapt inside me—a moment of pure, unalloyed joy!

But our loving and gracious God had still more for us. While the doctor and nurses were finishing up with Edith, one of the pediatric nurses came out into the hall to speak to me.

"Mr. Marshall, I have been a pediatric nurse for twenty-five years, and I want to tell you something. In all my years of caring for newborns, I have never seen a baby with such perfect muscle tone!"

Perfect muscle tone—the precise thing that Peter Christopher lacked. The nurse knew nothing of our previous infant, of course, yet the Lord used her to speak the words He knew would reassure me most.

Gloria _____

*C*atherine, spring 1969 . . . My search for my next major book project is over. It will be a novel . . . based on the life of a remarkable woman who lives here in south Florida. I will call her Gloria. In fact, *Gloria* would make a good title for the book.

I have been off-and-on about this project for months. Yet ever since meeting her I knew intuitively that I had a jewel in Gloria's story, although admittedly an uncut one. Others who know her, Tib Sherrill, members of my family, have not appreciated the gem, doubted that it was worth a book setting, suspected even that it might be fake.

But something inside has made me hang on. I've listened to the doubters, I've doubted myself sometimes, wondering if her far-out experiences are authentic. How can I be sure? For Jesus' sake, I cannot, dare not pass along anything to my readers that is not 100 percent genuine.

Evelyn Underhill's book *Mysticism* has impressed me. It tells me that (1) in Gloria I have on my hands a modern mystic; and (2) that there is a solid philosophical and psychological base for mysticism. So far, so good. Then comes my personal counterreaction. It goes like this: But what good will it do to write a book for general consumption on such a specialized example of mysticism as Gloria? Aren't the mystics, like the prophets, especially singled out and endowed people?

I am torn here between wanting to write a book that will have a broad common denominator, and one that will have much of the supernatural in it. I sense that they pay a heavy price who have supernatural gifts. So what can a book like *Gloria* have for the average reader today? Why not just spin a good story and let it go at that?

Now this morning an insight from God's Word: "And it shall come to pass in the last days, saith God, I will pour out of my Spirit upon *all flesh*: and your sons and your daughters shall prophesy, your young men shall see visions and your old men shall dream dreams" (Acts 2:17, NJV).

The question is, have we arrived at the time for this prophecy to be fulfilled? Can the hippie movement be evidence that the last days are upon us? Maybe the young in their restless search for "something beyond" are really hungering for the fulfillment of Joel's prophecy.

Perhaps the charismatic renewal is part of this, too. Sure, the wheat here has to be separated from the chaff. But let us not be misled by the chaff into thinking that there are no kernels of wheat.

So what does all this mean regarding *Gloria*?

That I am to trust my instincts here. Yes, Gloria has some silly foibles and goes off on tangents. But so did many of the saints.

My conclusion: I am to go full speed ahead with Gloria. Since I don't see how to write it, God will show me how. It's as simple and as magnificent as that.

Summer 1969 . . . I had this curious dream about Tib Sherrill. Something was wrong with her so that she had to make the decision to allow surgeons to cut off both her legs to save her life. She wept. I wept. In the dream I went through a period of rebellion for her. How could she make such an irreversible decision?

But she made it and the night came when she had to prepare to enter the hospital for the dreadful operation.

I went through agony and an emotional upheaval—and there the dream ended.

What is the correct interpretation of this dream? Is there a message in it—something I'm supposed to convey to Tib?

When I took it to my prayer group, one woman felt that the dream was not about Tib at all, but about me. I was the one about to lose my legs, meaning that I was about to go through the rest of my life maimed, a cripple, only half a person.

Is my subconscious trying to tell me through this dream that my household situation and marriage have made me half a person, that they are beginning to cripple my creativity?

Another possible interpretation—Tib Sherrill represents a portion of my own being. Probably the writer part. Perhaps even more specifically, the new book I'm working on, Gloria.

For many years Tib worked with me on Christy. I counted on her input so heavily that even during the year she and John and their children spent in Bolivia, chapters were constantly in the mail between Florida and South America. Now Tib does not feel she can be part of the Gloria project.

Therefore, one possible interpretation of the dream is that

I have been depending too much upon editorial help, using it as a crutch, and that my subconscious mind is terrified at the idea of going ahead without it. Perhaps the real problem in my subconscious is that I am grieving over Tib's unwillingness to see the potential in *Gloria*. Len has always been lukewarm to this book—and anyhow Len is too involved at *Guideposts* to give me the help I need.

I know that there was fear in the dream and that the fear probably has to do with my writing. So I can begin praying at that point anyway.

God *could* be asking me via the dream, "Are you *willing* to have Me remove all human props from your writing and rely only on Me?"

Tib ... I knew ahead of time that the editorial session on *Gloria* would be fiery.

Critiquing Catherine's writing was always hard because she identified so personally with her work. Fans of hers would often comment wistfully to me on my good fortune in knowing "the real Catherine." And to know her *was* good. For friends of Catherine, life was never dull. Her integrity, her high standards, her impatience with spiritual fence-sitting, made her friendship worth more than that of a dozen comfortable, undemanding souls.

But there was a part of Catherine that I felt was often concealed in face-to-face contact, even from intimates. This fear of exposure, this tendency to "run up the back stairs," in her own phrase, was to change in the early 1970s. Her time of darkness was to bring about this and other transformations.

But from the beginning, Catherine had no hesitancy in putting herself, all of herself, onto paper. Her readers—I among them—knew a "real Catherine" who might otherwise have stayed hidden. Her warmth, her vulnerability, her intense caring, flowed from her pen like the life blood that, in truth, it was for her.

I never had to ask Catherine how a morning's work had gone; her face across the lunch table told me exactly how many pages she'd written and how good or bad she thought they were. Suggesting changes in work so inextricably tied up with her very self was always an ordeal—both for me to make and for her to hear. All writers, no matter how bright the smile we glue to our lips, die a little when told we must redo something. We call a manuscript *it*, but it's really *us* and it hurts like surgery to reshape it.

With Catherine this universal writer's reaction was intensified. Catherine had no plastic smile to paste on at such moments; her face betrayed everything she felt. I think this is one reason person-to-person encounters were so threatening to her—the bland social cover-up was no part of her armory. Getting a negative reaction to the morning's work, her face would blanch as from a physical blow. Often she'd escape to some solitary corner of whatever house, hers or mine, we were working in, taking the imperiled pages with her as one would snatch a child from an attacker.

Soon, however, she'd be back, manuscript in hand. "What else is wrong?"

Her commitment to excellence made her pursue criticism, in spite of the pain, from Len, from me, from her publishers.

With *Gloria*, however, I knew the pain would be fiercer than usual. In spite of initial unenthusiastic responses from both Len and me, she'd invested months in interviewing, additional months in writing. She'd sent me an outline and a draft of the early chapters and was waiting now for my reaction.

The meeting took place at a country inn in New Hampshire where she and Len had gone for a brief holiday. John and I drove up one August day with the idea that Catherine and I would have an initial session on the book that afternoon, after which the four of us would have dinner.

That night nobody ate. At six o'clock John and Len arrived at the room where Catherine and I were working, to find her pacing the narrow space between the beds.

"You're telling me I'm not capable of getting a complex personality on paper!"

"I'm saying that Gloria sends mixed messages. And that a fiction writer has to find some unifying principle in his principal character. Real life doesn't have to be consistent. Fiction does."

"And you think I'm not capable of doing that."

"Of course you're capable. What I'm asking is, should you? Does this project have your name on it—or is it a distraction? A temptation, even, pulling you away from the book God has for you?"

"God told me to write about Gloria."

"Then do. Write *about* her. Write about the impact she's had on you. On Catherine. It's trying to write *as* Gloria that I question. To write in first person you have to feel some identity with your subject. Let me ask you bluntly, Catherine: do you like Gloria?"

Catherine stopped her agitated pacing to stare through the window at the peaks of the White Mountains on fire in the setting sun. "She baffles me," Catherine admitted. "But I certainly don't agree with what you write here—" She ruffled through the pages in her hands. "Where you say she's crazy."

"I didn't say crazy. I said emotionally unstable."

"It's the same thing."

"It's not the same thing. Rational people can have irrational areas."

"All right," Catherine said, "your term was *unstable*. And yet you say here—" she pulled out another page "—that you want the vision scene to show 'her genuine spirituality.' Which is it? Is she an authentic mystic, or a very mixed-up woman?"

"I think she's both, Catherine. And I don't think you'll ever be comfortable with those contradictions in her."

"Well, can you explain to me why God would lavish such tremendous spiritual gifts on a woman who's as kooky as you seem to think?"

"No. Indeed I can't explain it. But because I don't understand something doesn't mean it isn't so."

And so it went, as the shadows traveled up the mountain slopes beyond the window, with John from time to time forlornly suggesting dinner and Len trying to keep the peace between two opinionated women. The only thing the New Hampshire trip decided was that Catherine would continue, alone, with the writing of Gloria.

Len . . . I had some serious reservations as to whether or not Catherine should do the Gloria book, but these had less to do with Gloria herself and more to do with whether or not Catherine could handle this type of material, especially Gloria's promiscuous teen years. Tib Sherrill felt that Catherine's lack of sympathy for the adolescent Gloria would make those episodes unconvincing. A McGraw-Hill editor was partly responsible for Catherine's absorption with Gloria's seamy past. He told us, "Catherine Marshall writing sex scenes. That will sure get the public's attention!" Maybe. Maybe not.

To me Gloria's conversion and walk with Jesus seemed the most promising area. Gloria not only hears the voice of Jesus, but according to her own report, sees into the heavenly kingdom. I remember one day in particular. . . .

I had just returned to our Florida home from New York City. When I arrived home Catherine and Gloria were in the living room. The three of us chatted for a while and then I disclosed a problem situation at the office that was bothering me.

"Let's pray about it, Len," Catherine suggested. "Maybe we should lay hands on you."

I was willing and sat down in the chair facing the window. At that moment Catherine was called to the telephone.

She asked Gloria to go ahead and pray without her. Gloria stood behind me silently for a moment. I waited. Nothing happened. Instead Gloria picked up her purse, walked out the front door, got into her car, and drove off.

Somewhat nonplused, I took my bag to the bedroom and started unpacking. Catherine joined me a few minutes later.

"Where's Gloria?" she asked. "Did she pray for you?"

"No. She just walked out the door and drove off."

"How strange."

Ten minutes later I answered the phone. It was Gloria. "I'm sure you're wondering why I left when I did," she said.

"Well—yes."

"There was no need for me to pray," she said. "Two angels were already there praying for you, one on each side of the chair, kneeling by your side. I felt I should leave."

Stunned, I hardly knew what to say. Could it really be true? I believed in the existence of angels, but did they really have human-like shapes that could be discerned by certain people? And were they that involved with the workaday concerns of our lives?

Amazingly, the office problem was resolved by the time I flew back to New York. The whole episode haunted me for days, weeks—and helped me understand the fascination Gloria held for Catherine.

The Generation Gap _____

Catherine, January 2, 1970 ... Night before last the New
Year was ushered in with the "Episode of the Chair." Len
and I were flattered and delighted when Chester, 17, and
Jeff, 14, elected to spend New Year's Eve at home playing
bridge, just the four of us. Jeff was my partner, sitting
opposite me in the mahogany, velvet-seated armchair, an
antique that I especially prized. He and I lost the game, Jeff
going down with a hand he should have made. In a burst of
overdramatic frustration, he banged his hand on the table
and sprang to his feet, knocking the chair backward. One
arm of the chair was broken in two pieces.

Upset, I stormed at Jeff that all his privileges would be
taken away for the weekend.

Len, in turn, became angry at me in front of Jeff and Chester, saying, "This kind of punishment has to be decided between us apart from the boys."

We were all tired, all edgy. Household harmony had already been stretched to the breaking point by too many guests, too much activity over the holidays. When we went to bed that night, Len and I were scarcely speaking.

The next day, yesterday, our relationship was still strained when Len announced that two of his friends from Ohio Wesleyan were "dropping by," a Methodist preacher and his wife. I was less than enthusiastic at the news.

In our living room, however, the preacher told a story that has lingered with me. A friend of his lost a small child through illness. He was bitter that his prayers for healing had not been answered.

He told of the preacher going out into the starry night, realizing that he had but two courses: he could go on railing against God, hating God, and thus become estranged from Him.

Or, he could obey St. Paul's injunction, "In everything, give thanks," and praise God—even thought he didn't understand why God had let his child die, even though his praise would be mechanical and halting.

He chose the latter course and started in, "Thank You, God, for giving us such a beautiful child and for letting us have the joy of her for two years." The man reported to the preacher that from the minute he began this mechanical praise, a tremendous weight lifted from his soul and he began to see the face of his God again.

I thought about our loss of Peter Christopher and how our thanksgiving had lifted us out of the pit then. It came to me that the only way I could live with my present situation and keep my sanity was to actually find something in Jeff's outbursts, in Len's permissiveness with both boys, in a hundred things in our household, to praise God for.

So now I ask, "But how can I thank You, Lord, for situations brought about by human failure and sin?" My own included.

I hear You telling me to reread the story of Joseph being sold into slavery—certainly the result of sin in his brothers. But as Joseph examined himself during those years in prison in Egypt, he no doubt came up with the realization that sin in himself—arrogance, judging, bragging—had helped produce the sin in his brothers. So everyone involved had sinned. Yet Joseph found cause to praise God.

It would appear that praise is the only way, Lord. Even with all our mistakes, You have still "allowed" us to make them. Thus we are still under Your permissive will. Help me, therefore, to praise You in every circumstance.

Len, May 1970 . . . "Be firm now," I told myself as I drove to Stuyvesant Hall on the Ohio Wesleyan campus where our daughter, Linda, was now a junior. It was parents' weekend and I had flown up from Florida. An engagement kept Catherine from joining me, but before I left, she and I had agreed that we were not going to underwrite college expenses if Linda continued spending her time in peace marches and protest meetings.

This was shortly after the four Kent State, Ohio, students had been killed by the National Guard. At nearby Ohio Wesleyan the ROTC building had been taken over for a day in protest, the administration building partly occupied, classes suspended for two days. Linda had been peripherally involved in all this.

I remembered the past Christmas when Linda had given a talk from the pulpit of our church on her summer experience in a ministry to inner-city children in San Diego,

California. An offshoot of the ministry of our friends
Louis and Colleen Evans, this program seemed to have
deeply affected Linda. She came back talking about racial
prejudice, poverty, involvement, sensitivity. I'd been proud
of her then—but these student activities against the war
were something else.

I hoped for a relaxed lunch with Linda, during which we
could come to some sensible conclusions about the importance of education as against marches and demonstrations.
Linda greeted me with a question: "Would you like to see
what's going on here? Lunch can wait, can't it?"

Stomach grumbling, I drove her in my rented car to Gray
Chapel. "By the way, Dad," she said, "I didn't tell you and
Mom something the other night on the phone. Five of us
from Wesleyan went to Washington, D.C., for the march at
the Capitol. *The Transcript* [the college paper] paid my
expenses."

"Why didn't you tell us on the phone?"

"Well, you both seemed so uptight about everything."

While digesting this piece of news, my mind went back
fifteen years to the little girl who liked to jump on my lap
and throw her arms around my neck. In many ways I hardly
knew this twenty-year-old with the granny glasses, long
black hair, jeans, sandals.

We parked the car and joined some 500 students heading for the Chapel, the main assembly hall on campus.
Much in evidence were long hair, dungarees, open shirts,
bare feet.

Thirty years before when I was a student on this same
campus, we wore saddle shoes, loud socks, sports coats,
Joe College hats. Nothing had changed really; conformity
was still the rule.

But what the students were doing was definitely different!
Mimeographed literature was being passed out: statistics on
the Vietnam War, on taxes, on the draft. The students then

split into small groups to plan local action. Thirty years ago in May, I recalled, our big spring demonstration was a "panty raid" on the freshman girls' dormitory.

Linda and I walked across the campus to the recreation center, joining a group discussing a student plan to visit homes in the community. A girl with long, copper-hued hair was speaking.

"When you knock on a door," she was saying, "be friendly, be courteous, and for crying out loud, be neat."

"You mean we have to cut our hair?"

"Yes. Guys with long hair might just as well not go. Another point—let them talk. We want to get across our conviction about stopping the war, sure. But we also want to win friends. If the adults want to talk about campus violence, settle for that and let them know we're against this, too."

The girl read a summary of the instructions from a mimeographed sheet: "Communicate . . . talk, not tell . . . conversation with love."

I asked Linda if I could have a copy and she got one for me. We next visited a group discussing a proposed student boycott of Coca-Cola.

"Why pick a company that isn't making war materials?" someone asked.

The leader explained that students had to show their economic power in some way. They couldn't boycott General Motors cars with any effectiveness, but they could stop buying Coca Cola. The ultimate aim: have the Coca-Cola directors make a statement against the war.

I looked at Linda. "You're on shaky ground with this project." She nodded.

As we drove back to her dorm, I quizzed Linda about her trip to Washington. "I'm glad I went," she said. "It was an awesome experience and peaceful. We stumbled onto an SDS [Students for a Democratic Society] street meeting there. It was so far out it was ludicrous. We don't want to destroy America, we want to save it."

She paused for a moment. "Dad, I've been thinking about a lot more than politics. It began last summer when I woke up to the fact that the world is full of people who don't have the opportunities I've always taken for granted. I saw that I'd been living just for myself, and pretty superficially at that. Now I want to make a difference in the world.

"You and Mom have always talked about the importance of living out your faith. That's what I'm trying to do. I lead the high school group at William Street Church, I've been tutoring a sixth-grader, and I help plan the chapel 'Happenings' on campus. All this has meant more to me than the prayer group I attended for a while in the fall. I want to live for something bigger than myself, but I don't want to be tied down by religious labels."

Four hours had passed. Catherine might not care too much for Linda's social gospel approach, but I felt reassured by my daughter's idealism. Though I doubted that the Lord was first in her life, I sensed He had His hand on her. Now it was time for me to head for the airport.

Linda started to get out of the car, paused. "I hope you're not unhappy with me."

There it was. The little girl I remembered . . . uncertain . . . wanting love, reassurance. I reached out my hand and touched her cheek. It happened in a matter of seconds: generation gap, communication gap, parent-child gap all dissolved.

I drove to the airport feeling warmed inside. There's more to education, I decided, than books and classes.

Catherine, March 1971 . . . I had a dream last night that I should try to record. The exterior situation is that my sister and her family (with two teenage girls) arrived yesterday. Since Linda, Chester, and Jeff were all at home on spring vacations, that made five young people at the dinner table. I don't think that I've ever been so aware of the "generation gap." I felt as though we older ones were standing on the opposite bank of a great chasm.

In the dream, some people came into the bedroom where I was sleeping and forcibly kidnapped me. There were both males and females, obviously enemies who meant no good to me.

At one point, I remember being put on an operating table where a man shot something at me that hit my face. Immediately I knew that this would make me lose consciousness, and it did.

Len seemed to be somewhere on the edges of all this activity, by no means under the kind of assault I was, but also apparently a captive and unable to help me.

I can "get" no more of the dream except that the kidnapping seems to have arisen out of some statement I had made in a speech that did not please my enemies. Does the dream indicate I have an "adversary role" with teenagers? What am I to learn from this?

May 1971 ... Lord, this morning I'm in awe once more at what You've done. The report came from Chester who called last night all excited. He had gone from Taylor University in Upland, Indiana, where he is a sophomore, to a conference hosted by Roman Catholic charismatics at Notre Dame. Some 40,000 people had poured into South Bend, Indiana, nearly filling the Notre Dame stadium. Chester said he had never seen anything so powerful in all his life as 40,000 people on their feet, shouting and singing and praising the Lord.

What awes me is this. An article by one of the Catholic leaders attributes the origins of this Catholic renewal to three books: *The Cross and the Switchblade* by David Wilkerson (written by the Sherrills), *They Speak with Other Tongues* by John Sherrill, and *Nine O'Clock in the Morning* by Dennis Bennett.

Lord, memories flood back of that spring morning in 1960 when You prodded me into that confrontation with John Sherrill. What if I hadn't obeyed?

Obedience . . . obedience . . . obedience. How You depend upon it from Your children! How many great events should have happened but didn't because someone was not obedient! Scary to think about!

Husband/Wife Confrontation _____

*L*en, May 1971 ... After six years of commuting every other week from Florida to New York City, I felt quite literally split in two. Even members of my family were never quite sure where I was. Happily, *Guideposts* was doing well; in fact, becoming a major force in magazine publishing.

My major concern was the growing tension between Catherine and me. It was frustrating to come home after an exhausting week in New York only to be met with a new set of problems. Sometimes Catherine would start in as I was unpacking my bag:

"Jeff missed his school bus this morning. He overslept

because he stayed up late last night studying for a test. I had to drive him to school." (Jeff was then fifteen.)

"How did he do on the test?" I asked.

"He wouldn't tell me. I suspect he failed. Why don't you ask him?"

"I'll ask him tomorrow."

"If he did fail, I think he should be punished. Maybe no tennis this weekend."

I groaned. Tennis over the weekend was what Jeff and I most enjoyed doing together.

"If Jeff failed his test because he waited too late to study for it, he should be punished, I agree. But I'm not sure that depriving him of tennis is the answer."

"You'll let him off too easily."

I struggled to hide my annoyance. "At least give me a chance to unpack."

"You and I have never agreed on punishments for the children," Catherine persisted.

"I tend to be too easy on them, I admit it. But they're good kids. The boys have never given us trouble. You'll agree with that, won't you?"

"True," Catherine admitted. "Why do you think it's worked out that way?"

I had no trouble with that one. "Because we've prayed for them every day. And the structured home you set up for them when they were small. They thrived on this routine. I'll be eternally grateful to you for this, Catherine."

Catherine softened for a moment. "Then please don't resist me when I ask you to discipline them."

"The only time I resist is when I think you're being unloving."

"Like with Linda?" The edge was back in her voice.

"Well, yes."

"I wasn't really prepared to take on three small children when I married you."

We were back on rocky terrain. Familiar ground, especially in recent years. "Why do you keep bringing this up?"

"Because it's constantly on my mind. I feel that I'm living outside of God's will."

"You certainly didn't feel that way the first ten years of our marriage."

"At times I did. The pace of our lives back then was so fast I just didn't dwell on it."

"What you're saying, Catherine, is that when things were going well for you, you felt you were in God's will. Now that your book *Gloria* is not going well, and you have some relationship problems inside and outside the family, then you're out of God's will. And so you place the blame on the fact that you married a divorced man."

"It goes much deeper than that," Catherine replied. "I thought I'd heard God on the matter of your divorce before you and I were married. The unrest in my spirit began about five years ago. It came from—well I'm not sure just where."

"How about the women you meet with here in Florida?"

"The unrest began inside me first. I took it to them for prayer."

"And what came out of this prayer?"

Catherine was silent for a long moment. "I'm not quite sure. That possibly I was to have remained content in my single status."

I struggled with a growing irritation that I knew I had to keep under control. "All right, Catherine, you and your women prayer partners have come to the conclusion that possibly our marriage was not of God. What does this add up to now—today? Certainly not another divorce. Separation? How would that go down with your readers? We're really between a rock and a hard place, aren't we?"

Catherine nodded. "What you're saying is that I have to work this out between God and me."

"What I'm saying is, look at the positive accomplishments you and I have achieved together over the past twelve years. Shall I list them?"

"That's not necessary. I agree there are many."

"Then why would God bless our marriage so much if we are out of His will?"

Catherine shook her head. "I'm sure lots of people who are 'way out of God's will are accomplishing things that appear to be blessed. That has nothing to do with the feeling of unrest I have about our marriage. It's troubled me for years."

"Then let's go a different direction," I suggested. "Who would benefit most from a rupture in our relationship? Why don't you and your prayer partners come against the dark powers that would love to do us in?"

"We have come against all dark forces, Len. These women are not your enemies. They want the best for us, they want a healing here."

"What kind of healing?"

"We're not sure." Catherine took a deep breath. "You're always saying that my attitudes need to change. I agree and I'm trying. The question I have for you, Len, is: What about your attitudes? What do you need to change?"

"About our marriage?"

"Well, yes. But I was thinking more about your divorce."

"I don't understand. A divorce is a divorce. What can you change about that?"

"You can't change the fact of a divorce, but you can change your attitude about it."

Taken by surprise, I struggled to put my thoughts together. "Divorce is always a tragedy. It's a terrible failure. But for some marriages, it seems to be the only answer. I tried for years to save my first marriage. Nothing seemed to help. The divorce and remarriage gave my children a chance for a stable home, a normal childhood. For me . . . well, it freed me to find the creative life God had for me."

"Len, you're not really sure of that. God's perfect plan for you might have been to stick with the marriage, in spite of Eve's alcoholism, to work out a productive balance that could have had positive results beyond your wildest dreams."

I stared at Catherine in amazement . . . speechless for a long stretch as I got very busy sorting some papers. Deep down I had to admit Catherine had scored a point. And I realized something else. Though unsettling, there was also something deeply fulfilling in these confrontations with Catherine. How I loved to watch her mental processes in action. How I loved her. Period.

"So how do I go about changing?" I finally asked.

"That's between you and the Lord," she replied.

I didn't sleep too well that night.

Dark Threads _____

*C*atherine, June 1971 ... Lord, everything in my world seems to be going awry. I'm at odds with the people closest to me. All my projects are stalled. Everything seems to be out of sync except my relationship with You:

(1) The movie of *Christy*. MGM paid a lot of money for this, hired a writer at great expense to do the script, shot a lot of footage in the Great Smoky Mountains. Now it's all been shelved.

(2) My editor at McGraw-Hill has been fired. The situation in the trade book department there is total confusion.

(3) Tib Sherrill still can't (won't) be my editor. She's taken on other assignments: she thinks the *Gloria* project is wrong for me.

(4) The writing of *Gloria* is not developing as it should.

(5) Len's commuting to New York every other week puts an extra burden on me to be both mother and part-time father to Jeff and Chester (though I have to remind myself that our living in Florida is Len's accommodation to my fragile health).

(6) Linda's graduation from Ohio Wesleyan was not a happy occasion. The Vietnam War has many young people in our nation in a state of rebellion, including Linda.

(7) My relationships with Peter and Edith are not good. They resist almost every suggestion I make.

(8) Since U.S. troops have gone into Cambodia our college and university campuses are rioting, buildings being burned. We in the U.S. are a fragmented people, unable to hear one another.

O Jesus, You who cursed the fig tree so that, being unproductive, it withered and died, You who create, but must, at times, also destroy, I thank You that what is of God in all this will emerge.

Section II

The Summer
of 1971

Editor's Note: Catherine did little writing in her journals during this time. This section is based on twenty hours of tapes recorded by Catherine and me in September 1971, plus recollections by some of those involved in the events.

A Call to Do Battle _____

*E*dith ... Amy Catherine Marshall entered the world in the middle of the afternoon on July 22, 1971. Peter and I had again traveled to the Goddard Hospital in Stoughton, seventy miles from home, so that we could have the kind of childbirth experience we wanted. We were thrilled to be having another baby, never imagining that there might be a problem again.

This time Peter was permitted into the delivery room. My labor was normal from every point of view. But as soon as Amy was born I knew that something was wrong. The doctor didn't hold her up for us to see. He didn't put her on my breast while he cut the cord. She didn't cry. There was a scurrying among the nurses and a muffled hush that didn't ring true to my experience with Mary Elizabeth's birth. From my stirruped position on the table, I looked to the left where she was being bundled.

"Is she OK?" I asked.

"Well, she's a little blue. We're going to put her under a heat lamp and warm her up. I'm sure she'll be fine." But the doctor was grim-faced and nobody seemed to be looking at me. Peter kept patting my arm. They whisked her away to the nursery, saying she should have a little oxygen.

Throughout the evening, the nurses kept making excuses for not bringing Amy to me. She was having a little bit of trouble, they'd say.

"What's the matter?" I'd want to know.

"The pediatrician is looking her over now. He'll be in to talk with you a little later."

With every little bit of information I could glean, the reality was ever-so-slowly breaking through. My baby was not all right. She had poor muscle tone. She wasn't sucking. She wasn't wetting. She had a yellowish cast they needed to monitor. She was being fed fluids intravenously.

No, no, no. Every brain cell resisted taking it in. It couldn't be happening again. It couldn't be true. But it *was* true. And finally tears held back by a dam of denial came spilling out, uncontrollably, along with anguished questioning—why, why, why?

An angel of mercy visited me late on the first night. She was a nurse going off duty who had recognized our name on the patient sheet and knew that I would welcome prayer. She crept into my darkened room and sat next to the bed, taking my hand in hers. What she prayed I don't remember, but it provided for me the unmistakable assurance that God had not forgotten and that I could count on His presence even in my darkest, angriest, most despairing hour.

The next morning the pediatrician came again. He said

he'd noticed on my chart that we had previously lost an infant son. Would I authorize a release of those autopsy reports? They might have some bearing on a diagnostic assessment for Amy. He also felt the baby should be transferred to Boston Children's Hospital. They had good diagnostic capabilities there; would I authorize transferral and transportation in an ambulance?

Within a couple of hours a brisk young resident from Children's Hospital, Dr. Rubinstein, came to take Amy away. I watched from my second-story window as the tiny bassinet was loaded into the cavernous expanse of the shiny ambulance. The little body that I had never nestled in my arms was surrounded by hanging bottles and monitoring equipment. Technology was taking my place. Such feelings of uselessness were to recur often in the weeks ahead. With lights flashing the ambulance raced away.

The first hint that the doctors suspected a genetically related disease came the next day. Dr. Rubinstein came to see me armed with all kinds of questions about infant deaths in the family tree. He explained that they were seeing exactly the same symptomatology in Amy Catherine that existed with Peter Christopher four-and-a-half years before.

Now through a computerized search the doctors at Children's believed they had a diagnosis: an extremely rare, recessively inherited, genetically carried disease. This disease, Dr. Rubinstein explained, is manifested in babies as a result of defective genes, which both mother and father have to contribute in order to result in—I heard for the first time the dreaded name—cerebro-hepato-renal syndrome. Apparently the defective genes control the pathway of migrating cells during embryonic development. Should two defective genes meet at conception (a one-in-four probability in affected persons), proper migration of embryonic cells to the brain, liver, and kidneys is impeded and as a result these organs are malformed and virtually nonfunctional in the full-term infant.

Dr. Rubinstein concluded his explanation by saying that there had been only forty recorded cases of this disease, and that none of those forty infants had survived. Indeed, survival much beyond six months was impossible, given the fact that the brain was so incapacitated that it could not support life. His best guess was that Amy might live five to ten weeks.

There it was: cold, clinical reality. Overwhelmed, I longed to go home, to the stable life I knew of cooking for Peter and playing dolls with Mary, of raising vegetables and cutting flowers, of Sunday school teaching and singing in the choir. To life when "cerebro-hepato-renal syndrome" was just a string of unpronounceable syllables.

Catherine . . . Edith came home without the baby just as Len and I arrived from Florida by automobile. We explained to two-and-a-half-year-old Mary Elizabeth that Amy Catherine was sick and had to stay in the hospital.

Then we began to phone praying friends around the country. Peter used some previously scheduled speaking engagements to talk about Amy Catherine's condition and ask for prayer. On Sunday, four days after she was born, Peter asked his congregation in East Dennis to pray for the healing of his baby daughter.

The Marshalls had a sixteen-year-old girl named Debbie living with them to look after Mary Elizabeth and help around the house. The discussion about the table on Sunday evening focused on how negative all the medical personnel at Children's Hospital were about Amy Catherine's chances.

The weight of our negativism and anguish must have gotten to Debbie. In the middle of the night she became so sick to her stomach that at 4:30 A.M. Len drove her to the Hyannis Hospital. There she was medicated and released, with instructions to rest for several days.

Monday was unbelievable. First the dishwasher broke down, then the hot water heater. For two days we were without hot water. Edith, only five days after childbirth, had to minister to Debbie, answer a steady stream of telephone calls, and supervise the household, while I took care of Mary Elizabeth.

To top it off, Peter's car wouldn't start and he had to spend most of the day getting it repaired.

By Tuesday morning at breakfast time we were all so beaten by this string of mishaps that a spontaneous prayer rose from the table: "Lord, we need help."

The answer came in a totally unexpected way. Some ten miles further down the Cape, in Orleans, the leaders of a Christian community responded to the need of the Marshalls. Two women were dispatched in a van with enough food for two meals. They told us later that they had started out from Rock Harbor singing and praising God. The closer they got to East Dennis and to the Marshall home the darker the atmosphere got and the harder they found it to sing and pray. "It was as if we were coming against some kind of strange powerful force."

They arrived cheerily enough, bringing the food in from the van. Then they cleaned the house from top to bottom, cooked and washed dishes and took charge of the telephone, leaving Peter, Edith, Len, and me free to have long sessions of prayer that afternoon and evening.

The first prayer session was in Peter and Edith's bedroom, chosen not only because Edith could participate while lying down, but also because it was the only room with air-conditioning. We began by praying for that tiny, precious life at Boston Hospital.

Then I described how I'd been awakened in the middle of the night by the Lord who revealed to me why all my life I'd seen so few results of my prayers for healing—either my own or others'. "I was told that it was because I have a great fear of disease," I said, "and that if I could get rid of this fear then I could be better used by the Lord in praying for Amy Catherine."

"Perhaps," Edith suggested, "we can inherit fears as well as illness." She and Peter had been given some long forms to fill out by the geneticist at Children's Hospital. On these forms they were supposed to record not only the physical disabilities of their ancestors on both sides of the family, but the phobias, too—since apparently even these things can come down from generation to generation.

This led us to Exodus 20:5: ". . . For I, the Lord your God, am a jealous God, visiting the iniquity of the fathers on the children, on the third and the fourth generations" (NIV).

"Then," I said, "if I'm to get rid of my fear of disease I may have to look back to my parents and grandparents."

Immediately I found myself recalling my father's mother, Sarah Wood, for whom I'd been named. Sarah Catherine Wood was a name I'd disliked and seldom used.

Why had I resisted using the name *Sarah*?

As it dawned on me, I felt chills racing up and down my back. My Grandmother Wood had been so afraid of the night air that she wouldn't raise her bedroom window, winter or summer. In hot weather my grandfather would come out of their room in the morning white-faced and dripping with perspiration. After he died, my grandmother persuaded my Aunt Effie to sleep with her—with the same results.

Grandmother Wood was so afraid of thunderstorms that at the first peal she would plunge beneath the covers. And so it went. A fear-dominated woman.

In going back through my own life, I came up with a time when my specific fear of germs began. It was when we lived in West Virginia. Next door to us was a family named Fletcher whose Victorian home had a number of porches upstairs and down. The Fletcher boy was dying of tuberculosis. He used to lie out on the top porch where from my bedroom I could hear his terrible hacking cough. Then his sister caught the disease, ending up in the Trudeau sanatorium in New York State. This close association with lingering death planted in me a morbid fear of "contamination."

There in the bedroom Len and Peter laid hands on me and prayed that I be cut loose, in the spirit, from both inherited fears and acquired ones.

Next Peter began probing for the roots of his own fears. He recalled that around the time of his father's death, when he was nine, he had been harassed by some older boys on our block. Since he couldn't stand up to these bigger boys, he would end up running home. This memory still haunted him.

Peter's favorite Old Testament hero, he told us, was the young boy David, going out to fight the giant Goliath. "I would love to have this quality in me, this fearlessness," he said. "The ability to stand up against superior odds and not run away."

I found myself almost catapulted across the room toward my son. Laying my hands on Peter's head, I prayed this prayer: "My son, I hereby cut you free from me, from any fears of mine that would bind you in any way. Even as Samuel anointed David, so I now anoint you to go out and fulfill your appointed destiny in life boldly, whatever that may be."

Peter told me afterward that he felt something very real happened to him during this prayer, something he had been needing for a long time.

Our second family session took place in the living room after dinner. We invited Pat, a neighbor of the Marshalls, to join us because of her experience as an intercessor. We had also invited her for dinner, but she had declined. "I'm on a fast for Amy Catherine," she told us.

After we had prayed together, Pat had a strong message for us. First, we had to overcome the discouragement brought on by the medical diagnosis. Second, we had to fight for Amy Catherine's life. "The word I've received from the Lord is that Amy Catherine is a member of the Body of

Christ—a member in need of ministry. You have no right to deprive her of this ministry or back away from it, no matter what the doctors say."

These words hit me like a slap in the face. A call to battle! All my adrenaline began to flow.

Peter and I drove to Boston the next day, Wednesday. At last I was to have my first visit with Amy Catherine, now one week old. She was in a special section of Children's Hospital for babies with rare diseases. As we entered the medical complex through double swinging doors, we passed a large bulletin board covered with snapshots of babies and small children. A printed sign above it read *Our Graduates*.

This gave us a good feeling, indicating that there was a personal touch in this hospital, that it was not just a sterile treatment center. We had to put on gowns, though not masks, and scrub our hands with a particular kind of soap. Meanwhile the nurse in charge had picked up the baby, wrapping her in a tiny blanket, and was waiting to place her in our arms.

"We've come to pray for Amy Catherine's healing," I told her.

The nurse had been smiling. Now her expression changed. "The doctor has explained to you the prognosis, hasn't he?"

We nodded.

"The baby has many problems. There have been multiple seizures. Please don't get your hopes up."

"We believe God will heal her," Peter said firmly.

Peter carried Amy Catherine into a glassed-in small room where he anointed his tiny daughter with the oil he had brought with him. Then he placed her in my arms. I unfolded a corner of the blanket. She was such a beautiful baby, with her rosebud mouth, delicately shaped head, rose-petal skin. She did not open her eyes as my tears fell on her blanket.

Peter . . . The first crisis with Amy Catherine had come 36 hours after her birth when she still had not wet her diapers. This meant no kidney function, without which she would not live another day.

We'd called every prayer group we could think of to intercede for her. Members of my own church went into a special session. One prayer warrior there had a vision of an arterial system with vessels branching out from it like limbs of a tree. Then she saw fluid begin to work through the system. It was soon after this that Amy Catherine's kidneys had begun to function.

We had rejoiced. God had responded!

The Gathering
of Sixteen _____

*C*atherine ... On August 1, 1971, the second Sunday after Amy Catherine's birth, my son after much prayer mounted the pulpit of his East Dennis church and preached a sermon that rocked all of us. The subject was faith and the substance of it was this:

As you all know, my daughter Amy Catherine was born on July 22nd with severe genetic problems in her liver, kidneys, and brain. The doctors have given us no hope that she will live more than a few weeks. In fact, no baby with this genetic syndrome has ever lived beyond six months.

I am here to state this morning that the doctors do not have all the answers. Our Lord God does. He is the Creator of life. He decides when we are born and when we die.

I do not know what His plan is for Amy Catherine. But I do know that we are to believe for her healing. In fact, right here now before you all, and God almighty, I claim a miracle of healing for Amy Catherine.

I was sitting next to Edith during the service and felt her pride in him at that moment. Later I discovered that others in the congregation were troubled by the sermon because he'd left no loophole in case the baby died. But to me there was something very moving in the way my son stuck his chin out and said, "Lord, I believe."

Peter's sermon, plus Pat's exhortation to us, sparked something inside me. We had received our marching orders. *The time had come for action!*

What if our family crisis with Amy Catherine was part of the movement of the Holy Spirit sweeping across the country in 1971? Len and Jeffrey had recently returned from California to report the Jesus Movement among young people gaining momentum. *Guideposts* was putting together a special series of articles to be called "The Surging Spirit."

What if a miraculous healing of this "hopeless" situation was part of the Spirit's mighty plan for the '70s? Then the idea came: *Call together some prayer warriors. Have them come to Cape Cod to pray for Amy Catherine, to claim a supernatural healing!*

Len and I got on the telephone. Those we called were asked to come the following Sunday for a four-day, all-out prayer campaign. The place—yet to be decided. Probably somewhere on the Cape; possibly nearer Boston so we would be closer to Children's Hospital.

Edith . . . I seized eagerly on Mom's and Len's offer to gather some prayer warriors together to battle Amy's sickness. The fact that they were taking the initiative was especially welcome, for I was feeling helpless and inadequate.

Life seemed to have reeled out of control. It had nightmarish qualities about it. I couldn't do any of the things that to me seemed important, like nursing my newborn infant and helping Mary Elizabeth through this crisis and regaining my own strength and standing together with Peter to make decisions. Amy was hooked up to machines in a hospital ninety miles away, I was exhausted from the constant trips into Boston, and I couldn't seem to get a very good handle on all the "input" that loving and well-meaning Christian brothers and sisters were giving us. In addition to everything else, I was beginning to wonder if maybe there was something dreadfully wrong with me spiritually.

And so, if others would take up the slack in the battle lines and let me regain some equilibrium, I was only too glad to have them do it.

Catherine . . . Soon the details of the gathering on Cape Cod were worked out, both as to place and people. A Christian center in Orleans soon to be named the Community of Jesus offered its facilities: Rock Harbor Manor, a lovely location on Cape Cod Bay with sleeping accommodations and spacious meeting rooms. The two women who came to the Marshall home the previous Tuesday to clean, cook, and minister were from this community.

The people who responded to our calls made an unusual mix: John and Elizabeth Sherrill were long-time friends; Jamie Buckingham, a roving editor for *Guideposts*, was a new friend. Virginia Lively was a prayer partner of mine in Florida and a woman with a nationwide ministry of healing. Charles Hotchkiss, who came with his wife, Linda, was Virginia's pastor and an Episcopal priest in Belle Glade.

Bob Slosser was a *New York Times* editor; with him came his wife, Gloria. Scott and Nedra Ross had a Christian ministry to young people in upstate New York. These last two couples were close friends of the Sherrills. We invited Arthur Gordon, a close *Guideposts* associate, and his wife, Pam. Arthur couldn't come, but Pam did.

The final person invited was our 22-year-old daughter Linda. She was working in her Grandmother LeSourd's gift shop in Maine when I called her. Linda and I had gone through some difficult times in our twelve-year step-mother/stepdaughter relationship, but the Lord impressed her name unmistakably on my mind. Linda later told me she probably would not have come unless I personally had asked her.

By Sunday afternoon, August 8, all of these people had gathered at Rock Harbor Manor. Counting Peter and Edith, we totaled sixteen. It soon became clear, however, that there was anything but close compatibility among us. "Lord," I found myself praying, "are You sure these are the people You summoned here?"

Virginia Lively . . . The call from Catherine came in early August: her newborn granddaughter lay in critical condition at Children's Hospital in Boston. However, Catherine went on, God had told her that if a group of prayer warriors gathered on Cape Cod and prayed for a miracle, the Lord would heal this child. Would I be willing to come?

How could I refuse? I loved Catherine, and my heart ached for her family. I assured Catherine that I would come to the Cape.

As soon as I got off the phone, I knelt by my bed to pray. I believed implicitly in Jesus' desire to heal Amy Catherine; and Catherine had told me on the phone that God had promised to do this if we would ask in faith. But now, even before I began to pray for Amy Catherine and for Peter and Edith, I heard the inner voice I had come to know so well:

This child will not live. But any other child they have they may have in perfect confidence.

I was stunned. Never in twenty years of healing ministry had I received such a totally unexpected message from God—a message of great promise linked with a message of death. Why? I was investing my entire life in the belief that Jesus wanted to heal. Why would He choose not to restore a tiny newborn?

As I continued to kneel beside my bed, my mind reeled with questions. Could this message really be from God? It stood in direct opposition to the divine assurance Catherine believed she had received. Had I mistaken something else for the voice I thought I knew? If not—if I had actually heard from God—should I relay the message to Catherine, challenging her own spiritual discernment? In any case, was this the proper time to reveal so hard a word from God, as she was undergoing a wrenching family crisis? Shouldn't I simply wait and let events prove or disprove the message? God could reveal His will to Catherine in His own way, in His own time, without any help from me.

"Lord, is this message from You?" I asked.

Flooding me came the assurance that it was. "Then what do You want me to do with it? Do You want me to share it with Catherine? With the others at Cape Cod? I need Your wisdom, Lord."

For as long as I knelt by my bed, I heard nothing more.

I had come to the Lord back in 1951, with neither questions nor expectations, giving myself completely, wherever that might lead. He in turn had used me as a channel to bring His healing to others. Despite my previous suspicion of Christians who tossed off references to "hearing the Lord" as glibly as I might refer to a conversation with a neighbor, in the years that followed I had learned to distinguish His thoughts from my own. The inner voice, though inaudible, was very clear. There was His admonition, for example, to grieve for three days after my husband Ed passed away, then to let him go to his new life and I to mine.

There was one message I had not heard, however, which was coming to represent the biggest trial of my Christian life: I also had a daughter named Linda. For years I had been praying for her healing from an illness with symptoms of dizziness and lack of energy that seemed to defy diagnosis. With no results.

I knew by heart the Bible promises of healing, like verses 2–3 from Psalm 103:

> Bless the Lord, O my soul,
>   and forget not all his benefits,
> who forgiveth all thine iniquities,
>   who healeth *all thy diseases.* . . .
>   KJV

God said right in His Word that He would heal *all* our diseases. So why didn't He heal my Linda? I certainly believed He could heal her, just as He healed many through my own hands. But after thirteen years, Linda seemed no closer to healing than she had in the pediatrician's office as a pre-teen. My daughter continued to suffer this nameless affliction while I carried on a healing ministry! "I've seen You do so many miracles, Lord," I prayed with growing urgency. "When will You do this one?"

The Clarion Call _____

*L*en . . . From the very first Monday morning meeting of the sixteen in the spacious lounge of Rock Harbor Manor, there was divergence among us. When some of the group admitted that they had come for the fellowship as well as for the immediate emergency, Catherine reacted sharply.

"The purpose of this get-together," she declared, eyes flashing, "is to pray for a miracle. The word from the Lord is that if we would gather a group here to pray for Amy Catherine, the power of His Spirit will fall on us and Amy Catherine will be healed."

I stared at Catherine in amazement. During our prayers together for the baby she had never sounded so confident. Her all-out faith picked up where her son's sermon the week before had left off. I looked at the circle of faces focused on Catherine. Their expressions ranged from Peter's nodding approval to Virginia Lively's look of strange anguish to Gloria Slosser's stark amazement to a "let's-go-for-it" exuberance on the face of Charles Hotchkiss.

What a strange mixture of people, I thought to myself. Already it was clear that pastors Hotchkiss and Marshall would be strong, aggressive leaders; both had experience in healing ministries. But Catherine's clarion call for boldness of faith surprised me because of her long frustration in this area. "I certainly do not have the gift of healing," she often lamented, after vainly storming heaven for an ailing friend or relative. I surmised that what had changed her was that prayer time in the Marshalls' bedroom when she identified the roots of an abnormal fear of disease, and Peter and I claimed freedom for her.

A tremor of excitement shot through me. If God had promised Catherine a supernatural healing of Amy Catherine, this was going to be a momentous occasion.

My eyes moved about the room. The look on Linda's face was inscrutable. I didn't know my daughter very well. I was glad she was here.

John and Elizabeth Sherrill remained intimate friends, inextricably involved in Catherine's and my lives. Since Tib's negative reaction to the *Gloria* project, the relationship had suffered. Yet in this crisis Catherine had turned instinctively to them.

The Slossers and Rosses were friends of the Sherrills. "I think they will make a contribution," was John's simple explanation for inviting them. As a *New York Times* reporter, Bob Slosser seemed a most unlikely prayer warrior, yet we were to find his practical wisdom and sensitive spirit a good balance during the emotional scenes that were to occur. His wife, Gloria, was one of those quiet intercessors from whom power radiates.

Scott Ross, son of a Scottish Presbyterian preacher, intrigued me. In reaction against what he saw as the hypocrisy of the Church, Scott had turned to a "hippie" lifestyle, becoming a popular disc jockey, an intimate of the Beatles and the Rolling Stones. After his conversion he and his wife, Nedra, had started a ministry called Love-Inn: a large farmhouse in upstate New York where rebellious young people could "live in" for a period and encounter Jesus Christ.

How fascinating that Bob Slosser and Scott Ross some seventeen years later would have leading roles at the Christian Broadcasting Network, Bob as President of CBN University and Scott as a 700 Club interviewer.

Jamie Buckingham, formerly a Baptist minister, had become a roving editor for *Guideposts* after the Sherrills discovered his outstanding writing talent at the 1967 *Guideposts* Writers Workshop.

Linda Hotchkiss, like Gloria Slosser, was the kind of strong intercessor whose work would undergird all that was to come. Pam Gordon would be arriving that afternoon by plane. As perhaps the newest believer among us, she was to perform a mission she would never have contemplated.

As I studied these people and their various gifts, my own role seemed obvious. Someone was needed to handle the myriad details behind the scenes. As the executive editor of *Guideposts*, seeing that other people got their jobs done was a big part of my role. Working out the details of housing and travel for this gathering had taken a lot of doing, and I mentioned in that first session that it had required all my skill as an organizer. To my dismay, instead of praise, this simple statement drew fire.

"I think your focus here is wrong, Len," said John.

"What I'm picking up here is a managerial spirit," Jamie concurred.

I was chagrined. "I wasn't complaining, just stating facts," I said.

"Maybe," John persisted, "your concern for details is blocking the Holy Spirit from using you more in a ministry role."

"Len," Virginia Lively joined in, "I notice you're constantly looking at your watch. Your mind is not here. Is it on the plane you're supposed to meet—or perhaps the article you're writing for *Guideposts?*"

Edith Marshall spoke up. "I'll go meet Pam Gordon at the Hyannis Airport this afternoon. Len, you stay here and be a part of this body."

Later, as we prayed, the word came that three men should drive to Boston that afternoon to anoint Amy Catherine with oil. As an elder in the church, I should be one of the three.

Prayer for the baby followed. It began quietly, then grew in volume. "Thank You, Lord, for healing Amy Catherine. . . . We praise You, Lord, that You are doing a mighty work in her small body. . . . Hallelujah—right now the baby is being healed!"

The note was one of rejoicing. Why did it make me feel uneasy?

When Peter Marshall, Jamie Buckingham, and I arrived at Children's Hospital that afternoon, I found myself surprisingly nervous. I had never before anointed a person with oil for healing. In our Delray Beach Presbyterian church this was considered the pastor's role. Elders were expected to oversee finances and perform other mundane services. And yet the Scripture passage in James was perfectly clear:

> Is any sick among you? let him call for the elders of the church; and let them pray over him, anointing him with oil in the name of the Lord.
>
> James 5:14, KJV

Before going up to the children's ward, Peter, Jamie, and I stopped in at the chapel to pray. In the quiet beauty of that place I sensed that Jesus was looking on our efforts with love and compassion. He had certainly loved children during His time on earth. I had a surge of hope that we could be His instruments for healing Amy Catherine.

In the children's ward a nurse placed the tiny baby in my arms. I braced her awkwardly against one shoulder while I fumbled with the bottle of oil. As I moistened my fingers with several drops of oil, I wondered again why the least trained of the three of us should be doing this.

"Lord," I plunged in, "as an elder in the church and this baby's grandfather, I claim the promise of Your Word for Amy Catherine . . . I now anoint this small child of Yours and pray that a healing will take place in her body . . . in the name of Jesus."

It was a jittery performance by this grandfather. Sweat built up on my forehead and I nearly dropped the bottle of oil on the floor. My prayer was a stumbling sequence of uncertain words, so quietly uttered that a nurse and an orderly working on the other side of the room never even looked in our direction.

What I learned from that experience, though, has stayed with me ever since. *My willingness to perform a priestly function in my role as an elder in the church or head of my home is much more important than the skill with which I carry it out.*

Peter and Jamie held Amy Catherine in turn, cradling her tenderly in their arms and praying for her. Human beings invoking God for a miracle. *Lord,* I wondered, *just how important is our role in what You will do here?*

Then the thought struck me. I remembered the prayers of the group that morning, releasing me from a managerial spirit to assume a fuller role in the Body of Christ. Perhaps our ministry to Amy Catherine was not the only thing God wanted from us in the next few days.

Jamie . . . The afternoon we went into the hospital to pray for Amy Catherine I slipped away from Len and Peter to make another prayer visit. A couple of years before I had met a New England couple, Jim and Linda Byrd, who were thinking of moving to Florida. We had corresponded several times. In her last letter Linda had asked me to pray for the child of a dear friend. The little girl was dying of cystic fibrosis and had been taken to Children's Hospital in Boston.

I had prayed, but had forgotten the whereabouts of the child until the afternoon we drove from Cape Cod to Boston to pray for Amy Catherine. Suddenly it occurred to me that this other child—a little girl of eight or nine—was in this very hospital.

After our prayer time with the Marshall infant I excused myself and checked at the nurses' station. Yes, the little girl I was concerned about was located just down the hall.

I found the room and knocked gently. There was no answer, but I could hear activity beyond the door. I eased the door open and realized why no one had heard me. An emergency was taking place. The beautiful little red-haired child was lying on the bed, wired and tubed to all kinds of machines. Two nurses were working feverishly over her. Her mother was standing at the foot of the bed, weeping.

"I'm Jamie Buckingham," I whispered to her. "I'm from Florida and Linda—"

"Oh," she gasped. "You're a pastor, aren't you?"

I nodded. "What's happening here?" I asked.

"She stopped breathing. They've got her started now, but it could happen again at any time."

"Would you mind if I prayed for her?"

The young mother clung to my hand, her body still shuddering with sobs. I reached out with my other hand and laid it on the little girl's foot, protruding from under the sheet that had been pulled loose as the nurses thrashed about, bringing her back to life.

Suddenly the frantic activity stopped. The two nurses and the hospital attendant straightened up, looking at me for the first time, then bowed their heads. Even the machines in the room, gasping and gurgling, sucking and beeping, seemed to pause.

"Lord, heal this child in Jesus' name," I prayed.

It was brief. Just a few sentences, then I withdrew my hand and was gone.

It was not until after I returned to my home in Melbourne, Florida, more than a week later, that I got the news. Linda Byrd, who knew nothing of my visit, had called my wife. A miracle had happened, she reported. Remember the little girl with cystic fibrosis who had been dying in the Boston hospital? Well, she had just been released, allowed to go home. The doctors said they must have made a mistake. It wasn't cystic fibrosis after all—because that's incurable. And the child was fine now. Healed completely. She thought we'd want to know.

The Slugger _____

***C**atherine* . . . The moment Scott and Nedra Ross arrived, a struggle began inside me. I was aware of an inability to relate to them, which troubled me. Unless we were united as a praying body, would the Lord honor our prayers for Amy Catherine's healing?

Scott, I learned, had been born in Scotland to an evangelical preacher's family. That part intrigued me, for I had loved the Scottish people ever since my marriage to Peter Marshall. But when his family emigrated to America, Scott found himself—kilts, accent, kitchen table haircut—the butt of cruel teasing on the school playground. Worse, the small church his father had come to pastor broke every promise they had made to his simple, unworldly parents.

Before long Scott had shed his Scottish accent and his church background eventually to become a disc jockey with a focus on rock music.

Nedra, a beauty with both black and Indian blood, had a gift of spiritual discernment, which would emerge during the days that followed. The Sherrills were so high on the Rosses that they were doing a book with Scott that would soon be published under the title *Scott Free.*

Why was I resistant to them? The generation gap again . . . and yet the Sherrills are in the same generation Len and I are. Was it because I saw how our Linda was drawn to them? Because I sensed the attraction of rebellious spirits to each other?

The meeting on Tuesday morning took place outdoors on the lawn adjacent to Rock Harbor Manor. It began with a report on the trip to Boston by the three men. The nurses had been most cooperative as the three ministered to the baby; the condition of Amy Catherine was unchanged. Peter reaffirmed his belief that the Lord was going to perform a miraculous healing in his daughter.

After this positive opening, the tenor of the meeting changed. Peter offered to the group a Scripture passage he felt had been given him:

> And he shall enter into a strong and firm covenant with the many for one week; and in the midst of the week he shall cause the sacrifice and offering to cease; and upon the wing or pinnacle of abominations [shall come] one who makes desolate; until the full determined end is poured out on the desolator.
>
> Daniel 9:27, AMPLIFIED

This seemed to us a very strange passage of Scripture to apply to the present situation. It was to haunt some of us in the weeks that followed.

Peter then bluntly asked a question: Were we all supposed to be here? There was an uncomfortable silence; then somewhat defensively people began to share. One of the first to do so was Scott Ross.

Scott vividly described what it was like to be a preacher's kid in a strange land ... the loneliness, the poverty, the rejection. Bitterly he lashed out against the Church, which had mistreated them. "The leadership of the established Church is phony. They don't care about the people, they don't care about the clergy. They don't care that the pastor of a small church and his family hardly have enough to eat. They serve themselves and their own pet projects. They're a group of hypocrites. . . ." His voice rose despairingly. "The church is nothing but vomit. It's ... it's dog's vomit."

It was too much. I found myself on my feet, pointing a finger at Scott. "How dare you call the Body of Christ 'dog's vomit'! How dare you say that about the Church that Jesus said was His Body and for which He died! How can you say such a thing and still call yourself a Christian?"

My outburst was totally spontaneous. I was propelled to my feet without any conscious decision. What happened then was completely unexpected.

Instead of lashing back at me and defending his statements, a dam seemed to break inside of Scott. Tears streaming from his eyes, he began to sob convulsively. The cleansing lasted a long, long time. With Virginia Lively laying hands on his head, and me holding his hand, Scott was freed from the spirit of hatred that had taken root in him as a small, bewildered boy.

A healing also took place inside me as my habitual negativism about the lifestyle he represented dissolved, for once, in understanding.

Another surprising event took place during that same morning meeting. We'd agreed that each afternoon a contingent representing the group would drive to Boston to pray on the spot for Amy Catherine during the hospital visiting hours. The question arose: Whom should it be today?

We had a quiet time of prayer, then Jamie Buckingham broke the silence. "I feel that God has given me the name of one person He wants to go to Children's Hospital today—Pam Gordon."

I will never forget the kaleidoscope reaction on Pam's face: first incredulity, then fear, then pain. Finally, a torrent of tears. As with Scott Ross, some of us gathered about Pam to minister to her as she kept repeating, "I'm not worthy . . . I'm just not worthy . . . ."

"Being worthy has nothing to do with it," Jamie tried to explain.

Being asked to go and pray for a newborn baby girl, to hold her in her arms, had clearly opened up an old traumatic wound in Pam's heart. The tears and prayers that followed were the beginning of a second healing on that sunlit patch of lawn that morning.

The explosion of emotions had been so physically tiring, however, that I went to my room right after lunch to take a nap, leaving it to the group to decide who would accompany Pam Gordon to Boston.

Len . . . Most of us met again after lunch. We would have done better to have rested for an hour because there was little togetherness. Linda was upset about something. She and Scott Ross went off together to talk. The others couldn't agree on who should go to Boston and who should stay behind to support them in prayer. Pam, of course, was going. Edith said she had to go and finally Linda Hotchkiss became the third.

So ironic this selection, because we had spent much time that morning on the husband's role in spiritual leadership. Now here were three women on their way to Boston while the men went off to rest.

I went to our room where Catherine had gone right after lunch. "Who's going to Boston?" she asked sleepily.

"Pam, Edith, and Linda Hotchkiss."

Catherine jerked herself up to a sitting position. "You've got to be kidding!"

"That's the way it ended up. They're already on their way."

"What happened to the men?"

"None felt led."

"What about you—why didn't you object?"

"I was stripped of my managerial baton yesterday, remember?"

"And what about Virginia? She told me she felt she was supposed to go."

"The group chose Linda Hotchkiss."

To my surprise Catherine jumped out of bed and hurriedly began to dress.

"Where are you going?"

"I don't know. But three women going in to pray alone. Where's the spiritual authority there?"

"So you and Virginia will make five women."

"You're full of resentment, Len."

"No, I'm not. I had a great experience yesterday with Amy Catherine. It's changed my whole way of thinking about my role as a male. The men are copping out today because they're tired. You ducked out of the meeting after lunch because you were tired. So don't pass judgment."

She glared at me for a moment and stormed out of the room. I learned later what happened. Catherine went first to Virginia's room, got her up, then tracked down Peter and Charles Hotchkiss. Jamie joined them in the hall. Catherine lit into the men on the matter of their being "prophet, priest, and king" in intercessory situations. Soon Virginia, Peter, Charles, and Jamie were on their way to Boston, while

Catherine called the hospital and left word that the three women were to await the arrival of this second group.

The seven had a good prayer time at the hospital. They also agreed on a nickname for Catherine: "The Slugger."

Catherine . . . The next healing in the group occurred between John Sherrill and myself. Seven of us—Virginia Lively, Charles and Linda Hotchkiss, John and Tib Sherrill, and Len and me—had met in a special prayer session for Amy Catherine, little suspecting that a very different kind of restoration was going to take place.

After John Sherrill's experience of the Holy Spirit in Atlantic City back in 1962, a powerful ministry of teaching had begun for John. Often when he spoke of Jesus, he would choke up and have to struggle for composure, a sign of his close relationship with the Lord.

Four or five years after his baptism, I was dismayed to learn that John was going to a psychiatrist two or three sessions a week. When I challenged John on it, he stared at me in genuine bewilderment. John's entire family, he reminded me, had been active in the field of psychiatry for decades. His father, a seminary professor, had pioneered early efforts to reconcile religion and psychiatry. His mother and his sister (and Tib's sister, too) were psychiatric social workers. To John, psychiatry represented a medical breakthrough similar to—say—the discovery of the circulation of the blood. He couldn't see that going to a psychiatrist subtracted anything at all from his witness.

"But John," I protested, "you are switching authority figures in your life, substituting the psychiatrist for Jesus."

Again that baffled look. "Catherine, the doctor doesn't try to replace God! On the contrary—he can help someone find God, sort out neurotic ideas and holdovers from childhood, thus discover who Jesus really is."

"I've nothing against Christian psychiatrists," I agreed. "I know they can help people. But not you, John! My spirit rails against it for you."

As usual I came on too strong. A barrier went up between John and me, invisible, unacknowledged, but very real. On the surface the LeSourd-Sherrill relationship continued strong. Tib remained my editor—at least up to the *Gloria* project. We remained friends. Two years previously, in 1969, when Len and I returned to Kauai to celebrate our tenth anniversary in the same hotel where we'd spent our honeymoon, it was the Sherrills we invited to come with us. Still, I ached for the return of the old transparency among us.

Now, on Cape Cod, John prefaced our prayer time with this announcement: "You will be interested to know about a decision I've recently made, Catherine. I've concluded that I've made about all the progress I can in my psychiatric sessions. I'm grateful for the self-understanding I've gained, but I've decided that it's time to phase them out."

I was delighted to hear this, of course, but sensed that John had more to say.

John stroked his close-cropped beard for a long moment, then opened up. "You need to know that I've had a tremendous fear of making this break. The fear is not stopping the sessions per *se*, but of closing off the relationship. Twice before in my life when a major relationship was ruptured— by death in those earlier cases—the loss was followed by a bout with cancer. So now with this new separation I'm battling fear—the fear that the cancer will return."

Once he had gotten that fear out, John began to talk about the little boy John Sherrill, who had been skinny and not very athletic, growing up in a sports-centered Southern town. At this point, tears suddenly filled John's eyes.

Virginia Lively broke in. "The Lord has just given me these words for you: He says, 'John, I want you to know that *I* will *never* leave you; that you are and will always be one of My strong ones.'"

With this Virginia knelt before John and with great intensity of feeling said: "John, I wish I had the eloquent words to tell you the man that I see in you—the teacher, the leader, the prayer warrior, the communicator."

I sprang from my chair, moved across the room, and embraced him, saying: "John, I love you, I love you." By this time both John and I were weeping. There'd been a mystic, instantaneous reconciliation between him and me. I didn't quite understand what had happened or how; but my spirit was suddenly overflowing with joy in the reunion.

Something important was happening to the group through tears. Scott Ross had been embarrassed by his weeping, but healing inside him had begun the moment he let his emotions go. The same with Pam Gordon. And now John and me. The power and presence of God seemed to be in direct proportion to the tears that flowed. The men especially resisted this in our macho society where men are taught that it isn't "manly" to weep.

Yet we were discovering that tears were not to be feared, that often weeping opens the door to the *real* person inside and the reality of the situation to be dealt with. In fact, what we read in the Scripture about how God abhors hardness of heart should convince us that tears are the sign of the hard heart melting and therefore a very *true* *sign* of the Holy Spirit.

Still I went to bed that night troubled. Half of me was rejoicing over the restoration of my close relationship with the Sherrills, and over the other healings that were taking place. The other half of me was grieving over tiny Amy Catherine at the Boston hospital. Despite the massive prayer directed toward her, not only by our group of sixteen but from hundreds, perhaps thousands of people who had heard of her plight, there was no change in her condition.

What are we doing wrong, Lord? I asked silently, staring at the ceiling. *Are we missing something? Are we so busy talking to You and to each other that we're not listening for Your instructions to us?*

I turned toward Len to see if he was still awake. He was breathing steadily, asleep. How I envied his ability to drop off so quickly. The more I wanted to sleep, the harder it was for me to let myself go, as I endlessly replayed the day's events.

My dream that night turned out to be significant. It seemed there were two large houses that belonged to our family. There were many rooms in each house. Some were furnished, some were not. There was heirloom furniture in some of the rooms, but I was aware of the fact that a very great deal of work needed to be done in rearranging the furniture, adding new pieces, decorating. I was appalled at the task that lay before me and the rest of the family. Although other members of the family were about, the two main characters in the dream were my father and me.

Father's attitude in the dream was: we must get on with this refurbishing as quickly as possible. The episode seemed to be taking place rather late in Dad's life because he made the statement to me, "I'll stay with you to help as long as I possibly can." The fact that my father had passed away ten years before in 1961 didn't seem significant.

As I pondered this dream the next morning and then asked the Lord about it, I had the distinct impression that it referred to all the work that was going on in sorting out family relationships. Dad's repeated "Let's get on with it" stressed the urgency of this.

Linda _____

*C*atherine ... The next morning, Wednesday, I opened
the meeting with a plea that we stand together in spirit
against the pessimistic opinions of the doctors and nurses
at the hospital. There followed an hour's glorious prayer
time for Amy Catherine. Powerful intercession. Strong affirmation that the baby was being healed.

Then came individual sharing. My stepdaughter, Linda,
was sitting on the floor in front of her father. When I asked
her where she was personally at this point, she singled out
Scott and Nedra Ross as the two people who had been most
helpful to her over the past few days.

"Do you need prayer, Linda?"

She shook her head a trifle uncertainly.

"How about a healing of any bad memories?" suggested Virginia Lively. "Maybe some that go back to when you were a small child?"

A long silence. "Well, there was a birthday when I was very little." She glanced up at her father.

Len had been writing something in his notebook. Now his head snapped up. "You remember your third birthday, Linda?" he asked.

"I'm not sure when it was. We were living in an apartment in Glen Oaks. You and Eve had a big fight—and you left."

Len was staring at her incredulously. "That was your third birthday."

"I guess so."

"Did you understand what the fight was all about?"

"No. I just remember that I had been so excited about having a birthday party. Then I was sent to my room to be all by myself, as though I were being punished. I couldn't understand this because I hadn't done anything wrong. I cried my heart out. Eve came in to comfort me after a while, but I felt you had deserted me, Dad."

As Len and Linda faced each other, suddenly my mind went back to the dream I had had the night before . . . the importance of restoring and redoing the rooms in our family house.

Len . . . I was stunned by Linda's revelation, amazed that she could remember that unpleasant scene after almost twenty years. I described to the group how her mother and I had decided to have a special cake, candles, ice cream, and presents for that third birthday party. I had arrived home at six P.M. to discover an empty vodka bottle and a wife who could hardly walk. I couldn't believe Eve would do that to her daughter. Not understanding the disease that alcoholism is, I blew up at her. The party was ruined. Linda was plunked back into her room and I was so frustrated that I stormed out of the house and just drove about aimlessly for the next two hours. Linda never did have her birthday party.

John Sherrill picked it up at that point. "Linda, what are your memories of your mother?"

"Mixed. I have some great memories of her. She taught me little songs and dances, took me places. We did a lot of things together. She was so beautiful, and I knew she loved me, but I didn't understand why she changed moods so quickly. There are some bad memories, too."

"Did her drinking upset you?"

"I wasn't always aware that she was drinking—just that she acted strangely at times."

I was getting increasingly uncomfortable over the way the meeting was going. "Are we getting off the track here with all these personal disclosures?" I asked.

John can be blunt. "I know this is unpleasant for you, Len, but I think we should hear Linda out on her bad memories." Then to my daughter, "Anything else you want to share?"

She was looking at me now. "Dad, I wasn't old enough to understand that Eve's drinking was the main problem. What I do remember is feeling so alone and hurt and torn up inside. Looking back, I can't help but wonder why no one ever seemed to care about what was going on inside of me.

"Dad, I love you so much . . . ." Her voice broke. After a pause she went on. "And I know you love me, but I feel like you've been gone a lot. Not just physically, but emotionally as well."

Catherine now spoke up. "Len, maybe there is something you need to look at here. Didn't you tell me once of a period in your life when you ducked out on any situation if it got emotional?"

I suddenly felt stricken. There *was* something here I needed to look at. "Yes, that's true. When I was around twelve I cried in a sad movie and was so embarrassed I remember giving myself an order that I would never cry again. For the next seventeen years I'd close off any encounter if I felt tears welling up."

"Is there still a tendency in you to duck out of tense situations rather than staying to see them through?" John asked.

"Perhaps."

"Can you think of any reason why emotion is hard for you to handle? How about your father? Was he like that?"

I shook my head. "My father was as close to being a saint as any man I ever knew." Then I checked myself. "Yes," I said. "There were times when my father retreated from unpleasant household scenes. My mother was inclined to get worked up at such times and burst into tears. I remember during these upsets of Mother's, Dad would go off and smoke a cigar. Only when Mother calmed down a little would Dad return and try to restore the peace."

"The generation thing again," said Catherine. "Do you see, Len, why we have called you 'the peacemaker' so often?"

"There's a difference between being a peacemaker and running away," said John.

"But inherited patterns can make someone like Len do both," suggested Catherine.

I knew what the conversation was leading to and was beginning to feel a deep inner agitation. My hands were trembling.

"Len, I guess what is coming out here concerns your divorce," said John gently. "Tib and I remember only too well the agony you went through with Eve, the years you spent trying to help her, the prayers we all poured into the situation. But, Len, maybe Linda isn't aware of all this. Maybe she thinks you just walked out on the marriage, like you walked out on her birthday party."

I leaned forward and touched Linda on the arm. "Is John right?"

Tears were sliding down her face. She nodded and leaned her head against my leg.

Words of protest formed in my mouth. Defensive, self-pitying words. Linda needed to know that the last five years of my marriage to her mother were the most painful experience of my life, that nothing, ever, could compare to the frustration, the anguish, the sheer bafflement of trying to help a loved one who was unable to accept help, who kept on the path of self destruction no matter what you did.

I stifled those words. Something deep in my spirit told me that Linda already knew of my pain, that she needed something else. My silent prayer: *Lord, what do I say to her?* Then the words came.

"Linda, the truth is that I did quit on the marriage. Will you forgive me?"

She nodded and reached for my hand. My tears joined hers as I hugged my daughter.

Linda . . . I had come to Cape Cod not only because I was concerned for the baby, but also because Mom seemed to want me to come. Things had been very strained between us for as long as I could remember. The time with her at my college graduation had been awful. I felt we were worlds apart. Perhaps now Amy Catherine's need was providing a chance to find common ground. It was risky to be with Mom, for I wondered if she would ever accept me. And I was uneasy about being around Amy Catherine, as babies—sick or well—intimidated me. Yet my longing for family closeness propelled me to come—even over the protests of my Grandmother LeSourd, for whom I'd been working. In a strange way I even welcomed the fact that there was a crisis, for it seemed our family had experienced its greatest coming together in times of greatest pain.

After the emotional exchange between Dad and me on Wednesday morning I was about to take a shower. A particular moment is crystallized forever for me. I had one foot on the bathroom rug, the other in the bathtub. At that instant like a bolt of lightning the realization hit me that "one foot in, one foot out" was an accurate representation of my life. Several times in the past I'd gone through the motions of committing my life to the Lord, but always with part of me holding back.

Over the years I had sensed that God's hand was unmistakably in and on my life. But I resented the family pressure I felt toward Christianity. I was searching everywhere else for meaning in life, one time during college complaining in my journal, "Isn't there any choice for me but God?"

Standing half in, half out of the tub, suddenly I saw how He had allowed me to go my own way, had given me plenty of "rope," yet had always protected me from serious harm. Now it seemed He was saying to me, "Linda, it is time for you to decide—for Me, or against Me. You can no longer have it both ways."

At first I pulled back. Choosing the Lord's way would cost me, for some things in my life would have to change. And I doubted I would have much fun. But I couldn't bring myself to turn my back on Him entirely. Most of all, I was tired of living in two worlds and not enjoying either. I longed for peace and a sense of rightness about the direction of my life.

I took a deep breath and said aloud, "I choose You, Lord." Then I got into the shower. That shower was my point of no return.

Forbidden Feelings _____

*T*ib . . . That summer of 1971 our own daughter, Liz, was fifteen. Eight years later, in God's strange ecology, Liz was to marry a geneticist, Alan Flint, who works in the research laboratory of Children's Hospital.

Until Children's new building was completed last year, anyone visiting Alan at his lab entered the hospital through the same Greek revival portico that once admitted us to Amy Catherine's ward. Each time I passed between those gray concrete pillars on Longwood Avenue the familiar feelings would sweep over me—sorrow, anger, pity, guilt. The emotions of 1971 still painfully alive in the 1980s.

They haunted me so long, I believe, because at the time these negative feelings were never expressed. I remember my vigils at Amy Catherine's cribside chiefly as times of grief denied. She was so tiny, so beautiful, so unequipped for this alien world. I remember holding her in a kind of awed astonishment, as though my human arms cradled a being from some unimaginably distant realm.

All babies bring with them a bit of eternity. But this one especially. Amy Catherine was wrapped in a stillness and inwardness that had nothing of this earth about it. I remember trying to pray, the first time John and I visited Amy, and being unable to form any image at all of this child joining our clamorous world.

John held the baby next and prayed for us both, affirming what we both knew to be true: God can reverse the direst medical prognosis.

And, yet, the tears I had not allowed to surface, there in the hospital, kept flowing in some hidden part of me throughout the four days on Cape Cod. Hidden but terribly real—the part of me that was heartsick and outraged, not only at this second ordeal for Edith and Peter, but at all the tiny sufferers occupying the cribs at Children's Hospital. The part of me that knew how Edith's heart was torn and twisted. The part that wanted to put my arms around her.

But gestures, even thoughts, of sympathy were ruled out by the premise of our gathering. I'd come fully assenting to that premise. "I tell you the truth," Jesus said, "if anyone says to this mountain, 'Go, throw yourself into the sea,' and does not doubt in his heart but believes that what he says will happen, it will be done for him."

In Amy Catherine's diagnosis we were indeed up against a mountain of impossibility. And we'd accepted the challenge, as a group and individually. We'd come to the Cape to claim the miracle promised to Catherine. But there was a condition to Jesus' promise: *We were not to doubt in our hearts.* Any admission of grief, even to myself, it seemed to me, was a form of doubt that could threaten the miracle's occurrence.

Agreeing together for the victory was the key. Absolute unity was stressed so strongly that my unshed tears seemed to me monstrous intruders in a sacred place. Again and again I forced them down, berating myself for lack of faith. Sometimes, across the room as we stormed heaven for the baby's healing, I would see another tormented face and imagine another struggle like my own.

But no one spoke out. No one questioned the victory being proclaimed with such conviction. I hope it was not a desire to get credit for a greater faith than I had that made me keep silent. I don't think it was. I think it was a passionate hope that those who sounded so sure of healing were right. That my unexpressed sorrow was merely the result of human-sized thinking.

And yet, as the days passed, a sense of unreality seemed to steal over the impassioned prayers for Amy Catherine. Years before, after Peter Christopher's death, Edith and I had grown close during a stay at a retreat house in West Germany. I'd loved the steel-sharp honesty that flashed from her as she admitted, "I'm mad at God." Edith knew that this was not a mature attitude. But she also knew that gut-level reality is the road to maturity.

To all growth. It was happening again on Cape Cod. Out of realness and honesty—however painful—was coming healing for members of our group, time after time. Only in our prayers for Amy Catherine were negatives ruled out. Only in our prayers for her was power absent.

Edith . . . My overriding concern throughout the retreat was my own spiritual state; if others were to be believed, there was every indication that I must be dangerously "out of it." After all, Peter had gone out on a limb, stating emphatically and publicly that he believed God would heal Amy. And Mom was crystal-clear that no other stance could possibly line up with Scripture. Others in the group seemed to concur. But in my heart of hearts, I wasn't sure I believed it.

Afraid that I was alone in my disbelief, I couldn't risk being honest. Adding to the confusion was the fact that part of me was genuinely afraid that any doubt on my part might keep God from being able to do His healing work.

So throughout the time, I worked hard at mustering up a mindset and a belief system that would not jeopardize our baby's well-being—as though by an act of my will I could change the message my own heart was receiving. Any doubt was 100 percent unacceptable, wasn't it? I could not, I must not, allow doubt any room or voice. My baby's life might be at stake.

The kinds of messages I was getting, which I believe were authentic, were ones having to do with Amy's need for love, for acceptance, for as many hours of cuddling as we could give her. Though the doctors had insisted that she had so little brain function she could not feel pain, I knew that in the midst of that jungle of wires, tubes, and monitors, her spirit was crying out for our unconditional love.

On the Beach

*C*atherine . . . By the third day it was obvious to all of us that the Holy Spirit had descended on our small group of sixteen. People had become painfully aware of their sins; tears of repentance were flowing, lives being redirected. To me, it was a prelude to the main event—the healing of Amy Catherine. "When, Lord?" I kept praying. "What is Your timing? Give us Your instructions."

Meanwhile, as the ministry continued in our group, several asked for a water baptism in the nearby bay. What some call a "believer's baptism"—baptism by total immersion after a personal step of commitment—had become popular during the current move of the Holy Spirit. Some of the men went down to the beach to scout out a suitable place for the ceremony.

Pam Gordon had returned from Children's Hospital glowing from her prayer time with Amy Catherine. "The baby smiled at me," she told us. "She really did." Pam was the first to ask for the "believer's baptism."

As we trooped down to the beach as a body, Pam confessed that all her life she had felt an overpowering fear of water. She had had a bad experience as a little girl when in fact she had almost drowned in a pond. Then as an older child there was another occasion when she nearly drowned. All of this had contributed to an almost paralyzing fear of allowing her head to go under the water.

To vacationers in swimming, or lounging on the sand, our proceedings must have presented a strange sight. Jamie was the first one immersed. Then came Peter. They had to find a deeper place in the water for Peter and it was quite something to see my son's tall form dipped beneath the surface. Next they baptized Edith. Then it was Pam's turn.

Jamie and Charles talked to her first, then prayed that the Lord would simply remove her fear. Which He did— gloriously. Pam was radiant as she came out of the water.

Jamie ... When we walked down to the beach for water baptism that morning, I assumed that as a Baptist minister I would of course "officiate."

But God had other ideas and as the group left the house to make our way over the sand dunes and through the waist-high sea oats toward the water, I suddenly found myself in His presence. It was one of those rare times when I knew the Holy Spirit was teaching me. It developed into a dialogue as we headed toward the bay.

You're not going to do the baptizing, He said. The voice, although not audible, was just as real as if I had been standing in a classroom listening to a teacher.

"But I'm the most qualified. Besides, I want to. I need to." I had so little I could hold out as trophies to make others notice me.

*No, I am not going to let you do the baptizing, because
your own water baptism was out of order.*

I knew, of course, what He was talking about. It had
bothered me, on and off across the years, but like a lot of
other things that were not quite right, I had relegated it to
the back of my mind and tried to forget about it. During my
teenage years I had joined the First Baptist Church of Vero
Beach, Florida. In order to become a full member of the
church, I needed to be immersed—the outward sign, sup-
posedly, of an inward surrender to Christ. I talked to the
pastor and then on a Sunday morning, prodded by my
mother who also felt it was time for me to join a church, I
walked down the aisle and was received with what Bap-
tists call "the right hand of fellowship." A week later, on a
Sunday night, the pastor ushered me into the church bap-
tistry, suitably adorned in a white robe, and I was immersed.

But there had been no accompanying spiritual experience, no surrender of my will to Jesus Christ's. Even though
words to that effect were used, they were simply words. It
wasn't until several years later, when I found myself at a
campfire service on an island in Schroon Lake, New York,
that I made the necessary spiritual commitment to the
Lordship of Christ. Across the years ever since, I'd known
my water baptism had been premature.

But God is never finished with a man until he is con-
formed to the image of His Son. My baptism was one of
those things that I could no longer push beneath the surface
of my lake and pretend all was well. It was time to make the
correction. Publicly.

"But who will perform those baptisms if I don't?" I asked
the Holy Spirit.

Why, Charles Hotchkiss, who else? He responded.

I dreaded asking the next question for I already knew the
answer. "And who will baptize me?"

Charles Hotchkiss, the Spirit answered—and I could almost hear Him chuckle. *You'll be the first candidate when we get to the bay.*

"But God!" I protested. "He's an Episcopal priest and I'm a Southern Baptist minister."

This time it seemed the Holy Spirit laughed out loud.

However, in my obedience to the command of God, something else happened. In fact, it happened even before we reached the water. I began to think of the sins I had served—the substances that had controlled me. While others might be addicted to alcohol or drugs, I was addicted to food. In short, I was a glutton. I was also fat. Not "stocky," but blubbery fat. I carried around my waist more than 25 pounds of excess flesh. I had been on every diet imaginable, but all they did was set the stage for a subsequent weight gain.

I had resigned myself to remaining fat; yet deep inside I knew I wasn't supposed to be that way. Now I began to realize that water baptism was another key to inner healing, for in submitting I was actually appropriating the death of Christ to my own subconscious appetites:

> That like as Christ was raised up from the dead by the glory of the Father, even so we also should walk in newness of life.
>
> Romans 6:4, KJV

When we arrived at the water's edge, I pulled Father Hotchkiss aside and made my rather unusual request. He nodded, asked me a few questions, and agreed to take me into the water first. He quickly made it plain that if I was to submit to his baptizing me, I would also have to submit to his method.

I had no sooner agreed than he turned to the group that had assembled on the beach and said, "Jamie wants to go first, but before I baptize him he wants to confess his sins before you."

I hadn't counted on that. But I had come this far and meant to see it through. If my friends rejected me on the basis of my sins, that was their problem, not mine. I was determined to go all the way and leave my world under water.

So I named them: gluttony, lust, resentment, unforgiveness, pride, self-righteousness . . . on and on the list went. It was difficult and terribly embarrassing. If there was any group in the world I wanted to impress with my spirituality, this was it. Yet I knew God was pleased.

We waded out into the bay, which by that time was visibly receding. I crossed my hands in front of my chest, waiting for Father Hotchkiss to lower me backwards beneath the water.

"On your knees!" the priest said.

I started to protest, but I remembered that I had agreed to do it his way, no matter how strange it seemed. I dropped to my knees on the sandy bottom. The warm water came up to my chest. I felt the priest's hand on the back of my head and realized I was to go under face first.

I came up, shaking the water out of my ears, just in time to hear the priest say, "That's for the Father." Then, before I could catch a good breath, I was under again. This time the Son, and finally, a third time, for the Holy Spirit. I guess he figured he'd never get his hands on another Baptist minister.

Something did happen out there in the water, something in my inner spirit that had to do with discipline. I had begun a fast that day that I expected would last three days, which was the longest I had ever been without food. Instead, it lasted 28 days. During that time I began to experience a new surge of spiritual authority. Not only were my old appetites being broken, but by the time I returned home at the end of the week, I felt like Moses descending from Mt. Sinai with the tablets of stone in his hand and the radiance of God on his face. Apart from my experience with the baptism of the Holy Spirit, nothing had so visibly shaken and shaped my life as did my submission to baptism in the salty water of Cape Cod Bay.

Catherine . . . Thursday morning before sunrise the group met again on the beach, this time for a service of Communion. It was our final morning together, clear but cool; a covey of seagulls dove and swooped at the waves as they rolled onto the sand.

Before Communion, there was another water baptism. Linda had asked for this following the healing experience between her and her father the day before. It was good to see her come out of the water so joyous and alive, though I sensed that Len, Linda, and I still had more work to do on our relationships.

Next we gathered in a circle on the beach. Jamie and Charlie had brought a loaf of bread and some juice in a cup; these elements were placed in the middle of our circle. Jamie suggested that this be a different type of Communion, that each one of us should kneel down by the elements and go through a ritual of personal Communion in whatever form seemed appropriate. It could be a prayer, a meditation, a confession, a thanksgiving.

And so we did this, alone, or man and wife together. I was very much moved by the quality of reverence, the depth of repentance, the humility. Virginia Lively was especially affected; she slumped sideways onto the sand from her kneeling position, sobbing her heart out.

Virginia . . . The beauty of the Cape Cod beach, the summer surf pounding against the long, sandy shore, had given us the perfect backdrop for four days and nights of prayer and conversation. As the days passed, and God still did not give me clear direction about whether to share the prophecy He had given me about Amy Catherine, I remained quiet. At least this way I could know my words had no bearing on whether this precious infant lived or died.

Len noticed my silence one evening with a kindly, "Why so quiet, Virginia?"

"Just thoughtful, I guess," I replied.

Over those four days, most of those in our group of sixteen visited Children's Hospital, prayed, pleaded with God. When Amy Catherine got no better, some began to assert, in spite of the evidence, that the miracle was taking place. ("Lord, You are healing her right now!" "We're standing on Your promises, in the name of Jesus!") It seemed almost as if some of these prayer warriors needed to prove to themselves that they had sufficient faith. Did everyone really believe in his or her heart that Amy Catherine was being restored? Or were others, like myself, carrying a silent burden of grief?

My heart ached for the suffering family, while my mind echoed with the words of the prophecy I had received: *This child will not live.* What a contrast with the ringing affirmations of others in the group. The second half of the message, promising health and normalcy to all future offspring of the Marshalls, kept me from feeling completely despondent.

On the final day, in order to celebrate what God had done among us, we had our early morning worship service and Communion on the beautiful expanse of white sand below Rock Harbor Manor. As we walked out to the beach, someone remarked, "Virginia is the only one who hasn't needed ministry!"

Everyone nodded. I had seemed to be the strong one, the one to listen and encourage and pray for the others. Little did they know.

Someone placed the Communion elements, a small loaf of bread and a cup, onto a cloth on the sand. Then we stood in a circle around the elements as Jamie Buckingham led us in worship, offering songs of praise and thanksgiving to God in the soft dawn light.

After Jamie had blessed the elements, each person in turn knelt on the sand and either prayed aloud, meditated silently, or shared an insight. Then each one tore off a piece of the loaf and drank from the cup. Only the breaking of the waves onto the shore and the occasional cry of a seagull punctuated the awe-filled time of remembrance.

As my turn to partake of Communion neared, however, my throat began to ache and tears stung my eyes. Where were they coming from, now of all times? Had they been collecting deep inside without my knowing it, to surface now when I least wanted them to? I didn't even have a handkerchief with me!

As I knelt in the sand, a sob broke my voice. "O Lord," I heard myself cry, "why haven't You healed my daughter?"

What was I saying? I hadn't been thinking that much about Linda—not any more than usual, anyhow. But tears came boiling out as Virginia, the "strong" one who needed no ministry, fell apart before everyone's eyes.

"You promise healing in Your Word, Lord. And I've prayed every way I know how. But You still haven't healed her. It's been so long, and I don't understand. Why don't You do it, Lord? How long do I have to wait?"

My heart felt as though it were splintering and all the pent-up worry and fear of more than a decade pouring out through the cracks. Somehow I had collapsed onto the sand, sobbing like a small, abandoned child.

As I lay there, my own strength exhausted, I was given ears to hear how I sounded: *Why haven't You . . . ? Why don't You . . . ? I don't understand . . . . How long do I have to wait?*

Why, forever, if He chose! I suddenly realized, with stunning clarity, that I didn't have to understand at all! I needed only to come to a point of relinquishment. Never in thir-

teen years had I really turned Linda's problem over to Him.
I had hovered over her fretfully, watched her, nagged
her, assuming without ever admitting as much that I
could worry and pray at the same time. How many times
had I read verses in the Bible without really *hearing* them:
"Have no anxiety about anything . . ." (Philippians 4:6) or
"Cast all your anxieties on him, for he cares about you"
(1 Peter 5:7).

How far I had slipped from that inner awareness that
healing is always an unpredictable gift—sheer grace, unde-
served favor, nothing I could either work for or earn. His
desire to heal and restore, as revealed in Scripture, origi-
nated solely because of His goodness and was in keeping
with His purpose.

Now I knew what had struck me as familiar in the prayers
at Cape Cod for Amy Catherine: they reminded me of my
own prayers for my daughter, which had crossed the
boundary of expectant faith to the borders of demand!

Something hard inside was melting as I continued to
weep in the gathering dawn, surrounded by Christians
whom I loved. My attitude and my praying had to change.

"O Lord, You know I love You," I said aloud, struggling
back up to my knees. "And Lord, even if You never heal
Linda, I'll still love You. I always will. I trust You, Jesus. I
leave her in Your hands. Thank You, Lord."

My tears still flowed, but the splintering pain in my heart
was lessening. At last I was willing to leave the accomplishment of Linda's healing in the hands of the God who remained sovereign over His creation.

At the close of our bread-breaking service, one of my
friends touched my arm and silently handed me a handkerchief. As I turned, I looked into the compassionate eyes
of Bob Slosser, who wore the barest hint of a smile. Without
a word he opened his arms and enfolded me in them. I felt
warm, safe, comforted.

When the group started back to the retreat center for

breakfast—our final meal together before heading to the airport and home—I remained behind for a minute or two, waiting for the sun to slip red above the horizon. Suddenly it emerged, bathing the beach in light, almost as though somebody had flipped on a switch to let the glory of God shine forth.

Binding
and Loosing _____

*C*atherine ... Nine of the sixteen prayer partners departed Cape Cod by plane or automobile on Thursday. When we had first gathered in the living room of the Christian Center on Monday morning, we had been a disparate collection of people, with widely different beliefs and lifestyles. A few had been only nominal believers. Many were wrestling with deep personal problems.

In four days we had come together in unity, bonded by intense prayer, tears, and confession. We bid goodbye to the nine with deep emotion, grateful for the healings, but aware that the focus of it all, Amy Catherine, was still untouched.

Surely, Lord, You will not forget this little agent of so much healing.

After Peter and Edith left to spend the evening in their home ten miles away, Scott and Nedra Ross, Linda, Len, and I settled down in that same living room for what I felt would be a relaxed evening. We wanted to seek from Linda gleanings about her future plans, now that she had completed college. By now I realized that Scott and Nedra had been a very positive influence on our daughter and was grateful that they had come.

After we were seated in easy chairs, I asked Linda if she had any plans for the future.

She was silent a moment. "When I arrived here four days ago I had hoped to go to graduate school at Boston University."

"To what purpose?" I asked in some surprise.

"To study counseling at their School of Theology."

"Counseling!" Now I was incredulous. "That seems a bit peculiar, given—"

Len broke in. "Come on, Catherine, let's hear Linda out."

Linda guessed what I had not finished saying. "Mom, I know you think I'm too messed up to be able to help anyone else. Yet my friends—even people I know only casually—come to me with their problems. I'd like my life to count for something significant, and I feel the way to have the greatest impact is with one person at a time. I've gotten disillusioned with trying to change the world through politics or social work."

Though I felt relieved that Linda's political philosophy was changing, I had a sudden *déjà vu* feeling about her wanting to continue her rather aimless and costly education.

But Len was intrigued. "I'm fascinated that you want to be a counselor, Linda. I do think you have a gift for communication and I know you care about people. I'm just not sure you need to go to graduate school at this point. Maybe you should get a job first to find out more about your skills and aptitudes. Possibly do volunteer counseling on the side."

"Definitely," I concurred. "There are better uses for money than graduate school, especially since you haven't applied yourself during college. Forget graduate school, Linda. You need to find a job and earn some money."

Tears filled her eyes. "Why are you always so negative about any plan I come up with, Mom? You keep putting me down."

Len showed his agitation, too. "Catherine, we came here to have a relaxed conversation about Linda's future. You sound like a prosecutor badgering a witness."

Scott and Nedra Ross had been sitting there watching this exchange like spectators at a tennis match. Len turned to them apologetically. "Sorry to make you sit through this family matter."

Nedra shook her head. "Maybe there's a reason for our being here. As an objective listener, I have some insights on your relationships if you're interested."

"Go ahead."

"Each one of you is locked into a position you don't want to be in. Catherine by nature is forthright and pragmatic. Toward her stepdaughter now she is the interrogator, yes. But Catherine has a warm and compassionate side. So why doesn't she show it toward Linda?"

"I'd like the answer to that," said Len.

"Because when Linda finds herself in a shaky position, she has learned that if she gets tearful and plays the role of the 'put-upon' daughter, she wins the sympathy of her father. She almost sets up Catherine to criticize her."

"And Len," Nedra continued, "who is used to being a peacemaker, reacts against the unfairness of strong stepmother tearing into misunderstood stepdaughter. Yet because Len loves you, Catherine, these scenes make him miserable."

"Amen to that," responded Len.

"You, Catherine, don't like it when you find yourself reacting so negatively. And Linda hates playing the divisive role in your family. So all three of you are trapped and unhappy."

"What's the answer?" I asked.

Scott spoke up. "Let me come in at this point. Nedra and I have gotten to know and love Linda this week. She's been very honest with us and I think we have been helpful to her. A lot has happened in her life the last few days. Linda has made a new commitment to the Lord. She and her father had a real breakthrough in their relationship yesterday morning. Now she needs a healing in her relationship with you, Catherine."

"I would like to see that," I replied.

"I really want that, too, Mom," said Linda.

"Good," continued Scott. "The next step might be for Linda to be as open with you two as she was with us. What do you think, Linda?"

Linda nodded. We all sat back in our chairs while she took a deep breath. "Well, first of all. . . ."

She stopped, smiled apologetically, and moved forward in her seat. "What I want to say is this . . . ."

Long pause as Linda put her hand on her throat. A look of bewilderment crossed her face. More resolutely she gripped the side of the chair and started speaking—and stopped again without completing the sentence.

The four of us waited as several more times Linda tried in vain to express herself, each time putting her hand to her throat.

Len offered his daughter reassuring words. Scott and Nedra smiled encouragement. But though her voice sounded fine, Linda could only get out a few syllables.

Half an hour passed. I got up and walked about the room. "You can go to bed if you're tired, Mom." Linda looked relieved at the prospect.

I shook my head. "Linda, I don't know what it is you have

to say to us, but it must be important. So I intend to stay here all night if it's necessary."

"Linda, why do you keep massaging your throat?" Len asked. "Does it hurt?"

Linda shook her head. "No. I just have a funny kind of choking sensation there."

"It may not be funny," suggested Scott. "Let's come against dark powers and principalities right now." Together we prayed for Linda's freedom from any demonic interference.

Another hour went by. I couldn't believe what we were experiencing. "Linda, if you were to tell us at this point that you've had a baby out of wedlock and strangled her, I wouldn't be shocked," I said.

"Oh, Mom, please. It's nothing like that. Must you always expect the absolute worst of me?" She began to cry. But still something was holding her back.

We continued to wait. I placed some pillows on the floor and stretched out on the rug. "If it takes all night, so be it," I said.

Finally, Len had a suggestion. "Linda, maybe the problem is that you're trying to tell *us*. Why don't you kneel here in front of the couch and say whatever you have to say directly to Jesus. He will free you to talk to Him."

Linda . . . When the five of us gathered together that evening, I felt tied in knots inside. Was it distress over Amy Catherine, uncertainty over my future, the tension I habitually felt when with Mom, or something else entirely?

I was relieved that Scott and Nedra were present. Perhaps they could serve as a buffer between Mom and me, for I was always intimidated by her in these family sessions. I was glad that everyone else was gone, for I had some personal matters to address. I needed to "come clean" with my parents—confess where I had wronged them, ask forgiveness, and begin anew. Yet the early confrontation with Mom threw me off-stride.

How much I had anguished over our relationship. Why was it so unsatisfactory? I longed for that mythical, perfect mother's love, feeling abandoned by my first mother and not really accepted by my second. True, if my performance in school or elsewhere pleased my stepmother, she would be warm and loving to me. If not, I braced myself for criticism. And my behavior *had* left a lot to be desired in recent years, with the chasm between us widening.

Now why couldn't I get the words out? At first it seemed to be the ordinary reluctance one feels in admitting something unpleasant. As time passed, I was embarrassed, frustrated, frightened. How could I do this to my parents and the Rosses? What must they be thinking about me? This session going late into the night was only further exasperating Mom, who greatly prized her rest. Why did I always seem compelled to do the exact opposite of what I should around her, inviting her censure?

When she came out with her worst scenario statement, I was both angry and relieved. For certainly what I had to share wasn't *that* bad! And Nedra had said kindly, "Linda, even if that were true, it's not too big for God. There's nothing He can't or won't forgive."

When Dad suggested I get on my knees and talk to Jesus, the release came. Up until then, I'd been trying to confess to the other people in the room, afraid of what they'd think of me, fearful of further rejection. Now I was able to put those fears and my desire for approval aside. Haltingly at first, then in a torrent, I poured out my heart to the Lord. As I confessed my rebelliousness and irresponsibility, my tears no longer stemmed from my own pain—I began to grieve over how I had sinned against God Himself.

In the ensuing quiet, I began to sense the inner peace and freedom I had been longing for. Then I rose, turned to my parents, and asked their forgiveness. It wasn't an emotional scene. In fact, it was curiously matter-of-fact. There were embraces all around and goodnights exchanged with dispatch.

As I lay in bed that night I felt stripped and drained. There was no exhilaration but I didn't mind that. I knew the Christian walk wasn't based on feelings but obedience. Now I had done my part and I was in God's hands.

When I sat down to breakfast with Mom the next morning, I noticed that she had brought her Bible with her, which was unusual. I was curious as to how she would treat me, but I felt an odd new sense of detachment.

"Linda," she began, "I'm sure you recall the story of the Prodigal Son."

I nodded, for I had expected the comparison.

She opened her Bible and asked me to read that wonderful story from Luke 15:11–31. When I finished she looked at me and said: "I have a confession of my own to make, Linda. When you received God's all-restoring forgiveness last night, my reaction was: All those years of anxiety and turmoil you put your father and me through, and now you're forgiven by God *instantly*. Isn't that too easy?

"Well, this morning I received my answer. I was awakened to a clear, incisive, internal message: 'Remember My story of the Prodigal Son? Catherine, you're in grave danger of taking the place of the elder brother in that drama. *Let all negative thoughts about Linda go as of this moment.* As of now you are to take the lowest seat at My banquet table, below Len, below Linda. And you are to confess all this to her this morning.' "

There was an odd uncertainty in Mom's face as she continued. "So, as your brothers would say, I have been properly zapped. Linda, will you forgive me?"

Again I was at a loss for words, this time overwhelmed by the wonder of it all. The awareness that the Lord God

Himself loved, accepted, and forgave me began to bubble up inside. God cared enough about me to "zap" my famous and celebrated stepmother! He really did love me!

"Oh, Mom, I'm blown away. Of course I forgive you. But there's something else." I struggled to give words to my thoughts. "I think I went farther than you realize in blaming myself for the things that have gone wrong—Eve's alcoholism, my schoolwork, the problems you and Dad have had. Even though I believed in God all those years, I always felt He was in your corner—so I doubted He could really be in mine.

"What you've said to me this morning means more to me than you'll ever know. For in spite of all the misunderstandings and hurt, you've always been extremely important to me." My voice caught. Awkwardly we got up and embraced.

"Oh, Mom, I really love you."

"And I love you, Linda."

This time I cried from pure joy. If Mom, who always seemed so close to God, wasn't mad at me, God probably wasn't either! Perhaps He even had good things in store for me.

Black Friday _____

*C*atherine ... Our intense prayer time at Rock Harbor
Manor ended on August 12. Len and I stayed another two
days on the Cape, then drove to Boston to spend a day at
Children's Hospital before heading back to our summer
base at Evergreen Farm in Virginia. We'd been told that
Amy Catherine's condition had stabilized and I took this as
a sign that our prayers had begun to make a difference, that
the healing had begun.

When we arrived at the hospital, we discovered that Amy
Catherine had been moved to Division 20, which is Clinical
Research. A slim young Filipino nurse greeted us and took
us into a room where there were two large glittering steel
cribs.

I had a sinking feeling that this was the wrong place for Amy Catherine, that she belonged in a much smaller, cozier crib. This room seemed cold, stark. I picked up the tiny baby and held her in my arms. Then I sat down and began to love her.

Len and I both saw changes for the better in Amy Catherine. She was more active. She moved her hand to her face, a perfectly normal baby gesture. Then she began to cry. I concluded that Amy Catherine had gotten accustomed to being fed every time she was picked up. The fact that she kept turning toward my breast and opening her little mouth like a baby bird really got to me.

I looked her over carefully. The lovely pink face with the rosebud mouth reminded me of Mary Elizabeth. Both were such beautiful children. Only Amy Catherine's eyes weren't quite right.

The nurse came in and began feeding Amy Catherine from a bottle. It took a long time, about an hour, to get a few ounces of milk down her. Len and I walked about the hospital, stopping as always in the chapel. The stained glass window with a picture of a nurse and a child was somehow comforting.

As Len and I sat on the wooden bench meditating, my mind drifted back over the past week. So many lives touched. It was as though each person who came to pray for Amy Catherine received a blessing. Linda, most spectacularly. She was now on her way back to Maine to finish her summer stint at her grandmother's gift shop. *Lord, I pray You will guide her into a productive new life.*

I thanked God for the healing between myself and the Sherrills. For the way the Holy Spirit had moved in Peter's life, in Edith's, in Jamie's, in Len's, in Pam's, in Scott Ross', in Virginia's. And probably in all the others, too, in ways I didn't know at that time.

You were there, Lord! And You are here now healing Amy Catherine! Thank You, Lord!

Late that afternoon Len and I drove to New York City so that Len could catch up on his work at the office. I was most reluctant to leave Boston because in my heart I felt a continuous prayer ministry was needed at Amy Catherine's bedside. The medical personnel there felt her situation was hopeless, and though cooperative with our requests in every way, I feared that their unbelief in supernatural healing could impede the Spirit's ministrations.

What the doctors really wanted to do was perform certain tests on the baby, including a liver biopsy. I had urged Peter and Edith not to consent to this. I felt I had received specific guidance from the Lord that snipping out a piece of Amy Catherine's liver would traumatize her and undo the progress she had made. To my alarm, Peter and Edith had allowed the doctors to persuade them to agree to the biopsy. Then at the last moment the doctors themselves canceled the operation because they felt the baby was too weak.

This was the status of things at the hospital when Len and I left New York to continue on to Evergreen Farm where my mother was expecting us. Since Peter had a canoe trip with the youth of his church scheduled long beforehand for the end of August, Edith and Mary Elizabeth joined us at the farm for the week that Peter was gone. For the first time since the baby's birth a month earlier, Edith was able to relax for a few days.

I found myself struggling again with the passage in Daniel that Peter had been given a few days after Amy Catherine's birth:

> .... In the midst of the week he shall cause the sacrifice and the oblation to cease, and for the overspreading of abominations he shall make it desolate. ...

How did this relate to Amy Catherine? I looked it up in the Interpreter's Bible and got little help. It seemed to allude to some kind of decree by Antiochus of Syria that suspended sacrifice and offerings for a period of three-and-a-half years. In their place would be offered the abomination of heathen sacrifice.

A footnote, however, grabbed my attention: "The abomination ... is the idol set up in the temple—a common theme throughout the Bible. Idols have a terrible fascination for men [who] want to put something of their own creation in the place of God. This is a clue to the whole tragedy of humanity."

A thought began to germinate in my mind. What was the Lord trying to say to Peter through this verse? Was He saying that men (including Peter) are distracted by things like work and sports, which become idols and keep men from a closer relationship to Him?

Nothing particularly new about this. Men have always made idols of their cars, their sports ability, their work skills, their sexual prowess, and so on. Was the Lord trying to warn Peter of something here? The canoe trip, for example? In view of Amy Catherine's condition I questioned Peter about taking such a trip, when he would be out of communication with us for days. He considered canceling it at one point; then, when the baby's condition stabilized, he decided not to disappoint the young people in his church.

Friday, August 27, at Evergreen Farm began with a call by Edith to Children's Hospital. She talked to the doctor who told her, "Your baby has responded so well to blood transfusions that we're going ahead with the liver biopsy."

When Edith reported this to us at breakfast, my heart sank. I begged Edith to call the doctor back and ask him to cancel the surgery. Edith refused to do this. When the four of us—Mother, Edith, Len, and myself—gathered in the living room to pray about it, I found myself in a difficult situation. Both Mother and Edith had always placed doctors on a pedestal, were too quick, in my opinion, to accept their verdicts and opinions as gospel. Len was neutral, again inclined to play the role of peacemaker. He certainly did not share my strong conviction about the biopsy. I sensed, too, that he was resistant to what he felt was my "slugger" approach.

I confess that I handled this confrontation badly. Instead of simply reiterating what I believed I had received from the Lord, that the biopsy should be avoided at all costs, I bore into Edith.

"Since Peter is on a canoe trip, Edith, you're the only one who can stop this awful procedure."

"I'm sorry, Mom, but I don't feel I'm supposed to do that. Peter and I together gave them the okay. I have no new reason for asking them to stop it."

"You have a very good reason. It will do great harm to your baby."

"The doctors don't feel that way. They say it's only a minor procedure."

"Edith, cutting out a piece of a baby's liver is not minor. The doctors have given up on Amy Catherine. They're only interested in her for medical research. As the mother, how can you let your own flesh and blood go through this unnecessary operation?"

Tears of anguish formed in Edith's eyes and I calmed down a bit. "What time is the biopsy to be done?" I asked.

"Early this afternoon."

"Would you do this? Would you call the doctor and ask him to postpone the biopsy until Peter returns from his canoe trip and the two of you can review the situation?"

Edith turned to my mother and Len. "What do you think I should do?"

As I expected Mother sided with Edith. "If you and Peter

prayed it through, and then decided to allow the biopsy, it must be right."

Len put the cap on it. "Peter as the spiritual head of his household gave the go-ahead for this biopsy. I can understand why Edith is reluctant to change that decision."

I was furious with my husband.

We stopped talking at this point and prayed together. The substance of the prayers: "We turn this situation over to You, Lord. If You do not want the biopsy to take place, we know You will stop it as You did before."

Later that day northern Virginia was hit by violent thunderstorms, rain, and hail. The wind tore down several trees on the farm; we lost our electricity for a while.

Completely appropriate, I thought to myself. This is *Black Friday* in every way. That evening I went upstairs to our room, lay down on the bed, and sobbed and sobbed.

On Saturday, August 28, I awoke in an agony of spirit. During our early morning prayer time together Len was tender but firm with me. I had overstepped my position. I was the grandmother, not the mother of Amy Catherine, so owed Edith an apology for my overbearing attitude. And I needed to act quickly since Edith and Mary Catherine were taking the noon plane back to Boston.

It was difficult for me to apologize because my guidance about the biopsy was so clear. When I knocked on Edith's door, she answered sleepily and invited me inside. I sat on her bed and asked her to forgive me for the way I handled the situation. We both wept, then hugged each other.

The call came from Edith the following day, Sunday afternoon. "Amy Catherine is in critical condition. She has jaundice and seizures. Her body is on a machine." She began to sob.

"I'll check with Len," I told her. "If he's free we'll both fly up to Boston tomorrow morning. We'll take a cab from the airport and meet you at the hospital."

As I hung up the thought struck me: *I was right about the biopsy. But being right may be a bigger burden to carry than if I had been wrong.*

Len was able to switch some dates so we both took the morning flight. Edith met us in the lobby of the Children's Inn, an accommodation for families of patients. We registered, then walked over to the hospital together. Peter was driving up from the Cape and would join us later in the day.

When Edith and I walked into Amy Catherine's room, my heart broke. Her naked little form had been placed on a tilted heat bed in the middle of the room. Over it was a small canopy with a lamp from which the heat flowed. On a table nearby the heart monitor gave a steady beep beep beep. Wires seemed to be attached to every part of her body: one to record the heartbeat, one for her breathing, one as a catheter, a tube in her foot for intravenous feeding. Another tube ran down her nose into her stomach.

Edith was crying and my own chest was heaving with sobs. The whole scene was so grim: aside from the tilted bed, there was a bulletin board on the wall filled with notices, a washbasin for the nurses and doctors, a nurse's table, a few chairs, a linoleum floor, and all these machines. The room was coldly sterile in every way.

When Edith left to make some phone calls, I was alone with the baby for several minutes. I studied Amy Catherine. She was a pasty yellow color from the jaundice. I wanted so much to hold her. The nurse entered and proceeded to bathe the tiny infant within and around the life-support paraphernalia. At first she seemed disconcerted that I was there watching her. Then as she finished she said impulsively, "You know, I don't see any reason why you couldn't *hold* Amy Catherine."

"I would certainly like to do that," I replied, wondering

how I could pick Amy Catherine up with all these wires and tubes protruding from her.

The nurse gave me a white gown to put on and instructed me to sit down close to the tile-bed so that nothing had to be disconnected. My hands were trembling as I lifted her onto my lap.

The moment I touched Amy Catherine it was as if the stench of death left the room. Her eyelids fluttered; gurgling noises came out of her mouth; she moved her hands about as if she wanted to touch back.

Edith soon joined me and we took turns holding Amy Catherine, clucking and exclaiming over every nuance in her response to us. Our need at that point was to pour out love to this helpless and internally damaged child.

The realization soon hit us that the simple fact of being held and cuddled was making a difference to her physically. Even the doctors and the nurses began commenting on how well she was responding. Clutching at hope we decided to continue this kind of treatment night and day between Peter, Edith, Len, me, and others who came to visit and pray for her.

That night Len and I spent a long time praying in the hospital chapel before going to bed. In the morning I awoke with a Scripture passage in my mind about the paralytic man let down through the roof by his four friends: "Jesus seeing their faith healed him" (Mark 2:5).

It was as if I had received a thunderous answer from God the Father Himself: that disbelief in God's goodness is the worst sin of all. Not only is it God's will to heal, but for us to believe that He desires anything else saddens Him more than any sex sin. The way He wants us to deal with unbelief is exactly the way we deal with any other sin: bring it to the foot of the cross, confess it, ask forgiveness and cleansing, and receive back faith as a gift.

Over and over in the Gospels Jesus stresses the all-importance of faith. "Go, and it shall be done for you as you *have believed*" (Matthew 8:13). Or in the case of the woman with the issue of blood: "It's *your faith* that has made you well" (Mark 5:34). To the two blind men: "Do you really believe that I can do this for you?" And when they answered in the affirmative, then: "According to *your faith* be it unto you" (Matthew 9:28–29).

Most definitive of all was the statement He made to His disciples when they had been unable to heal the demoniac boy. "Why weren't we able to do this?" they asked Him. And He answered clearly and unequivocally, "*Because of your little faith*" (Matthew 17:19–20).

Above all other qualities, Jesus calls us to faith. Furthermore, He tells us that the *difficulty* of the situation has nothing at all to do with its solution. He says that there is never any doubt about whether He is *able* to handle any situation. The only question mark points to me and my faith in Him. Jesus tells us: "Everything is possible for one who has faith" (Mark 9:23).

Thus my question "Is it really God's will to heal today?" was answered. Here I had been trying since Sunday to relinquish Amy Catherine, while Jesus seemed to be saying, "Sorry, that would be far too easy. The minute you turn your back on the situation, and don't count any unbelief in you as the sin it is, you are also turning your back on the living God."

My faith was rejuvenated.

During the second day of our holding Amy Catherine, she showed decided improvement. Her heart was so much stronger that the doctor decided there was no need to monitor it every minute. The heart machine was just turned off. Silently Edith and I cheered.

The next two days we were in and out of Amy Catherine's room at all hours, having some rather strange yet cozy times with her and with the night nurses who weren't used to all this company. During this time Edith really got to know her baby as she cuddled and mothered her. The atmosphere in the room became noticeably cheerier, and from a tiny, wired-up patient, Amy Catherine turned into an individual. It was during these days that the baby got to me totally.

Walking on Water _____

*C*atherine ... Linda returned from Maine on August 30 and settled in the Marshall home in East Dennis to help care for Mary Elizabeth and free Peter and Edith to spend more time at the hospital. By now there was a steady procession of visitors, mostly from Peter's church, to help with our prayer vigil. When Len had to return to Florida to help our two sons get off to school, I stayed alone at the Children's Inn, going back and forth from my room to the hospital.

Two couples from the Boston area heard that Peter Marshall's granddaughter was critically ill at Children's Hospital and came to visit one night when I was there alone. People from Rock Harbor Manor agreed to come during the night so that Edith and I could sleep while prayer continued 'round the clock.

The hospital personnel were cooperative and friendly, if a bit incredulous at our tenacity. An English physician, in this country on some kind of exchange arrangement, was in charge of the case. As he bent over the crib to peer closely at Amy Catherine, with his full beard almost tickling her stomach, he seemed like something out of a Dickens novel.

Once after examining the baby, he turned to me and asked in a pleasant voice, "Will you be going on holiday on the Cape this weekend?"

I shook my head. "Until Amy Catherine gets better, I'll be here."

He seemed puzzled. "There's really nothing you can do for her."

My response: "As long as there is breath in Amy Catherine's body, I'll be here to pray for her."

To the doctor and the nurses coming in and out of the room I must have seemed like a complete fanatic. I'm sure I was, during the whole six weeks that had now elapsed since Amy Catherine's birth. It was an all-out faith walk on my part, the most exhilarating experience of my life. If you talk about adventure, there is no adventure like totally trusting God. It was like spending six weeks walking on the water, or parachuting out of a plane, or climbing Mt. Everest.

The closest comparable experience was just after Peter Marshall's death when I was living in the Kingdom of God on earth and knew with great sureness what I was to do each moment. This was different in that we were walking in blind faith. We really were. I mean there was no sight in it—literally no way to see what lay before us. Perhaps it wasn't a faith walk at all, and we were running far ahead of the Lord. But at the time we felt we were being obedient. The highs were thrilling, the lows devastating.

One such low came Friday night, September 3. Amy

Catherine had had a restless day. One of the nurses had seemed so callous and brusque that I asked another nurse what was wrong. "She's going through a divorce," she replied.

The baby's body seemed more jaundiced than usual. Again I agonized over the damage the liver biopsy had done to her. What had it accomplished, really? From my room at Children's Inn I called Sandra Ghost, one of my Florida prayer partners and a woman who was going through a faith walk with her own child. She had a specific word for me: *I was to raise my eyes from the immediate situation in the hospital room and see the heavenly hosts struggling to help us.*

She called my attention to a passage in the Old Testament where help was slow in reaching the prophet Daniel. Eventually an archangel appeared to Daniel and told him that he'd been delayed "in the heavenlies" 21 days, fighting evil forces in the spiritual universe in order to battle his way through to earth (Daniel 10:12).

The next morning, Saturday, September 4, I was up early and reread this chapter of Daniel. Whenever we ask for a miracle, apparently, we can expect to engage in this kind of spiritual warfare. *Lord, help me to continue to be strong in battle,* I prayed. Once more I marveled over how I was able to overcome my usual limitations of shortness of breath, lack of energy, early fatigue—all surmounted in my total concentration on the baby.

How have I managed this, Lord? I'd spent long hours of prayer, watching and ministering there in the hospital, day after day after day, and well into the night. I just didn't have this kind of vitality. *Are You giving it to me, Lord?* I know that Len and others think I'm doing this not only because Amy Catherine is my grandchild, my flesh and blood, but because she bears my name. There may be something to this, Lord. I've always been a battler for what I felt was right. You gave me this competitive quality and I've had to use it in life over and over again. Now I see this same quality in Amy Catherine. I see it in her now as she fights for life against all the odds. All my own determination and drive reach out to this child to establish contact with the fighting spirit in her. I'm saying to her, "You'll make it and I'll fight with you. Two Catherines slugging it out together."

Edith joined me at the hospital Saturday morning. Again we took turns holding Amy Catherine, cooing to her, loving her. She was not responding as well as she had earlier in the week. Her color was bad and the heart monitor had been reattached.

Because Amy Catherine had not taken the bottle very well after the biopsy operation, the doctor had been feeding glucose to her through the tube in her nose. A few ounces of glucose were given to her this way every couple of hours, after which they had to pump the bile out of her stomach through another tube.

The mid-morning feeding went routinely. But when they began pumping the bile out of her stomach, Amy Catherine protested with cries and whimpers. I was sitting by her crib at the time, my stomach protesting, too.

After the second feeding several hours later, Amy Catherine was put into my arms while the nurse began pumping out the bile. This time Amy Catherine began crying loudly. She didn't like it at all and was telling us so.

The nurse kept on pumping and would not stop even when I urged her to. Suddenly her eyes darted to the heartbeat machine. The rhythm had slowed. "I think we'd better put her back in the crib," she said, then went running for the doctor.

The doctor and Edith, who had gone for snacks, arrived at the same moment. When she looked at the baby, Edith exclaimed, "Something's wrong! Why is her skin so mottled?"

The doctor bent over Amy Catherine for several minutes then looked up and said gently, "The baby has expired. I'm sorry." I will never forget that he used the word *expired*.

Edith began to cry. Somehow I could not. The time was 2:18 P.M. How strange that I remember this fact!

I went over to the crib, placed my hand on the baby's head, and quite blatantly asked God to restore her to life. Somehow I was not willing to believe that it was going to end like this. I kept my hands on her for quite some time. Her little head was turned slightly to one side away from me. She still had no clothes on. Her mouth was so much like Mary Elizabeth's—the one thing that I had noticed over and over during these weeks. Perhaps from the heat above, her body was still perfectly warm. But, oh, so quiet.

I checked out of the Children's Inn, eager now to get away from the scene of so much pain. Edith and I were silent during the drive to the Cape.

That night I stayed with Mary Elizabeth while Peter, Edith, and Linda went over to the church to the Upper Room Fellowship. It was a very hot night and Mary Elizabeth was restless, so I went up to her room and sat down in a chair by her crib. Somehow I was able to relate to this child whereas I had been silent during the grown-up conversation at dinner.

We sang some songs and talked. Mary Elizabeth kept pushing her stuffed animals and her dolls through the bars of the crib until my whole lap was covered with them. And so a two-and-a-half-year-old ministered to me in a way no adult could have.

Searching for Reasons _____

*C*atherine ... Peter's church had an overflow congregation the following day, Sunday, September 5. In fact, Peter had had overflow congregations all summer long, for the drama of a tiny infant's fight for life had gotten to many people on the Cape.

I was in such a state of depression that I have little recollection of that service. It was an especially difficult assignment for Peter, the bereaved father, to try to explain to his church why God would take this precious child when Peter didn't understand it himself. It was especially awkward for him since he had gone all-out for a supernatural healing.

Peter did the best he could. In essence, he took the blame upon himself, which may have been right for him to do as head of his home, but which left many with theological questions.

I certainly had questions. What had made me so certain that God was going to heal Amy Catherine? Like Peter, I had gone out on a limb in this regard. Had God told me He was going to heal the baby? I certainly thought He had. There were several occasions when I had felt His assurance about this. Obviously I had been wrong and, yes, I was angry about it. And I was still deeply upset with Peter and Edith about the biopsy.

The thought settled on me that but for the biopsy Amy Catherine would have made it. God's plan for Amy Catherine was thwarted by the disobedience of His children. How often that had happened in the history of mankind!

The rehashing of our words and actions began on Monday night at 6 P.M. in Peter and Edith's living room. Len was still in Florida but was flying to Washington the next day to meet us there for the burial service at Fort Lincoln Cemetery, where Peter Marshall and Peter Christopher had also been laid to rest. Linda was at the Marshalls' along with another couple. The six of us planned to go out for dinner.

Something was said to the effect that we had "missed it" with Amy Catherine and we were off. It would be almost 10 P.M., four hours later, before we would think about food. At the beginning a lot of anger, resentment, and pain came out. I admitted my sense of defeat. "I have never given myself so completely to anything in life as I did to Amy Catherine. When Peter Marshall died, painful as it was, I felt God's presence in the hospital room. Not with Amy Catherine's death. It was as if God had left us, too, along with the baby."

Then Linda spoke up. "I've been doing a lot of praying the last few nights. Would you all be interested in what I feel God has been saying to me?"

A bit self-consciously she read from a yellow pad some of

her journal entries, concluding with this passage from Scripture:

"My thoughts are not your thoughts, neither are your ways My ways," declares the Lord. "For as the heavens are higher than the earth, so are My ways higher than your ways, and My thoughts than your thoughts."

Isaiah 55-8–9, NIV

"Maybe," Linda concluded, "we're not supposed to understand all that God was doing through Amy Catherine. He certainly touched a lot of lives."

"That's true," Peter responded. "Yet I sensed that the sixteen of us were not in unity in our prayers for her."

"What you're saying, Peter," I said, "is that we failed, not God. How do you feel that you failed?"

Peter shifted about uncomfortably on the floor where he was sitting. "I should never have gone on that canoe trip. It was all wrong." Suddenly he began sobbing. "I simply did not care enough to give everything to the baby."

For a moment I was back in our home in 1949 at the moment I received the telephone call telling me of Peter Marshall's death in George Washington University Hospital. When Peter, age nine, had cried then, I had taken him in my arms. Now I moved over beside him and put my arms about him.

Edith's turn was next. Haltingly and painfully she confessed that throughout the six weeks of Amy's life she had harbored a hidden fear that God would not heal the baby in spite of our fervent prayers. She suspected that her faithlessness was rooted in past experience. After all, her own mother had died when she was a little girl; then Peter Christopher. With sobs, she broke down. "I just don't know what He wants of us! What kind of God is He, anyway?"

It was a powerful time of honesty and ministry one to

another. The evening ended on a single note: *It was not God who had failed, but we who had failed.*

The funeral at Peter's church the next morning stressed this same theme. I spoke briefly at the service. "When you go all-out to claim one of the promises in Scripture," I said, "and the baby dies, this can be devastating to your faith. Yesterday I was prepared to resign as a roving editor for *Guideposts* and tell McGraw-Hill that I would be doing no further books on religious subjects. But as we prayed and shared together last night in the Marshall home, it became so clear to us. God hadn't failed us. He had a plan for the healing of Amy Catherine. Through our disobedience we thwarted His plan."

After the funeral, Peter, Edith, and I drove to Hyannis Airport and boarded a small private plane for the flight to Washington, D.C. In the baggage section of the plane, beside our luggage, was Amy Catherine's tiny coffin.

The burial service at Fort Lincoln Cemetery was a simple one. Len joined us there, along with my brother, Bob, my sister, Emma Lynn, and their families, plus a few close friends. Peter's message was much the same as he'd given in East Dennis earlier that day, identifying our lack of faith and unity as the hindrance to God's perfect plan. I wept only when I saw Amy Catherine Marshall's little coffin about to take its place beside the equally tiny coffin of Peter Christopher Marshall.

Afterward Bob and Len were talking about Peter's burial message and I overheard Bob say, "We certainly have a bigger God than *that*, don't we?" That statement troubled me.

The next day Len and I flew back to our home in Florida. In the evening I placed a call to my friend Sandra Ghost whose gifts of wisdom and discernment had been so helpful to me during this crisis. I told her about the repentance time Monday night and our conclusion that we, not God, had failed.

Sandra was silent for a long moment after my report. Then she said, "Catherine, that seems to imply a huge emphasis on works, as though the healing depended upon man. God's grace is much greater than all that, isn't it?"

By the time I hung up the phone, the heaviness had returned to my spirit. I turned to Len and remarked, "I sure wish I hadn't called Sandra tonight."

Somehow I wasn't ready to consider the question both Bob and Sandra had raised.

Virginia Lively . . . One of the hardest things I've ever done in my life was to go to Catherine and share the prophetic word I'd had about Amy Catherine: "This child will not live. But any other child they have they may have in perfect confidence." Several days after Catherine's return to Florida I made a date to see her at her Boynton Beach home.

When I arrived I could tell that Catherine was despondent. "I've had trouble sleeping," she confided. "My mind keeps going back to Children's Hospital. There on the heat bed is that helpless, dear little baby with all those tubes sticking out of her. I just start weeping." Her eyes filled as she spoke.

We reminisced for a while as I tried to summon the courage to confess what I had withheld from her and the others at Cape Cod. Finally, it came out: the prophecy about Amy Catherine.

Catherine blinked as though I'd struck her in the face. Moments of silence.

"Why . . . why . . . why, Virginia, did you keep silent? It would have made all the difference."

"But would it have really?" I replied. "I don't think you would have accepted it. And there would have been a negative pall over the whole week, interfering perhaps with all the good things that did happen. When the baby died I would always have wondered if my nay-saying had affected the outcome. Can you see my position, Catherine?"

Catherine nodded, but I knew her well enough to tell she was deeply angry. There was darkness in her spirit. Intense misery. It frightened me. I loved her so.

We talked about other things, awkwardly. Catherine could not, would not bring up again the subject of Amy Catherine. Driving back to my home in Belle Glade, I reviewed the situation for the thousandth time.

Would my talking to her earlier have prepared her for Amy Catherine's death, and alleviated her depression to some degree? Would it have brought on the depression sooner? Would it have antagonized her, since it flew in the face of what she believed she had heard? Should I have spoken up anyway and let the chips fall where they might, letting the Lord handle the problem? Or was it right, what I did do—hide it in my heart, using it as personal information only, until receiving a further word from God?

So disturbed was I that I shared my concern with Freddie Koch, a close friend of Catherine's and mine. Freddie was troubled about a vivid dream she had just had, resulting, she felt, from her prayers for Catherine. We decided we should share the dream with both Catherine and Len.

The four of us gathered together in Boynton Beach and Freddie described her dream. It seemed that Freddie was trying to get to Amy Catherine in the hospital and was having a very hard time doing this because nurses and doctors kept stopping her. But Freddie felt that she simply had to get to the baby's side and pray for her. Finally Freddie did reach Amy Catherine, but, instead of praying for her, she found herself coping with the remnant of a very dirty diaper.

The rest of the dream involved the details of cleaning up the messy diaper, disposing of it, and so forth. Freddie never did get back to Amy Catherine to minister to her. And there the dream ended.

The vividness of the imagery startled us. My interpretation of it was: "The Lord is trying to tell us that we are spending a great amount of time trying to deal with something that the baby has finished with, gotten rid of. What I see is that Amy Catherine is with Jesus. What we are doing here, in our human way, is dealing with all the after-effects of the experience, the residue of the whole affair. We are spending a lot of energy on this residue, trying to decide about where to put everything, trying to find neat solutions to it all, and this is not what the Lord asks of us at all. *He is saying that the baby is with Him and that we are to forget all the why-this and why-that and get on with worshiping the Lord and praising Him for the way that Amy Catherine ministered to so many people while on earth.*"

Catherine, I could tell, was not satisfied with that interpretation of this dream. On the contrary, she felt that the dirty diaper represented the mess, the impurities, the sin in our lives, and that the mess was so big that we never did get around to praying effectively for Amy Catherine. The reason the baby died was that there wasn't enough prayer power, that we weren't clean enough channels through whom God could work.

Catherine seemed determined to see man's failure as the culprit; nothing Freddie and I could say could convince her otherwise. My heart ached for Catherine. She was having trouble praying. There was deep hurt in her voice. I think she felt that God had betrayed her, that in a smaller way I, too, had betrayed her. *O Lord,* I pleaded, *be tender with her.*

Peter . . . After Amy's burial in Fort Lincoln Cemetery, Edith and I stayed on in Virginia for a much-needed recuperation period at Evergreen Farm. But although there was physical rest, there was no rest for our souls, for we were spiritually depressed and defeated. Amy was dead; we had blown it. I was burdened by the thought that it was somehow all our fault.

It was only when Edith and I got back to Cape Cod, and I resumed my life and ministry at the East Dennis Church, that the bigger picture of Amy's life and death began to come into focus. I saw that I had fallen into the trap of believing that if we could just muster enough faith, God would have healed Amy.

I knew better than this. As a pastor I had walked through deaths with people whose healings had been prayed for with utmost faith; I knew perfectly well that human failure was not to blame.

The New Testament is full of Jesus' healings, but He didn't heal everybody, every time. At the pool of Bethesda where Jesus healed a cripple, the healed man walked out of the place past all the prone bodies of the other invalids.

Eventually, these truths emerged from the birth, brief life, and death of our little girl. Our God is the sovereign Lord of life and death; our times and seasons are truly in His hands. Healing is truly a divine mystery, and God has His inscrutable purposes for each person's life. The healing power of Jesus is not a supernatural power source that can be tapped into by a special group of Christians who learn the secret formulas of faith. The Lord of the universe will be controlled by no man's faith. God is never under man's influence; He is always free. Healing remains in the hands of the One who triumphed over man's sin and sicknesses on the cross . . . yet it is often His good pleasure to express His healing love through the prayers and ministry of His servants. But not every time and not solely in response to our initiative. Sometimes our God has plans and designs for people's lives that we cannot possibly fathom.

Had I lost my faith in divine healing? Only temporarily, until I realized that Amy's death had not resulted from a lack of faith. In the weeks following Amy's death I found that I believed in spiritual healing as much as ever, for I had learned that our faith is not to be in healing, but in the God who heals!

I believe that Mother knew all this, too. She was simply blinded for a while by her intense involvement with our baby. I can understand that; most of the sixteen of us who met on the Cape lost our perspective, too, during those incredible days. Though Amy Catherine's death was the immediate trigger, I believe it was the combination of things going wrong in her life that brought on Mother's time of darkness.

Section III ————————
The Dark Night
of the Soul ————————

"Are you in the dark just now in your circumstances,
or in your life with God? Then remain quiet. If you
open your mouth in the dark, you will talk in the
wrong mood: darkness is the time to listen."

Oswald Chambers

Editor's Note ... I suspect that if Catherine had been assured by the Lord that it was lack of unity of the sixteen and disobedience by Peter and Edith that prevented Him from healing Amy Catherine, she would have accepted that. That would have been human failure, and Catherine was never surprised at human failure. Her sorrow would probably have lifted fairly quickly. When she learned of Virginia Lively's foreknowledge about the baby's death, however, directly opposite to the word she felt she had received from God, Catherine was devastated. She had gone all-out in faith and felt that God had let her down. In addition she felt humiliated in front of family and friends: Virginia had heard God correctly, she herself had not.

At this point Catherine entered a period of darkness. Her regular journal entries for the next six months virtually ceased. The following section is pieced together from notations she made to herself, her letters to family and friends, some dreams she recorded, and my own memories of conversations and confrontations we had. She stayed angry at God for many weeks; then when she sought to renew the relationship there was nothing. Only silence—and darkness.

The Clouds Descend _____

*C*atherine ... I believe that Satan won the victory last summer in the Amy Catherine situation. His handwork is all through it.

As I told the family the night before the funeral, there was a vast difference between the day of Amy Catherine's death and that of Peter Marshall back in 1949. I felt Jesus' presence in the room where Peter died. For a week after his death I walked in the glory of the Kingdom of God on earth.

At the time of Amy Catherine's death I could not feel Jesus' presence in her hospital room. On the contrary, I sensed evil there. We did not walk in any glory in the days following. Far from it! There was dissension, blame flung about, nitpicking over various decisions, a sense of failure.

Despite the good things that happened to some of the people who gathered to pray on Cape Cod, I have seen no good come from Amy Catherine's death itself. Only misunderstanding and confusion. I have not understood why the results were so negative. I have not understood what was behind all this.

Could Amy Catherine's genetically damaged body somehow have been demon-possessed? If so, was it wrong to anoint her with oil and claim a healing? Would a completely different kind of deliverance prayer have worked the miracle?

But *how* could we have gone ahead with an exorcism over an innocent newborn child without a specific revelation from God?

I dreamed last night that I was in my own home, though it was a larger house than our actual one, with several floors. Climbing to the top floor I found to my surprise six people living there. They were not overtly antagonistic toward me, but were obviously intruders; they had moved in secretly and were doing their housekeeping with inadequate equipment, a scruffy broom, etc.

Today in trying to interpret this dream, I sought the identity of my "squatters" so that they could be ousted. The first appeared to be "depression," the second "unshed tears," the third "grief." That's all I've gotten so far.

The fourth one of the "squatters" in my dream of several days ago has to be "sleeplessness." On the way to the airport to fly to New York yesterday, I realized that I had left my sleeping pills behind. So last night in the New York hotel I did my usual lying there, hour after hour, waiting for dawn. Just a bit of dozing the last few hours. Then I awoke with a raging headache. And still no feeling of Jesus' presence at all.

Yesterday I was struck by a phrase I read somewhere long ago: *We learn humility through humiliations.*

Having gone through a humiliation last summer, I should have much more humility today. Yet I don't feel that I've grown spiritually in this area. I don't feel that I've grown spiritually in any area these past months.

Humiliation. The dictionary calls it "a painful loss of pride, dignity, and self-respect." I feel I represent every bit of that description and I don't like it at all.

My humiliation, of course, is a paltry nothing compared to the humiliation suffered by Jesus on the cross. Yet somehow Jesus and His suffering seem remote, unconnected with me and my present misery—that's all I seem to think about these days. I'm aware of a fatal self-centeredness here, but seem incapable of breaking free.

I woke up this morning with a Scripture passage running through my head: *No one is able to come to me unless he [or she] is drawn by the Father* (John 6:44, MOFFATT).

"Does that mean," I asked myself, "that I can't have a relationship with Jesus unless God instigates it?"

My mind whirled back through the years. Had God drawn me to Jesus as a child? Obviously so. The Father in heaven had drawn me to the Son. But now I feel no relationship with either Jesus or the Father. It seemed to end the day Amy Catherine died. So the Father must be blocking me from this relationship. Why?

I don't want to pursue it further. It's too painful. The hurt over my grandchild's death has to heal. I'm incapable of seeking understanding by going back over the events yet again.

So where does this leave me? Wallowing in my sin? Clearly this is so, but I feel helpless to do anything about it. I'm reminded bitterly of an article I wrote for Guideposts titled "The Power of Helplessness." I sure don't feel any power in my present state of helplessness. Nor do I sense God coming to my aid. All above me, it seems, is a heaven of brass.

My dreams recently have certainly reflected my state:

In one I was the preacher's wife in a church where an elaborate wedding required "tickets" of those invited. I seemed to have arrived late and not really dressed correctly. There was some discussion as to whether I was to be let in without a ticket. Whatever was decided, I never saw the inside of the church in the dream. Instead, because something was missing, a whole group of us had to go and get it—whatever it was. As we went on this errand I kept losing things. First my fur stole, then my gloves. The group grew angry at me; there were even physical threats. I woke with the sense of being odd-man-out, rejected by those who counted.

In another dream I was in an apartment where the plumbing was badly out of order and about to flood the place. I knew where the leak was, but instead of attending to it I left the apartment to go to a meeting where President Nixon was speaking. I was seated in the front row. Since I had left the apartment while sorting the laundry, I still had in my hands a pair of my dad's old dirty work pants and two dirty socks.

During the meeting, I dropped the soiled laundry to the floor and to my chagrin, the President came to where I was sitting, picked up the dirty work pants, looked at them wonderingly, and handed them back to me. Though humiliated, even in my dream came the thought, *But they are soiled not in any shameful way, but through honest work!*

When I got back to the apartment, water covered the floor and the plumber had to be called immediately. Here the dream ended. Clearly, the overflowing water represented some situation that my subconscious knew to be wrong, which I was neglecting to put right.

And still another dream: I was due to make an important speech, but had no time to go back to the hotel and change my clothes. I was told, "No, you'll just have to wear what you have."

This was dreadful because I had on an old skirt and ankle socks. Behind the stage at the auditorium I started to make up my face while several people watched me impatiently. By now I was acutely aware of an auditorium full of people waiting, too.

The makeup was a process of bungling and stumbling. I could not find a lipstick in the various cluttered purses I had with me. Finally I found it and with shaking hands tried to apply the lipstick, while trying to collect my thoughts about what to say in my speech. Thinking about the talk, I absentmindedly applied lipstick around my eyes. Those watching were startled. I tried to wipe off the lipstick, then apply powder on the area. *I'll go in there looking like an old hag,* I thought. There to my great relief the dream ended.

All these dreams have features in common: clutter, disorganization, unpreparedness, unacceptance of me by those around me, unhappiness with myself, a feeling of being threatened by circumstances and the critical attitudes of others.

And in them all—a state of humiliation.

Len ... I found Catherine sitting in her chair by the bed, listlessly looking through some catalogs. It was 11:30 A.M., a time when ordinarily she would be in her office hard at work on a manuscript. *How do I penetrate the darkness of her spirit?* I asked myself.

"We need to talk," I began.

"What about?"

"You cannot go on like this. We're all deeply concerned about you."

Catherine shrugged. Her eyes went back to her catalogs. My concern for her shifted to irritation. "How can you go against the advice you've so often given to others about wallowing in self-centeredness?"

For a moment her eyes flashed. I welcomed this, preferring anger to apathy. The sparks quickly subsided, however, and she shrugged again. "Just say that I'm wallowing in my sin."

"You are doing exactly that, and what's more, you're enjoying it."

Catherine shifted about uncomfortably. "What do you want me to do?"

"Put the Amy Catherine matter to rest and get on with your life."

The pain inside suddenly shone through. "I can't put it aside."

"Why?"

"I keep seeing her little mouth crying out for help. I can still feel her body in my arms, wanting so much to be held and loved, yearning for health. Every time I try to do any writing these images return to haunt me."

"Why don't we take off for a week? Go down to the Keys, perhaps, or to one of the islands," I suggested.

Catherine brightened for a moment, then shook her head. "I don't think I'd be good company. It's my problem and I'll work through it." She thought for a moment. "What was the title of that Guideposts piece by Joe Bishop? 'The Way Out Is the Way Through'? Maybe I should read it again."

"The point of the article is that you don't duck a painful issue, you meet it head-on. Are you doing that?" I asked.

"I'm trying to." She paused for a long moment. "In some ways you know me better than anyone else in the world. In one area you don't know me at all."

"What's that?"

"There's a part of me, deep down, that since my childhood has belonged only to the Person of Jesus Christ. He and I have had some wonderful sharing times together. He has been with me in every crisis—until now." Her lip began to tremble. "Now He just isn't there anymore. Each morning when I awake, I seek Him, to no avail. I must have offended Him terribly this past summer."

I put my arms around her, feeling her pain, fighting back my own tears. "You've been through these dark times before, haven't you? What about those occasions during your widowhood when you felt estranged from God?"

"They were more like dry periods when I was simply unproductive. And they never lasted very long. Sure, I'd be sunk in self-pity for a stretch, but Jesus was somehow close to me even then. For months now there has been real darkness. I feel like I'm talking to the ceiling. And you know how listless my prayers have been."

I nodded. Listless was the right word. "When did you first feel this rejection—if that's what it is?"

For a while Catherine didn't answer. In fact, I had to repeat the question. Her thoughts seemed many miles away.

"I'm not sure," she said at last. "Probably right after Amy Catherine's death. Possibly after hearing about Virginia Lively's prophecy. She heard correctly. I didn't."

"And that hurt your pride."

"She should have told me."

"If she had come up to you in Cape Cod and reported this revelation to you, you would have rejected it flat. I've never seen you so convinced, so determined about anything as you were about Amy Catherine's healing."

"I'll never go out on a limb like that again—for anything or anyone—ever," she snapped.

I took a deep breath. "I think it's your anger at God that has shut the door on your relationship with Him."

She shook her head vigorously. "I've been angry at Him before and He still comforted me. I believe God encourages us to be honest, to express anger when we feel it. So I don't think you're right, Len. Sure I was angry when Amy Catherine died, rebellious, too . . . ." She stopped, hearing her own words.

"There's a big difference between anger and rebellion." I voiced her unspoken thought. "Feelings of anger are often justified, and usually subside fairly quickly. Rebellion is more long-lasting and destructive. Remember that Bible class we taught last year? How you kept stressing that it was the rebellion of the Israelites that kept them from the Promised Land?"

She nodded. "One's words can come back to haunt one, can't they?"

"Think about it, Catherine," I urged. "You're miserable without Jesus. Maybe you should go off somewhere alone and pray it through."

Catherine . . . Inside I am dry and lonely, unable to accomplish anything, really, just going through the motions of life, barely able to do that. It is more than a dry period. I've been through those before and did not lose the Presence. This is darkness. Deadness. Awful in the way it numbs you, makes you cold and indifferent. You do the very thing, say the very word, you know you should not. Frightening!

This morning in an effort to find a handhold to pull myself out of this pit, I reread C.S. Lewis' *Screwtape Letters.* In advising the junior demon, Wormwood, how to turn Christians away from God, Screwtape warns that at times their Enemy (God) will withdraw all support from His own subjects. He continues:

> He cannot "tempt" to virtue as we do to vice. The Enemy wants them to learn to walk and must therefore take away His hand. . . . Do not be deceived, Wormwood. Our cause is never more in danger than when a human, no longer desiring, but still intending, to do our Enemy's will, looks round upon a universe from which every trace of Him seems to have vanished, and asks why he has been forsaken, and still obeys.

I find myself convicted by these words. For I know that God not only asks us to bear these dry and barren stretches of life, but even to thank Him for them. This is what Glenn

Clark called "radiant acquiescence," a phrase I always thought was a bit much—and still do, I guess.

I must get down on paper some of the passages I've encountered this week in my reading of Scripture. Though my prayers are hollow and uninspired, I am receiving instruction from His Word. If the Lord will no longer speak to me directly, then I will go this route.

Here are the passages I have been led to:

And when you spread forth your hands in prayer, imploring help, I will hide My eyes from you; even though you make many prayers, I will not hear; your hands are full of blood! Wash yourselves; make yourselves clean; put away the evil of your doings from before My eyes; cease to do evil.
Isaiah 1:15–16, AMPLIFIED

The Lord is far from the wicked, but He hears the prayer of the [consistently] righteous—the upright, in right standing with Him
Proverbs 15:29, AMPLIFIED

You do ask and yet fail to receive, because you ask with wrong purpose and evil, selfish motives. . . . You [are like] unfaithful wives [having illicit love affairs with the world] and breaking your marriage vow to God!
James 4: 3–4, AMPLIFIED

These verses are like arrows piercing my heart. Lord, have mercy.

During my afternoon nap I had yet another version of a dream that has recurred over and over again. I am always in a very large house. I go through corridors and rooms, from one floor to another. There are many people around, but they pay no attention to me, and I have nothing to do with them, do not appear to know them. I am searching, searching for my own room, my own place, but *cannot find it*. I cannot even find which floor it's on. Fear is in the dream, building to panic. Sometimes, in exhaustion, I even stop in someone else's room to take a nap in order to get strength to rise and start searching again.

Usually I awaken from this recurring dream with my stomach hurting and symptoms of severe tension, probably with raised blood pressure.

"In My Father's house are many mansions. . . ." This passage used to comfort me because it promises a place for everyone. I do have a place in the universe. Why am I now so lost?

This terrible feeling of lostness—apparently deep in my subconscious—must reflect my separation from God. When one has lost one's way and can no longer feel the Shepherd's hand, when the Valley of the Shadow is dark with the light of faith withdrawn, what does one do then?

Trust God in the dark and wait and hope and hang on as best one can, I suppose.

Len . . . Christmas in our home had always been a lively family time. I had hoped that Christmas 1971 would lift Catherine out of her darkness. It did not.

I'd expected her to be impressed with the changes in Linda when she came home for the holidays. Linda seemed more disciplined, was handling her finances well, and hadn't asked us for a penny. Gone was the confusion of the '60s as she launched into her new job in full-time Christian work with college students. But though Catherine complimented Linda on these things, the compliments seemed dutiful rather than heartfelt.

Chester was enjoying his second year at Taylor University in Upland, Indiana, a rising star on the Taylor tennis team. Ordinarily Catherine would have drawn him out about the semester's experiences; this Christmas—beyond a few perfunctory inquiries—she showed little curiosity.

Jeffrey, attending a local prep school, had found work for the holidays in a nearby restaurant. As he regaled us with tales of difficult customers and crises in the kitchen, Catherine seemed miles away, her mind wandering down a dark road where none of us could follow.

Peter, Edith, and Mary Elizabeth had not been able to come to Florida this Christmas because of Peter's heavy responsibilities to his congregation at the holiday season. Amy Catherine's brief life and death had left unresolved questions with which both families were still struggling.

Catherine . . . I have received some illumination about this shut-in place in which I have been so confined. It came from a section in *Mysticism*, by Evelyn Underhill, entitled "Dark Night of the Soul."

She explains that for those who have trod the Christian way for some time, a spiritual and psychic fatigue can creep in. In this state one knows anew the helplessness of the human condition. In fact, here, for a time, we can be in a worse state than at the beginning of our Christian walk. The reason: when one first becomes a Christian, along with new awareness of one's own frailty, there is the sure and wonderful knowledge of God's *adequacy*. In the darkness that assails the long-time Christian, the skies seem totally deaf; no light breaks through at all. Nothing, inside and outside, seems to work.

This is certainly my state at this time.

According to Evelyn Underhill, if one can ride it through on sheer, blind faith, just hanging onto the rock of salvation, then it has to pass, and we go on to a higher state in the spiritual life.

What was a fresh thought to me was that this dark state is *necessary* in our Christian growth. It comes when we've reached a kind of plateau of faith where nothing is changing, where certain areas of our life remain *not* committed to Jesus Christ, *not* being taken over by Him. So we have to find fresh truths in our helplessness and in our need, become desperate in a new way, in order to get on with the next stage in our Christian development.

Even many great Christian saints went through a "dark night" experience, some pretty gruesome, according to Underhill, before they came out into the light again. This is encouraging for us ordinary strugglers!

More on "The Dark Night" from Evelyn Underhill: "The most intense period of that great swing-back into darkness . . . is seldom lit by visions or made homely by voices. . . . Stagnation . . . impotence, blankness, solitude, are the epithets by which those immersed in this *dark fire of purification* describe their pains."

I paused a moment to reflect. Was I being purified? I saw none of that, at least not yet. There was stagnation, all right, more like sloth.

"Psychologically considered," Underhill wrote, "the Dark Night is an example of the operation of the law of reaction from stress. It is a period of fatigue and lassitude following a period of sustained mystical activity."

Again I paused to consider. Yes, stress had built up to an incredible high during the six weeks of Amy Catherine's life. Then the awful letdown, followed by total fatigue. But I've been through these highs and lows before and never lost contact with Jesus.

When one's mental machinery has been overworked, continued Underhill, "when the higher centres [of the mind] have been submitted to the continuous strain . . . with its accompanying periods of intense fervour . . . the swingback into the negative state occurs almost of necessity.

"This is the psychological explanation of those strange and painful episodes in the lives of great saints—indeed, of many spiritual persons hardly to be classed as saints—when, perhaps after a long life . . . with growing consciousness of the 'presence of God,' the whole inner experience is suddenly swept away, and only a blind reliance on past convictions saves them from unbelief. The great contemplatives . . . emerge from this period of destitution, however long and drastic it may be, as from a new purification. It is for them the gateway to a higher state. But persons of a less heroic spirituality, if they enter the Night at all, may succumb to its dangers and pains. This 'great negation' is the sorting-house of the spiritual life."

Many succumb to its pains. That certainly describes my unheroic reaction to the current darkness. Yet it is reassuring to know that those who hungered most for God were often the ones deprived for the longest stretches. I want to learn more about the saints. . . .

Evelyn Underhill went on to describe the "dark night" experience of Madame Guyon (1648–1717). Looking further into her life I found that this fascinating woman was a member of high French society and the mother of five children. Jeanne Guyon above all else was an all-out woman of God. She was imprisoned in the Bastille for four years because of her religious beliefs, which were at odds with the Roman Catholic Church of that period. She wrote forty books, including a twenty-volume commentary on the Bible. Though one of the leading exponents of Quietism— which teaches that spiritual perfection is attained in an attitude of total acquiescence to circumstances in life— Madame Guyon was noted for her Christian philanthropy: dispensing bread to the poor, taking the sick into her home, establishing hospitals in several cities.

Yet Madame Guyon experienced painful periods of what she called "aridity" (what writer hasn't gone through that?), during which she lost for a time all interest in "the divine realities" that had previously filled her life. "How dearly I paid for those happy periods when the presence of God was so real," Madame Guyon wrote in her autobiography. "For this possession which seemed to me so perfect was but the preparation for times of total deprivation."

During these dark times intellectual life sank to a low ebb. She suffered trials of every kind: "exterior and interior crosses abounded."

When her consciousness of God was extinguished, a state of mental and moral chaos seems to have invaded Madame Guyon. "As soon as I perceived happiness or beauty or a virtue," she stated, "it seemed to me that I fell incessantly into the contrary vice: [for example] if I was given an intense perception of the purity of God, so far as my feelings went, I myself became more and more impure. My imagination was in a state of appalling confusion. . . . I could not perceive any good thing that I had done in my whole life."

Self-control and the power of attention were diminished. She became attracted to the worldly things around her, which she had previously renounced. The neat edifice of her spiritual life was in ruins.

"It is an amazing thing," said Madame Guyon, "for a soul that believed herself to be advanced in the way of perfection, when she sees herself thus go to pieces all at once." Although she watched her husband and their two eldest children die early on, faced the hardships of travel as a missionary of the Gospel, relinquished her life as a wealthy socialite to minister to the poorest of the poor during the days of Louis XIV, then for years suffered the "dark night" when she felt that even God had abandoned her, Madame Guyon was restored to health in her final years to teach the word. "He did return with more goodness and strength and with great splendor." In her last will and testament, Madame Guyon wrote:

It is to Thee, O Lord God, that I owe all things; and it is to Thee, that I now surrender up all that I am. Do with me, O my God, whatsoever Thou pleasest. . . .

Within Thy hands, O God, I leave my soul, not relying for my salvation on any good that is in me, but solely on Thy mercies, and the merits and sufferings of my Lord Jesus Christ.

I've never approached either Madame Guyon's total dedication or the total breakdown she went through; the thought that the road back to communion with God leads through such suffering terrifies me.

In the Valley _____

*L*en ... As the months went by, those of us in daily contact with Catherine—her mother, our secretary Jeanne Sevigny, our housekeeper, Mary Moncur, our son Jeffrey, and I—were baffled and distressed by Catherine's state. To outsiders she appeared to be living a normal life; to the five of us (Chet was back at school, Linda at work in Washington, D.C.) she was but a shell of the woman we knew and loved.

Catherine and I arose early as always, having a time of Bible reading and prayer together before beginning our work day. But the prayer time was wooden; Catherine was mouthing words by rote. There was no vitality, no joy, no power. Whether I was tender or scolding, patient or angry made no difference. She responded lethargically.

After breakfast she went to her office to write. "How is she doing?" I would ask Jeanne Sevigny. Jeanne, by now a close friend and a participant in our ministry as well as secretary, would just shake her head. "Productivity about zero."

"Nothing at all?"

"Nothing for me to type. She keeps reading over parts of the *Gloria* manuscript, but we all know that project is dead. A part of her seemed to die with it. We do get the mail answered, but I have to push and shove and prod her even with that."

"What's your diagnosis, Jeanne?"

"Grief and frustration. Anger, too."

"Aimed at whom?"

"God, mostly. And at us, too. All of us, even her mother."

"Buried anger, isn't it? She doesn't explode as she used to."

"You're right. I think the explosions were a lot healthier."

My efforts toward dialogue with Catherine were mostly unsuccessful. After receiving a series of one-word answers to my questions, I would usually back off. Yet I knew I had to keep trying. If only something would go right for her! The movie version of her novel *Christy* seemed permanently shelved; likewise her novel *Gloria*, though she kept pulling the manuscript from the file drawer and going through the motions of working on it. Amy Catherine had died. The relationship with Peter and Edith was strained. In fact, none of her relationships was working very well.

The best news I had to give her was about Linda, who continued to astonish me with the changes in her life. "Linda has found a most remarkable group of Christian friends," I told Catherine one day in our bedroom after I had visited Linda in Washington at the nonprofit organization "Cornerstone" where she worked. "In addition to her administrative responsibilities and leading a Bible study, Linda writes a newsletter. I think she has a gift for writing."

No response.

"Tell me something, Catherine. Why do you refuse to see the many positive results of Amy Catherine's short life? She was used in a mighty way, you know."

Catherine looked at me wearily. "I'm glad for Linda, and for Scott Ross and Pam Gordon and Jamie Buckingham and all the others who were helped. It's very self-centered of me not to be more grateful for this, I know. Forgive me."

"You say that, but you don't mean it. Words are coming out of you, but there's no emotion to back them up. It's as if the real you has gone somewhere else and I'm talking to a cardboard figure."

"Thank you for those kind words."

I shifted to a different line. "You said several days ago that you felt you were moving about in a dark cage. Do you mean something like a prison?"

"That's pretty close."

"What are you doing to get out?"

"Not enough, I guess. I feel like a dead person. Abandoned."

"Not by those of us here in this house. We love you. We're praying for you."

"Thank you."

I sat down on the bed where she was sitting and reached for her hand. "I've heard you say many times that when a lot of things go wrong in a person's life, the Lord is trying to get that person's attention. I'm sure you've been applying this to yourself."

For the first time, Catherine's eyes met mine. "I sure have."

"What do you think He's saying to you?"

Long pause. "That I'm probably out of His will. That I may have been out of His will for some time."

There was sudden tension between us; a warning light within me cautioned me to cease the probing. Yet another part of me knew I must push ahead.

"How long do you think you've been out of His will?"

The question lay there between us for a moment. Both of us knew where we were heading. Catherine's eyes left mine and her lip trembled.

"Since I married you," she finally said.

"You know and I know that everything hasn't gone wrong since we were married," I challenged her. "Forget all the books and articles we've worked on together and their impact on people. Look at the lives of our four children. Has our marriage made things better for them or worse?"

"Better, I guess. But I think you could have married any number of women who would have been better mothers to your children. I just think that I was supposed to stay single after Peter's death."

"And live all alone in that comfortable sanctuary you were building ... a snug retreat ... well away from the action. That's not the guidance you got before we were married. After warning you that it would be difficult at times, the Lord nudged you to say yes to a new life with me."

Catherine nodded. "I remember. But I'm not at all sure about my guidance anymore. I thought I heard the Lord say He was going to heal Amy Catherine. Obviously I heard Him wrong. Maybe I heard Him wrong about us."

I sat there a moment struggling with a decision. How to reach Catherine? Gentleness and patience? Or confrontation? I made up my mind.

"Would you like to hear my opinion as to when you began to move away from God's will?"

Catherine stared at me stonily. "Go ahead."

"It all began with the enormous success of *Christy*. I watched the change in you. It was gradual over many months. The plaudits, the adulation, the bestseller lists, the movie sale, all heady stuff. When we flew to New York for interviews, the publisher insisted on providing a limousine. We both loved it. Then came the bowing and scraping by the editors when you described your next book, another novel.

What they were saying, essentially, Catherine, was that you could do no wrong. That's when the change in you really began. Deep down inside, you bought it. You began to think you could do no wrong. Every book you'd written, a major success. Magazines eager for articles."

I paused, watching Catherine's reaction. She didn't appear resistant so I plunged ahead.

"It was at this point, Catherine, that I began to feel the arrogance. Before the success of *Christy* you had what I felt was a delightful sense of inadequacy. Especially for one who had been so successful. It was this inadequacy that I related to when we first met. You needed God. Without Him you were incomplete. In a lesser way you needed me. We made a good team in both work and play. On your book projects you needed Tib. Then after *Christy* you changed. Ask yourself, Catherine. Did you come to a point where you felt you didn't need God anymore? Or me? Or anyone?"

Catherine flared. "I've always needed God."

"If you've always needed Him, why can't you reach Him now?"

A stricken look clouded Catherine's face. Tears welled up. I tried to embrace her, but she turned away. I patted her shoulder for a few minutes, then left her alone.

Catherine . . . I am forced to the conclusion that Len is right. I did become spiritually arrogant after *Christy*. I became selfish with the use of my time, not wanting to be bothered with people who bored me or disagreed with me. I forgot too easily what I owed to the skills of others.

God was right to discipline me. I deserved it. Len was right to correct me.

But did the punishment fit the crime? I now feel so completely abandoned, rejected. The pain of Amy Catherine's death still immobilizes me. It's so dreadful to be in a state of darkness that I can understand better the fear of hell. How awful eternal darkness must be!

Reading about the "dark night" in Evelyn Underhill's *Mysticism* both helps me and depresses me. Her description of the pain and anguish suffered by St. Teresa of Avila, the sixteenth-century Spanish Carmelite, is agonizingly real to me.

Is there something inside those great saints that invites, even seeks this kind of suffering? The holy men and women of medieval times actually even inflicted torture upon themselves as a way to subdue their flesh and thus come to know God better. I confess I'm baffled by this. Life is painful enough without making it more so. Some of these godly people make it sound as if the dark night experience should be deeply relished because it will end up being good for you.

Reading further in Evelyn Underhill's book, I see that St. Catherine of Siena was another who went through intense suffering and spiritual warfare. She came out of a well-to-do Italian family and as a girl was described as "pert, pretty and pious." Early on, she determined to remain a virgin, with Jesus only as her Bridegroom. Despite strong parental resistance she entered a convent.

After enjoying the presence of Christ for many years, however, there came a dark night experience. For months on end Catherine was tormented by fiends who filled her small cell in the convent "with obscene words and gestures inviting her to lust."

Try as she would, she obtained no relief from this assault until she ceased her opposition. Her surrender consisted of this simple statement: "I . . . will gladly bear these and all other torments in the name of the Saviour, for as long as it shall please His Majesty." With this act, the evil spirits fled and she was comforted by a vision of the cross.

St. Teresa had a similar experience that she attributed to the action of the devil. "The soul," she says, ". . . loses all control over itself, and all power of thinking of anything but the absurdities he puts before it. . . . It is impossible to describe the sufferings of the soul in this state. It goes about in quest of relief, and God suffers it to find none."

St. Teresa then goes on to describe the inner pain there is in separation from God: "The pain thus grows to such a degree that in spite of herself the sufferer gives vent to loud cries, which she cannot stifle, however patient and accustomed to pain she may be, because this is not a pain which is felt in the body, but in the depths of the soul. . . . You will . . . ask why this soul does not conform herself to His will. . . . Hitherto she could do this, and consecrated her life to it; but now she cannot, for her reason is reduced to such a state that she is no longer mistress of herself and can think of nothing but her affliction."

I'm not ready to identify with Teresa's former consecration and total self-surrender, but I can relate to the loneliness she felt, her self-centeredness, her inability to take the positive action, to do what would get her going in the right direction. Until one has been immobilized, one does not understand this kind of paralysis. I feel like a person suspended in midair, who can neither touch the earth nor mount to heaven.

Evelyn Underhill points out that all these forms of the dark night—the absence of God, the sense of sin, the loss of the self's old peace and joy, and its apparent relapse to lower spiritual and mental levels—are considered by the mystics themselves to be a purification of the will so that it may be merged with God's will.

The starved and tortured spirit going through a dark night, Underhill writes, learns "to accept lovelessness for the sake of Love, nothingness for the sake of the all, [to die] without any sure promise of life. It sees with amazement the most sure foundations of its transcendental life crumble beneath it, dwells in a darkness which seems to hold no promise of a dawn."

Then in her *Dialogue* St. Catherine records these words, which she felt God spoke to her:

"In order to raise the soul from imperfection," says the Voice of God, "I withdraw Myself from her sentiment, depriving her of former consolations . . . which I do in order to humiliate her, and cause her to seek Me in truth. . . . Then, if she loved Me without thought of self . . . she rejoices in the time of trouble, deeming herself unworthy of peace and quietness of mind. . . . Though she perceives that I have withdrawn Myself . . . [she] perseveres with humility in her exercises . . . and it is to this end . . . that I withdraw from her. . . . I leave her so that she may see and know her defects . . . and learn how incapable she is of stability or perseverance. . . . This should be the end and purpose of all her self-knowledge, to rise above herself. . . ."

There is much in this statement to ponder. My mind accepts the idea that God may be doing a purification of my soul by withdrawing Himself. Humiliation is something I am now very familiar with. I have always seen God as a tender, loving Father. That He can also be rigorous and stern is now abundantly clear to me as well.

In reading about these Christian saints and mystics, I'm reminded that though the way we talk about our faith changes, the basic truths of Christianity do not. *Ego-slaying* is a modern term for the process St. Catherine went through. It was a concept I thought I'd come to grips with in *Beyond Our Selves*. I'm forced to the conclusion now that though I may have assented intellectually to this principle, I have done little to live it out.

There are other popular phrases to describe it. "The Cross life" is the one used today in many Christian groups; "self-abandonment" is another. Whatever the words used, the underlying reality is the same: *For there to be more of God in a person's life, there has to be less of self.*

No one demonstrated that principle better than the Ger-

man saint Heinrich Suso. Evelyn Underhill was greatly
intrigued by Suso and I can understand why.

Len ... Catherine's interest in Heinrich Suso's dark night
experience led me to do some research of my own on this
German saint. It's a story that would have made front page
news if it had happened today.

Suso was born about 1300 in the German province of
Swabia, the son of a knight and a patrician mother. His
early life was lived on the banks of Lake Constance, with
the towering Alps in the background.

By nature young Heinrich was a poet. Even his prose was
full of the song of the birds and the scent of flowers. His
father is described as "a very worldly man" whose life
centered on hunting, hawking, and tournaments. Heinrich,
however, took after his religious and tenderhearted mother.

His frail health preventing his becoming a knight,
Heinrich entered the Dominican friary of Constance at thirteen. At eighteen, hungering for more of God, he entered
into strict seclusion which was to last for nine years. He
practiced severe bodily mortifications: he wore a hairshirt
and an iron collar around his neck to which his hands were
fastened. A wooden cross with iron nails in it was attached
to his back. When his health had been broken by these
excesses, one day in a vision the Lord told him to desist.
The very next day he threw all his torture instruments into
the river.

Suso went to Cologne to complete his studies, then returned to Constance to teach there in the friary house. This
was difficult for him at first because he loved to be alone in
rapt communion with God. At once artist and recluse,
utterly impractical, he had the dreamer's dread of the world
of men.

Suso was a born romantic. Images of a spiritual chivalry
color his devotional writings: again and again he turns to
the language of the tournament. Suso was exalted by the

stories of hard combats, the knightly fortitude that pays no attention to its wounds.

"O my sweet Lord," he exclaimed one day, "if only I could become Thy spiritual knight!" When he experienced trials, however, Suso went off by himself to sulk. In his writings he reported the Lord's response: "Well, now, Heinrich, what has become of your noble chivalry? Who is this knight of straw? It is not by making rash promises and drawing back when suffering comes that the victory is won."

"Alas! Lord," said Suso plaintively, "the tournaments in which one must suffer for Thee last such a very long time!"

The Lord replied, "But the reward and the honor which I give to My knights endure forever."

God was calling Suso to give more of himself to others, to have more contact with the unfriendly world. Instead of the quiet cell and the secret mortifications, the reality of his renunciation was to be tested under the unsympathetic gaze of other men. For the outside world was to test Suso to his utmost.

It happened during one of his teaching tours. A woman who attended one of his services accused him of being the father of her child. This kind of news always spreads like a forest fire on a windy day. Poor Suso was utterly crushed by the ensuing uproar, "wounded to the depths of his heart."

"Lord, Lord!" he cried. "Every day of my life I have worshiped Thy holy name, and have helped to cause it to be loved and honored by many men: I am blameless in this situation and now Thou wouldst drag my name through the mud!"

The Lord did not answer.

When the scandal was at its height, a woman close to the pregnant woman came to Suso in secret. To his speechless horror she offered to destroy the child that was the cause of this gossip, in order that the tale might be quickly forgot-

ten. "Unless the baby is somehow disposed of," she
warned, "you will be forced by public opinion to accept it
and provide for its upbringing."

How would an intrepid knight handle such a dilemma?
Suso wondered. To the woman he said, "Your plan is unthinkable. I have confidence in the God of heaven, who is
rich, and who has given me until now all that which was
needful unto me. He will help me to keep, if need be,
another beside myself. Please go and fetch the little child
that I may see it."

When the woman returned with the baby boy, Suso put
him on his knees. Sighing deeply, Suso said, "Could I kill a
pretty baby that smiled at me? No, no, I had rather suffer
every trial that could come upon me!

"Oh, my poor, poor child," he continued. "Thou art an
unfortunate orphan, for thy unnatural father hath denied
thee and thy wicked mother would cast thee off. The providence of God hath given thee to me, in order that I may
provide thy upkeep. I will accept thee, then, from Him and
from no one else."

How different a response would have come from the
early Suso, an aesthetic man interested in little but his own
safe spirituality, a man who would have rejected the child
self-righteously as someone else's problem.

Heinrich Suso found a suitable woman to care for the
child at his expense. When the news of his decision to
support the baby circulated through the community, his
reputation was further damaged. Now even his friends for-
sook him and he narrowly escaped expulsion from his
religious order. For by assuming the expense of rearing the
child, Suso seemed to admit that he was, in effect, the real
father—though he was not.

This all-out act of chivalry should have won for Suso the
approval of heaven, if not of men. But if heaven applauded,
Heinrich Suso could not hear it. He entered a darkness

where even God seemed to have turned His back. In despair, he implored his Lord, "Why have You allowed this to happen to me?"

There was only silence. Suso traveled to Ulm where he tried to begin a new ministry. But the story of "his child" followed him and he was forced to flee again.

From Suso's biography it appears that his "dark night of the soul" lasted a full ten years. He remained a friar, he continued to write and teach, but he was bitter and rebellious and not very productive. At some point near the end of this dark period there came a dialogue with God. It began with Suso asking the question, "Where are You in my travail, Lord?"

After years of silence, he at last heard God's voice: *Heinrich, where then is your resignation? Where is that equal humor in joy and in tribulation which you have taught other men to love?*

Suso replied, weeping, "You ask where is my resignation? But tell me first, where is the infinite mercy of God for His friends? Thou knowest that Thou art my only consolation, that all my trust is only in Thee. So long as it was only a question of preaching resignation, that was easy: but now that my heart is pierced, now that I am wounded to the marrow . . . how can I be resigned?"

Then, abandoning himself completely, he concluded, "If it cannot be otherwise, *fiat voluntas tua* (be it done according to Your will)."

This act of self-abandonment was at once followed by a vision from the Lord in which the end of his troubles was announced.

Suso summed up his experience thus: "When God judged that it was time, He rewarded me for all my suffering. I then enjoyed peace of heart and received in tranquillity and quietness many precious graces. I came to praise the Lord from the very depths of my soul for those same sufferings which, for all the world, I would not now have been spared. And God caused me to understand that by this complete abasement I had gained more, and was made the more worthy to be raised up to God, than by all the pains which I had suffered from my youth up to that time."

Catherine ... The suffering saints—and I should include Job here, too—make my troubles seem small and paltry indeed, but their ordeals continue to frighten me. Is this the kind of cross life the Lord wants all of us to live?

If so, why does the Bible promise in so many places "good things" for those who love the Lord?

Did Suso and the others have a certain kind of spiritual pride that the Lord found obnoxious and that needed to be demolished?

More to the point, do I have this same kind of spiritual pride and is my dark night experience His way of chastening me?

I find myself with many questions and few answers.

I have never had a problem facing up to the fact that I am a sinner. Since the fall of Eve in the Garden of Eden human nature has been sinful. Glibly I can repeat, "I am a sinner saved by grace."

By saying this, however, I place myself in a general category of sinners, enabling me to avoid facing up to the fact that I have committed, am committing, specific sins. It is much more comfortable to be general than specific. The other day I ran up against this phrase in *My Utmost for His Highest* by Oswald Chambers: "Sin is red-handed mutiny against God."

That hit me like a sledgehammer blow. I am in rebellion against God. I have been for many months now. I am in despair about it, but cannot seem to change. All is darkness in my life. Nothing is working. I read books, I go to church, Len and I pray together, but Jesus is not in any of it.

My sin is separating me from God—Father, Son, and Holy Spirit. Chambers also says, "If sin rules in me, God's life in me will be killed; if God rules in me, sin in me will be killed."

How do I make that switch so that again God rules in me?

I do not want to go through a ten-year period of darkness as Heinrich Suso did.

A Shaft
of Light _____

*L*en ... One morning in the spring of 1972 two of Catherine's closest women friends—Virginia Lively, Freddie Koch—and I asked Catherine to join us in the living room of our Boynton Beach home. We were all struck by her joylessness, her heavy spirit, and by the deep circles under her eyes. Sleeplessness was becoming more and more of a major problem for her.

We talked aimlessly for a few moments, then Catherine, always blunt, cut it short. "You're here to confront me," she stated. "Let's get on with it."

"We've tried to be helpful to you several times since Amy

Catherine's death," Freddie began. "You admit you're in trouble, we pray together, and nothing happens. Why?"

Catherine shrugged, then waved her hand in a helpless gesture. "I wish I knew."

"Are you still angry at God?" asked Virginia.

Catherine hesitated a moment. "Who am I to be angry at God? He is our almighty Lord, who knows all, sees all, and has His own ways that are mysterious and incomprehensible to us. It would be awfully silly for me to pit my puny anger against the Almighty."

"Yet that's what you've been doing for the past six months," I stated.

For a moment I hoped Catherine was going to deny it, argue back with her old zest. But she quickly subsided into passivity.

"What's happened in the past six months isn't as important as what happens in the future," Virginia enjoined. "We love you, Catherine, and it hurts us all to see you suffering."

Freddie Koch drew a deep breath and said, "Catherine, I feel the Lord is telling me something that He wants me to tell you. It's about your self-pity. You're neck-deep in self-pity."

Catherine nodded unemotionally. "I think that's probably right. I confess to being a mess. So how do I get out of this hole? I'm sick to death of the darkness in my life."

"You could really be sick to death unless you do something about it, Catherine," said Virginia.

"The first step is to confess the rebellion and self-pity to the Lord," I suggested softly. "Confession and repentance."

Catherine shrugged hopelessly. "I've already done this, again and again. I honestly have. It's the complete lack of response that confounds me. I've never, ever lived in this kind of vacuum before. I talk, I pray. Nothing. For most of my life I've felt God's presence, heard His voice, received thoughts that I knew came from Him. No more. He's gone from my life. I know I terribly offended Him last August. I guess I offended most everybody. But I was so totally caught up in the Amy Catherine battle. It was all-out warfare, you know. Nothing ever like it." Tears began spilling out of her eyes.

"What is destroying me is that I understand nothing about it, nothing about anything that happened. What's wrong with going all-out for something you believe in? God likes single-eyed people, doesn't He? It says so in Scripture. Well, I've always tried to be one hundred percent in everything I do. And always before, God honored my efforts. Why not this time? Why have I been flattened so completely? I know it's happened to others. Great saints have gone through dark nights a thousand times worse than mine. But they almost seemed to ask for it, seeking some higher plane of spirituality. I didn't ask for anything for myself, only that a tiny baby be healed, and God not only refused that request, but turned His back on me. I don't understand."

"Maybe it's that insistence on understanding that's the problem, Catherine," suggested Virginia.

Catherine stared at Virginia for a moment with a hint of surprise in her eyes.

Something stirred in me. Had we made a small breakthrough in Catherine's impenetrable shell?

When the session broke up after a prayer time, I was still not sure.

Catherine . . . Something happened to me yesterday when Virginia, Freddie, Len, and I met. For a moment a shaft of light seemed to break through the darkness. When I awoke this morning, however, the darkness still surrounded me. My prayers still seemed to bounce back from the ceiling.

Then for the first time in months a new and gentle thought came to rest on my mind: Read Isaiah 53. It didn't come from my thoughts, nor would Satan likely be sending me to Scripture. With a surge of hope, I knew it had to be from the Lord.

I read the 53rd chapter of Isaiah eagerly, struck anew by this foretelling of how Jesus would suffer hatred and rejection, of how alone He would be on the cross. These passages leapt out at me:

> He was oppressed and he was afflicted, yet he never said a word. . . . He was buried like a criminal . . . but he had done no wrong. . . . Yet it was the Lord's good plan to bruise him and fill him with grief.
>
> Isaiah 53:7,9–10, TLB

I had read this passage many times before, even since Amy Catherine's death, but it had not affected me as it did now, particularly the tenth verse. God made His own Son suffer, but it was a "good plan." More than "good," it was perfect as only something from God could be. It was terribly important to the future of the human race that Jesus Christ have His dark night experience on the cross. Yet what a desperately dark night it had to be for Him, a time of despair and abandonment for Him to have cried out, "My God, my God, why hast thou forsaken me?" (Matthew 27:46).

Suddenly I was overwhelmed with feelings of remorse, embarrassment, gratitude, and relief, all mingled together. Reading about the saints and their trials had not touched or enlightened me the way this sudden realization had. For reasons of His own, God had allowed Amy Catherine to be born genetically damaged. Her death served God's purposes, fulfilled His plan in some specific way not revealed to us, just as Christ's death on the cross at first baffled and dismayed His disciples, but did not destroy their faith. I heard my own words, "What is destroying me is that I don't understand." I, from my tiny human vantage point, demanding to see into the secrets of eternity!

Virginia had challenged me on it: "Maybe it's that insistence on understanding that's the problem, Catherine."

How many others had tried to caution me? Linda, reading from Isaiah: "Maybe we aren't supposed to understand why God does certain things."

Tib, with one of the best minds I know: "Just because I don't understand something doesn't mean it isn't so."

What about the weeks after Peter Marshall's death when my plea for understanding had been met with something infinitely greater?

Instead of feeling rejected and abandoned, I suddenly felt ashamed. When Amy Catherine died, I demanded that God explain Himself to me, and when He didn't, I proceeded to sulk like a child. A petulant child who had failed to get her own way.

In the days that followed this new understanding, I began to pore over the Scripture accounts of Jesus' humiliation and death; also Bible commentaries on this theme. I was especially moved by this passage from a book by Hans Kung, *On Being a Christian*, portraying how the death of Jesus might have looked to a news reporter the day after the crucifixion:

Jesus found himself left alone, not only by his people, but by the One to whom he had constantly appealed as no one did before him. Left absolutely alone. We do not know what Jesus thought and felt as he was dying. But it is obvious to the whole world that he had proclaimed the early advent of God in his kingdom and this God did not come. A God who was man's friend, knowing all his needs, close to him, but this God was absent.

The unique communion with God which he had seemed to enjoy only makes his forsakenness more unique. This God and Father with whom he had iden-

tified himself to the very end did not at the end identify himself with the sufferer. And so everything
seemed as if it had never been: in vain. He who had
announced the closeness and advent of God his Father
publicly before the whole world died utterly forsaken
by God and was thus publicly demonstrated as godless
before the whole world: someone judged by God himself, disposed of once and for all.

What better description of estrangement from God—yet
this was His dearly beloved Son!
If Jesus could suffer this humiliation before the whole
world, what right did I have to sulk and pout because I had
been made to look foolish before a few friends and fellow
Christians?

Day after day in our Florida home, I shut myself away
with my Bible and notebook to work through my new
discoveries, seeking a new relationship with my Lord.
Again and again I read the crucifixion account, feeling
the aloneness, the agony, the abandonment Jesus must have
felt. I was there in the crowd, looking up into His face.
Flooded anew by contrition one afternoon, I burst into
tears and stumbled to my knees. "Forgive me, Lord. Forgive
me for my rejection of You, too."
Then came this revelation: when life hands us situations
we cannot understand, we have one of two choices. We can
wallow in misery, separated from God. Or we can tell Him,
"I need You and Your presence in my life more than I need
understanding. I choose You, Lord. I trust You to give me
understanding and an answer to all my 'Why's?'—*only if
and when* You choose."
Understanding. That seemed to be the key word in my
difficulties. I had sought it from the Lord most of my life
and in His gentle tenderness He had often provided it. So

often, in fact, that I had begun to take it for granted, assumed I had a right to understanding. What arrogance! What presumption!

Then a new thought hit me like a thunderbolt. Presumption was my sin. During the prayers for Amy Catherine I had taken the lead in telling God what He was to do about Amy Catherine: "Thank You, Lord, for healing this tiny, precious baby." Had I really heard Him say what His plan was for her? Or had I wanted the healing so badly I simply imagined He must, too? Presumption. I had assumed something I had no right to assume. God would always be God. We will never fathom His ways, but I had presumed to try. "O Lord, forgive me for my presumption."

Then still another thought struck me. Worse than my presumption, even, was the fact that with Amy Catherine I had really wanted to play God, to be God in her life. Appalled, I tried to detach myself from this sin. There was no detachment. I had tried to usurp the power of almighty God. "O Lord, can You forgive me for this abomination?"

And He answered me. At long, long last, I heard the Voice that had been silent for so many months: *I, your God, am in everything. The baby died, but Amy Catherine is with Me. And while she lived, she ministered to everyone who prayed for her. You alone, Catherine, were too stubborn to see it.*

Section IV

The Coming of the Light

A Journey Begun _____

Len ... During the months that Catherine walked the valley of apathy, I had looked at every hopeful sign as a possible turning point. It came with her words of submission: *I want You, Lord, more than I want understanding.*

I thought back to a time when my own insistence upon "understanding" from God had gotten me into trouble. "Why haven't you healed Eve of alcoholism since we both had committed our lives to You?" I had pleaded. We never seem to learn that God's ways are almost always different from ours.

Now that the turning point had come for Catherine, I sensed that the way from darkness to light would not be easy; her spiritual well was dry. Fortunately for this book, Catherine wrote daily in her journal.

Catherine . . . The message to me yesterday was most specific. I am to arise each morning at 6 A.M. and rejoice in the Lord. I am to praise Him with a grateful heart. I am to pour out my love for Him. I am to thank Him for everything that has gone wrong in my life. I am to do this indefinitely.

Resistance wells up inside me. I have trouble enough sleeping at nights without rising an hour earlier. But so be it. Len agreed to join me.

So this morning we sit on our patio watching the sunrise. First there was total darkness, then a deep rose above the blue. Now the edges of clouds are showing lighter rose. The birds have awakened and started twittering.

To put the focus on praise, I turned to Psalm 66:

> Make a joyful noise unto God, all ye lands: Sing forth the honour of his name: make his praise glorious.
>
> verses 1–2

Lord, my praise seems so hollow and shallow.

Then I came to verse 18: "If I regard iniquity in my heart, the Lord will not hear me." That is a jolting thought! I have spent so much time in recent months taking my spiritual temperature, bemoaning my sins and faults. The implication of this verse is clear: I am to take my eyes off myself and fix them on Him.

Again this morning I am so aware of my spiritual emptiness. In the days ahead I am to fill myself with spiritual refreshment through beautiful writings the Lord will bring to my mind. I am to let my soul bask in these words until it is aglow. I am to write them down. I am to keep doing it even though my heart is not in it.

Right away these words come to mind:

> *Still, still with Thee,*
> *when purple morning breaketh,*

> *When the bird waketh,*
>   *and the shadows flee;*
> *Fairer than morning,*
>   *lovelier than daylight,*
> *Dawns the sweet consciousness*
>   *I am with Thee.*

Harriet Beecher Stowe, 1811–1896

I feel a flutter in my spirit, Lord. These lines were given me. I could never have recalled them word for word on my own.

This morning, Lord, I am reminded of the pastor and his wife who visited us that New Year's Day (after the "Chair Episode" with Jeff the night before). I remember the story the pastor told of the man who lost his young daughter through an illness. Only by praising God was he healed of his bitterness. This is happening to me now, Lord. I am feeling Your presence again after so many months of darkness. Today I am led to the 90th psalm and these words:

> O satisfy us early with thy mercy; that we may rejoice and be glad all our days.
>
> Make us glad according to the days wherein thou hast afflicted us, and the years wherein we have seen evil.
>
> Let thy work appear unto thy servants, and thy glory unto their children.
>
> And let the beauty of the Lord our God be upon us....
> verses 14–17, KJV

The word *mercy* reverberates within me. You are a merciful God. You saw my rebellion, my arrogance, and chastened me by withdrawing Your presence for a time, but You did not abandon me. Thank You, Lord, for being so loving and patient with me.

The Lord is showing me this morning that my rebellion against Him following Amy Catherine's death was the central element in my sin. Rebellion was the pivotal point on which all the other unlovely qualities turned:

Presumption
Hardness of heart
Self-centeredness
Self-pity
Anger
Resentment

I am beginning to see it all now. The instant we are in a state of rebellion, we have not only lost our contentment and our joy; we have also declared personal war on God. If God is truly God, then He is Lord and Ruler of circumstances. So if we are rebellious against the circumstances He has allowed, then we are, in practical fact, rebelling against Him.

No wonder God withdrew His presence from me! My spirit of rebellion shuts the door in His face. It is saying, "I will do it my way from now on. I will be the boss of my own life."

Afterward, when the darkness descends and desolation overcomes one, a few halfhearted statements like, "Well, Lord, maybe I was a bit too self-confident . . . I guess I do need You after all . . . why don't we work out a sort of partnership?"—these little gestures won't restore the relationship. All-out repentance is needed.

So I'm having to go back to my childhood to try to locate the root of my rebellion against circumstances—and thus ultimately against God. I think it centered in the deprivation our family suffered during the Depression. Dad as a pastor of a small church made such a pitifully small income that we had but the barest essentials. I'll never forget the embarrassment of going with him to the market on Saturday and watching him whisper to the grocer, asking if he could receive credit until the first of the week.

I rebelled against our poverty, against the "missionary barrel" gifts of Dad's parishioners to our family, used and often soiled clothes that seldom fit properly. In college, my rebellion turned toward inequality of all kinds. Not having the right clothes for social affairs, I affected scorn for this part of college life. My non-acceptance of these situations never became serious enough to separate me from God back then, but seeds were sown—seeds of dissatisfaction, lack of gratitude. I'm having to search back through my life to each such occasion, confess the wrong spirit there, then ask the Lord's forgiveness.

I am beginning to look forward to these early morning times. There is an air of expectancy inside me as I watch the sun rise and wait for the Lord. What guidance will He give me today? Will it be a verse of Scripture? A hymn?

Today it was a poem:

> *Awake my soul, and with the sun,*
> *Thy daily stage of duty run;*
> *Shake off dull sloth and joyful rise*
> *To pay the morning sacrifice!*
>
> *Shine on me, Lord, new life impart,*
> *Fresh ardors kindle in my heart;*
> *One ray of Thine all-quick'ning light*
> *Despite the clouds and dark of night.*

Thomas Ken, 1637–1711

Thank You, Jesus, for revealing to me that to rise at six each morning is to travel from "dull sloth" to "fresh ardors." How glorious is the early morning air, the dazzling colors of the sunrise, the sweet bird sound, the fresh smell of the foliage and flowers!

Thank You, Lord, for the opportunity of this firsthand audience with the King. How privileged is that person who is admitted to Royal Presence, to listen to the almighty King, to watch Him, to bask in His majesty. In earthly courts, such a one would be considered favored indeed. Yet this is the status and the privilege You give to each of us, Lord.

This morning, Lord, I need to record my dream of last night. My dreams usually involve people and places. The one last night had neither, no pictures at all, only an idea. I don't believe I've ever had this kind of dream before.

The idea or thought was about You, Jesus. Not surprising, since I have felt closer and closer to You recently. The thought was about Your death on the cross. This was redemption for us, and You being who You are, God as well as man, insisted upon doing our redemption right, doing it to the last awful detail, all the way to the end. You could have taken so many shortcuts that would have made dying so much easier for You, but You would not.

And in my dream, as this realization swept over me, I wept.

The depths of meaning in this strange dream will be given me in time, I'm sure, because I'm convinced that it came from You. And how I rejoice that once more I have a relationship with You.

It was an example of a concept I received years ago from author-teacher-friend Glenn Clark: Prayers are answered and marvelous things happen when the unconscious and the conscious are of one piece and track perfectly together. What is tracking here—and how much this delights me!— is that the truth of Christianity is not just in my wide-awake mind, but deep down in my unconscious mind also.

Then You led me to these words:

> Yes, even when I am old and gray-headed, O God, forsake me not, but keep me alive until I have declared Your mighty

strength to this generation, and Your might and power to all that are to come.

                                        Psalm 71:18, AMPLIFIED

Lord, I make this prayer for myself, that You will use me in the years ahead to *declare* You and Your works in a mighty way to this generation.

Changing _____

*L*en ... All of us rejoiced as the weeks passed and Catherine emerged from her isolation. There was a new softness in her demeanor. She laughed and joked more. My morning prayer time with her had a new vitality.

"What have you learned from all this?" I asked her one morning as the two of us ate breakfast together.

"Not to take myself so seriously," she replied with a smile. "I need to remind myself at least once a day that the world can get along just fine without me."

"How will all this affect your work?"

"I don't know yet. I'm not ready to begin a new book. Maybe later this year. I feel a great need to get myself better organized—papers, clothes, personal belongings. I need to give away a lot of things. The Lord has really zapped me about this."

Mary Moncur, our faithful housekeeper of many years, refilled our coffee cups. She was relaxed and smiling, too. During Catherine's long months of lethargy and moodiness, Mary had in some ways absorbed these attitudes into her small frame, trying to take the weight of Catherine's despair upon herself.

I felt lighter, too, somehow. It had been an extra strain to commute every other week to New York City, knowing my wife was going through a time of agonizing reappraisal of everything, including our marriage. Meanwhile, *Guideposts* magazine was entering a period of turbulent growth with more demands on my creativity. I sensed the time was approaching when I would have to make a hard decision as to whether I could continue as the full-time editor of a New York-based publication while living in Florida.

"Catherine, any revelation as to what got you into your— your dark state?"

An almost imperceptible shrug. "My usual overreacting and intensity, I guess. Also trying to play God with my family. The controlling mother syndrome, as my son would say."

"And being a perfectionist?"

"Yes, that fits."

"Do you think you're changing?"

Catherine tensed slightly. "I have always had high standards for myself and every member of our family. Even as a young girl I would listen to my father's sermons, knowing when his points were weak. I agonized when I felt he hadn't done his best.

"It was the same with Peter Marshall. He had a tremendous gift for communication, but I knew when he had not done enough preparation for a sermon. That's when I began to help him with research. I'm always straining for the best, in myself and in others. It hurts me when people do shoddy work. I tend to take it personally."

"I hope you never change, Catherine. Your quest for excellence shines through all your books. You get the absolute maximum from your talent. But how much can you— should you—transfer this to those close to you?"

"I know what you're getting at, Len. You think I'm too hard on Linda and Chester and Jeff."

"Yes, you're tough on them. More so than I. It used to bother me a lot. I didn't feel enough of your love went along with this toughness. I'm beginning to change my mind about this, however, and you need to know this."

"In what way, Len?"

"The past months have been a real learning time for me, too. In looking back at my first marriage, I see how I tried to smooth over the difficulties, rationalizing that I was a peacemaker. When his home situation is in chaos, a man tends to seek peace at any price. When you and the others pointed this out to me on Cape Cod last summer, I resisted it. But it's true. In my first marriage I now think I did damage to Eve by not confronting her more. I covered up for her too much, ducked the truth. If a father is obsessed with being a peacemaker, he tends to be overly permissive with his children. I thank God now for the way you came into our family of four confused, bruised individuals and set tough, high standards for every one of us."

Catherine's eyes teared up suddenly. "Len, you don't know how much this means to me. I've felt so guilty at times because I just couldn't manufacture the love I knew you wanted me to feel toward the children. I've never had a problem with your professional standards; I think you know how much I respect your editorial skills. I just hated to see your oh-so-casual approach to disciplining the children."

It was a beautiful moment at the breakfast table. I took her hand, then kissed her.

"I think I know what else you're thinking," Catherine said softly. "It concerns our marriage."

"Your perfectionism has made it difficult at times. My divorce, for example, is the essence of imperfection."

"That's true, Len. I wanted to ignore it, pretend it never happened. That was foolish of me. I let it fester inside."

"But God heals these wounds. He restores. He reconciles."

"I know that, and I'm struggling with all that right now. Forgive me for being the way I am. I can't seem to help it. I need to hear from the Lord. He is guiding me in so many ways now. I'm sure He'll give me His word about this, too."

Catherine . . . As Len and I continue to arise for worship each morning at 6 A.M. I do feel changes taking place inside me. Since I asked the Holy Spirit years ago to indwell me, then I conclude that He is at work, turning "bad" attitudes there into "good" ones.

Perhaps this is an analogy: It's as if the Spirit within me is the photographer's developing solution. By praising Him I have ceased fighting bad situations, so that these "negatives" can be bathed in the divine solution. Once bathed, the "negative" turns into the "positive"—black turns into white—and lo, we have a beautiful and acceptable picture.

Relinquishment is the key here. Certain evils (negatives) need to be turned over to God through praise so that He can work His powerful chemistry on them.

Paul told us, "Most gladly therefore will I rather glory in my infirmities" (2 Corinthians 12:9).

An "infirmity" can be interpreted as anything that bugs us persistently. For me, insomnia. It need not be a big thing, just something we live with day after day, but never seem to get on top of in our own strength. The healing can begin when we praise God for it. The words of a familiar hymn can start the process:

> *When morning gilds the skies,*
> *My heart awaking cries,*
> *May Jesus Christ be praised!*
> *Alike at work and prayer,*
> *To Jesus I repair;*
> *May Jesus Christ be praised!*

Tr. by Edward Caswall, 1814–1878

I was shaken this morning while reading the eleventh chapter of Paul's letter to the Romans. Three sins of which I have been guilty during the Amy Catherine ordeal:

(1) *Not trusting Jesus.* There was soul force in my determination that the Lord was going to heal Amy Catherine. I need to dig in on this: Why my almost frenzied take-charge attitude during those crucial days? *I did not trust Jesus.* I did not want anything but that the baby be completely healed. I was blind to the work Jesus was doing in the others: Pam, Linda, Jamie, Scott, Virginia, Len, and, of course, Peter and Edith.

(2) *Not valuing His grace.* I entered the Christian life by grace, but have had trouble living my life on that basis. Instead, I keep falling into the trap of thinking that being accepted and loved by Jesus depends on how I measure up. In turn, I relate to other people on the same basis.

Linda nailed me on this last summer. "Your love for me seems to depend on my performance. If I'm good there is acceptance; if I'm bad, rejection." All I can say to that is, "Ouch!"

(3) *Not abiding in His kindness.* What depths of meaning in the words *abiding* and *kindness!* Just the steadfast, constant love, the positive, simple, homespun kindness of Jesus. When will I learn to abide?

The ultimate statement of the inscrutability of God is made in these verses:

Oh, what a wonderful God we have! How great are his wisdom and knowledge and riches! How impossible it is for us to understand his decisions and his methods!

For who among us can know the mind of the Lord? Who knows enough to be his counselor and guide?

And who could ever offer to the Lord enough to induce him to act?

For everything comes from God alone. Everything lives by his power, and everything is for his glory. To him be glory evermore.

Romans 11:33–36, TLB

This morning I'm an hour late in getting up. Len is in New York. The temptation is to make it 7 A.M. from now on instead of 6. Would love that extra hour of sleep. What about this, Lord?

No answer. I guess I don't need an answer. The original word from Him stands. Starting at 7 A.M. cuts short my time with Him. I want You, Lord, more than I want sleep.

This morning before our prayer time I walked into the yard and over to the roses. An urge came over me to kneel in the dew-sparkled grass and bury my nose in the flowers' fragrance. My heart seemed to explode with, "Thank You, Lord, for such beauty! Oh, how it feeds my spirit!"

In my devotion times I find my mind still coming up with verses from old hymns. What a treasure lies in great words that have been sung millions of times by millions of people! What healing power!

Often just a single line of an old hymn will come to mind. I write it down and wait to see if the Holy Spirit gives me the whole verse. Sometimes He does. If not, I search out the rest of the words in my collection of old hymnbooks.

There is therapy in this for me, because as I look through these old hymnals additional verses jump out at me. I sit down and read them over and over. God is planting them in me to help my spirit grow. Like this one:

> *My hope is built on nothing less*
> *Than Jesus' blood and righteousness;*
> *I dare not trust the sweetest frame,*
> *But wholly lean on Jesus' name.*

> *[Refrain:] On Christ, the solid rock, I stand;*
>   *All other ground is sinking sand,*
>   *All other ground is sinking sand.*

> *When darkness veils His lovely face*
> *I rest on His unchanging grace;*
> *In every high and stormy gale,*
> *My anchor holds within the veil.*

Edward Mote, 1797–1874

I underlined the words *When darkness veils His lovely face I rest on His unchanging grace.* Here are the words that fill my cup. I need to repeat them over and over until they are deep in my unconscious. Then when the next crisis, or time of darkness, or merely His silence, comes, I have something to draw upon.

It is raining this morning, so Len and I are inside listening to the raindrops pelt our roof. We need the rain, Lord, so thank You for the moisture that will sink into the earth and nourish our flowers and fruit trees.

Gratitude wells up inside me, Lord, that Your Spirit, too, is sinking into me, Your words nourishing the roots of my being.

Here's a song I haven't sung in years. It spells out exactly how my spirit is being revived:

> *For the beauty of the earth,*
> *For the glory of the skies,*
> *For the love which from our birth*

Over and around us lies:
Lord of all, to Thee we raise
This our hymn of grateful praise.

Folliott S. Pierpoint, 1835–1917

A feeling rises up inside me that little trickles of praise
are now running together, merging, beginning to form a
small river of praise. It began mechanically, yet now has
increasingly the feel of spontaneous emotion.

Slowly but surely my mind is being cleansed. Rich,
beautiful, positive words are taking over, chasing away the
negative ones. I am being filled with Your light.

Lord Jesus, how radiant and glorious is that light of
Yours! Yesterday afternoon You gave me a glimpse of Your
Kingdom that I cannot reflect on even now without tears of
gratitude.

I was seated in a chair in the living room alone, thinking
about all that I have been learning these past few months. I
did not fall asleep, so this was not a dream. Nor was it an
ethereal, other-worldly "vision." It seemed real, as real as
the fabric on the chair, or the Florida sunlight pouring
through the windows, or the trilling of a mockingbird in a
ficus tree outside. Suddenly I felt the living presence of
Jesus. What joy to have this again in my life!

"We're going on a journey," You told me.

Soon we were in what seemed to be a large and impressive throne room. Crowds of people lined the walls on all
sides. As we walked the length of the room approaching
One whom I knew to be God the Father, I spotted in the
crowd those I love who had gone on before: my father; Peter
Marshall; my grandson, Peter Christopher—now not a
baby, but a curly-haired five-year-old. Crawling delightedly
about his feet was a bright-eyed one-year-old I recognized
as Amy Catherine.

Then I looked down at myself. To my horror I was dressed in rags—torn, unwashed, filthy. How could I bear to stand before the Father, the Lord God omnipotent, clothed so vilely? When we stopped before the Throne, I could not even look up. I had never felt so unworthy.

In the same instant, Lord Jesus, You spread wide the voluminous robe You were wearing, completely covering me with it. "Now," You told me, "My Father does not see you at all, only Me. Not your sins but My righteousness. I cover for you."

Then I was aware again of the living room and the chair where I had been sitting—and of inexpressible joy and gratitude washing over me.

Sleep

Catherine . . . That magnificent "journey in the spirit" last week prompts me to step out in greater faith and trust. It is time to confront an old enemy—sleeplessness. My remedy for this in the past has been sleeping pills. And even these do not always work. I've gone through a real agony of spirit about this.

Finally, before I went to sleep the night before last, I was promised that Jesus would speak to me regarding this. He did. It happened while I was standing before the kitchen sink last evening after dinner.

"Do it [ditch the pills] for love of Me. Sleep is probably your most cherished possession. Therefore, lay your cherished possession on the altar. Make this your alabaster box of ointment poured out for Me."

I had already, that afternoon, promised Him that I would do whatever He asked—so, of course, I will. It's one of the biggest steps I have ever taken.

This is a day to praise God. For I did it: flushed the sleeping pills, more than $50 worth of them, down the john. Then I spent two hours trying to sleep yesterday afternoon, just lying there on the cot in my study, tossing and turning in a state of inner terror. Of what I do not know.

It's been a week of sleepless nights, exhausted days—and always that nameless fear. I prayed about it and the answer came: "Make a list of the positive things you accomplished last week."

I did so, a good list of steps taken, drawers cleaned, clothes given away, and so on. My mind tends to veer off on another track, however, thinking of the long, wakeful hours, resenting the fact that God has not rushed immediately to my rescue during these torturous times. But then the counter-insight comes: "I want to do more than handle your sleep problem. You're demanding an instant miracle in one area. I want a healing of the whole woman."

This will undoubtedly include things undreamed of at this moment. But I do know that it will include a real cleansing of my subconscious. So much debris, so much negativism, so many fear thoughts, so many thoughts of nonacceptance by God have piled up.

Tomorrow will be the one-week anniversary of this pill-dumping adventure. But because I've slept so little during this time, it seems more like a month.

Last night was the worst night of all when I was truly desperate and in tears. This morning the Holy Spirit dropped a single phrase into my mind: Blessed assurance, Jesus is mine. . . .

I recognized it as the beginning of the old Gospel hymn. I went to my hymnal and reviewed the rest of the lines:

> Blessed assurance, Jesus is mine!
> O what a foretaste of glory divine!
> Heir of salvation, purchase of God,
> Born of His Spirit, washed in His blood.
> This is my story, this is my song,
> Praising my Saviour all the day long;
> This is my story, this is my song,
> Praising My Saviour all the day long.

Fanny J. Crosby, 1820–1915

After singing these words several times, I understood the Holy Spirit's message: Settle down to knowing that you are accepted by the Father, by Jesus, and by Me. Be assured of Our love. Rest in it.

After another night of sleeplessness these words from the 121st psalm:

> My help cometh from the Lord,
> which made heaven and earth.
> He will not suffer thy foot to be moved:
> he that keepeth thee will not slumber.

verses 2–3

How comforting to know that God never sleeps in His watchfulness over us. If we are awake, so is He, never wearying in His constant care. And another thought this morning: As long as I "battle" for sleep, it will not come. For sleep must be essentially a giving-up process and my releasing myself to it.

Lord, this morning I am astonished and delighted with the variety of words You bring to my mind, songs and

poems I memorized years ago but thought I had forgotten.
Here is the verse You gave me today:

> O God, I cried, no dark disguise
>   can e'er hereafter hide from me
> Thy radiant identity!
> Thou canst not move across the grass
> But my quick eye will see Thee pass,
> Nor speak, however silently,
> But my hushed voice will answer Thee.
> I know the path that tells Thy way
> Through the cool eve of every day;
> God, I can push the grass apart
> And lay my fingers on Thy heart.

Renascence, Edna St. Vincent Millay, 1892–1950

Lord, You are indeed a "radiant identity"!

This morning I must deal with a prophecy I received
some time ago in my prayer group. I confess my reluctance
to follow through on it. It was that I must allow myself to be
"hid with Christ in God" (Colossians 3:3). I read about this
admonition years ago in one of Hannah Whitall Smith's
books, and avoided it then, too. I must have been afraid it
would mean my being wiped out—that if I were "hid with
Christ," I, as a person, would be no more.

Today I'm convicted. For what my reluctance means, of
course, is that *I want the world to see me, not Jesus.*

So I confess to You this morning my divided will on this.
You know how much I have loved being with You, talking
and listening. But I confess that I find being hid completely
by Your cloak and Your personality difficult. I've enjoyed
the world's acclaim, reveled in my "own" success. This
desire to be noticed and admired has been going on since I
was a teenager—and before.

So will You take the part of my will that still wants "fame

and fortune" in this world and tame that kicking child part of me? Will You make me all of one piece so that I'm willing, even eager, to be hid with and in You? I hereby not only give You permission to do this, but I ask You to do it.

And I do now—by faith and with gratitude—accept the forgiveness and the "hiddenness" that You held out to me in that vision of Your Throne room.

Thank You that when I am hid with You, standing before the mercy seat of the Father, it is a Throne of mercy and not of judgment.

Thank You that You, Lord Jesus, are willing to—and do—stand for me before the Father, so that He does not see my sins and failures at all, but only You.

Thank You for hiddenness. Make it complete and lasting, so that the sweet freedom of forgiveness will be lasting, too.

Following my confession of last week about my reluctance to be "hid with Christ," I had an extraordinary Communion experience today in church. In a moment of pure faith and illumination, I was able to take the bread and wine, believing that Jesus Himself, His physical body, His attributes, the essence of His being, were flowing into me, was becoming an integral part of me. During that exhilarating moment I was truly lost in Him.

The fact that I had said yes to Him last week in an all-out assent of my will must have made it possible. In thinking back through the years, I have said yes to Him many times. I see now that this is the way it must be, given our egotistical natures, bending our will to Him over and over.

This morning I'm grappling with an old enemy, fear. Just when I seem to be winning one battle, something else happens to defeat me.

I've tried to keep my mind on You, Jesus, praising You for the renewal of our relationship. Then I keep feeling this lump on my right side. It has been there for over a month now. The doctor isn't much concerned, seems to think it's just fatty tissue. "If it doesn't go away in a few months, come back and we'll look at it again," he told me.

Len and I have prayed about it, but it hasn't gone away. Now I'm battling perhaps the oldest enemy I have.

All my life I seem to have had a problem with fear. My mind goes back to the sessions Peter, Edith, Len, and I had last summer on the Cape, trying to trace the roots of fear back through the generations. Clearly we got only a start with this.

This morning I keep repeating over and over again, "Faith overcomes fear." That has helped. Then I focus on this verse, repeating it over and over:

> For God hath not given us the spirit of fear; but of power, and of love, and of a sound mind.
>
> 2 Timothy 1:7, KJV

The Writer _____

*C*atherine . . . It is almost 8 A.M., Lord, and I seem to have fallen back into the pit again. Len is in New York and I've had a miserable night. It must have been 4 A.M. before I fell asleep. Then I slept through my 6 A.M. rising alarm.

The main reason for my heaviness this morning is my manuscript *Gloria*. It has had more lives than a cat. I've buried it and then resurrected it so many times.

Recently I gave it a new look as a nonfiction book, a suggestion from an editor at *Guideposts*. Len was skeptical because of Gloria's unpredictable marriage situation. But I spent several weeks doing resuscitation work.

At 5 P.M. yesterday, I telephoned Gloria and for a few minutes chatted with her about the project. Then came the bombshell: "Catherine, my present plan is to go ahead and use the new no-fault Florida divorce law to terminate my marriage. I won't be accepting any engagements after the first of the year because I know how some Christians feel about divorce. But the marriage is over."

So after four years' work, endless hours of recorded interviewing, and the expense of transcribing all that—300-plus pages of manuscript written in three versions—this time we tell Gloria goodbye and finally bury her. Once again others have been right, while I've been wrong.

Lord, I need help to get over this death!

Another factor in my spiritual decline this past week is this lump in my side. Yesterday Len and I went to see the doctor about it. He said that if I had to have a lump in my body, this was the kind to have, a cyst in the fatty tissue. Once again he said he thought it harmless. But of course, he added, you never know for sure until you operate. He suggests I have it removed as a hospital outpatient under a local anesthetic.

I am puzzled as to why with all our praying about this, we have not been able to get it dissolved or absorbed by prayer. It's apparently not a big problem in any case. Doctors consider it about on a par with having wisdom teeth cut out. So far, the only word from the Lord I've been able to hear is that it does not matter in this instance whether I rely on doctors or not. By which He, too, must be telling me that the cyst is harmless.

Yet it is a negative that weighs down my spirit.

This morning I am back again at my 6 A.M. arising. Last week when I repeatedly flunked the 6 A.M. test, nothing went right. I need this morning time with You, Lord. These words now penetrate my darkness, but I do not know the source:

> *Thank You, Lord Jesus,*
> *for the mysterious mind of man*
> *that can think*
> *and retain memories,*
> *that can plan ahead*
> *and question*
> *and put ideas together—*
> *new with old, for that is creativity.*
> *Thank You for the beating of my heart,*
> *so that I am still alive on this earth;*
> *for the mysterious mechanism of breathing;*
> *for ears to hear the birds*
> *trilling their greeting to*
> *the morning outside my window.*
> *Thank You for darkness that turns into day.*

Special words, Lord, as I begin all over again to learn how to praise You and trust in You.

I'm beginning to understand why it is so important that I begin my recovery period early in the morning with praise. There is a progression here that I'm slowly perceiving.

First, the time of day is crucial. In the early morning we are freshest in body, mind, and spirit. There is the freshness of the day itself. It is quiet. Fewer distractions and voices to jam the wavelengths between us and the Lord.

Jesus always seemed to be up and about early in the morning. It was His favorite time. He sets the pattern for us.

Second, I'm discovering that praise is the only valid taking-off point for prayer. We have to establish the connection between us and the Lord before we can ask Him for anything in faith. Only worship can establish this connection. And worship begins with praise—praise that focuses our attention on the beauty and love and saving power of Jesus.

I'm indebted to the Holy Spirit for teaching me this. He did it through bringing to life for me one of those little vignettes or snapshots tucked into the pages of the New Testament. This one was of the time Jesus and His disciples sought overnight lodging in a Samaritan village and were turned away. When His disciples asked Jesus to bring down the fire of heaven upon these villagers, He rebuked them:

> "You do not know what manner of spirit you are of. For the Son of Man did not come to destroy men's lives but to save them."
>
> Luke 9:55–56, NKJ

I've recently been in the same mood as Jesus' apostles. My "righteous" indignation has been directed toward the officials of a church who have been most insensitive in dealing with a troubled woman.

Then the Spirit led me to that story in Luke. Such gratitude rose in me that Jesus never falls into the negative traps we do! Always and always He remains the Savior, staying immovably on the saving side—always constructive, always upbeat, always creative. No wonder He is the only One worthy of our worship!

In the days that followed I had only to let my spiritual eyes glimpse this snapshot again, and the praise would rise. In turn I discovered what a boost this gave to faith. Small prayer requests were answered during those days grounded in praise. There would be throughout the day the delicious feeling of no out-of-jointness, of my life all in alignment.

Third, the Holy Spirit showed me that I was constantly being trapped by one of Satan's oldest tricks: looking at the problem instead of at Jesus and His power. I had listened, really paid attention to Old Scratch's suggestions, for example, as to how difficult it would be for me to get going again on another book after the *Gloria* fiasco. I got to thinking that this was going to be the most difficult prayer God ever had to answer. The reasons *why* I couldn't do it seemed so massive, so logical.

The Comforter told me that all of this had been Satan's technique for discouraging me unduly and that I must never fall for this temptation again. Here again, it is my joyful praise that thwarts the enemy and negates his sly suggestions.

The Spirit
of Control _____

You have been speaking to me, Lord, about my children
and grandchild. In the early morning times You have been
showing me quite firmly that *they are not mine but Yours.*
You love them far more than I ever could. You loaned them
to me for a season. Now I am to take my possessive, managing hands off—strictly off.

This is never easy for me. I have tried to be involved in
my son Peter's life and family. Peter and Edith resist this,
though sometimes they need me and call for me, as they did
a year ago with the Amy Catherine crisis. But I see now I

went too far in that situation; took too much of the burden onto myself; even presumed to assign blame for the outcome, deciding that Amy Catherine's death was Peter and Edith's fault for allowing the liver biopsy, or the result of the group's lack of singleminded prayer power. God has shown me unmistakably over the past year that He is sovereign over our flawed nature!

When I first became stepmother to Linda, Chester, and Jeff, I did not have the love for them that I did for my own flesh and blood. But a surprising thing has happened the past few months. I feel myself yearning for a closer relationship with each of them. This is Your doing, Lord.

The other morning came the crowning touch. I was reading in the Psalms when suddenly these words leapt from the page:

> The Lord will perfect that which concerneth me: thy mercy, O Lord, endureth for ever: forsake not the works of thine own hands.
>
> Psalm 138:8, KJV

I could—and did—claim this promise promptly and with such rejoicing! You will perfect my children and grandchildren in Your way and in Your timing. Years ago You began this work. It is Your business to complete what You start. You have promised that You will. I've claimed and accepted this promise. It's as good as done. My heart is rejoicing. Weights and weights have been lifted from me.

Today this verse is given to me:

> . . . God who began the good work within you will keep right on helping you grow in his grace until his task within you is finally finished.
>
> Philippians 1:6, TLB

And to top it off, the Holy Spirit is reminding me that "Jesus is the Author and Finisher of our faith." Of course! The Finisher!

Praising You is the key to letting You get on with the job.

I need to record here how my morning times of praise have opened my heart in a new way. The Lord has been leading me to certain passages of Scripture to teach me things about myself that in the past I have not wanted to hear.

One of the most quoted sections of Scripture is the thirteenth chapter of 1 Corinthians. I have not wanted to face up to the truth it expresses:

> Charity suffereth long, and is kind; charity envieth not; charity vaunteth not itself, is not puffed up, doth not behave itself unseemly, seeketh not her own, is not easily provoked, thinketh no evil; rejoiceth not in iniquity, but rejoiceth in the truth; beareth all things, believeth all things, hopeth all things, endureth all things. Charity never faileth. . . .
>
> 1 Corinthians 13:4–8, KJV

Perhaps the biggest point of contention between Len and me in twelve years of marriage has been my unloving attitude toward Linda. I knew I was in the wrong here. God pointed it out to me early in our marriage when we were living in Chappaqua. Because Linda was willful and stubborn (qualities I recognize in myself), I became judgmental toward her.

Then came that memorable moment in the Chappaqua Congregational Church so many years ago. The winter sunlight was coming through the tall windows. I even remember that we were sitting on the right side of the church. The Spirit said so clearly, *If you can't love Linda, you can't love Me.*

A devastating statement! Queer about love . . . is it then of one piece, so that when we deliberately withhold it from any single human being, we deny love itself and, in the end, are rendered incapable of loving?

My attitude about Linda during her early teens was—all right, Lord, since You say I must, I'll go on forgiving her for her deception and for her poor grades that, to me, were incomprehensible for a girl with an IQ of 169. I would forgive her, but love her? Impossible! We can't manufacture love, can we? Toleration and politeness were as far as I could go.

The real problem here, of course, was my will. I wasn't willing to let God give me the gift of love for Linda, or to let Him love her through me.

Many times I've asked myself, What's behind the inability of a parent to love a stepchild? It's widespread in our society, and as divorces multiply, it becomes an increasing problem. I've heard experts on family life talk about stepmother/stepdaughter relationships as though there is almost a chemical factor here that causes jealousy, resentment, friction. It's been said that different generations are always in understandable conflict. And that whenever two broken families are merged, relationship problems are inevitable.

I'm sure there is truth in all this, but that does not let me off the hook. The Spirit of God can work miracles in all these situations. He has shown me that my arrogance and pride in my own opinions go hand-in-hand with my being a very controlling person. That means that I try to play God with husband, son, stepchildren, other relatives, even with friends. So highly do I regard my convictions, pet theories, and tastes that when anyone resists them, I become angry and resentful, even to the point of turning against that person.

This is what happened between Linda and me. I really had not wanted to do anything about it until a year ago on Cape Cod. A start was made when I confessed to her my "elder brother" attitude and we hugged each other. But it was only a beginning.

Now the Spirit is showing me that this root of bitterness toward Linda, no matter how much I went through the motions of forgiving her and releasing her from my judgment, was poisoning other relationships—especially with Len. Nay, even more it was rendering me incapable of loving anyone, even the Lord Himself.

Charity endureth all things. That spells it all out for me. So in Len's presence—the Lord stressed that I was to do this with him—I got down on my knees this morning, confessed all this, and asked God to give me the gift of love for Linda. I don't know how or exactly when He will achieve this, but achieve it He will. Nothing could be more in line with His will.

The Spirit is continuing to teach me about control. I need to understand, for example, the difference between the parental authority that is approved—established—by God, and the tendency we have to dominate our children in the wrong way.

I can see that when parents have a *spirit of control*, our children feel this and react against it, even when they haven't consciously analyzed the problem. A case in point is Jeff and the advice I gave him (in a spirit of control) regarding his choice of courses this year in prep school. He resisted some of my suggestions and I reacted emotionally rather than objectively.

The Spirit pointed me back to the years of my girlhood in Keyser, West Virginia. I was undoubtedly a peculiar, introspective child, not a good mixer, lacking in social graces. In the early grades I got my satisfaction from proving how superior I was in schoolwork, pulling down excellent grades. When I was a teenager, while others were beginning to date, my lack of social adjustment became more obvious.

It was to this period that the Spirit pointed me. He asked

me to repent of the way I had justified my lack of popularity by retreating even further into my "superiority."

So this morning I've had to renounce the lie that I ever was, or ever will be, "superior" to anybody. Then I was told to accept and embrace the truth that of myself I have no value, that what I achieve or what I amount to depends on the degree that Jesus is allowed to live in me and work through me.

What the Spirit showed me is almost a lifetime of the Pharisaical attitude: "Lord, I thank Thee that I am not as other men." No wonder I have been super-critical and judgmental! No wonder I have sought to be controlling! No wonder I have not been able to express love to others.

Len has a constant hunger to get close to me, to see into my thoughts, to have a deep togetherness. I have resisted this because I have always been a solitary person.

The other morning when I was being shown that I not only had to be willing to love Linda but to be more open to Len, I wanted to make this confession to Jesus alone. But Jesus said, "No, do this before Len. You have to begin to make your prayers *real*. There's no other way except the kind of honesty that bares your soul to another human being."

When I did, it was not as difficult as I anticipated. Afterward, I felt as if I had had a spiritual bath and cleansing.

Now this morning, in retrospect, I have further insight about this: If I will continue to make my prayers real in this way, the glimpses this will give Len into my innermost heart will supply him the emotional satisfaction of togetherness that he so craves. Has not my ghastly sense of superiority, even toward Len, resulted in my wanting my "real" communications with Jesus alone, thus making my prayers with Len shallow and phony, and shutting him out? He has felt this deeply and reacted with resentment.

Could it even be that one of the reasons Jesus withdrew Himself from me was to force me into a closer relationship with Len?

Relinquishment _____

*V*irginia Lively ... In the spring of 1972 my daughter Linda called me with wonderful news. She was fairly bubbling over the phone. "Mom, know what my problem has been all these years? Low blood sugar. I can do something about that!"

I was overjoyed. It was the answer to my prayer on the beach that morning on Cape Cod six months earlier. All those years Linda had had a severe case of hypoglycemia. How well I remembered scolding her for eating nothing but doughnuts and a cola drink for breakfast! Now, as she began drinking milk (which she'd always hated), cutting out sweets, and eating balanced meals, her mysterious symptoms disappeared, one by one, until she was completely healed.

Lord, when I placed Linda's healing in Your hands—and took my own anxious ones off—how swiftly and sovereignly You acted!

Catherine . . . I have something else to praise God for this morning. After waiting and hoping for months now that the lump in my side would dissolve, and after bombarding it daily with prayer, yesterday I went to the doctor for surgery. The lump was removed in a simple and painless procedure. The fatty tissue was examined and found not to be malignant.

This morning I also began using my concordance to trace the words *light* and *darkness* in Scripture. In the process came the discovery that God uses both for His purposes:

> I form the light and create darkness. . . .
>
> Isaiah 45:7, NIV

> He made darkness his covering, his canopy around him. . . .
>
> Psalm 18:11, NIV

> If I say, "Surely the darkness will hide me and the light become night around me," even the darkness will not be dark to you; the night will shine like the day, for darkness is as light to you.
>
> Psalm 139:11–12, NIV

As I arise early each morning for praise and prayer, the "dark" of my experience is revealed as God's loving provision, just as much as the days spent in the sunshine of His blessing.

Reading Agnes Sanford this morning about the drama of the Garden of Eden, and Adam and Eve being required by their Creator *not* to eat of the tree of the knowledge of good and evil, has started a train of thought in my mind. . . .

The food we eat provides the building blocks out of which the tissues of our body are made. In the same way, what we "eat" via our thought and imaginative life provides the building blocks out of which our souls and spirits are built. They are either nourished and grown in the knowledge and love of God, or else they atrophy and die.

God means for us to look at the good, the beautiful, the true, the pure.

But how can we do that when all about us in the world is full of evil and pain?

The answer Agnes Sanford gives confirms what I've been learning elsewhere these past months: Learn to look steadily at Jesus Christ. Jesus points out to her the areas of the world—the issues or persons—about which He wants her to pray on a given day. Then not only does He keep her informed of all that she needs to know about these particular situations (thus becoming for her the knowledge of good and evil), but also this knowledge does not depress her mind or hurt her body in the way the continual absorption of evil tidings across the board can hurt the rest of us. Agnes Sanford is doing something constructive about specific evils rather than simply bemoaning and wallowing in negatives.

The Lord is teaching me something every day about myself. Some of it has been painful. I see ever more clearly how off-the-track I was in the summer of '71, wanting to play God with Amy Catherine, rather than take the lower seat at the banquet table (Luke 14:7–11) and watch God in action.

Now the clear insight comes to me that the undying ember underneath my guilt over marrying a divorced man is not so much that I disobeyed one of God's laws (no such lofty remorse), but rather that I have set for myself the God-playing role of always having to be right. I keep giving an order to myself subconsciously that I must never make a mistake with a major decision. It's really sheer egotism all the way. What an insight! Lord, thank You. What a fool this mortal has been.

Back to my childhood again. I must be the best. I must get top grades. I must win debates and prizes for speaking. I must never be wrong. This has been my bondage ever since. Those areas like sports and popularity, in which I couldn't be tops—those I left strictly alone.

Then this insight: The true definition of a fanatic is one who is playing God in some arena of life—political, medical, educational, theological, relational. He is certain that his ideas and stand are necessary to "salvation" in his particular domain.

What happens is that Satan hoodwinks all of us terribly sincere folk through his age-old trick of tempting us to act as gods, the sin as old as Lucifer of usurping God's place. This, of course, leads to all kinds of excess, taking oneself too seriously, coming to believe that one is indispensable. Thank You, Lord, for exposing me as one of these misguided fanatics.

Len and I had been trying to find a time to be with Tom and Debby, a young couple having trouble in their marriage. I contacted Debby by phone; she suggested Saturday morning. I had a conflict, so we came up with Sunday afternoon, if it checked out with Len.

"Is Sunday afternoon okay to meet with Tom and Debby?" I asked him.

Len grimaced. "Not good for me."

"Why not?"

"There's a football game on TV I want to see."

"You put a TV program ahead of ministry?"

Len looked uncomfortable. He had constantly made the

point with our children that any TV-watching came second
to activities in which they participated in person, such as
family outings, sports, or church events.

"Don't Tom and Debby have any other time free?" he
asked me.

Now I was on the defensive. "Yes. Saturday morning."

"That's fine with me."

"Well, it's not for me."

"Why not?"

"I have a date to get my hair fixed."

"You put a hairdo ahead of ministry?"

It really was funny, only neither of us was laughing. Len
had often accused me of giving my hair too great a priority.
He had no understanding of how we women feel about such
things. So we glowered at each other, ending up seeing Tom
and Debby Sunday evening.

Later that still, small voice said, *Ask Len why he has such
resentment about your hair appointments.*

I did. He responded with vigorous denials of any resentment. As we talked I realized that my hair appointments
were not the issue. Our relationship for the past few years
was the issue. The Lord was trying to tell me something
here.

As a result I've begun praying harder for answers to my
questions about our marriage.

One morning soon afterward, Len and I were sitting up
in bed having our morning prayer together, when out of
Len's mouth came an insight, a word that was clearly not
his at all, but the Lord's.

I cannot recall the exact words Len spoke, but the essence was this: "In every onward step in the Christian's life,
you can only come to the Lord *as you are.* You learn that
first in connection with salvation itself. It's the same with
each subsequent step, because everything you receive from
God is a gift—unearned, solely by grace."

This spoke directly to my current concern with Christian growth. But the further lesson for me was: *God had spoken through Len.* Clearly, God was saying to me through this: "Your criticism of Len has been off-base and displeasing to me. It's the same spirit that Michal had when she looked down on King David [2 Samuel 6:16]. It's dangerous to your spirit. Cut it out."

Then this dream the other night. In it several of the stones had come out of the engagement ring Len gave me before our marriage thirteen years ago. I was sifting through a box half-filled with sand and bits of debris, hunting for the diamonds and the sapphire that is the center stone. At last I located the gems.

The next morning as I was pondering the dream, I reached these conclusions: Despite the debris in our lives, God has brought good out of our marriage and will continue to do so. More pinpointedly, marriage to Len might well be God's tailor-made human situation to correct what is wrong in me.

Thus as I recognize God's hand in our marriage (and I have increasingly resisted this during the past few years), I am now able to praise Him more genuinely and enthusiastically for my situation. This darkness, too, will be turned into light.

New Life _____

Catherine . . . This morning, Lord, I need to be with You, listen to Your words, drink in Your wisdom. So much has happened to me recently that I can hardly absorb it all. I know now that You didn't leave me during that long, dark period last year. You withdrew for a while to let me grow up a bit.

In a few days I'll be sixty years old. Some months ago I faced this milestone with gloom and foreboding. I was like those melancholy men who came to see me after Peter Marshall's death and told me that my financial picture was very bad, that I would have to sell the house, the car, and find a job in an office somewhere. I was 34 then and refused to accept this verdict. Instead I began to put together a book of Peter Marshall's sermons. This gave God an opportunity to activate in me His gift of writing. This launched a new career—and a new life—for me.

Today I hear You saying that as of right now I'm to stop playing the role of those gloomy men who put limits on what God can do in my situation. God is telling me that I am poised on the edge of another new life now at age sixty just as surely as I was at 34. "Believe in it," He says. "Believe in Me. Open your eyes and see My invisible chariots standing all around you to rescue you and move you on your new way."

This morning I can feel my next writing project groping for its deep roots, thrusting down in search of the life-giving water at some deep level in my being. Bit by bit, stroke by stroke, I watch the chapters emerging on such subjects as praise, forgiveness, healing, the move of the Holy Spirit.

The creative process is a little like the bulbs one plants that must begin their growth in the dark for a time. Even the formation of the earth began in darkness. What a different perspective this puts on the dark night I've so recently emerged from. For the first time I'm beginning to understand how the saints could praise God for this experience!

I've shared this project with Len, who is enthusiastic and has already come up with a title for the book: *Something More.*

November 30, 1973 ... Unexpected news from Edith and Peter! Edith is pregnant and expecting a baby next May. We'd understood that in view of the heartaches with Peter Christopher and Amy Catherine, they'd decided not to try again. And they did not. This pregnancy is strictly unplanned; neither Peter nor Edith can figure out when conception took place. Thus, how else can we take this except as an "act of God"?

May 4, 1974 ... Last Saturday at about three in the afternoon Peter Jonathan Marshall was born. Weight: eight pounds, thirteen ounces. I have never heard Peter so excited as he was over the telephone. "Mom, you have a grandson! He's normal. Perfect." Praise God! How can we find words in the English language adequate to express our joy and thanksgiving?

Jonathan means "gift of God."

God knew that if this baby had been defective, there was no fight left in us. It would have been too much for us to bear.

I've never heard Edith so bubbly and happy as when she described the baby. As she studies his little face, she sees features and characteristics of all the children, especially the two deceased babies. She reports that he has Peter Christopher's beautifully shaped head and chin; Amy Catherine's mouth; Mary Elizabeth's large eyes. It's as if God is saying, "See, I am giving you all the babies in one beautiful, perfect baby."

At his church service the day after Peter Jonathan was born, Peter read these selections from the 66th psalm:

> You have purified us with fire, O Lord, like silver in a crucible. You captured us in your net and laid great burdens on our backs. You sent troops to ride across our broken bodies. We went through fire and flood. But in the end, you brought us into wealth and great abundance.
>
> Now I have come to your Temple with burnt-offerings to pay my vows. . . .
>
> Come and hear, all of you who reverence the Lord, and I will tell you what he did for me. For I cried to him for help, with praises ready on my tongue. He would not have listened if I had not confessed my sins. But He listened! He heard my prayer! He paid attention to it!
>
> Blessed be God who didn't turn away when I was praying, and didn't refuse me his kindness and love.
>
> Psalm 66:10–20, TLB

September 24, 1980 ... Another joyous family event—
David Christopher Marshall was born to Peter and Edith;
weight, nine pounds, three ounces. Normal and healthy in
every respect.

It was Virginia Lively who heard this message: *This
child will not live. But any other child they have they may
have in perfect confidence.*

Thank You, Lord, for blessing our family so richly.

Afterword _____

*L*en . . . Catherine came out of her dark night experience with greater maturity and a new creativity. The result was a flow of articles, books, and teachings on the deeper walk. Her books published in the next ten years would include *Something More, Adventures in Prayer, The Helper, Meeting God at Every Turn*, and the novel *Julie*.

The experience was life-changing for me, too, in several ways. In 1974, after much internal agony and struggle, I listened to the Lord about a career change. Trying to be the full-time editor of *Guideposts* while living in Florida was hurting my marriage, making me a divided person, and shortchanging the magazine.

After 28 years at *Guideposts*, I resigned and waited for God to guide me. He did—into Christian book publishing. Catherine and I became partners with John and Elizabeth Sherrill of a company we named Chosen Books, which went on to publish most of the titles listed above, plus other bestsellers like *The Hiding Place*, *Born Again*, and *Life Sentence*.

In addition to writing regular articles for *Guideposts* up to the time of her death in 1983, Catherine and I jointly taught a class on the Christian walk for seven years at our Presbyterian church in Delray Beach, Florida. Later, with Pastor George Callahan, the two of us helped start the New Covenant Presbyterian Church in Pompano Beach, Florida.

Then in 1979 Catherine was given a vision by the Lord for an intercessory prayer ministry, with this instruction: *There is a great untapped reservoir of people who have the heart for intercession and are not being used. Call them into service.*

This prayer ministry was launched by Catherine and me in 1980 as *The Intercessors*, a part of the nonprofit *Breakthrough*. Today we have nearly 2,000 intercessors mobilized to pray for the needs of people whose letters pour into our office by the hundreds each week. A bimonthly teaching newsletter on intercession goes out to 15,000 prayer partners. (One may receive it without charge by writing to Breakthrough, Lincoln, VA 22078.)

During the last year of Catherine's life, as she was in and out of the hospital, there was a constant flow of family members to her side. It brought tears to my eyes the way Catherine reached out to Linda. The healing between them was complete, the love bonded in eternity.

Catherine and I had rejoiced in 1980 when Linda married Philip Lader, a man with special skills in law and business whose speaking gift reminded Catherine of Peter Marshall, Sr. Both Linda and Phil wanted children, yet years passed without a pregnancy.

Then there was our last visit to the Lader home in Hilton Head Island. One morning after Phil had left for work, Catherine received guidance that she, Linda, and I were to kneel by the Lader bed and pray that a conception would take place—in that very bed.

In March 1983 Catherine passed away. When Phil was named president of Winthrop College two months later, the Laders rented out their Hilton Head home and moved to Rock Hill, South Carolina. Soon Linda, as the president's wife only twelve years after her own college experience, was amazing me with her poise and organizational skills as she served as a hostess and model to young people on campus.

On February 2, 1985, Linda and Phil called me with great elation to announce that their first child had just been born: Mary Catherine Lader, named after Phil's mother and Catherine.

Catherine, not only do you have a namesake, but as it turns out, Mary Catherine was conceived on a visit back to Hilton Head, in the very bed you prayed over!

On June 17, 1987, a sister was born to Mary Catherine—Linda Whitaker Lader—Whitaker for Catherine's mother, Leonora Whitaker (Christy) Wood. Leonora passed away quietly and beautifully in her sleep on February 19, 1989, at the age of 97.

In August 1980 Chester married Susan Scott, a talented interior designer and tennis player he met while he was a student at McCallie School, a prep school for boys in Chattanooga, Tennessee. On May 8, 1981, Jacob Leonard LeSourd was born; on September 18, 1983, his sister, Hadley Johnson LeSourd entered the world.

At the time of Catherine's death Chester was an English

teacher and tennis coach at McCallie. In a moving and memorable talk in the school chapel, Chet honored Catherine for her tough but prayer-centered discipline. "It was the best possible launch pad I could have into adult life," he told the teenage boys.

In October 1986 Jeffrey married Nancy Oliver, a partner in a Washington, D.C., law firm. Jeff opened the marriage ceremony by paying an unusual tribute to his stepmother. He told the church packed with friends and family that it had been his dream as a boy that Catherine would live long enough to meet the girl he would marry. When Catherine passed away in 1983, it seemed his dream would not come true.

Then, while courting Nancy, he discovered that she, like Catherine, was a graduate of Agnes Scott College; that Nancy's mother and Catherine had served together on the school's Board of Trustees; and, best of all, that Nancy, a gifted communicator, too, had been Catherine's special hostess one year at an Agnes Scott alumni gathering. So Catherine and Nancy had met—not knowing, of course, how the future would bring their two families together.

In June 1985, two years after Catherine's death, I married Sandra Simpson, a joyous Christian, budding writer, and mother of three children in their mid-twenties. Sandra's book, The Compulsive Woman, was published in 1987 and led us both into a ministry to compulsive-addictive people. In the process, Sandy and I became aware that God had further healing work for us to do in our own family relationships . . .

Sandy, with her children and their father. And I, with my first wife, Eve.

When Linda called one day in the fall of 1988 to say she planned to take sixteen-month-old Linda Whitaker to visit Grandmother Eve, I found myself saying, "I'll go with you."

Like Catherine with Amy Catherine, I had tried unsuccessfully to understand why God had not healed Eve, who is now in a nursing home, unable to move about except in a wheelchair. All of us had maintained contact with Eve; the children had visited her; we had helped her financially. But it had been almost thirty years since I had seen Eve face-to-face.

When we arrived at the nursing home, Eve was sitting in her wheelchair finishing breakfast. Her body was ailing, but her face was alive, her eyes warm. The meeting was awkward at first, but not for long. Soon we were going back thirty years to reminisce over the good times we had had together.

There was no trace of bitterness in Eve, only gratitude. Gratitude that Catherine had been such a good mother to her children. (In fact, Eve had written to Catherine to express this.) Gratitude that her children had visited her in their adult years. Gratitude that her material needs had been provided for. I was astonished. Eve was blessing us.

We all went to church together and met Eve's friends; in fact, Linda and I were asked to stand and be introduced publicly during the service. It was a dramatic moment, as though we were acknowledging before the world our responsibility for our relationships and giving testimony to God's unlimited power to heal. Before our departure, the three of us held hands and prayed together while baby Whitaker played on the floor beside us. The healing tears flowed as we asked forgiveness for the hurts each one of us had brought on the others.

Later I reflected: Why do we underestimate the Lord's power to transform even the most damaged relationships?

Catherine held off raising the divorce issue in her writings because, although as recorded in her journals, she finally reached a point of peace about our situation, it was never clear to her what the meaning of her experience was for others. She was horrified at the thought that by disclosing the fact that she had married a divorced man, she might seem to be endorsing a practice she abhorred.

Today, when half of all marriages begun will end in divorce, many Christians are questioning whether biblical teaching on this subject is relevant to our times. To me, the dismal statistics seem ample reason for our society to return to scriptural principles regarding marriage and divorce. I was impressed by the total agreement in our family to cover the divorce issue in this book. "Bring it out in the open so people can see the anguish divorce brings," each member of the family concurred.

We also agreed that Jesus was concerned not with legalism, but with our well-being, when He spoke out so forcefully against divorce. Our Father in heaven wants to spare His children the grief, the pain, the spiritual and emotional damage that go with broken family situations.

The final truth is, of course, the forgiving, healing love of our Lord. He is in the business of repairing and restoring broken homes and hearts.

Catherine was His principal agent in my life and those of my children during our 23 years of marriage. She stepped into a chaotic home situation and welded five diverse personalities into a family. It was not a sense of her own adequacy that impelled her—on the contrary, she was all too aware of her shortcomings as a wife and mother. It was the certainty that God was adequate.

Throughout her life, in every tough situation—the loss of her husband, the challenge of single parenting, the death of two grandchildren, the clash of strong wills in a household—Catherine turned to her Redeemer. Even when He seemed farthest away, in the darkness of her own rebellion and alienation, she clung to the simple *fact* of His existence—in the absence of all feeling or evidence.

In Catherine's life He proved infinitely faithful. He longs to prove it in your life, too.

SOMETHING MORE

Something More

Catherine Marshall

Hodder & Stoughton

LONDON SYDNEY AUCKLAND

To

Peter Christopher

and

Amy Catherine

children of the King, now with Him

and to

Mary Elizabeth

and

Peter Jonathan

whom He has loaned to us

CONTENTS

ACKNOWLEDGMENTS

I want to express my gratitude to my long-time editor and friend, Edward Kuhn, Jr., who believes in excellence, hard work, and humility for authors; to Elizabeth Sherrill for sensitive and penetrating critique; to Dr. William R. Felts of Washington, D.C. for information on medical details; to Marguerite Shuster who contributed her insights as well as her knowledge of Biblical Hebrew; to my talented and versatile secretary, Jeanne Sevigny, who has patiently typed and retyped manuscript with unflagging enthusiasm; to Emma Mulrean and Frances Orgain who also helped with last-minute typing; to my husband Leonard LeSourd for many constructive suggestions and for being always an honest and discerning sounding-board.

Finally, to all the friends who through the pages of this book have been willing to share so generously of their innermost joys, sorrows, and victories, I offer my deepest appreciation.

C.M.

FOREWORD

The other day I pulled a copy of my book BEYOND OUR SELVES from the bookshelf and was startled to note again its date — 1961. Thirteen years! It scarcely seemed possible!

Writing it seems like only yesterday. Yet there have been so many changes that the thirteen years might have been fifty. For the world of the 'seventies is very different from the world of the late 'fifties and early 'sixties.

My personal world has seen changes too. In the Foreword of *Beyond Our Selves,* I wrote,

> Just at the point when I thought child-rearing was over, Len's three children have joined Peter John in calling me 'Mother' ... A man swimming a horse across a turbulent stream does not stop to take a picture of the experience. I'll get my colts across the stream, see them thoroughly dried off, well fed, and on their way — then perhaps the picture.

Well, it has happened. The colts are on the far bank. Jeffrey, a tot of five when I wrote *Beyond Our Selves,* is now a senior at the Mcfallie School. Chester is a junior at Taylor University. Linda has graduated from college and has a job with Cornerstone, a Christian organisation, in Washington. Peter John and his wife Edith minister to a lively, bursting-at-the-seams congregation at East Dennis, Cape Cod.

At times during the crossing, the stream was rough, the current swift, the wind shifty. Yet these thirteen years have been exhilarating, a learning process all the way. The pages that follow are not a photograph album of the crossing, but here and there snapshots are tucked in.

The setting of our lives has changed from Chappaqua, New York to the east coast of Florida with frequent stops at Evergreen Farm in Loudoun County, Virginia where my mother, after whom I modelled the heroine of my novel *Christy*, still lives, delighting in organic farming and conservation and enjoying her family and friends who come to her from all over the world.

The involvement of first, Peter John Marshall and then Linda LeSourd with facets of the rebellion of the young, together with the death of two grandchildren have forced me to re-examine my faith, groping for ever-surer foundations.

At farther range, the rapidly changing world scene creating its own uncertainties, has challenged the tensile strength of our faith. In the early 'sixties most nations were still full of hope. Surely, we thought, progressive education and our expanding social consciences would gradually eliminate the problems of society? As the dark side of human nature was educated out and away, together with the marvellous advances made possible by scientific knowledge, a golden age, Utopia, would eventually emerge.

Now we are in a position to see clearly that the progress we hoped for has not been achieved: we are not golden men living in a Utopia. Violence and crime have risen to new heights. The home and family units, the chief crucible from which our stability and creativity should have come, are a shattering vessel.

The present generation looks with sceptical eyes on both education and science and refuses any longer to regard either as a god. Standards of ordinary truthfulness, honesty, unselfishness, reverence for life, cherishing children, sexual morality previously accepted by past generations (even when individuals did not themselves measure up to those standards), are now under serious attack as not being necessarily desirable.

Situation ethics have got us into increasing difficulty. Moral and sexual perversions are being flaunted in books and motion pictures, with crusades mounted to make the perversions 'legal'. Superstitious practices involving witchcraft and the occult have reappeared from the subterranean depths in which they had lain since the Middle Ages and are quite literally courting the devil. Confusion reigns.

Principles, laws, institutions, positions of trust on which we have depended for structure, are crumbling all around us. Over most of the world a leadership vacuum has left man feeling rudderless with a sense of betrayal. Fear seeps like dank fog across the earth creating suspicion and mistrust, damaging relationships, and raising the spectre of economic disaster.

Where do we turn for help in times like these? Is there nothing on which we can depend?

A long time ago when Roman civilisation had also reached an impasse because of its corruption and state of decay, one small group of people who were certain they had the answer, called themselves followers of 'The Way'. They were disciples of a Jew named Jesus who had been executed about the year A.D. 29 in an obscure province of the Empire under the Roman governor Pontius Pilate.

'Seek a new way' ... The Way, they called it.

But is it really? If the way advocated by Jesus is the way for us today — then why hasn't it worked? Why hasn't Christianity eliminated poverty and war and brought us the good life? Because we have still never tried Jesus' way. Not enough of us. Not on a large enough scale.

Could it be that His way contains an answer that we have almost completely overlooked? Perhaps the reason we haven't found the answer all these centuries is that all the while it has lain in that portion of man we have mostly ignored — the spirit. Is it possible that the sole agent who can knit each human being back together, heal the wounds, and bridge the gaps between the heterogeneous elements of society is the one agent neither secular society nor the organised Church really takes seriously — the Spirit? By which I mean a specific: the divine Spirit tabernacling within each man's spirit. The Creative agent in life writ small enough to live within each of us, to work through mind, body, emotions, will, and conscience, not only synthesising them, but demonstrating a new and creative way — The Way — in every one of life's arenas.,

The itinerant rabbi Jesus told us that we — you and I — would be living in the era of the Spirit of Truth.

We have never needed truth so desperately.

The pages that follow offer you experiences from my life and the lives of people well known to me as case histories of what happens in the twentieth century when we say 'Yes' to the Spirit of Truth allowing Him to invade us and lead us out into the light. These are men and women from all walks of life with backgrounds and temperaments as varied as humankind itself is varied. Their experiences come from every aspect of life — where evil· strikes into the lives of 'good' people, in matters of health, family relationships, rebellion, business and money, safety, remorse, resentments, and estrangements.

There are some surprises in this raw material from life. For the Christian the emphasis is usually on the original commitment to the religious life as symbolised by joining a church. Most sermons and religious books do not lead us to expect much to happen spiritually between our 'entering in' and the end of life. The 'rewards' are to come in after-life.

Yet the true stories related here tell us that commitment is only our birth into the new life. Then begins learning and growth. The process of being moulded into a mature person in Christ Jesus becomes more challenging with each year that passes. I am finding that the knowledge of God grows often by means of the very experiences that would sweep us downstream, the turbulence I would prefer to escape.

As we grow older the pace and dimension of physical life must wind down. But it is meant to be just the opposite with the spiritual life — growth at an ever-accelerating pace. The heights and depths of the spirit and enthusiasm for God aren't for children. In the latter half of life, the normal Christian almost breaks into a jog or a run. Excitement and aliveness build. A new quality of joy is given to us. It has little to do with the circumstances of our lives — good or bad — but everything to do with knowing Him who is managing the circumstances. It is joy that has the feel of permanence, even of eternity about it. Deep within we know that nothing that befalls us today or tomorrow can ever defeat that joy.

There are other reasons for the joy too. How great it is to realise, for instance, that the Holy Spirit did not limit His revelations to the truths contained within the canons of the Old and New Testaments. 'I have much more to tell you,' this Jesus told His companions around the table during His Last Supper talk with them, 'but you cannot bear to hear it now. When He, the Spirit of Truth, is come, He will reveal all.'

All — more and more. Always something more.

No matter how late the hour, no matter how desperate the moment, we cannot despair; the joy and the riches He has promised us stretch like a shining road into the future!

CATHERINE MARSHALL

BOYNTON BEACH, FLORIDA
MARCH 4, 1974

CHAPTER ONE

YES, GOD IS IN EVERYTHING

At last we were safely airborne. December winds buffeted the little Cessna 205 four-seater as if it were a helpless leaf tossing in the vastness of the sky. There was room only for the pilot, my son Peter, his wife Edith, and me. Directly behind Edith and me was the baby's casket — so tiny with a spray of pink rosebuds atop it. It was the casket of my first grandchild, Peter Christopher Marshall, who lived for only two weeks. The special flight was the only way we could make it that day from the funeral service in West Hartford, Connecticut to the graveside service at Fort Lincoln Cemetery outside Washington.

Inside the plane the noise shut out conversation. Pictures kept intruding on my thoughts. So much had happened in only fifteen days ... Peter's first telephone call on December 3rd, 'It's a boy, Mom.' But his voice was not as excited as a man's should be over his first child. Then it came. 'Something's wrong, Mom. "Poor muscle tone," the doctors say.'

Lung congestion had followed, the threat of pneumonia. That Sunday Peter had crawled in under the oxygen tent to christen the baby Peter Christopher — 'Christ-bearer' or 'light-bearer'.

I remembered that morning in Florida thirteen days later when the inner release to go to Connecticut had finally been given me. The message had been so clear, 'Go — and crown My prince with thanksgiving.'

Then that seemingly interminable three-and-a-half-hour

delay at New York's Kennedy airport. Something was happening to the baby. I could feel it. Later I found out: Peter Christopher had stopped breathing; he had turned blue, then stony white. Loving hands had been laid on the baby in prayer and miraculously, he had begun to breathe again.

But not for long enough.

Sitting there in the bumpy little plane with the roar of the engines and the shriek of the wind in my ears, I could shut my eyes and remember my first glimpse of my grandson — pink and normal looking, that perfect round head with its suggestion of blonde hair.

I had wanted to cuddle him — but first, I must do what He had told me to do. So there in the hospital room we offered up our sacrifice of thanksgiving, crowning His little prince with His own blessing.

Thirty-five minutes later, the young doctor had spoken. Simply, 'He is gone.'

Lord, I don't understand. When Peter Marshall died Your sure word to me was that 'goodness and mercy would follow me all the days of my life.' Lord, is this goodness and mercy?

Scarcely a person but knows similar earthly partings or heartache or loss. The mail I read day by day dramatises our shared human plight: the young wife who had received one of those dreaded telegrams from Vietnam: 'Killed in action'; a grandmother struggling to save her grandson from drug abuse; a husband with an alcoholic wife; a doctor's verdict of terminal cancer; a fire that destroyed one's home and possessions; a business man cheated by a dishonest partner; a marriage breaking up in disillusionment and bitterness.

'How can God permit such things to happen?' is the cry that rises from our hearts. If He exists at all and is a loving God, He would not want such evils to befall us. Yet how could He be God and not have the power to prevent these disasters? These are the most difficult of all questions for those embarked on the Christian walk. Certainly, for me this problem of evil has been a real stumbling block.

In my groping to understand, back in the 'forties, during a long illness, I 'discovered' a body of Christian literature unknown to me. It was experiential, the true personal experiences of other people. Compared to most church literature which I knew so well — largely theory — this was exciting reading. I gobbled up everything that A. E. Simpson, Glenn Clark, Starr Daily, Rufus Mosley, Frank Laubach, Rebecca Beard, Dorothy Kerin, Roland Brown, and later on, C. S. Lewis and Agnes Sanford wrote. In addition, I began to search out the journals and letters of some who lived in other eras — Brother Lawrence's *Conversations*, John Foxe, John Wesley, Hannah Whithall Smith, George Müller, Evelyn Underhill. These journals and letters proved a rich mine of personal experience.

I recognised that the experiential approach had firm New Testament precedent. For example, when John the Baptist sent messengers to Jesus to ask if He was really the long-awaited Messiah, Jesus' response was not a theological discourse. Instead, He pointed John to His miracles — the healing of all manner of disease, of the blind, the deaf. These facts were the evidence.

And I remembered the ringing words of Jesus' apostles to those who would silence them, 'We cannot but speak the things we have seen and heard.'[1]

But thrilling and helpful as those books were, there was one chapter in Hannah Smith's *The Christian's Secret Of A Happy Life* over which I had stumbled. Able to accept and profit from all the rest of Hannah's book, my rebellion was violent against chapter twelve entitled 'Is God in Everything?' I asked myself how God could be 'in' the death of a three-year-old who wandered into the street in the path of a truck? Was God in War? In cancer?

The answer that welled up inside me was a resounding 'Certainly not!' Further, I even considered such submissiveness wrong — when Christians, confronted with such tragedies, intoned, 'Then it must have been God's will' ... and piously quoted old harassed Job, 'The Lord gave, and the Lord taketh away; blessed be the name of the Lord.'[2] To me this seemed an especially cruel and offensive form of piety.

But despite myself, there were two bits of Hannah's chapter twelve that stuck to my mind like glue. The first was an illustration. The author related how at an informal prayer and sharing meeting one night, a woman had risen and told this story ...

She had been much troubled by the seeming contradiction of a God supposed to have all power in heaven and on earth versus human instrumentality or 'second causes'. It seemed to the woman that stubborn, evil mankind was always messing up God's perfect plans. So she had pleaded with God to set her straight on this question.

The result had been an interior vision:

She thought she was in a perfectly dark place, and that there advanced towards her, from a distance, a body of light which gradually surrounded and enveloped her and everything around her. As it approached, a voice seemed to say, 'This is the presence of God! This is the presence of God!' While surrounded with this presence, all the great and awful things in life seemed to pass before her — fighting armies, wicked men, raging beasts, storms and pestilences, sin and suffering of every kind.

She shrank back at first in terror; but soon she saw that the presence of God so surrounded and enveloped herself and each one of these things that not a lion could reach out its paw, nor a bullet fly through the air, except as the presence of God moved out of the way to permit it.

And she saw that if there were ever so thin a film, as it were, of this glorious Presence between herself and the most terrible violence, not a hair of her head could be ruffled, nor anything touch her, except as the Presence decided to let the evil through. Then all the small annoying things of life passed before her; and equally she saw that there also she was so enveloped in this presence of God that not a cross look, nor a harsh word, nor petty trial of any kind could affect her, unless God's encircling presence moved out of the way to let it.[3]

So for this woman (and subsequently for Hannah Smith too), one of life's most thorny questions was for ever settled: God is in everything. The events of our lives do come to us, moment by moment as from His hands, no matter how evil the instrumentality or second causes may appear to us to be.

The acceptance of this principle, Hannah Smith asserted, was the only possible basis for the Scriptural admonition (repeated over and over — Old Testament and New) 'In everything give thanks; for this is the will of God in Christ Jesus concerning you.'[4] And 'everything', she insisted, did mean everything — bad things as well as good.

It was Hannah's warning that unless we do accept God in an all-inclusive 'everything' we can know no contentment. In that case a life of faith and victory becomes a romantic mirage. For how can we accept or give thanks for what is less than good, or even evil, if we do not believe that God's shielding Presence has deliberately stepped aside to allow those forces to get to us? Even more, that His purpose in stepping aside is for good — not evil?

Well, the matter may have been settled for Hannah Smith. But not for me. I could not understand her explanation fully. I convinced myself I was hanging the matter on a hook for further consideration. Practically speaking, this was simply rejection.

But surely few are as stubborn as I! I held out on Hannah

Smith's thesis from 1945 until 1972. Twenty-seven years!

In those twenty-seven years a great deal happened including the worst I could imagine: on the morning of January 25th, 1949, with only a few hours' warning, my husband Peter Marshall slipped over into the next life.

For the first week, I was supernaturally carried over and above grief. Then inevitably, I fell to the bottom of the pit asking 'Why? Why?' Even — 'Have I been mistaken to put my faith in God? Has everything I've ever believed been wrong?'

In essence, my husband's death at only forty-six had thrown me squarely back once more against Hannah Smith's assertion that God *is* in everything — either to accept or refuse it . . .

> What is needed is to see God in everything, and to receive everything directly from His hands, with no intervention of second causes . . .
>
> An earthly parent's care for his helpless child is a feeble illustration of this. If the child is in its father's arms, nothing can touch it without that father's consent, unless he is too weak to prevent it. And even if this should be the case, he suffers the harm first in his own person before he allows it to reach the child. If an earthly parent could thus care for his little helpless one, how much more will our Heavenly Father . . . ![5]

But I was still not quite ready for that 'completely restful' life of the spirit. Perhaps my mind, always questioning, always seeking the answer to 'Why?' got in the way of the deeper life, the longer view.

I did understand and could accept the difference between God's ideal will and His permissive will. For the Creator refused to make His creatures puppets whose strings He could manipulate to force us to obey. He took the risk of giving us free will. Therefore, men are sometimes going to go their own stubborn way, bringing unhappiness, grief, and horror into human life. Upon those occasions, God 'permits' the disobedience. Thus the permissive will of God is a fact of our life on earth.

In Peter's case, I am certain that it was not God's ideal will that he die of coronary occlusion at forty-six. Why then, did God 'permit' it? I had some clues, but not the final answer.

In the meantime, I forced myself to stop asking 'Why?' and face stark reality: I was a widow with a young son to rear without his father. So what was I to do next? What was God's ideal will for me right then?

Lovingly and surely, I was taught one of the greatest lessons any of us can ever learn. In essence, it could be summarised like this ... Sin is in the world. And sin is 'missing the mark', missing God's perfect plan. There is so much of this missing the mark that it is going to impinge on every person's life at some points.

If God left us with only this, real happiness or victory in this life would be an impossible mirage. But the Gospel truly is good news. The news is that there is no situation — no breakage, no loss, no grief, no sin, no mess — so dreadful that out of it God cannot bring good, total good, not just 'spiritual' good, if we will allow Him to.

Our God is the Divine Alchemist. He can take junk from the rubbish heap of life, and melting this base refuse in the pure fire of His love, hand us back — gold.

Out of that understanding I was led to claim for my personal crisis and for my young son, the promise that for me, is gold:

> And we know that all things work together for good to those that love God, to them who are called according to his purpose.[6]

The results of this claiming were amazing. Gently and tenderly, God brought to my mind the teenage dream of wanting to write. 'Now is the time,' I seemed to hear God saying. 'Go forward and I'll open the doors before you.'

The words soon became fact. The first venture was my editing some of Peter Marshall's sermons. This became *Mr. Jones, Meet The Master.* I was hard at work on it within six weeks of Peter's death. A year or so later, thousands of people were reading Peter Marshall's words. Clearly the Lord was telling me, 'Catherine, your job is to spread his message.'

From that time the path has gone on and on through my delight in the editing and writing of eleven books. Of course, the 'good' that God, the Alchemist, worked for me has gone far beyond merely a satisfying career as an author. Blessings have been heaped upon me, including eventually, eleven years after Peter's death, marriage to Leonard LeSourd and the challenge of taking on a new family — Linda, Chester, Jeffrey. The new family responsibilities in addition to my writing have taken all my resources of physical and spiritual strength and have given back a full life.

There have been many joyous experiences. Like that when my granddaughter Mary Elizabeth Marshall was born. On the second day of the baby's life, the head nurse on Maternity had bounced into Edith's room. 'Of all the babies I've seen born in this hospital,' she announced jubilantly, 'yours has the greatest muscle tone!'

'It was like a direct message,' Edith told us later. 'That nurse didn't know about Peter Christopher. It was like the Lord saying, "See, I've handed you a special joy. I've heaped it up." '

My cup overflowed . . . The total rapture of a one-year-old as she received her first doll . . . The fun of painting Christopher Robin and Pooh Bear figures on a little girl's bedroom furniture, of reading to her and watching understanding grow and unfold.

In the midst of such joy it seemed to me that I could forget Hannah's challenge: that God *is* everything, good and bad. I left it on the hook where I had hung it years before. I still wasn't convinced.

Then in 1971 a family crisis brought it to the forefront again. On July 22nd of that year, a third child was born to my son Peter John Marshall and his wife Edith. It was apparent from her birth that Amy Catherine had suffered severe damage to internal organs because of some unknown genetic difficulty. Medically speaking, there was no hope.

The family decided that we could but pray in total faith, asking for a miraculous healing. We were joined by Peter's congregation on Cape Cod, by a group of sixteen who flew in for days of intensive prayer in a retreat situation, and by many, many others. If ever a family went out on the end of a limb of faith, we did. As for me, not since Peter Marshall's first heart attack had I thrown everything I am and have, every resource of spirit and mind and will into the battle for a human life.

Meanwhile, the sixteen people gathered there were experiencing in the space of a few days extraordinary answers to prayer: one of the group prayed for a little girl on the same floor with Amy Catherine at Boston Children's Hospital and later found that the child's miraculous recovery had begun that day; our daughter Linda experienced a cataclysmic reordering of her life lifting her out of darkness and confusion into a new beginning; our friend Virginia Lively was given the key to her daughter's health; a woman's life, blighted twenty years before, which no amount of prayer, counselling, and psychotherapy had alleviated, was lovingly restored; a man's resentment against his father, festering since childhood, was healed; a floundering marriage was made right again.

It was as if the baby Amy became a divine catalyst, calling forth a concentration of God's power and love for others.

After the retreat, I stayed at the Inn near Children's Hospital in Boston while Peter and Edith took turns keeping the vigil over Amy and driving back and forth to Cape Cod to be with Mary Elizabeth. Day after day we sat beside the baby who was stretched out on a slanting 'Heat Bed' under a big light. Amy was hungry and would open her mouth expectantly like a baby bird, yet she was too weak to suck; she had to be fed intravenously, the seemingly endless tubes sticking out in all directions.

'She needs to feel loving arms,' my heart kept telling me. Finally, the nurses assented and one morning carefully placed her in my arms, tubes and all. She cuddled up, nuzzling me. After that it became a ritual, and I was holding our baby only minutes before her heart stopped beating. Amy Catherine's time on earth had been but six weeks.

Had I long before received the truth of 'Is God in Everything?', I could have endured Amy's death in the spirit in which I had accepted Peter Marshall's. But the years of non-acceptance had taken a larger toll than I knew. I fell on my face. There followed months of rebellion against God, sharper questioning than ever ... 'What can we believe about healing through prayer?'

I experienced the most intense misery I've ever known. Life went grey. Nor was it all psychological or spiritual. Events in the exterior world began going against me. Things like: a major Hollywood studio purchased my novel *Christy*, then decided not to produce it. The fiction manuscript on which I was working was presenting problems so great that I began to see that after pouring myself into the manuscript for three years, I was going to have to suspend work on it. An almost wild succession of small, vexing personal inconveniences came on in waves: the dishwasher went out; the bathroom plumbing went awry; a truck driver backed into our mailbox and demolished it; the lawn developed chinch bugs; the car kept stopping cold on us.

> 'When sorrows come, they come not as single spies,
>   But in battalions!'[7]

wrote Shakespeare. It is true. Trials do have a way of piling up. The question is — why?

Once again I was brought back to Hannah's thesis. If we don't accept the circumstances God's permissive will has allowed, and ask, 'Lord, what is Your will for me in the midst of these circumstances?' — then He permits the difficulties to heap up. For most of us that's the only way He can get our attention.

In my misery He had my attention all right. Obviously, I was meant to turn off my grumbling and wait upon Him. I was to listen and to learn.

Finally the words of truth began to break through ... 'His loving allowance for us' ... 'Must see all of life as coming directly from His hands.' Hannah Smith again! After twenty-seven years of rejecting her!

To explain the evolution of my belief to that moment when I knew that I'd made connection with the transcendent power of God, I must backtrack briefly. When still in my twenties a lung condition had put me to bed. After a year and a half of the four walls of my bedroom, desperation had set in. Every other way medically and spiritually had failed me. I had been forced to the Prayer of Relinquishment, 'I stop demanding anything. I want only what You want for me, whatever it is.' There I had touched the hem of His garment and found health. And is not relinquishment very close to the 'acceptance' Hannah wrote about?

Yet I had been puzzled, as had others, about a seeming contradiction between relinquishment and praying with faith. For how can we pray 'Thy will be done, whatever it is, even unto death' and mean it, and at the same time have faith for healing?

Suddenly, it was as if a searchlight played upon my own experience of relinquishment[3] to illumine it for me further. Having ascertained through reading of the four Gospels that God's will is for health (as Satan's is on the side of disease,

death, and destruction), I had felt myself to be in accord with
God's will in asking for healing. I loathed the idea of disease
and of being sick and had self-righteously set myself not to
submit to illness. Thus in my mind there was the sharpest kind
of dichotomy between on the one hand, disease and sickness — the Destroyer's territory, and on the other, wholeness of
spirit, mind, body — God's kingdom.

Yet back in 1943 a year and a half of asking on the basis of
that dichotomy and of 'believing' to the limit of my ability
(what I thought was faith) had resulted in — nothing. The
reason was, I perceived now, that God would not allow me to
get well *until I saw Him even in my illness.* Disease is of
Satan's kingdom, but God had allowed it for me. Blame it on
Satan, I might, but see God *in* it, I must. He would hold me at
that point until I did.

He held me firmly right there, until out of desperation, I
bowed to Him. That was all He required. I had dropped my
human 'reasoning' — the basis of my authority in asking — and
had laid everything, including mind and emotions, at the feet of
the Creator: He had taught me through hard experience that as
His creature, I had no authority of my own. When I finally
acknowledged that, He raised me up speedily.

I realised then what I'd really been saying to Him. 'I'll keep
a certain amount of rebellion and pin it to a good cause (against
disease).' Then I had added with due piety, 'Of course, God, I
only insist on this because I know it's Your will.'

But God's reply had never varied. 'You can't insist on anything. I will not let you harbour rebellion for any cause. Lay
your arms down.'

I had also been guilty of a Pharisaical stance in relation to
my understanding of prayer, healing, and the like — a fearsome
trap laid for those who have done their homework by reading a
lot of books, attending many meetings, complemented by a
minimum of experience. I cringed as I saw myself alongside

that Pharisee in the temple,[9] standing and praying with myself, 'God, I thank thee that I am not as other men are. I've done so much reading and thinking and praying. I have more understanding than most of them.'

My situation was perfectly set forth in this incisive statement in Romans 1: 21:

> Because that, when they (rebellious men) knew God, they glorified him not as God, neither were thankful, but became vain in their imaginations, and their foolish heart was darkened.

No wonder God had been unable to 'justify' me! No wonder I couldn't hear His voice at all until I had deposited my 'understanding' along with my 'proper rebellion' at His feet. Then I heard (I don't know about other people, but He doesn't always speak to me in King James's English), 'You did read the Gospels correctly about healing. But the important thing is not whether your ideas are right. Learn this: you can't trust in your own understanding any more than you can trust in your own righteousness. I am offended by even one odious whiff of spiritual self-exaltation.'

Thus it was that the searchlight playing on my healing through relinquishment lighted up some ugly facts about myself. I saw that previous to being willing to bow before God and worship Him, lifting only empty hands, I had been steadily refusing to recognise the totality of God's authority in my situation. God *is* in everything — even illness.

I recognised better what Hannah had meant by God being 'in' everything. Further, new light was shed on one of Jesus' teachings in the Sermon on the Mount:

> Are not two sparrows sold for a farthing?
> and one of them shall not fall on the ground
> without your Father.

> But the very hairs of your head are all
> numbered.
>
> Fear ye not therefore, ye are of more value
> than many sparrows.[10]

The Greek word for 'without' (verse 29) is a strong word implying more than sympathy or even empathy. I was told by those knowledgeable in New Testament Greek that this word 'without' can be used not only as 'without the knowledge or consent of' but also as 'without the Father's *participating presence*'.

Then I was given an insight on a facet of Jesus' teaching that had before now escaped me — His identification with every human being in trouble. The Gospel accounts show Him with a passion for helping those in trouble. He has not changed! The minute we need saving from anything, He stands ready in His role as Saviour.

He illustrated this identification in a variety of ways to show us that it is a real fact of our world ... When we minister to someone hungry or poverty-stricken or ill or in prison, we are ministering to Him.[11] When we persecute others, we persecute Jesus.[12] When we receive and welcome one little child, we receive and welcome Him.[13] Frank Laubach has put this in a memorable way, 'At the centre of every need He stands pleading with us to help Him as He moves to help others.'[14] He is not only 'in' trouble and sorrow, but is there in a particular way — to have dialogue with us, to teach us, and then to rescue us.

Putting this together with the Sermon on the Mount passage, Jesus was telling us that since not even one insignificant sparrow can perish without the knowledge and consent of a loving Father, and more, His participating presence (since He stands waiting at the centre of every need), then we should have no fear. Each of us is infinitely precious in the Father's sight, so much so that He knows every detail about us, even to the number of the hairs on our head.

Therefore, nothing can happen to us without His knowledge, His consent, and *His participating presence* as Saviour. All of that Hannah had meant by God being 'in everything'.

Now, so many years later, God had given me this new insight to illuminate the heartbreak of Amy Catherine's death. Once again, I had been making the same errors: once again, I had been leading with my 'understanding' that it was surely God's will to heal an innocent baby. As before, I saw Satan's work all over the physical problem, the tiny, genetically-damaged body. And just as steadily, I was refusing to see God 'in' the situation at all. So I had been attributing Amy's death to the combined factors of our failure in prayer plus the power of evil. Seeing it that way, I had not been able to receive the baby's death as from God's hands in a greater scheme of things not yet given to me to understand.

It was a shock to realise that as a result of this defective thinking I had actually ascribed more power to evil than to God. To the mind of Jesus, as consistently portrayed to us in the Gospels, this would be unthinkable. For any one of us to believe that His Father could be frustrated or vanquished by any rival power, would surely call forth His sad, 'O ye of little faith! How long must I bear with you?'

Nor is this the viewpoint of the Gospels alone. Like a great bell tolling and tolling over all the land, deep-throated, its echoes ringing in our ears, the consistent voice of the sovereign power of God reverberates throughout Old Testament and New. He is the God of the supernatural — omnipotent, omnipresent, omniscient in this life and the next. We cannot believe this and also think that our God is no match for the evil of the world.

Yet even believing in God's power doesn't help in our crisis situations if we cannot also believe that He wants to help *us*. Frequently, we hear people say, 'I know God has power — but "if it be His will" to use it . . .' Like that Leper who pleaded with Jesus, 'Lord, if You choose, You can make me clean . . .'

Jesus' ringing response leaves no doubt: 'I do choose. Be clean.'[15] And Jesus is the portrait of God. Here is the One who leaves the ninety-nine sheep safely in the fold and goes out after the one lost lamb — because He cares.[16] By every word and deed, Jesus made it clear that His Father not only cares, but that no detail of any life is too insignificant for His loving providence.

The accounts of Jesus' miracles portray Him working out His Father's love for each man, each woman, each child. He went about demonstrating the Father's delight in restoring deranged minds to sanity, sight to blind eyes, hearing to deaf ears, the joy of unfettered motion to the lame and the paralysed; in satisfying hunger, dispelling pain, curing diseases of all sorts — no matter how far gone or how hideous.

So often the styluses of the Gospel narrators etched the word 'compassion'. No wonder! In Jesus they had encountered a caring of such depth and magnitude, yet often stooping to attend to such minute detail, that language failed them in describing it. He who was the embodied revelation of God had the profoundest sense of the sacredness of human personality of any man in history. The Galilean's tender love for any human being in misery or pain or need is the Gospels' eternally true message about God. In the eyes of Jesus today, our Contemporary Lord, no set of facts in any century should ever shake this central core of truth about the character of His Father.

Yet as the twentieth century has progressed, men have found the truth that God cares about each one of us increasingly difficult to believe. We need to be searchingly honest here. As children of a scientific age, we have grown up indoctrinated with the concept of a mechanistic universe. Machines have all but taken over our everyday lives. The individual has come to feel lonely. Is anyone at home in the cosmos? Perhaps God *is* dead. And machines are not much company.

To loneliness is added helplessness. The individual feels like an all-but-worthless cog in the machinery of huge industrial bureaucratic nations. No wonder we find it a long leap from our century's framework of thinking to Jesus' sure teaching about the Fatherhood of God.

Yet whenever we are emboldened to accept and act on Jesus' revelation of the Fatherhod of God, always and always we find solid ground beneath our feet.

With a love and patience beyond imagining, God brought me slowly back step by step to take a fresh look at Hannah Smith's thesis, at what's wrong with grumbling about our lot in life — even baby Amy's death — and at the relinquishment that brings such miraculous results. He seemed to be saying, 'Now that you're fully persuaded of the value of relinquishment, you're ready for the next lesson. *But relinquishment is only a stopping place on the way to praise. It's as nothing compared with the power of praise.* Now begin to praise.

My thoughts went back to the Apostle Paul's 'In everything give thanks: for this is the will of God in Christ concerning you.'

'You mean, Lord,' I asked, 'that in the midst of tragic circumstances, by an act of will I'm to praise You? How can I make it real? Wouldn't it be just words, almost hypocritical?'

'Obedience means turning your back on the problem or the grief and directing your eyes and attention towards Me. Then I will supply the emotion to make the praise real.'

One early morning not long after Amy Catherine's death I went out on the patio to begin. Hadn't nature always brought me closer to God? Birds sang in the branches of the Fiscus tree in the back yard. The sky was still grey-white with the faintest suggestion of blue. I began to praise that first time hesitatingly, woodenly:

'Lord, I think I'll begin with the small irritations first — that truck driver demolishing the mailbox. Surely, I'm not supposed to thank You *for* that! I can see, Lord, as I talk to You that the mailbox is of no consequence. Looking at You puts petty problems into perspective in a hurry. I can feel Your humour that I took it so seriously. So thank you, Lord, for perspective. Yes, and humour. Thank You for You.'

As I persisted on down the list, another instruction was given. 'Now write down every situation in your life that seems less than good, that you would like to see changed.'

That wasn't hard. I went inside to get my red notebook and a pen and proceeded to fill five pages. But what came next *was* hard: 'I want you to go down the list and praise Me for every item.'

'Lord, I can see praising You for bringing good out of all these things, but I still don't understand how I can praise You for the bad things. Doesn't that make You the Author of evil?'

'I am Lord over all — good and evil. You start praising. I'll supply the understanding.'

Step by hesitant step, I was being led on an exciting spiritual adventure.

CHAPTER TWO

THE GOLDEN BRIDGE OF PRAISE

My first discovery was that I knew almost nothing about praise, neither what it was nor how to praise. Beyond some joyous hymns and a few 'Praise Gods' and 'We adore and worship Thee' with the lips, what then? We Protestants sitting so properly in straight rows of pews staring straight ahead, how can we know how to praise? The subject is mentioned occasionally as a nice worship exercise, a sort of icing on the cake as a gesture to God, but praise as the key to answered prayer, no. That was a new concept altogether.

A short time after I began my amateurish praise efforts with the five-page list, a new book came in the mail one day: *Prison to Praise*[1] by a former Army chaplain, Merlin Carothers. The author's thesis is that God steps in to change unhappy or even disastrous situations in our lives when we thank Him *for the situation itself*. This makes sense only when we see that life as it comes to each of us day by day is our schoolroom. That, in turn, can be true only when we at last understand that God is 'in' every circumstance — good or bad — that He allows to come to us. Growth comes at the point of our hang-ups and problems when we take an active step towards God who stands waiting for us at the centre of the problem. The quickest way to go to meet Him is through praise. No wonder we meet Him there, for Scripture goes on to teach us that God actually 'inhabits' (lives in) the praises of His people.[2]

Carothers concedes that when most people are first presented with the concept of praising God for unhappy situations, they are resistant and even incensed as I was when I was told to offer praise after baby Amy's death. But Chaplain Carothers records incident after incident of miraculous answers to prayer following praise.

There is such a thing as the 'fullness of time' for an idea. Following Carothers' writings on praise, books by other writers on the same subject began appearing on booksellers' lists, such as *Let Us Praise* by Judson Cornwall and *Praise the Lord Anyway* by Frances Gardner Hunter.

The Scriptural basis for this is not only solid but overwhelming, such as:

> Rejoice evermore.
> Pray without ceasing.
> In everything give thanks: for this is the will of God . . .[3]

> Continue in prayer, and watch in the same with thanksgiving.[4]

But out of many such passages,[5] it was the concept of praise as a sacrifice which began to show me the way:

> By him (Jesus) therefore let us offer the sacrifice of praise to God continually, that is, the fruit of our lips giving thanks to his name.[6]

The fact that the word 'sacrifice' is used tells us that the writers of Scripture understood well that when we praise God for trouble, we're giving up something. For sacrifice means 'the surrender or destruction of something prized or desirable for the sake of something considered as having a higher or more pressing claim.'[7] What we're sacrificing is the right to the blessings we think are due us!

We are also sacrificing our human desire to understand everything. Obviously, praising God for trouble makes no sense from the earthly side. Human reason asks, 'Why should I thank God for dark and negative circumstances when He is the Author of light and goodness alone?' So when we bypass our 'right' to understand and offer up suffering to God in praise, the Bible is right in calling this a 'sacrifice of praise'.

When we offer thanksgiving in the face of circumstances such as Habakkuk set forth, that's a sacrifice.

> Although the fig tree shall not blossom, neither shall fruit be in the vines; the labour of the olive shall fail, and the fields shall yield no meat; the flock shall be cut off from the fold, and there shall be no herd in the stalls:
>
> Yet will I rejoice in the Lord, I will joy in the God of my salvation.[8]

The Bible gives us many illustrations of praise being the hinge upon which great events turned. Just one example among many is the story of how King Jehoshaphat of Judah pleaded with God for help when the Moabites joined with the Ammonites to come against his little country. The answer came: Jehoshaphat and his people were to turn their back on their enemies and spend their time worshipping God . . .

> And when he (Jehoshaphat) had consulted with the people, he appointed singers unto the Lord, and that they should praise the beauty of holiness, as they went out before the army, and to say, Praise the Lord; for his mercy endureth for ever.
>
> And when they began to sing and to praise, the Lord set ambushments against the children of Ammon . . . and Moab, which were come against Judah: and they were smitten.[9]

When we turn to the New Testament there are many examples. There was the time Paul and Silas were cruelly

beaten at Philippi and put in jail under maximum security with
their feet chained in stocks.[10]

In this crisis the prisoners gave themselves to prayer, which
is understandable. But to praise? So exuberant did their rejoicing become that it flowed over from words of thanksgiving
into songs of praise.

Praise for what? we might ask cynically. That their backs
were raw and bleeding from the 'stripes' so cruelly laid upon
them! That they were in prison with all the city authorities
against them? That with their feet in stocks, they couldn't even
move around their cell? Thanking God for that? From any
human point of view, it makes no sense. It's foolishness, maybe
even hypocrisy. Foolishness, that is, so long as we are looking at
the human circumstances and not at God.

Paul admits to us that anything about Christ's cross or about
the crosses you and I bear in life is 'foolishness' to the world.
But he had learned that God allows us to have disappointments,
frustrations, or even worse because He wants us to see that our
joy is not in such worldly pleasures as success or money or
popularity or health or sex or even in a miracle-working faith;
our joy is in the fact that we have a relationship with God.[11]
Few of us ever understand that message until circumstances
have divested us of any possibility of help except by God Himself.

It is a stripping process that we experience as we go on in
the Christian life. The process has gone by many names in
Christian literature: 'the dark night of the soul' . . . 'inward
desolation' . . . 'the winter of the soul' . . . 'the way of the
cross' . . . 'the Valley of the Shadow' . . . 'the Dispensation of
Darkness.'

Once we have only God to depend on — as Paul and Silas
had at Philippi — then we can *with joy*, 'draw water out of the
wells of salvation.'[12] We draw out the precious water by rejoicing in Christ, our Deliverer, not in our circumstances or in

anything about ourselves. Not even pride at our wonderful experiences or our faithfulness, or what we've learned, or even our joy.

About midnight, as Paul and Silas, still bruised and bleeding, turned their minds from self and sang their thanksgiving to the Lord, rejoicing in Him, an earthquake rocked the city of Philippi, shook the foundation of the prison, burst the gates and wrenched the chains from the walls. Two other miracles followed quickly. The jailer and his entire household became followers of The Way. And when morning dawned the city authorities in a complete about-face withdrew all charges and bade Paul and Silas 'depart, and go in peace.'

As the former prisoners strode on their way, Paul could exult, 'I have learned in whatsoever state I am to be content.'[13]

Out of such a framework, we would do well to listen to this giant among apostles when he admonishes us to

> Rejoice in the Lord *always*: and again I say, Rejoice ... in everything by prayer and supplication with thanksgiving let your requests be made known unto God.[14]

Just to be certain that we fully understand, Paul carefully details for us some of the difficulties he has undergone in the midst of which he had practised 'rejoicing': official scourgings of thirty-nine stripes — five separate times; three times beaten with rods; stoned once; three shipwrecks; innumerable journeyings in peril of robbers and other enemies; weariness; pain; hunger and thirst.[15] Few of us can match Paul's list.

Even as God asked praise of Jehoshaphat and of Paul and Silas, so He asks it of each one of us. And the longer one ponders this matter of praise and experiments with it, the more evidence comes to light that here is the most powerful prayer of all, a golden bridge to the heart of God. No human situation is too burdensome, no circumstances are too calamitous for praise to bring as marvellous results today as it did then.

Gladys, a missionary in Ecuador, has written me several times. One of her letters related her brother Clem's story. His marriage had broken up after the couple's only child, a three-and-a-half-year-old boy, had died in a drowning accident. Clem was an efficiency expert for an industrial consultant firm, travelling a great deal, usually staying in one place about three months until he could get a particular company's problems straightened out. Yet he was handling the problems of his own life with anything but efficiency; Clem was miserably estranged from God.

Clem's and Gladys' father had died suddenly when Clem was fifteen. Ever since, the boy had been angry at God. Whatever church services she and her brother would attend, he viewed every preacher and every congregation with a critical eye. Gladys had been praying for her brother's change of heart for twenty years. So far as she or anyone else could see, nothing had happened as the result of these prayers. Indeed, a deterioration process was apparent in her brother's life.

Then the Prayer of Praise came to Gladys' attention. She decided to praise God for Clem's life just as it was, believing that God was working in spite of outer circumstances.

Almost immediately a chain of unexpected events began. Clem's employer, based in Chicago, sent him to Seattle on a six weeks' consulting job. There he met some distant relatives who were retired missionaries. He had long talks with the missionaries, finding them easy to confide in. They took Clem to their church where for the first time he found the atmosphere to his liking — warm and friendly and loving.

Then Clem's work in Seattle was over and unwillingly he went back to Chicago. The rest of the story was in Gladys' letter:

Clem decided that he would get right with God someday, but he could do this best in Seattle where the atmosphere was more to his liking.

In the ensuing months Clem consistently put the cart before the horse by trying to solve his problems and *then* he would give his heart to God. Dejection set in.

At last there came an opportunity for him to be in Seattle over a week-end, staying at the home of the same relatives.

On that Sunday morning Clem awoke overwhelmed with the knowledge that Jesus loved him. At a Sunday evening service Clem was also aware that many of the people there were praying for him. That night the pastor asked anyone who wanted to hand his life over to God and to become a follower of Jesus to stand.

Secretly (so Clem told me later) he had told the Lord that he would go forward if the pastor asked. But he would not rise.

After the service, outside in the church parking lot, Clem felt that God was talking to him. 'You have to have your own way even in this? You are saying, "I will accept God on my terms." The terms will have to be Mine, none of yours; or there will be no acceptance.'

Clem drove as rapidly as he dared back to the relatives' home. 'I can't hold out any longer,' he announced as he rushed into their living-room.

It ended up with their shoving the piano bench to the middle of the room to double as an altar. There my brother knelt and handed his life over to the Hound of Heaven who had pursued him for so long.

Gladys' letter ended with these words:

Five months of praising God for Clem *just as he was* was more effective than twenty years of begging God in prayer to rescue my brother.

Or here is another incident . . . Redeemer Temple in Denver, Colorado, is an unusual church. Its worship services are attended by a cross-section of Christians from the main-line Protestant denominations — Lutherans, Presbyterians, Methodists, Disciples of Christ — as well as by Roman Catholics. Many of these worshippers are still members of their own denominations and of a Sunday morning attend an early service in their own church before going on to Redeemer Temple. 'It's because in this church the Book of the Acts is being lived out before our eyes,' one of them told me, 'that we can't stay away.'

As in the Acts a large group in the church has been led to communal living. A group of hippies who had stumbled into Redeemer Temple one Sunday and subsequently had their lives turned right side up, were led to buy a run-down house in the heart of the Ghetto and renovate it as the headquarters of a Christian commune. There at the 'House of Grace' they minister to other hippies. The Redeemer Temple congregation enthusiastically agreed to sponsor and help finance it.

On Sunday, May 17th, 1970, the sanctuary at Redeemer Temple was crowded to the doors. Suddenly a young man sitting in the centre block of pews got to his feet and stumbled down the aisle towards the platform. His appearance suggested that he had come from the hippy commune. Since the services at Redeemer are more informal than most and often filled with surprises, no one reached out to stop the man.

But it was apparent to everyone that he was drunk. 'My name's Clarence,' he announced, his voice thick. 'I'm a man of colour and proud not to be a white, proud to be a Black Panther.' He was waving a black beret aloft.

At first Pastor Lou Montecalvo had courteously stepped back allowing the young man the floor. As it became obvious that this was a drunken speech filled with clichés and memorised hate talk, the pastor walked over to the intruder and put one arm around his shoulders. 'Clarence, you're delivering your speech to the wrong people. We care about you here.'

Gently, the pastor began leading Clarence back towards his seat, talking to him as they walked. 'See all those people out there? They love you, Clarence, not for the usual human reasons, but because they know how much Jesus loves you.'

The congregation was hushed. At the foot of the chancel steps, two ushers took over from the pastor and quietly escorted Clarence back to his seat.

Pastor Lou returned to the pulpit and began the morning prayer. But as he began to pray, the voice of the drunk man in the pew was heard again, muttering and complaining. It was rapidly becoming a duet between the complaining from the pew and the praying from the pulpit.

Then a strange thing happened. All over the church people began quietly praising God aloud. 'Thank You, Lord' . . . 'We praise You for what is happening . . .' First a quiet steady hum of voices, then a harmonious chorus of thanksgiving and praise. After a few moments of this, the chorus diminished again. Finally the voices ceased.

Then everyone saw — Clarence was no longer there, somehow in the midst of the praise he had slipped out of the church. As the people were realising this, a member of the congregation rose. 'I believe that I have a word of prophecy for all of us. It's this . . . "My children, this day I have been showing you, teaching you this lesson. Satan, the enemy, is routed by praise, and only through praise." '

Then he sat back down and Pastor Lou quietly picked up again, incorporating into his prayer gratitude for the tremendous object lesson that pastor and people alike had just been taught. Not long afterwards in the same church, Clarence rose and made a public apology for his behaviour on May 17th. Then he asked for prayer for the Black Panther organisation.

'We know,' one of those who heard him told me, 'that it is only a matter of time until Clarence will have his own personal confrontation with Christ and become one of us.'

It was a sign of the spiritual maturity of the Temple people that they responded to this situation by:

Giving thanks *always for all things* unto God the Father in the name of our Lord Jesus Christ.[16]

'Always . . . for all things' is inclusive. It offers us no loophole, however awkward or irritating the situation, wherein we are not to praise. Even in the relatively minor emergency of an interruption to a worship service, praise wrought its own miracle.

Grim circumstances of quite a different nature faced our Dutch friend Corrie ten Boom and her sister Betsie during World War II in Ravensbruck, the Nazi concentration camp. The sisters had been hauled off to prison for aiding Jews in the Dutch underground movement in their native village of Haarlem.

Corrie is now a vigorous eighty-two, travelling and speaking all over the world. She remains one of the most enjoyable guests who has ever graced our home and has often regaled us with anecdotes of her prison life. One of my favourites is her flea story . . .[17]

At one period of their imprisonment Corrie and Betsie were transferred from crowded cells (where they had been separated for months) to Barracks 28. Within the hour they discovered that their reeking straw bed-pads were crawling with fleas.

'How can we live in such a place!' Corrie wailed softly.

Without answering, Betsie immediately began praying, 'Show us Lord. Show us how.' Then a moment later excitedly, 'Corrie, He's given us the answer! I read it in the Bible this morning. Here — read that part again.'

It was in I Thessalonians . . . 'Rejoice always, pray constantly, give thanks in all circumstances, for this is the will of God in Christ Jesus . . .'

'That's it, Corrie! We're to thank Him for every single thing about the new barracks.'

'Such as?' Corrie was trying to look with fresh eyes at the half-dark, foul-smelling room.

'Such as being together here.'

'Oh, *yes.*'

'And having managed so far to hang on to that Bible.'

'Yes — Oh, yes. Thank You, Lord, for *that.*'

'And for the fleas . . .'

'Betsie, I see no way I can thank God for fleas.'

'But fleas are part of this place where God has put us. "Give thanks in all circumstances," it says. Not just pleasant circumstances.'

So the two women thanked God for the fleas.

As the days wore on the prisoners in Barracks 28 discovered that there was an astonishing lack of supervision or interference. Corrie and Betsie used the unprecedented freedom to talk to the other prisoners, read the Bible to them, minister in myriad ways.

Then one day a supervisor tipped her hand as to why they were given so much latitude. Some of the women had called through the grilled door to ask the supervisor to come and settle a dispute. She refused, as did the guards. 'The place is crawling with fleas,' the supervisor said. 'I wouldn't step through that door.'

Corrie's mind rushed back to their first hour in the barracks and to their rueful prayer thanking God for fleas. When she looked up, Betsie was chuckling, her eyes sparkling, 'So now we know why we were supposed to praise Him even for fleas. Even the fleas had to be His instrument for our good.'

As time has gone on, I have begun to see why praise is such a miraculous key. As we begin our praising in each

circumstance, ever-fresh insights follow. This much I already
see ... Just as a genius in mathematics can skip over many
interim plodding steps to get the answer to the algebra or
calculus problem, even so praise is the genius-shortcut route to
our answer — God. This is because praise is faith in action,
faith in its most vigorous form. When we praise ...

> We are letting self go by turning our backs (through an act
> of will) on the problem or grief where self has been most in-
> volved.
> We stop fighting the evil or less-than-good circumstances.
>> With that, resentment goes;
>> Self pity goes.
>> Perspective comes.
> We have turned our back on the problem and are looking
> steadily at God.
> We are acting out our belief in the character of God — His
> goodness, His love.
> We are acting out our belief in the present power of
> God — in His participating Presence.[18]

We have to experience the delights of it to know what glory
His participating Presence adds even to life's unpretentious
moments. Soon I made a discovery that thankfulness — as
nothing else does — enables us to live in the present moment.
Not often do any of us grasp one shining moment, live fully in
its 'presentness', and consciously enjoy it. I shall not soon forget
one such moment ...

After dinner one evening my mother and I were comfortably
settled in our living-room. Through the room and around us
flowed the music of a fine recording, the London Philharmonic
Orchestra playing Mendelssohn's *Violin Concerto in E Minor.*
As we listened, our hands were busy working on some table
mats that were to be a gift. The singing, soaring melody was a
delight not just to the eardrums but to the emotions.

All at once it happened. My heart overflowed with praise. Silently, I lifted all of it to Him, aware now of His presence . . . *This quiet room, the comforts and the peace of it. No bombs are falling outside. No Gestapo is going to pound on the door . . . By Your mercy and grace, Mother is still with us, the inimitable Christy, so gentle, yet so full of her own kind of ginger. You love her too. Isn't it great that she and I have such rapport that often conversation isn't even necessary . . .! This music, so glorious. It must be pleasing You too. Work for my hands to do, work that I enjoy. You know all about work with the hands. This moment — what delight — what an oasis in the midst of busy life.*

The thankfulness bubbled up and up and still, I had not spoken.

Three evenings later at the dinner table I shared the experience with Leonard and Mother and in the telling, found tears in my eyes.

Then I marvelled that such a quiet, unassuming moment had meant so much. Why, I wondered?

The word 'consciousness' is probably the key to the answer. The thankful heart raised in praise and adoration, verbal or silent, becomes the vessel to hold the sense impressions and the distilled essence of the presentness of life.

In my sorrow after Amy's death, I had been promised that when I obeyed God by beginning to praise, He would show me how and why. Some of the understanding He has supplied has been given directly, some through others. At my request a friend who knows Hebrew and Greek made a study of Old and New Testament verbs and nouns denoting praise. Here are some of the insights which resulted:

An arresting Biblical concept is that true praise and thanksgiving actually blesses and magnifies God; that what we do and our attitudes are important to Him for His sake, not just for ours.

The Hebrew root for 'thank' also means 'to acknowledge', 'to confess'. It is also related to the word for 'hand', probably meaning the gestures used in worship.

Confession of wrongdoing goes hand in hand with praise because it is the other side of God's sovereignty.

Anything but praise attributes more power to someone or something than to God.

Now I began to see how God's Presence can be the catalyst to turn evil events and situations into good ones. We could compare it to the process that a photographer goes through to develop a negative into a beautiful print. (The word 'negative' is intriguing here.) When we hold a photo negative up to a light, all objects are reversed: black is white, white is black. Further, the character lineaments of any face in the picture are not clear.

Once plunged into the developing solution, what photographers call 'the latent image' is revealed in the print — darkness turns to light and lo, we have a beautiful picture.

Even so, we must begin by obeying Jesus' injunction 'Resist not evil'. So we stop fighting whatever form evil is at the moment taking in our life, even as the worshippers in Redeemer Temple did not resist the interruption of a drunken man.

'Resist not evil' however, does not mean mere passivity or submission. That would make us 'slaves of sin', which is hardly what Jesus meant. When we praise by an act of the will, by our own free choice, first we accept present circumstances, then we take up a positive position. By beginning to praise God for the evil, we take our less-than-good situation and plunge it into the photographer's fluid — the Presence of God.

Even as the photographer has to wait while the chemicals in

the solution do the developing work, we too have to wait — meanwhile continuing to praise — while the Spirit does the work. And as we wait and praise, often unable to see any change in exterior circumstances, we understand what Paul meant when he wrote, 'I am become a fool in glorying.'

Paul was right. There are times when praise makes any one of us feel foolish. I remember the pain, the agony of my loss as I resolutely but awkwardly began the Prayer of Praise for my granddaughter Amy Catherine. 'Lord, thank You for being with all of us during those weeks of Amy Catherine's battle to live. You certainly were a participating Presence, else that other little girl wouldn't have been healed, all those other great answers to prayer would never have happened.

'Lord, I see it: There's still a lot of selfishness and introversion in me, or I would be as overflowing with praise for those others getting blessed as I would have been if Amy had been gloriously healed. Thank You for showing me this.' Now the pain was subsiding, the praise flowing more naturally.

'Lord, I see now what You mean about everything that happens being part of the lesson material in Your schoolroom. I really can praise You that You refuse to let us stay children, that You keep insisting on our growing up. Thank You for caring that much about us.

'And thank You most of all that Your love for each one of us goes right on despite our stubborn refusal to understand until You have shown us the light again and again.'

The matter of praise is obviously still one of my growing edges. I am convinced that living at the point of praise and seeking it will lead us to the richest discoveries we have ever made.

CHAPTER THREE

FORGIVENESS: THE AUGHTS AND THE ANYS

Joan is forty-six years old, a successful merchandiser of women's clothing, yet extremely unhappy. She resents her father to the point of hatred because she blames him that she never married. Her father so missed having a son that he pressed Joan into a too-masculine role from childhood on.

Roger, another acquaintance, is sixty, ill with a series of physical problems. He has drifted in and out of undemanding jobs beneath his ability. Roger's heart knows seething bitterness for a business partner who cheated him. Roger was the one who had to pay with a six-months' jail sentence. Constantly he harks back to this so that people do not like to be with him. His face looks so angry that children are always thinking he is mad at them.

In both Joan's and Roger's situation the inability to forgive has built to a point where all the people involved are frustrated and miserable.

Most of us are aware that Christ requires us to forgive. Yet forgiving is not easy when the other person is clearly in the wrong. This is especially true in actions that violate God's and man's laws and the good that God wants for His world . . . The rape-murder of a little girl. Ruthless exploitation of a small country by a large and powerful one. The Dachau extermination camps. Did Jesus mean that we must also forgive evil of that kind? And if He did, how can we?

For years I attached a condition to my forgiveness: if the

other person saw the error of his ways, was properly sorry, and admitted his guilt, then — yes, as a Christian, I was obligated to forgive him. Finally I had to face the fact that this was my fixed set of conditions, not Christ's. For He said, 'Forgive, if ye have aught against any ...'[1] 'Any' can have only one meaning — anybody — everybody — all-inclusive. As for the particular wrongs we are to forgive, Jesus is just as demanding on us there too. His instructions are to forgive 'aught'. The dictionary definition of 'aught' is 'anything whatsoever'. Again, all-inclusive.

The scope and inflexibility of Jesus' teaching on forgiveness staggered me. Obviously I was missing something. Basically, two questions clamoured for answers. Firstly, how can a righteous God ask us to forgive a rapist, an exploiter, or a murderer with blood on his hands? Would not forgiving the unrepentant murderer be the same as saying that all value-judgments are wrong?

Secondly, approaching it from the psychological side, Jesus, we are told in Scripture, 'knows what is in man'. He understands human nature all through; furthermore, the Carpenter of Galilee is intensely practical. Therefore, He would not command human beings to forgive in a way that is impractical, cuts across all morality, and is frankly impossible for us.

Now I knew I was missing something.

When a pastor listens to an individual pour out his problems, often he sees clearly that at this point or that one the person on the other side of his desk has been in the wrong. If the pastor has been trained in non-directive counselling, he will carefully withhold these opinions.

Even so, he is caught in a dilemma. The minister knows that a spirit of condemnation in him, even though unexpressed, will set up an immediate barrier to further confidences. Yet liberation for the needy one can only come from seeing himself as he really is and wanting to change. Without that there is no hope, as experience in a group like Alcoholics Anonymous has long demonstrated.

I remember Peter Marshall coming home from many such confrontations in his church office, marvelling, 'Nothing — but nothing — is as difficult as for one human being ever to bring another person to the conviction of sin. Why, oh why do we ever try it?'

And that's exactly what the Bible tells us. 'When He (the Comforter, the Holy Spirit) is come, He will reprove the world of sin . . .'[2] Here we have Jesus telling us that convicting one another is not, and never was, our work: it's the Holy Spirit's business. The pastor can point to the ideal, even be specific about what the Bible teaches. Beyond that, each of us must receive illumination about his guilt from the inside.

But can we? Is there any way we can facilitate the work of the Spirit? I was given help on that by David du Plessis, a minister formerly of South Africa.

Back in 1961 when I was writing about David du Plessis' insight that there is no such thing as inherited Christianity because 'God has no grandsons,'[3] I wrote of him as 'a new friend'. Now that the du Plessis' live in the United States, we see them more often. In 1971 at a time when certain family prayers were still unanswered, David gave us an insight as powerful as the 'no grandsons' one.

Over coffee in our living-room he pointed out to us a verse of Scripture that had long puzzled me:

Verily I say unto you, whatsoever ye shall bind on earth shall be bound in heaven, and whatsoever ye shall loose on earth shall be loosed in heaven.[4]

'For a long time I was puzzled,' David told us, 'about what "loosing" and "binding" meant. Then I found out: it means that by hanging on to my judgment of another, I can bind him to the very conditions I'd like to see changed.

'By our unforgiveness, we stand between the other person and the Holy Spirit's work in convicting him and then helping him. By stepping out of the way through releasing somebody from our judgment, we're not necessarily saying, "He's right and I'm wrong." Forgiveness means, "He can be as wrong as wrong can be, but I'll not be the judge." Forgiveness means that I'm no longer binding a certain person on earth. It means withholding judgment.

'How I wish,' David continued, 'that I'd been taught that from the beginning. My whole Christian life would have been different. Judge, judge — there are no more judgmental people in the world than Christians. It was certainly so in my life! When the Lord made me face up to that, He told me, "You're not forgiving. You're a public prosecutor, judging everybody in sight. And I want you to be a public defender — not public prosecutor." '

David put down his cup of coffee. 'Weren't you and Len telling me that you're troubled by some unanswered prayers? Well, in my life I've found this forgiveness business a key to getting prayers answered. A couple of years ago I was going through one of those prayers-not-getting-beyond-the-ceiling periods and I prayed, "Lord, I don't have enough faith. Give me the gift of faith."

' "It isn't your faith," the reply came. "I can see faith even if it's as small as a mustard seed. No, it's something else . . . When you stand praying — forgive if ye have aught against any. That's your trouble. That's why your prayers aren't answered. You go about with a lot of aughts against a lot of anys." '

As David concluded his story, I thought to myself, 'Our aughts against all the anys . . . What a shaft of light!' So now we saw why certain of our prayers had not been answered and we set ourselves to the work of forgiveness.

My husband Len and I started on a systematic releasing of our 'aughts against all the anys' in our respective lives. We agreed to spend about thirty minutes each morning, each with a cup of coffee in a separate room, getting our 'aughts' on paper. After that we would meet together for verbal prayer release of each person on our lists. Then we would tear the lists into small bits and put them in a large manila envelope. Eventually we would burn them.

Long ago we had learned the principle that it is necessary to get the past confessed and straightened out (as far as is possible) before we can live abundantly in the present. So we began as far back as we could remember, working on a different period of our life each morning, searching out people and situations buried deep in our unconscious.

For instance, since I've always been fascinated with history, many long-dead characters are as large as life to me, like the English Tudor king, Henry VIII. For reasons not altogether clear, I have always had a personal loathing for that man. On each trip to the British Isles, I could never seem to escape him. In the Tower of London, his coarse, obese presence hovered in the shadows as I would peer through the slit of a window to the green below where such a procession of his subjects had their heads chopped off at his instigation — Sir Thomas More, Bishop John Fisher, the aged Margaret Pole, and two of Henry's wives — Ann Boleyn and Catherine Howard.

Even in Scotland at the ruins of Dryburgh and Melrose Abbeys, who should appear but Henry VIII! As I stood in the grassy aisle, the guide intoned, 'In May, 1544, Henry VIII commenced what he called his "rough wooing" of Scotland. The Earl of Hertford marched on the Border, looting, murdering, burning. Behind them in England, 3,219 abbeys already lay in ruins, which had added treasure to His Majesty, the King, of £161,000. Scottish abbeys including Melrose and Dryburgh, were also soon put to the torch.'

So that's why Dryburgh was a ruin! Even as my eyes rev-
elled in the beauty of the stone fretwork looking like delicate
lace against the sky, I seethed at the thought of all those cath-
edrals and abbeys destroyed by order of Henry.

Now back home in Florida, during one of those quiet thirty-
minute periods of a morning, my 'aughts' against Henry VIII
kept hammering at me. How, I wondered impatiently, could
someone I'd never known in the flesh be such a personal affront
to me? And this historical 'aught' seemed too trivial and silly to
bother with. After all, this particular character had already
been dead 425 years and more pressing forgiveness work
awaited me nearer home.

But the answer came, 'No, this is valid for you. Get on with
the cleaning out. That's real emotional energy you've been
spending on history. The point is not whether the target for
your emotions is past or present, the dead or the living, valid or
invalid. The point is to get into the proper relationship with
Me: assume your creaturely role, and give back to Me the sole
right to judge.'

So ... marvelling at my own foolishness, I released His Majesty King Henry from my unforgiveness. After that, I could
rejoice in no longer having to arraign Henry for his black deeds
and let God handle that one.

On another morning, I tackled all my Aughts in connection
with my hatred of war, like the armament makers of World
War I, the Senate leaders who had defied Woodrow Wilson and
blocked America's entrance into the League of Nations; more
latterly, certain gentlemen of the Pentagon.

Some Aughts surfaced from my childhood. Childish resentments, to be sure, but needing to be unloaded. My baby brother
Robert had crawled in amongst my doll furniture, wrecking
everything. Not only that, fascinated with dolls' eyes that open
and shut, with an exploratory forefinger he had punched the
dolls' eyes back into their heads. When I discovered sightless

sockets looking up at me as Mrs. Eagen's and Mrs. Ogen's 'eyes' rattled around in their heads, I was so angry that Mother had to restrain me from pummelling Brother Bobby with my fists.

Mornings later an especially difficult Aught surfaced from Peter Marshall's first heart attack. Sometime before that attack he had stopped smoking. Nine days into his convalescence, the doctor had put a cigarette in Peter's mouth because he was so fearful of 'nervousness'. The passing of the years with all we know now about smoking and heart disease only made this Aught harder to release.

As Leonard and I dealt with our respective Aughts out of the past and proceeded to present areas needing forgiveness, we had continually to guard against merely flashing around our negative opinions and analyses rather than relying on God to remedy the situation. Gradually we found that by dropping personal judgments we could clear out tons of emotional debris that had obscured the real issues involved.

It did not take many mornings to see that the contemporary parallel of my Henry experience involved that category of persons who had never injured me, but whom I would rather avoid. There are many ways of expressing the feeling. 'He rubs me the wrong way' . . . 'Oh, I don't know, some chemical reaction between us — not good' . . . 'Just allergic to her, I suppose.' That would not do in Jesus' eyes, I discovered. So those people too, had to be released to be themselves whether or not I happened to like their looks, their habits, or their life styles.

Jesus' direction about love is clear: 'You shall love the Lord your God with all your heart, soul, and mind . . . and love your neighbour as much as you love yourself.'[5] In all honesty, we know how little genuine love we bring to God even in moments of what is supposed to be worship, how feebly and selectively we love our neighbour. The love God demands can only be the gift of God. Yet He cannot give us that gift so long as bitterness and resentment have slammed shut the door of the heart and unforgiveness stands sentinel at the door lest love open and enter. Forgiveness is the precondition of love.

The 'how' of forgiveness is through knowing how to use our will — the rudder of our life. We are responsible for the set of this rudder; once we have willed a course of action, God will be responsible for our feelings if we will hand them over to Him. Otherwise, nothing we can do would change these feelings.

When I put that conclusion alongside David du Plessis' statement, 'Forgiveness means, "The other person may be as wrong as wrong can be, but I'll not be the judge," ' I saw that forgiveness is simply the decision of our wills to release a particular person followed by verbalising that to God. It can be a simple prayer like, 'Lord, I release —— from my judgment. Forgive me that I may have bound him and hampered Your work by judging. Now I step out of the way so that heaven can go into action for —— ' Obviously, there is nothing impossible about praying like that.

As for faith that such a non-emotional release would result in changes in the other person's life, I confess that we began with deficient faith. The process of releasing the Aughts seemed too simple, too pat.

We were about to be shown that when we follow Jesus' directions, the simplest ways are the most powerful.

Every human being has problems of relationship with other people. The other (positive) side is that in interaction between people we learn most of life's needed lessons. Yet grown-ups as well as children are inclined to avoid correction. Any of us can plan a life style which skirts around our foibles, hang-ups, and selfishness.

By 1959 after ten years of widowhood, with Peter John in college, I realised that I was developing exactly such a life style. Though I had decided to build a house and settle down in Washington, there were inner warnings. I saw that too much protected solitude was a danger to me. It jeopardised aliveness and those fresh discoveries that are part of spiritual growth. By then I also understood that even the most earnest prayer and disciplined Bible reading leaves out another whole area through which God reaches us — people. What to do about it?

Today many people who seek an answer to all this are entering into communal living so that interaction with others can deal with character flaws. In the 'fifties and 'sixties however, there were only faint rumblings of movements towards community living.

For my solution I had turned my eyes towards the Church of the Saviour. This was a small interdenominational church shepherded by Gordon Cosby. One of its requirements of church membership included a high degree of commitment not only to the Lordship of Christ but to the group itself. I had all but decided to take this important step when Leonard LeSourd and his three children walked into my life.

Soon it became apparent that for me God had planned a different sort of involvement and commitment. The house I was building was almost finished. Inside its insulated, climate-controlled walls I could have slipped into the rut of a padded middle age much too early. There I would have been secure from the jostles and jabs of normal family living. In that perfect step-down office adjoining my bedroom, I might even have completed my novel *Christy* in three or four years rather than the nine years it took.

But what growing pains of the human spirit (my own included) I would have missed! How little I would have understood of what life is all about compared to what I've learned during the hurly-burly years since. Though I have still had little experience with living in community (only an occasional retreat and a three-generation household) I now see the family as another one of life's important training grounds for learning how to deal with the Aughts.

So I sold the house and undertook the rearing of a second family. The years since have dramatised what I already knew, that I am no expert in child rearing, only a constant learner. I know that I share with other parents those situations in a family where varying interests and personalities whittle away at selfishness and impatience, force us to run the risk of sharing our innermost selves, so that we are bent and then rebent into flexibility. The bumps and bruises and turbulence that are part of the price you pay for life's richness.

During the early years of my marriage to Leonard, some of the turbulence came from in-fighting between Chester and his young brother Jeffrey, two bear cubs frolicking about the house, rolling over rugs, colliding with furniture.

There was the morning I heard loud noises from the direction of the boys' room. Then came the sound of a slap and a door banging. Chester and Jeffrey were at it again!

Chester's angry voice met me as I crossed the living-room. 'Jeff, open that door. *Open* it!'

From the bedroom side of the door came an impudent reply that further infuriated fourteen-year-old Chester. He hauled back his right foot and kicked the door. There was a crunch. With dismay I saw that the toe of Chester's shoe had punched through the wood panelling.

I rapped sharply on the door. 'Jeff, unlock this door this instant — or I promise you such a scorched bottom you won't sit down for the next week!'

He slid back the bolt and stood there looking sheepishly at us.

'He hid my English paper and I have to turn it in today.' Chester's voice was still shaking with rage. 'He refused to give it to me.'

'Did you do that, Jeffrey?'

'Yes-s.'

'I'm disgusted with you. That's baby stuff.' Then I turned on Chester. 'When are you going to control that temper of yours? The door,' I moaned. 'Just look at that door! It's ruined.'

Such a bear-cub scene was not made easier for me by Len's genial disinclination to punish for in-fighting. His attitude tended to be a relaxed, 'Well, that's the way boys are.'

Soon after Len and I were married and were living in Westchester County, New York, my new daughter Linda was entering the sixth grade. It became apparent that my stepmother role was not going to be easy. There was the usual playing off one parent against the other and the tussles over clothes and curfews most mothers have with their daughters.

In the sixth grade, Linda was bright and freckle-faced with the instincts of a tragic actress. This was the period when the fad was to wear dirty plimsolls to school — preferably with no socks. One day Linda and I had just returned from purchasing a new pair of plimsolls. Several minutes later, I looked out of the front window and saw our daughter in the rock garden on her hands and knees, the shoe box open on the ground beside her, carefully dragging one white plimsoll, then the other through the black soil.

Loudly I voiced my objections, 'Do you really want to look as if you've come out of a pigsty?'

The gaze she turned on me was withering. 'Mom, everyone wears dirty plimsolls. I'll look ridiculous if mine are all new and white.'

The emotional temperature was soaring, so I dropped the subject. That afternoon when I happened to be near the junior high school, I dropped in to see for myself. Classes were just changing. Sure enough, all the way down the corridor moved hundreds of pairs of dirty plimsolls. Standing there, I remembered how humiliated I had been when Mother made me wear galoshes to school on a rainy day when my classmates didn't.

But plimsolls and the like were minor points compared to something that neither Len nor I understood. When fun times were planned especially for Linda, such as a party or a shopping trip, immediately afterwards she would turn into her worst self. This odd sequence happened so often that we knew a warped force was at work. It was as if she was saying, 'Please, I can't stand any special demonstration of love.'

On the other side, when punishment was necessary (usually the withdrawing of some freedom or privilege) no sooner was the discipline given than Linda would become a veritable angel with a winsome disposition.

Such behaviour was especially discomforting to a stepmother. The relationship was not what I had looked forward to with such hope. I felt like a rejected parent. Then I caught myself resenting this child and her attitudes. Since this was not my image of the 'good mother', I tried to ignore or bury such emotions.

I still remember some moments of realisation one Sunday morning in the First Congregation Church in Chappaqua. The winter sunlight was streaming in the tall arched windows laying long patterns of light across the white Colonial sanctuary. I was sitting there thinking about Linda. Suddenly in my mind and heart His voice was speaking to me with particular clarity and intensity. *Unless you love her, you don't love Me.*

'Lord, I know that's true.' The thought stabbed me. 'But *how* do we love a person when we hate some of the things they do? Please tell me how. And Lord, I have another problem. I can't manufacture love. Nobody can. I need help.'

With the issues thus clearly drawn I struggled on. Over and over I would take a fresh grip on my willingness to love Linda, no matter what she did — all the way from minor infractions to slipping out of her bedroom window after midnight for a date with a high school senior football star five years older than she. As I willed to love, I asked God to take care of my emotions and make my love real. For a time it would work and our home would know contentment and harmony. Then another crisis would develop and I would fall on my face.

The difficulties that had surfaced in early adolescence grew until Linda was finding life all but unmanageable. For years, schoolwork had been difficult. Here was a bright girl whose grades see-sawed wildly between A and Flunking. Almost every term report carried teachers' comments about 'Poor attitude and motivation' and 'Work not up to a level of ability'. Tutors and extra sessions and a prep school brought no demonstrable results.

During these years her father and I had tried everything we knew — guidance counsellors, a child psychologist, counselling with Christian friends, group prayer, prayer at Linda's bedside while she was asleep — every type of prayer we could think of. There had been some minor breakthroughs, but Len and I knew that the root of the problem remained. It seemed to be centred in her will. She appeared to be unable to want to be any different.

In college the trouble grew. To academic difficulties was added the Youth Revolution of the late 'sixties. Linda plunged wholeheartedly into it — life pattern; clothing styles — Levis, long hair, wire-rimmed spectacles; protest meetings, campus sit-ins, hitch-hiking to peace marches and rallies.

Most of us parents with children caught up in all this know the feeling ... wondering whether our sons and daughters might be ensnared in experiences dark enough so that we would prefer not to know specifics. Especially when they are away from home, we told ourselves that 'what we don't know won't hurt us', meanwhile knowing full well that the ostrich never solved anything with his head in the sand.

Graduation day came for our daughter. Linda's father, grandparents and I got to the graduation scene to find a very

tense girl on our hands. Tense and uptight, nothing gave her
any satisfaction. Apparently she could find no way to enjoy
what should have been a great moment in her life. Watching
the academic procession walk by on plimsolls, dirty white
shoes, T-thong sandals with mortar-board caps tilted on the
heads at every possible angle, I wondered what the other graduates were feeling? Were most of them unhappy too, with life
somehow out of order, all values a-jumble?

The scene left me with such heaviness of spirit that after our
return home to Florida, I spent one morning working on the
release of all Aughts against Linda stretching back over the
years to age ten. To my astonishment, I filled three pages.
Neither Len nor I told Linda anything about our prayer or
release.

We did not have long to wait to see results.

Several weeks later on Cape Cod during that tumultuous
summer of 1971 came the climax to our long years of struggle
with this particular situation. When my grandchild Amy Catherine Marshall was born on July 22nd with severe liver and
kidney problems, a group of us gathered on the Cape for concentrated prayer. On an impulse I telephoned Linda who was
working in her grandmother's gift shop in Maine. Would she
care to join us?

There was a moment's silence. Then, 'Yes,' she said, 'I'd like
to be there.'

Afterwards Linda told me that she wanted to come because I
was the one who had telephoned and invited her. What happened when she got there literally reversed the direction of
Linda's life. The details of the story are hers alone to tell. As is
usually the case, people other than Len and me — her
parents — were used by God as the catalyst for our daughter.
Repentance was involved for Linda, followed by confession.
Tears flowed. All of this took many hours of confrontation with
herself and with us in agonisingly honest dialogue. We heard

things we didn't want to hear. Rebellion carried on in darkness is not pretty. After that I understood why the direction given me in the Chappaqua church — *Unless you love her, you don't love Me* — had been so difficult for me.

'Mom, all along you never had a chance with me,' Linda admitted with tears. 'I resented you so completely when you married Dad. I just wanted to wreck things.'

No wonder this deliberate courting of darkness had brought us so much of it. Yet all was washed away during this long evening of honesty among the three of us when barriers came crashing down. For Linda it was the release of long years of hostility and guilt. Then, being a true child of this age, even in the Christian framework, Linda reached for the far-out thing. She wanted a 'believer's baptism' in the ocean followed by a communion service on the beach.

That was not the finish of this particular Aught–Any episode. I was to get my come-uppance the morning after the communion service.

During the intervening hours, my mind must have flicked at some secret thoughts along the line, '*All that* . . . all those years of agony she put her father and me through, then she's forgiven by God *instantly*. Isn't that too easy a forgiveness?' Ugly secret thoughts — except God knew.

The next morning I was awakened to the clear incisive internal message, 'Remember My story of the prodigal son? You're in grave danger of taking the place of that elder brother.⁶ That morning in Florida, you didn't quite mean business about finally releasing all those Aughts against Linda, did you? I heard and answered anyway. *Now let them go.* For now, take the lowest seat at My banquet table, below Len, below Linda. And I want you to confess all this to Linda this morning.'

Thus I was properly zapped, as our boys would say. Humbly and a trifle haltingly, at breakfast I made my confession to

Linda. She wept again, this time from joy, and then ecstatically hugged me.

Now that Len and I had released Linda of our aughts against her, she was free to become the very person we had longed for. A new life began for her. For several months she stayed with Edith and Peter Marshall under their direction and guidance. Gradually she began to get answers to those crucial questions, 'Who am I? Why am I on earth? Where am I going?' Linda now lives in Washington where she is part of a unique Christian fellowship at Trinity House, living co-operatively and ministering to students and young career people.

All of this give and take with my new family enabled me to identify with many friends who were having trouble with rebellious teenagers. One close friend, Sybil Jones, who lives in Virginia a few miles from our Evergreen Farm, was having a problem with her niece Fay. Because of the personal nature of the events, I have changed names and some unimportant details.

One night in Florida I received a call from Sybil. 'Catherine, I just have to talk to you. It's about Fay.'

As Sybil talked on, I was remembering Fay's family. I have known her parents, Loretta and Tim Randle, for many years and have watched with apprehension the way they have catered to their only daughter. Each Christmas would come a family picture of the three of them with the golden-haired Fay always the centre of their adoring smiles. As the years passed the Christmas cards showed the child was growing up into a beautiful girl — a pert face, slender body, lovely. Except that when she was fifteen a look was developing in Fay's face that bothered me — a touch of arrogance in the eyes. Selfishness around the mouth? Or was I imagining?

We would see the three Randles in the summertime when they came to Virginia to visit my friend Sybil who was

Loretta's sister. Aunt Sybil had always been a sort of spiritual godmother to Fay. She read Bible stories to her as a little girl, taught her special prayers. Fay stayed with her Aunt Sybil while her parents took long cruises or trips abroad. During those periods she would try to provide the disciplined home life that Fay was obviously not getting. While the Randles were hit-and-miss church-goers, they saw no connection between Christian faith and the way they structured their home. And whatever Fay wanted she usually got.

When Fay reached her seventeenth birthday that May, she wanted a Corvette hardtop automobile. Her parents gave it to her. Then Fay began to want things not even they would give her — like drugs and week-end trips with boys.

Soon an ominous personality change developed in their daughter. Fay became withdrawn, moody, secretive. She had been a good student; suddenly she didn't seem to care. That was when they discovered the marijuana.

'I've no idea how long Fay had been smoking marijuana,' Sybil told me. 'As if that isn't bad enough, her father found a big supply of "downers" in her room. When he discovered the marijuana and the downers — she had been using six or seven of them a day — he hit the roof. He took her car keys for a month. One night about a week ago Fay packed a bag and drove off in her Corvette. Apparently she had a spare set of keys.

'Her father almost went out of his mind,' Sybil continued. 'Days passed with no word from Fay. He alerted the police, then hired a private detective to find her.' There was a long silence as I prepared for — I did not know what. 'Last Friday they found her and some boy named Bart living together in a dirty apartment in the French Quarter of New Orleans.'

I commiserated with Sybil the best I could, promised to pray for Fay and hung up the phone thinking, 'How many many parents are going through this same kind of experience!' I knew of ten or more friends who had watched in anguish as rebellious children left home. Some had returned; one had died of a drug overdose; two had been killed in car accidents, others injured with one paralysed for life; some were still missing.

When Fay's father confronted her and her boy-friend in the New Orleans apartment, there was a stormy scene. 'I'm tired of your respectable middle-class life,' Fay shrieked at him. 'It's phony. You and your friends kill yourselves with cigarettes and booze. Let me alone to do what I want to. Bart is the only real thing I've ever found in life. Except maybe Aunt Sybil.'

Her father stared at her, at the long-haired boy beside her, then turned around and left. 'I don't have a daughter any-more,' Tim told his wife when he got home. During the next few months his wife and friends watched him age ten years.

That Christmas no card came from the Randles.

But while Tim Randle had given up on his daughter, his wife and Sybil had not. They persisted in keeping in communication with the young couple.

The next summer while at Evergreen Farm, I had an unex-pected visit from Sybil, visibly upset.

'I'm afraid I've done the wrong thing,' she began. 'Yesterday morning Fay and the boy-friend Bart arrived suddenly at my house. I had sent them some money to visit me, but they didn't tell me they were coming. They had hitch-hiked all the way from New Orleans. I guess they've had to sell Fay's car.

'I greeted them lovingly, fed them a big meal. Then sud-denly they asked where they were to sleep. "Are you married?" I asked. They shook their heads. "Then I'll give you separate rooms," I said.

' "Separate rooms!" The look on their faces was something. "You're a phony like everyone else," Fay shouted at me. Before I could stop them they'd picked up their things and walked out the front door.'

Sybil looked at me, her eyes full of tears. 'Did I do the wrong thing?'

We talked and prayed together. The answer to our prayers was clear guidance: Sybil had done the right thing. She had showed them love, but since Fay and Bart sleeping together as an unmarried couple violated the moral code of Sybil's faith and her home, she had to ask them to take separate bedrooms.

During our time together I told Sybil about the 'aughts against the anys' principle. For a long moment she considered the question, was there judgment and condemnation in her heart for Fay and Bart?

'Yes, I do think there is judgment on my part,' she admitted. 'But how can I honestly pray to get rid of it?'

We did it together. Then Sybil raised a new point. 'My releasing judgment against Fay and Bart may help my relationship with them. But the real problem is between Fay's parents and these kids. And the Randles are coming to visit me next week.'

Sybil had before her the formidable task of trying to bring the Randles to the point where they not only forgive and release their daughter from judgment, but do the same for Bart.

'You know, Bart isn't hard to like,' Sybil confided to me as she was leaving. 'Behind all that hair there's a gentleness and yes, even a sweet spirit. Fay calls him "a hip beautiful person".' Bart, too, had left a middle-class family situation in Arkansas in rebellion against his parents.

When the Randles came to visit, there was complete stubbornness on Tim's part towards any reconciliation. Finally, Sybil bluntly told them that their hardness of heart would keep God from doing His forgiving work in all the lives involved. It had not been a pleasant time.

Months later she was on the telephone again, her voice jubilant. 'Fay and Bart have moved into a small apartment just two miles from here. They hitch-hiked from New Orleans weeks ago, both now have jobs. I had them to dinner last night. Do you know what they asked me? Did I know a minister they could talk to? I sure did.'

The next letter had good and bad news. Bart's and Fay's talks with the minister had resulted in their deciding to get married. Living together unmarried had seemed racy and amusing. But they had few close friends and could find no real place in the community. There also came an inner dissatisfaction they couldn't define. They then had decided that marriage made more sense than they had thought.

So Bart and Fay were married one afternoon in a quiet church ceremony. The bad news was that Fay's parents had refused to come to the ceremony.

I had trouble sleeping that night, grieving over the Randles' unforgiving stubbornness. What was the Lord trying to tell parents through experiences like this? That what we have called love for our children is largely sentimentality, not strong enough to be redemptive? That the permissive giving of so many material possessions to children is really a form of self-gratification without the quality of love Paul talks about in the thirteenth chapter of Corinthians?

Fay's mother, it turned out, had desperately wanted to go to the wedding, but felt she should not come without her husband. Heartbroken by the situation, she thought of Sybil's words about their hardness of heart and the necessity of releasing their aughts against Bart and their daughter Fay.

The morning of the wedding, Loretta Randle alone in her quiet bedroom took two important steps. She gave her life to the living Lord she had never known. Then she spent two hours getting on paper her aughts against Fay stretching back to about age ten. She had not realised how many resentments against Fay she had acquired.

Loretta felt light-hearted, happier than she had been in years. So she persuaded Tim to work on his aughts too. He found it especially hard to release Bart, who in his eyes, had 'seduced his little girl'. All of this was done with no communication with Fay and her new husband Bart. Slowly, painfully, hundreds of miles away they were being released from judgment.

There came the memorable day in Sybil's living-room when Fay and Bart were reconciled with her parents. Fay asked her father's forgiveness for the harsh statements she had made that day in New Orleans. She hugged her mother — and wept. Then to Sybil's astonishment, her niece knelt at her feet. 'Aunt Sybil,' she said revealingly, 'you were right that day — when you wanted to put me and Bart in different rooms. One reason I got so mad was because I knew you were right. That's the reason Bart and I came here to live because we felt you were the one person we could trust. You stood for something and deep down we wanted what you had.'

Later Sybil wound up her report to me with a little vignette. 'The Randles,' she wrote, 'arrived two days ago for a week's visit. From my window I can see Bart and Tim Randle out by the front fence. Bart is handy with tools, so Tim has enlisted his help in making a new gate for me. Already there's an easy camaraderie between the two men. Isn't it great the way this has turned out! How can I ever thank you for the Aughts and the Anys?'

After we had seen such miracles of restored relationships, I began to understand why Jesus gave us the 'Aught–Any' command immediately following His clarion call to 'have faith in God' and His challenge to get on with a mountain-removing faith.[7] The sequence can mean only one thing — that our Aughts, big or just annoying, are always the chief block to prayer power.

Once we see this truth, many examples spring to mind, such as that of Stephen, that personable, eloquent young man who became the first Christian martyr. As the murderous stones flung by a frenzied mob bruised his flesh and broke bones and the bloody stones piled up at Stephen's feet, Saul of Tarsus stood watching, holding the witnesses' outer garments so that they could better hurl stones at the condemned man. Saul heard Stephen's last words before death, 'Lord, lay not this sin to their charge.' So it was Stephen's release of his Aughts against his executioners that made it possible for heaven to go into action for Saul of Tarsus.

Shortly thereafter, as Saul travelled towards Damascus, heaven opened to bring Saul to his knees in one of the most dramatic turnabouts in recorded history. He would become Paul, missionary–traveller over all the known world, great apostle to the Gentiles, and spiritual father to all of us in the western world.

As each of us bemoans the severing of so many relationships, we may recognise that we can't really expect anything else when we leave God out of our lives. As always, Jesus challenges His followers to be out in front showing the way: 'Forgive, if ye have aught against any . . .'

There's no way to get our world back together again except as each of us begins with himself and with his own family.

CHAPTER FOUR

THE LAW OF THE GENERATIONS

For years I felt the same despair as everyone else under the continual barrage of articles and true-life situations telling of estrangement between parents and children and issuing dire predictions of the imminent demise of the family.

The cover of a national news magazine dramatised it, a picture of a father, mother, son and daughter — square, robot-like people, with the caption, 'The U.S. Family: "Help!" '

Statistics followed: one in every four marriages now ends in divorce; a high 70 per cent rate of divorce exists in some California communities; 40 per cent of all married women with children hold out-of-home jobs; half a million teenagers run away from home each year; the rate of school drop-outs is steadily rising; the 'new morality' with utter rejection of pre-marital chastity has been accepted by a large percentage of young people.

During the 'sixties the world's youth had centre stage. The young had become our obsession: either they were glorified with even their hair and clothing styles copied by their elders; or they were feared, resented, and blamed for everything. After a while, it became apparent that neither extreme could be right since we had found so few solutions.

It was about then that I was startled to find in the Old Testament a brief but applicable description of society's plight in our time:

> Thou shalt beget sons and daughters, but thou shalt not enjoy them; for they shall go into captivity.[1]

All of us know the ways in which we do not enjoy our children. We are afraid of what is happening to them. Or we feel cut out of their lives. Then there's the basic fear that our children will 'go into captivity'. In the 'seventies, we are discovering that the captivity of drugs, of the occult, of sexual promiscuity is every bit as real a captivity as it was for the Israelites who were physically carried into Babylon centuries ago.

How different is this from those other descriptions in Scripture of parents who do enjoy their children, described joyfully as 'a fruitful vine by the sides of their house' . . . 'a quiver full of arrows' . . . 'the crown' of old age . . . 'olive plants round thy table'.

Startled by how pointedly the Deuteronomy verse speaks to our hearts today, I sought out the original setting of the words . . . The author and compiler of Deuteronomy[2] has Moses speaking them as part of a prophetic warning as given him by God. The forty years of Israel's wilderness wanderings were over. The second generation then stood poised, ready to enter the Promised Land. Moses would soon die; he would not enter Canaan with them. Before formally commissioning Joshua as his successor, the venerable leader gave a farewell charge to Israel. This charge is the book of Deuteronomy.

Reading this book is like looking through a window into the amplitude of Moses' spirit. In his speech there is no note of an old man's sentimental nostalgia, rather the entire thrust is into the future. Warm with feeling and persuasively eloquent, Moses focused on this one significant point:

> See, I have set before you life and death, the blessing and the curse . . .
> Therefore choose life . . .[3]

The rest of the Old Testament narrative tells us what

happened: all too often the descendants of those to whom Moses had given his charge did not 'choose life'. History records that these descendants did go into captivity literally as well as spiritually.

Each generation then, as now, has a choice: life or death ... the blessing or the curse.

Yet not understanding, we are hearing frequently today, 'Why shouldn't I do as I please — so long as it doesn't hurt anyone else?'

The truth is that not one of us can do as we please without hurting other people in the process. As Dr. Francis Schaeffer, philosopher and theologian, states it, 'Man is drowning in cosmic alienation.' Scripture continually insists on the principle of our connectedness as a fact of human life: 'We are every one members of one another.'⁴ In this Law of Generations, as I call it, we are linked to previous generations behind us. Our ancestors are in our genes, in our bones, in our marrow, in our physiological and emotional makeup. We, in turn, will be written into the children who come after us.

I was at home alone one night recently when I heard a noise in the kitchen. Dropping my mending in my lap, I tensed, listening for any other sounds however faint. Those cat burglars I'd been hearing about ... was someone there?

Hearing nothing more, I went to investigate. The kitchen was so dark! Suddenly, I felt that familiar prickling at the base of my neck.

Then came a surge of annoyance at myself. 'You're not going to let that fear of the dark return,' I told myself sternly. Resolutely, I walked into the kitchen and flipped on the light. A tray had toppled from its place beside the refrigerator.

Most of my life I've struggled with an assortment of fears, many of them foolish ones. As I sought through prayer for a reason for so many fears, I was pointed back to my father's mother, Grandmother Sarah.

My girlhood recollections of this grandmother are rather negative ones. I remember that she spent most of her days sitting in a comfortable chair in the bay window of the living-room, often with a huge Bible open on her lap. She used it as a sort of scrapbook; it bulged with clippings, cards, letters, and snapshots tucked between its pages. The expression on her face was usually dour. I cannot recall any of her grandchildren sitting in her lap to be cuddled.

Yet Grandmother Sarah had an immense capacity for friendship and hospitality. I can remember no meal in that home without guests and boarders, not even breakfast. She and the two daughters who ran the house were superb cooks in the best of Southern tradition.

But I began to see that the overall effect of my grand-mother's fear-ridden personality on me was not good. My mother remembers a significant event that occurred when I was six weeks old. Grandmother and Grandfather had agreed to babysit for me one night while my father and mother went to a lecture.

'About midway in the evening, an usher handed a note to the lecturer,' Mother recalled. 'He asked if a Mrs. Wood was in the audience? If so, there was a message for her at the door of the auditorium. There stood your grandfather. "It's the baby," he panted. "She's cried herself blue in the face."

'He and I started for home almost on a run. Half way home I could hear you screaming. Yet the instant I dashed into the room and picked you up, the crying stopped as though a tap had been turned off. You were frightened and my presence re-assured you. Grandmother had searched so fearfully for an open safety pin, a Florida mosquito chewing on you, or a rash — she had made you more afraid. She was so tense.'

Can it be that a baby's sensitive antenna can pick up the

tone of people surrounding him? If his family is happy and their relationship harmonious, the baby's reaction is contentment; if there is strong negativism like fear, the baby senses this and protests. Child psychologists and those who work with babies in institutions affirm that this is exactly so.

As I grew up, I discovered the nature of Grandmother's fears. Since she thought the night air dangerous, she would not allow Grandfather to raise any windows in their bedroom winter or summer. Many a morning we would see Grandfather stagger pasty-faced and dripping with perspiration from the sweatbath of their stifling sleeping quarters.

To this was added an abnormal fear of thunderstorms. As the skies would begin their fireworks, Grandmother Sarah would dash for her feather bed, cover herself with a quilt and stay there until the last bit of lightning had faded and the last drop of rain had fallen.

Later, when I was about eleven, Grandmother Sarah kept me and my younger brother and sister while my father, dangerously ill, spent three months at Johns Hopkins Hospital with Mother there beside him. It was a time of real fear and tension for all of us. At this impressionable time of my life, I somehow focused on Grandmother's fears of night air, drafts, thunderstorms, the dark, washing hair too often, staying out of the sun — things which seemed to me ludicrous and absurd. Such phobias were the last things I wanted to imitate.

Yet so strong is the Law of the Generations that even what we scorn can come down to us. In my case it was not Grandmother Sarah's particular fears — rather simply an over-inclination to fear. In my life it centred on a dread of germs and illness; a horror of mice or small dead animals, and during my childhood, fear of the dark, ghosts, and the like.

The time came when I realised that in Jesus' eyes, fear is a sin since it is acting out a lack of trust in God. Then my attention was drawn to that part of the second commandment which follows the injunction not to 'make for yourself a graven image'; 'For I the Lord thy God am a jealous God, visiting the iniquity of the fathers upon the children unto the third and fourth generation . . .'[5]

I had always wondered about this: was that fair? Or like a loving God?

But in the light of the revelation about my fear and Grandmother Sarah, I saw that the Exodus verse was simply stating a fact of life. And I *was* the third generation from my grandmother to be beset by those petty fears.

As is often the case when we are being taught something, this matter of sins being passed down from generation to generation seemed to be everywhere I looked in the Bible.

We are accustomed to the idea that we pass on to our children physical inheritance — colour of eyes, colour of hair, a number of diseases — tendencies towards gout, diabetes, certain skin diseases. Handing down a material inheritance is such standard practice that the laws of every country make careful provisions governing wills, probate, death and inheritance taxes. I began to ask myself, is it possible that our spiritual inheritance is as real as the others?

It soon became apparent that just as we can inherit either a fortune or debts, so in the spiritual realm we can inherit either spiritual blessings or those liabilities (unabashedly called 'sins' in Scripture) that hinder our development into mature persons. These blessings or liabilities do not come to us solely by heredity. Obviously they are also passed on by example and by teaching — conscious or unconscious. For instance, I think of a mother with a habit of keeping an untidy bedroom; her daughter now fights a continual losing battle with cluttered closets and drawers.

I've a friend who can scarcely go to sleep at night without reading herself to sleep; her father before her had the same habit, as do both her grown sons.

My husband Leonard dislikes tomatoes, sweet potatoes, liver, broccoli; so do sons Chester and Jeffrey. My grandmother used heaping teaspoons of sugar in her coffee or tea; my father did too, and also my brother.

These are trivial matters. Above this lowest level, more serious bequests are handed from generation to generation . . .

A man whom I'll call Sam found himself hindered by a terror of any emotional involvement with other people. At an office farewell party for a secretary who was moving to another city, the girl began to weep as she opened her gifts and read the enclosure cards. Even though she was weeping from gratitude and fond memories, Sam was still uncomfortable and found himself sidling out the door. 'But this is silly,' he told himself. 'Why am I doing this?'

It was a pattern he had repeated over and over — this ducking out of emotional scenes. As he pondered this fact, a picture came into his mind . . . It was a dinner table scene in his boyhood home. Angry over criticism directed at her, his mother had jumped up from the table and flounced out of the house. For a minute or two his father just sat in his chair, weary and lifeless. Finally, he left the table to seek out his wife to placate her. The scene ended with husband and wife returning home arm in arm, surface harmony restored. But there would be other occasions when Sam heard his mother crying and saw his father retreat out the back door to sit in the car and smoke a cigar.

Sam realised that these scenes had been repeated over and over through his growing-up years. How he had dreaded them! Whenever possible he had left the house. He sensed that his father had wanted to retreat from those scenes as much as he had. Now he could understand better one of his father's traits that had long puzzled and annoyed him, a sort of peace-at-any-price stance in any situation involving disagreements.

About three months after this revelation, Sam was caught up in a mild argument with his wife. He did not know that she was unusually tired from a difficult day. When she burst into tears, they were both startled to see their shy six-year-old son hastily leave the living-room and run up the stairs. Sam followed the child. He found him in bed rocking his body rhythmically back and forth in the way he had comforted himself as a very small child.

'Oh no!' the father thought as the significance of the chain reaction now into the third generation was borne in upon him. His son knew nothing of the similar episodes in his father's life when he had fled from emotion. Nor of his grandfather's tendencies along this line. Yet here was the child acting out the emotional hang-ups of his father and grandfather. It was uncanny! As he sat on the edge of the bed comforting his son, then and there Sam vowed to find the way to break this particular inheritance; surely this bondage to the fear of negative emotion had harassed his family long enough!

Intellectually, Sam knew that many of life's greatest experiences take place in emotional confrontations involving people. Yes, the man knew that, but the little boy still in the man remained terrified of all emotion.

Up to that time in Sam's life, he had had little use for religion. Yet one day at the noon hour, impulsively he slipped into the back of a church. There were several other worshippers sitting throughout the sanctuary. He could feel growing within him a desire that seemed ridiculously emotional — to stand up, walk down that long aisle, kneel at the altar rail and say, 'God, I need You.'

But he could also feel rising resistance. What if he got to that altar and actually shed tears? Those people sitting there . . . if they saw him kneel weeping at the altar, would they not think him some kind of exhibitionist?

A deep instinct told Sam that this was a true crisis point in his life. Here he was, again backing off from emotion.

Knowing that the answer had to be 'yes' if that vicious chain was ever to be broken, resolutely he got to his feet, walked down the aisle and knelt. Immediately, he forgot all about the other people. He even shed a few tears, but they were glorious tears, a moment Sam could never forget. The chain *was* broken and though not everything was healed instantaneously, that day in the church was the beginning of a new level of maturity for Sam and his family.

All of this gave me ample proof that the Law of the Generations is a fact — the sins or the blessings of the fathers *do* come down to the children.

It is the nature of sin to divide, to build walls, resulting in strained relationships or estrangement. I wondered if the Law of the Generations could give not only clues to the difficulties between the generations in our time, but even constructive answers. How might we pray so that the negatives could be transformed to positives?

In the process of searching for an answer, I was surprised to find that the last words of the Old Testament have to do with these problems between the generations. They are words of great promise. At the last days, God promised to send another prophet who:

> . . . shall turn the heart of the fathers to the children and the heart of the children to the fathers.[6]

The date of the book of Malachi has been placed at about 450 B.C. The writer mentioned Elijah as the forerunner of that 'Sun of righteousness' who would 'arise with healing in his wings'. All these centuries later we know who the Sun of righteousness is, the greatest of the prophets — the Lord Jesus Christ.

At the beginning of His public ministry Jesus made it clear that He had not come to destroy the Law, but to complete and fulfil it. Jesus would recognise the Law of the Generations, like all law, as part of His Father's world. But until then, there had been that missing dimension, exactly the question I had asked ... After we struggle and find that we can't keep the law by our own effort, then what? Is there any hope for us?

It is at that point that Jesus gives us the good news of His Gospel. He who is Truth and therefore is above the Law, will do for us what we cannot do for ourselves. So there is not only hope, but a real answer. We cannot turn the hearts of our children to their parents, but Christ can.

It was my son Peter who helped me to apply these new insights about my fears and Grandmother Sarah at a time several years ago when both of our families were coming to grips with the negatives in the Law of the Generations. No doubt Peter's place in the intertwining generations put him in the perfect position to help me with my fears. We found that our prayer work fell into three parts.

Firstly, having brought into the light all remembered dark heritage from previous generations, I had to forgive all these ancestors and release them from my judgment.

Secondly, Peter prayed that I be cut loose from these negatives. As I remember it, his prayer went something like this:

> Lord Jesus, You have told us that Your Word is the Sword of the Spirit,[7] that it is sharper than any two-edged sword known on earth. Whatever You say to us cuts deep and lays bare even the thoughts and intents of the heart.[8]
>
> You've also assured us that You came to earth to loose all bonds, to set every captive free.[9] Lord, Mother has been captive to these fears that we've been laying out before You. Yet You've declared that where the Spirit of the Lord is there is liberty.[10]
>
> So now, Lord, I take that Word and claiming it and wielding it as the Sword of the Spirit that it is, in Your Name and by Your power I hereby cut Mother free from every chain and

shackle from the past. I release her now to her rightful heritage — the glorious liberty of the children of God.[11] Thank
You, Lord Jesus, thank You. Amen.'

This powerful prayer led naturally into the third step, praising God for every part of this experience. For we found that the
release would not be final unless I received it in faith, and, as I
had been discovering, praise is the swiftest, surest route to
faith.

So now I began to understand how Christ makes the Law of
the Generations work for us. It was our friend, the late Starr
Daily, who gave me some further insights about what our part
is in this process.

For many years Starr, originally an expert safebreaker, had
been in and out of penal institutions, finally pronounced hopeless by the judge who sentenced him to prison for the third
time. Later, in the penitentiary hell-hole, he experienced one of
the most dramatic conversions of the twentieth century. After
the prison doors opened for him in 1930, he wrote ten books,
gave innumerable lectures, conducted hundreds of interviews
with youthful criminals.

Out of the totality of Starr Daily's great contribution to
prison reform, I'm concerned here with but a single facet of
what he learned — how a change in the attitudes of parents can
effect changes in a son who is in prison. A number of his
examples[12] demonstrated to me that the Law of the Generations works positively in as precise a way as it does negatively.

The father of a twenty-four-year-old prison inmate sought
an interview with Mr. Daily one day to ask for help. 'I've tried
everything with my son,' the man mourned. 'There's nothing
left but God.'

'Well, He's quite a left-over,' was the dry reply.

Wordlessly, the man handed Starr Daily a summary of his
son's record. It looked bad indeed:

. . . excessively quick and bright in intelligence, but infantile in emotional reactions and responses. Reformatory, jail and prison record of nine years. Type of crime: sex offences, burglary, robbery, forgery, confidence games, picking pockets, purse snatching, drug and narcotic peddling.

'Looks hopeless, doesn't it?' the father commented.

'Don't you believe it,' Starr told him. 'While there's life, there's hope. It's up to you.'

'Up to me!' the father almost shouted back. 'What do you mean by that? What can I do at this late date?'

The father and mother made no pretence of being 'religious'; they went to church twice a year, at Christmas and Easter. The home had always swung between two extremes — great leniency when the parents were not busy and in good humour, and unusual severity when they were out-of-sorts or rushed.

Starr next prescribed a spiritual rehabilitation programme for the couple. 'I'm going to be hard on you,' he told them, 'because I sense that you mean business.'

The programme was to be carried out in a way that would funnel into it tremendous spiritual power: husband and wife were to be 'in agreement' about what they were trying;[13] they were not to discuss it with anyone, keep all of it a secret between them.[14]

Then Mr. Daily wrote out a prescription for the couple. In relating this particular story Starr did not detail the prescription. However, it was not too difficult to cull out of Starr Daily's writings[15] the sort of spiritual rehabilitation programme he recommended:

(1) Rise early enough to start the day by giving one hour to the programme. During this hour, use only the Bible and a notebook and pen or pencil. Start with reading the Gospel of John. Jot down in the notebook:

Any verse or promise about faith.

Make notes about the character traits and attitudes of Jesus, remembering that when you want to know what God is like, look at Jesus.

Together try conversational prayer aloud — no 'thees' and 'thous', honest, straightforward; talk about anything that comes to mind.

(2) Begin to focus on the fact of Jesus' identification with anyone in need. Keep reminding yourself that He stands at the centre of each person's need ready to help, to be the Saviour.

Pick out three situations each day in which you in secret and silently pray for another person, visualising the Saviour spreading His light within them and their affairs.

Then practise trying to trust other people — not because they necessarily deserve trust, but because you are trusting the Spirit of the Lord in them.

(3) For now, do not ask anything for your son. He is God's child as well as yours; God loves him even more than you do. Turn him over completely to that light of Christ within him.

Whenever you think of your son, picture the light spreading as God does His own work within this boy.

Mr. Daily explained to this father that he and his wife were the key to the situation in the sense that the Law of the Generations enabled God to use them as His divine catalyst to change their son.

'As you work on this programme,' Starr explained, 'you'll be reclaiming your spiritual parenthood. You see, God's order for the home is that husband and father must shoulder spiritual along with financial responsibility. In a real sense the man is to be God's representative — priest or prime minister, as you will — for his own household. When the man takes this rightful place, then God promises His protection and blessing for that home.'

'My wife's been the spiritual one in our family . . .' the man objected.

'Maybe that's part of your problem. With both parents alive, in God's eyes there's no such thing as the woman being the spiritual head of the house. When that happens, strength and vitality go out of Christianity every time.'

'Why? I don't get it.'

'When a father thinks so little of God that he leaves any slight gesture towards Him up to his wife, how important are children — especially boys — going to think religion is anyway? Maybe,' Starr added gently, 'that's part of the problem with your boy.'

The father ruminated on that for a moment. At last he said slowly, 'Looks like I've got a lot of work to do.'

The father left with new hope. But it took him and his wife two months really to get under way with the programme Starr Daily had assigned them. Disregarding the initial awkwardness and unreality they felt, they took up prayer separately and together.

Though these parents did not understand why, during these months they no longer worried about their son. Later on, they understood that Starr's prescription had helped them put first things first: they were actually living out the Scriptural promise, 'Seek ye first the kingdom of God and his righteousness and all these things shall be added unto you.'[16]

Three and a half months passed. The father had long since finished the Gospel of John and had gone on to the Acts. One morning he had got to Chapter 10 where he was reading the story of the Apostle Peter and the Italian centurion Cornelius. Suddenly, a particular verse leapt out of the page at him:

God hath shewed me that I should not call any man common or unclean . . .[17]

His eyes were riveted to the words. An insistent thought kept hammering on his mind for admittance. Was God trying to give him a message through that verse?

The story was plain enough. Peter was given a vision of a huge sheet let down from heaven filled with all manner of creatures including some that the Jews regarded as unclean. The meaning: Peter was to disregard the Jewish taboo on certain foods. This led into the larger truth that Gentiles who wanted to ally themselves with the infant Christian church did not have to become Jews first. That, in turn, burst into a truth so big — here the father held his breath — that it embraced the whole world: God was asking Peter and all of us to love everything He had made, all His other creatures and one another. Nothing — no one — is to be refused the grace and love of God. So that had to include his son, the boy in prison.

Since God had accepted and welcomed him, the father, God expected him, in turn, to have the same openness of heart towards his son.

A warmth the man had never before felt flooded his heart. Here was a message to him straight from God. He would hold fast to that and no longer believe the prison official's negative prognosis about his son. Now he could receive every thought of his son into his mind with thanksgiving.

Here is Starr Daily's brief summary of what happened:

As this father turned from fear of and doubt in his son and looked steadfastly at the good with more and more praise, the boy began to respond to the new parental conviction and attitude. And it was done *'across space' without personal contact.* When the father visited his son six months later, the young man was cured of his criminal mind and well on his way to total rehabilitation.

When the parents — and especially the father — allowed God to become the Head of their home, the immutable Law of the Generations worked just as Starr had predicted — from sharply negative, the situation was turned upward to a glorious positive.

I have been fascinated to read about what happened in one entire family where the blessings of the Law of the Generations were joyously fulfilled through many generations.

In her delightful book about 'the uncommon union of Jonathan and Sarah Edwards'[18] Elisabeth D. Dodds gives us a composite portrait of the Jonathan Edwards family. Edwards, the Puritan, has been wrongly pictured as an overly-serious ecclesiastical sour-puss, remembered chiefly for a single sermon, 'Sinners in the Hands of an Angry God.' The full picture of him is very different.

Sarah Pierrepont and Jonathan Edwards were married in 1727 after a courtship of four years. Edwards was over six feet tall, towering over most of his contemporaries. His bride was a vibrant brunette with erect posture, gracious manners, and a gift for conversation that put people at ease.

The Puritan view of marriage was not the restrictive and spiritless one usually assumed. Most Puritans had a healthy viewpoint towards marriage, sex, and family life. Sarah's wedding dress was 'no white wraith mistily drifting towards some vague spiritual experience ... but she wore a pea-green satin brocade with a bold pattern as she stepped joyfully towards her lover.'

Sarah and Jonathan were to have eleven children. Edwards believed in rising very early, so everyone in the house was routed out even in the dark winter pre-dawn for prayers by candlelight. The family heard the father read a chapter from the Bible and then ask God's blessing on the day ahead.

Each child had chores. As the child's taste developed, his or her tasks were chosen as largely as possible on the basis of special talents and wishes. For example, Esther gardened, while Mary claimed that she was the champion maker of chocolate. The house functioned efficiently because all these highly individual children were taught to work together.

Courtesy was the rule. The parents approached the discipline of their children united; and this may be one reason why the children, in turn, married happily.

One Samuel Hopkins, who spent many months with this family, wrote in his quaint style:

> Sarah carefully observed the first appearance of resentment and ill will in her young children towards any person whatsoever, and she never connived at it ... Her system of discipline was begun at a very early age ... She wisely reflected that until a child will obey his parents, he can never be brought to obey God.

Edwards always gave one hour a day of complete attention to his children. Towards evening, he would take his place in his chair, one with a high back, unmistakably the father's. No one else presumed to sit in this particular chair. During this hour the children could ask questions, get help with lessons, or anything else they wanted.

Today it staggers us even to think about the work involved in such a household. How did Sarah Edwards stand up under this? Here security and fulfilment came from her certain assurance of her husband's love and the place of great honour always given her in their home. Jonathan treated Sarah with total courtesy and serenely expected that each child would follow his example. His wife always sat next to her husband at the table. Their children were able to observe daily the small affectionate demonstrations of their parents' love for one another.

About four o'clock on fair afternoons, Edwards would emerge from his study and suggest that Sarah join him in a horseback ride. The couple would ride together in the hills above the river. Edwards would test the day's harvest of ideas against Sarah's practical intelligence.

Sarah depended on her husband for her own spiritual replenishment. Whenever she felt an acute need of it, she would dive into his study during the day, confident that no matter how intent he was on his writing, he would put down his pen and turn to her with a lighted face. She fed on his leadership in family prayers and on the quiet times she and Edwards spent together on devotions after the children were in bed, a time together that put a benediction on the bustle of the daylight hours.

In those Colonial days, most women lost their looks early. Not so, Sarah. Her husband appreciated her beauty and her style. Everything she did was with flair. She took the trouble to tie her hair with a ribbon for breakfast and found time to arrange bouquets of the day lilies, pansies, and pinks she grew.

Though the Edwards had little money, Jonathan once spent eleven pounds for a gold chain and locket for his wife. So unusual was this for the time that his parishioners were critical of what they regarded as an overly-lavish gift.

On another occasion, Sarah went through a bad emotional time for a number of weeks. Long before anyone had thought of psychotherapy, Jonathan had Sarah sit down and tell him everything she could remember about the weeks past. Using a shorthand system he had invented, he took down her words in full. By promptly reliving the difficult weeks, Sarah was able to put into perspective the pressures which had built up over fourteen years of never-ending household demands. From then on, she sailed through strains that might have sent another woman into bitter seclusion or whining invalidism.

In this family where 'the hearts of the fathers and the children' were so visibly turned one to another, it is possible to see how God blessed them down through the generations 'unto thousands of them that love me, and keep my commandments.'[19] In 1900 A. E. Winship tracked down 1,400 of the Edwards' descendants and published a study detailing what astonishing riches this family had contributed to the American scene. By 1900 this single marriage had produced:

13 College presidents
65 Professors
100 Lawyers and a dean of an outstanding law school
30 Judges
56 Physicians and a dean of a medical school
80 Holders of public office:
    3 United States senators
    Mayors of three large cities
    Governors of three states
    A vice-president of the United States
    A comptroller of the United States Treasury

Members of the family had written 135 books ranging from *Five Years In An English University* to a tome on *Butterflies Of North America*. They had edited eighteen journals and periodicals. They had entered the ministry in platoons, with nearly 100 of them becoming missionaries overseas.

The Edwards family is a beautiful showcase of how God fulfils His promises when we do our part. For the greatest blessings that God has for us are never offered just to the individual. Always, 'the promise is unto you, and to your children . . .'[20] And the early Church held up as the ideal not individual salvation but household salvation, thus demonstrating the outworking of the Law of the Generations in the love and interrelatedness of the Christian community.

God is sending us a ringing call to understand that we cannot escape the blessing or the curse of the generations. If we will allow Him to, our Lord:

    . . . shall turn the heart of the fathers to the children and the heart of the children to the fathers . . .

Here is God's singing, soaring promise of what this could ultimately mean to nations of splintered families.

'The generations' can start to assume their creative function *at any point*. Even if most of one's life is in the past and certain children and grandchildren are acute problem cases, yes, even then God can turn this curse that goes down through the generations into a blessing. Moreover, this redemptive work can even work backwards, as in Peter's prayer for me, when my son was the instrument used to stop the fear inheritance up through an older generation as well as down to the generations to come.

For each of us — no matter what our situation or how we feel we have failed — there is hope.

See, I have set before you this day life and death, the blessing and the curse . . .

Therefore, choose life.

CHAPTER FIVE

THE JOY OF OBEDIENCE

Have you ever had an inner nudge to do something but have resisted it? Then later you found out why you should have obeyed the nudge? Most of us have experienced this.

Of course, we are right to be careful about obeying hunches because they can come from selfish desires or from negative forces outside us. On the other hand, when a person has asked God to take over his life and guide his actions, disregarding the inner Voice can be costly. I have heard story after story dramatising how the Lord tries to reach us with His wisdom and help.

The latest comes from Nancy De Moss. She and her husband Art, on that unforgettable Sunday night, September 3rd, 1972, were living in a spacious English Tudor house not far from Valley Forge, Pennsylvania. He and Nancy have seven children.

The week before Labour Day week-end, Nancy received a telephone call from her sister Lynne. She and her husband were going on a short trip for the holiday. Would Nancy be willing to keep their baby? With seven De Moss children in the sprawling house there was always room for one more. Nancy readily agreed. She thought the eleven-month-old Brandon was one of the most beautiful babies she had ever seen: tow-headed with big blue eyes and a smile that melted everyone who saw it.

But this time taking care of Brandon turned out to be difficult. The baby was restless from teething. For two nights the household got little sleep. On Sunday Nancy decided to move the baby's crib from the guest room (where it was proving difficult to hear him) to the playroom down the hall. That way both Nancy and the housekeeper could hear Brandon.

While the family was at dinner that evening, Ginny, a good friend of Nancy's sister, dropped in. 'I've come to take Brandon home with me,' she told the family.

When Nancy protested, Ginny explained, 'Lynne had asked me to keep Brandon. I was the one who should have taken him. I just know it. But we had something on for the week-end and I let this loom too large in my mind and turned her down. Ever since I've known that was wrong.'

'But my sister will be home soon,' Nancy said, 'and I don't mind keeping the baby a bit.'

'I know. But Brandon usually does stay with us, you know.'

When Nancy saw that nothing she could say would change Ginny's mind, she agreed and Ginny drove off with the baby.

Later on that night Art and Nancy had been asleep several hours when they were awakened by violent pounding on the door.

'The house is on fire!' shouted the housekeeper. 'I'm getting the children out.'

By the time the De Mosses had worked their way through dense smoke to the front lawn, they discovered that the three oldest girls were still inside the burning building. Nancy and the other children huddled together praying. Art ran around to the back to try to get to the three girls. The De Moss home is well out from the nearest town; the fire trucks were slow in arriving.

Inside the burning house the girls tried the back stairs only to have flames and smoke cut them off. Two of the girls groped their way to safety down another flight of stairs. But Charlotte, stumbling through the smoke, turned the wrong way and found herself back in the bedroom. She started out again only to find that in the crucial minutes lost, all escape routes had been cut off.

Running to the bedroom window, she screamed for help. The policemen, feeling helpless not to have ladders, tried to form a human net, then told Charlotte to jump. It seemed a long way down, but the thirteen-year-old leaped. Though the men did their utmost to break her impact, she fell hard and injured her back.

'Charlotte's fine now,' Nancy told me. 'Actually, she's received amazing blessings from the experience. During her time in the hospital she got so much attention that she's blossomed under it, sort of found her identity.'

'Did you ever find out how the fire started?' I asked her.

'No. The fire started in the playroom just a few feet from where the baby would have been sleeping. No one could have got Brandon out alive.' Nancy's eyes opened wide at that point. 'I get chills every time I think of what would have happened to Brandon if Ginny hadn't come for him.'

'It certainly puts a frightening priority on obeying those inner nudges,' I commented.

'Yes, it does — except that Ginny said it was more like a distress signal, then after that like an inner shove. She's been wondering for some time now how a person gets God's guidance. In this situation the signal was loud and clear. She was restless that particular Sunday afternoon. Her thoughts kept going to Brandon and her refusal to take him in the first place. But the child was obviously all right with us. Then suddenly Ginny had this strong feeling that she *must* go and bring Brandon back to her house.

'She was afraid she would sound silly to us. It could be embarrassing. She tried to shake off the feeling, but by dinnertime Ginny knew she had to obey. Instead of calling me, she left a message with the housekeeper to have Brandon's things ready. She knew that if she came in person, I couldn't turn her away without the baby. So the baby's life actually hung on Ginny's determination in obeying what she so deeply felt.'

As I pondered this story in subsequent days, I remembered how often Jesus had told us that we would be wise men and women to obey His instructions. He even went on to say that when we go through great difficulty — such as torrential rain and floods and storm winds beating against our house, it will not collapse and we won't be in real danger — if we obey Him.[2]

Yet how difficult it is for most of us to believe that the obedience God asks of us is for our benefit. A story like Nancy's makes it clear that it is *not* obeying that poses the appalling risk. No wonder Jesus had so much to say about obedience!

Unlike earthly kings, God does not want our obedience out of fear. Our obedience to Him is the fruit of lives growing in the rich soil of love and trust. Our obedience is to be at once both the result of our loving God and also the proof of our love.[3] As with our human love, we are going to be capable of loving only to the extent that we abandon ourselves to another with no reservations.

Nancy's story made me eager to search out Jesus' words on obedience. I found an amazing assortment of riches promised those who learn the joys of obedience:

Salvation is given to those who obey.[4]

When we purpose in our will to obey Jesus and tell Him so, then we shall know whether Jesus' teachings are from God or merely His own.[5]

We become members of Jesus' family when we obey Him.[6]

The Father will come to a man who obeys and make His abode within him.[7]

Jesus will manifest Himself to those that obey.[8]

The Holy Spirit is given to those that obey.[9]

Our deeds will be blessed when we obey.[10]

As we obey Jesus, the Father will shower us and our affairs with His love.[11]

Certainly, these are impressive dividends from obedience. But what exactly are we to obey? Since Jesus often mentioned His commandments, I found it helpful to read the Gospels through, setting down in a notebook the commandments which Christ Himself gave us. There are a remarkable number of them and many are surprisingly precise.

In addition, Scripture clearly points out other kinds of obedience God requires of us:

(1) To law and governmental authority.

As citizens of transient earthly kingdoms (along with the eternal kingdom of God) we are voluntarily to subject ourselves to law and the national government over us.[12]

(2) To the individual's Christian fellowship — what the Bible calls 'the Body', meaning the true Church, the Body of Christ on earth, we are to 'be subject one to another'.[13] Thus the individual's inner guidance is to be checked against the wisdom of the group mind.[14]

(3) To our human family.

Depending upon our individual position in the family unit, God asks of us obedience and responsibility in a chain of Divine Order which He has established ... Christ is the Head of each human family.[15]

The husband is under Christ's authority as he assumes leadership of his home and final authority over the children of the household.[16]

The wife is the helpmate to the husband, protected by him from stresses outside the home and even from any abuse from children. God would elevate woman, not plunge her into servitude. Rather, her husband is to honour and love her with an unselfish love even as 'Christ loved the Church and gave Himself up for her.'[17]

Children are to obey both their parents 'in everything, for this pleases the Lord.'[18]

This Divine Order gives us necessary safeguards so that the individual does not mistake the Shepherd's voice. With such solid support, we can relax into the freedom of a living Lord's dealings with us individually. It is when we try to hear Christ's Voice for the daily decisions that we begin to know Jesus personally. Most people are astonished at His interest in the details of this relationship: how well He knows us, all the little things we thought we had successfully hidden; how realistic and relevant are the directions that He gives us.

Substituting a type of super-spirituality for Jesus' homespun practicality can be one subtle way many of us try to keep a safe distance between Him and us. C. S. Lewis humorously illustrates this by telling us one way we can 'render our prayers innocuous'; make sure that they're always very 'spiritual', that we are concerned with the state of another's soul, for instance, rather than his rheumatism.[19]

It may turn upside down one's preconceived notions about Jesus to realise that He *is* concerned about rheumatism and not especially interested in the lofty generalities in which we tend to take refuge. The Bible also tells us that He is concerned about the fall of sparrows and the baby's teething and our little habits that have us bound more than we realise.

Insomnia may seem an odd affliction through which to learn the Lord's definition of obedience.

Not long ago I was still one of those unfortunates struggling with sleeplessness. In 1955 my physician had suggested a mild sleeping pill as the best solution. After years of using these, I was aware of the still small Voice on the inside calling the pills into question. But I kept ducking. There was the fear, not even admitted to myself, that if I listened to the Inner Voice, He would say something I didn't want to hear.

On those sleepless nights when my churning mind would not be turned off, wearily I would finally get up to find the cylindrical plastic bottle with the tiny capsules, pink on one half, blue on the other. Sometimes half-aware of a 'Stop' on the inside, I would pause even as my hand reached for the bottle. 'But I'm so exhausted', would run the counter thought. 'Surely this isn't the time to fight spiritual battles. I need sleep to get on with that important work tomorrow.' Once again I would take the sleeping pill.

Then one morning in 1972 *en route* to the airport to catch a plane, I realised that I had left the sleeping pills at home. I thought, 'Great! God has a wonderful sense of humour. The joke's on me! So this is the way He's going to give me the breakthrough I've been wanting.' Then I asked Him to see to it that I slept naturally.

As usual, His ways were not my ways. That night I did not sleep at all. Dawn found me weary from tossing and from praying in what seemed to be a vacuum and fighting a losing battle with self-pity. But leaving the pills behind had uncovered in a stark way how over-dependent I was on barbiturates.

Upon returning home, my prayers took the form of direct questions, 'Lord, am I hearing You correctly on this? Is this false guilt I have about something really unimportant, like these foolish little pills?'

When His answer finally came, there was no difficulty about recognising His voice, 'Yes, pills are foolish. But the more important point is, you desire sleep more than Me. Therefore, lay your cherished sleep on My altar. Make this your alabaster box of ointment poured out for Me.'

His words rang true, like the notes of a clear bell perfectly in tune. Obviously He was applying to my life His 'If you love Me, keep My commandments.' I realised then that obedience was going to be the key to some fresh new understanding. I was also to find that this is the way to get understanding rather than by the intellectualising, library-digging route — obey first, then the illumination comes.

That September afternoon I searched through the medicine cabinet for all the sleeping pills. There was a large supply on hand. Taking a deep breath, I flushed them away and watched as the swirling mass of pink and blue disappeared from sight. Then I told God that I was going to depend on Him alone for sleep.

There followed eight rough days and nights. My dependence on God was real enough but so was my sleeplessness. How was it, I would marvel over and over, that both body and mind could be so fatigued, yet I would be unable to sleep? Isn't it man's natural state to sleep?

Quickly I found that continued loss of sleep was resulting in over-sensitised nerves day and night. The slightest noise was amplified many times ... Someone would turn the pages of a magazine and for me it would be a loud rustling flip-flop. A bug would hit the windowpane and I would jump. I would turn over in bed and the freshly-laundered sheets crackled in my ears. I couldn't even nap of an afternoon. Something was inhibiting the sleep mechanism.

That God would let the struggle be so brutal came as a shock. Having taken what I fondly considered a positively heroic step in dumping the pills, I had expected my reward: an instant miracle.

I was given one, though not what I had expected. Even in the midst of my deepest fatigue there was no real temptation to go back to the sleeping pills even for one good night's sleep. The set of my will was firmly held by Someone else, astonishing to me because it was not of my doing.

I was learning about the part the will plays in our relationship with God. First, there is that period of initial struggle of the will when we know full well that a decision has to be made. God won't force it on us; it must be entirely our choice.

Once the struggle is resolved to the point of saying 'Yes' to Him — especially when it's accompanied by some irretrievable step such as pill-dumping — then the struggle in the will subsides. Grace is given an individual at that juncture, in the sense that the decision has been made. God regards it as a binding contract. It's as if by saying 'Yes' to Him, we pick up the ball (the will) and throw it to Him. He takes it then; He carries the will for us.

Even so, during these days I was given no relief on the sleep front. In an effort to understand, I began doing some reading about sleep. Some scientists believe that the brain has both a sleep centre and a wakefulness centre,[20] much as one's heart action is regulated by one set of nerves to stimulate activity, another set to reduce activity. It is theorised that natural sleep comes through reducing the wakefulness centre's activity partly by withdrawing nervous impulses to the brain. Artificial sleep from pills comes through a chemical that enters the blood stream and may depress or inhibit the waking centre's activity, thus changing the brain's chemistry. So for me, long use of even mild sleeping pills obviously had knocked my sleep mechanism all askew.

The nights seemed endless. I would hear a dog barking somewhere. Then the electric refrigerator clicking off. There would be the sound of a train in the distance, the five-after-two-in-the-morning freight. The engineer was blowing his whistle for that long straight stretch just before town.

The long periods of wakefulness required sharp disciplining of thoughts and emotions. I had had a lifetime tendency to let my thoughts sink to the bottom every time I would let my mind go fallow. Now a new level of obedience was being asked of me where negative or critical thoughts, doubting and worrying must be turned off immediately. After a few nights I noticed that I could take more authority over the negativism. This then, was another bonus of obedience.

I was also having to battle another by-product of barbiturates. These drugs tend to inhibit dreaming. In sleep experiments[21] those deprived of dreaming begin to show nervous and behavioural disturbances. Since much of my dreaming had been inhibited, conflicts and tensions had been building up in my unconscious.

It was a great night when I got three to four hours' sleep. When I did sleep, my dreams seemed continuous and wild and persistently pointed to two deep anxieties — rejection and danger. In an effort to understand, I wrote down the dream of September 23rd ...

I am the preacher's wife in a church in which an elaborate wedding is being solemnised — more gala than solemn. There are tickets to present at the church door and a fashion show is also to be part of the affair.

I am acutely aware that I am not part of the 'in' group. I seem to have arrived late and am incorrectly dressed. There is some discussion as to whether I am to be allowed into the church without a ticket. Fashionably dressed women are milling all around me looking at me curiously.

The dream ends without my knowing whether or not I will be admitted inside to see the ceremony.

There were also many dreams in which there was actual danger...

A group of us have been told that something important (unidentified) is missing. We are asked to go and get it. We have to walk a long way — uphill and down, through several houses, in one door, out another. I feel threatened. Some of the women argue with me, some are belligerent.

There are even physical threats — one especially vivid one: as we pass through one house near the front screen door, the man of the house warns, 'Look out! Pull your hat over your forehead. And watch the angle that you open that door.'

On the porch a rifle is mounted on a stand to the left of the door. It is connected to the door like a booby-trap, so that when the door is opened to a certain angle, the gun fires.

I wake up shivering with fear.

Sometimes resentment would rise in me. 'All right, Lord,' I would protest, 'I obeyed You and look where it's gotten me. I've been miserable ever since.'

Eventually the answering insight came, 'When you obey, I do more than handle one little thing. You've been demanding an instant miracle for sleep; I want a healing of the whole woman. You've been asking for *one* blessing; obedience is the door through which I plan to flood you with blessings.'

Following that, on the eighth day came the first breakthrough. After the worst night of all, I slept a little towards dawn and awoke with a single clause in my mind, presented to me in an authoritative and luminous way: *Blessed assurance, Jesus is mine.*

I recognised it as an old gospel hymn, one I had not thought about for years. When I looked it up and got all the words, God's message to me was plain and oh, so welcome:

> Blessed assurance, Jesus is mine!
> Oh, what a foretaste of glory divine!
> Heir of salvation, purchase of God,
> Born of His Spirit, washed in His blood,
> This is my story, this is my song,
> Praising my Saviour all the day long . . .[22]

This came as if in direct answer to the rejection aspect of my dreams. Obedience had helped me identify and face the rejection. Here was God's reassurance of His love and care for me, as if He was saying in terms of sleep, 'You may fall tranquilly asleep any time you need to, for I love you.'

So obedience in the little area of pills had led to the beginning of this deep healing of a basic need. The last line of the hymn pointed me to the next step in the healing — praise. That now-familiar way of praise — the open door to God!

After that, the threat-fear aspect of my dreams diminished, then disappeared altogether. In their stead delightful dreams of promise surfaced. Such as the one on September 30th . . .

I am wandering from room to room in a large house. In the spacious dining-room is a large and beautiful rug, and on it, an intricately-designed carved mahogany table, with portraits on the walls. An air of mustiness pervades everything as if these rooms have long been in disuse. Though I have never seen such a room, in the dream I have the impression that it is mine.

Going on to the adjoining room, I stand looking at tall cupboards with glass doors all around. They are filled with china and glassware that I recognise as belonging to me, but these possessions have not been used in a long time. I stand staring at all of it wonderingly, thinking how beautiful it is and what happiness to know that it will now be used again.

Whatever else this meant, certainly there was implied the picking up again of joyous activities that had somehow been set aside. The quantities of china and glassware suggested entertaining as a reactivation of human relationships in a creative outgoing way and an end to the unconscious mind's conviction of rejection.

The ninth day saw real victory, the wonderful feeling of sinking blissfully to sleep without fear and resistance.

Now, all these months later, I can say, 'Yes, it's natural to sleep.' And how great not only to be free from the chains of dependence but to know that lifelong problems are being healed.

Yet the road to freedom had to be through that low door of

obedience. Best of all is the closer fellowship with the Lord that always follows obeying a specific He asks of us.

After such an experience the Shepherd usually allows us a plateau for rest and refreshment. Then we learn that this obedience is a steady daily discipline and that the discipline is for life. But being fickle creatures, we use our freedom of will sometimes to take back what we've already handed over to the Lord.

It took my friend Pat Baker several years to conquer the cigarette habit. But finally breaking the habit was the least of her rewards. She was given insights about her own personal motivations; about the difference between real and counterfeit sacrifice; about how important it is to let God design the blueprint for obedience rather than trying to fabricate it ourselves.

After many tries, Pat had at last achieved a four months' conquest of the smoking habit. The victory had come through a simple step of obedience. For weeks Pat had been feeling God's inner 'Stop' each time she reached for a pack of cigarettes. There came a day when she said 'Yes' but added, 'If I'm going to have to quit, You'll have to do this for me.' Lying on the dresser before her was a pack of cigarettes. Deliberately, she left them there. Every time she was tempted to pick one up, she would think, 'If this were my idea to stop, I'd already have a cigarette in my mouth by now. But it's just not me at all.'

She found it exhilarating — the most joyful experience of her life. Then one evening she and her husband Dick had an argument. In a spirit of rebellion, Pat fled the house and drove around town trying to dispel her anger. All at once, she found herself reaching for a pack of cigarettes her husband had left on the front seat. Even as she did so, she was saying on the inside, 'Lord, I know You've told me to stop. And I really will stop — but not quite yet.'

For a year after the argument with her husband, Pat found

herself waging a losing battle in her struggle with tobacco. She asked prayers from all and sundry friends. Some of them suggested that one way of tackling the problem was to probe why she had started smoking in the first place. Yet Pat could find no answer to the question.

At last she got to that point of desperation I knew so well. 'O Lord, I want to be free. I really do. And I won't take the cigarettes back this time.' There was no immediate answer.

Then one Sunday afternoon she felt as if she was coming down with a cold. She decided on a nap. When she awakened she instantly recognised that there was something not of herself in the clear thought of her mind, 'Get up. Get dressed. Go down to the Bethany Church.'

Pat was inclined to argue, 'Lord, that's a wild church. I'm an Episcopalian. I've never been in that kind of place ...' Then more humbly, 'Lord, if this is really You and this is what I'm supposed to do, would you please let Dick agree to it?'

Ordinarily her husband Dick would say in a situation of this kind, 'Don't be ridiculous. You've been out three nights this week. Be sensible and go back to bed.'

This time, however, when she told him of this strange nudging, he answered, 'Go ahead, I think you should.'

When Pat got to the church she found that some sort of evangelistic services were going on. She slipped into the back hoping that she wouldn't be noticed. After all, this was a small town. What would her fellow Episcopalians think of her attending this kind of church?

Then the preacher's words caught her attention. He was speaking about Cain and Abel and about Abel's 'more excellent sacrifice.'

'Perhaps,' the young preacher said, 'Cain never liked the idea of killing innocent little lambs as a sacrifice to Jehovah. Why would Jehovah ask them to do that? Wouldn't it be better to wait until he understood why, and then obey?

'Meanwhile, if God wanted a sacrifice, how about that beautiful mound of fruits and vegetables he had grown! Those perfect bunches of grapes! Those luscious pomegranates and figs! Surely Jehovah would like those!

'You see, the problem with Cain,' the young preacher summarised, 'was that he was offering a sacrifice all right, one that he had thought up, but *not the sacrifice God had asked for.*'

Sitting there listening, Pat thought of all her multitudinous church and civic activities, of her generous giving of time and money, of her sacrifices during Lent. But the clear counter-thought came to her, *None of this is any good unless you do the particular thing I'm asking you to do.*

'O Lord,' Pat answered in her thoughts, 'I hear You loud and clear, but I can't do what You're telling me to do. I've tried. I just can't.'

Now the evangelist was giving an altar call, but it wasn't the usual one. 'All those,' he said, 'who came here expecting God to do something for them, come forward to receive it.'

That sounded the right note to Pat. She knew that being there hadn't been her idea in the first place. 'But,' she struggled with herself, 'I'm just not going down there. I know that young man will shout like those other evangelists do . . . "Lord", do they *have* to be so loud about it?'

Moments later she was astonished to find herself kneeling at the altar rail. The evangelist made his way to her first of all. Without saying a word, he knelt quietly on the other side. Pat looked across the rail at him, surprised at his quietness. Finally he said, almost whispering, 'The Holy Spirit never gives one of us a message for another person in order to hurt or embarrass them. The message is always given to help another. Do you understand that?'

'Yes, I do,' Pat replied, marvelling at the way the young minister was speaking directly to her thoughts.

'Would you like to hear what God has for you this afternoon?'

She nodded.

'Well, He's ready to deal with you about your problem with nicotine.'

Pat stared at him in astonishment. How could he possibly know that? She listened wide-eyed as he began telling her when and why she had started to smoke. 'It started when you were a teenager and it grew out of the soil of rebellion. Even then, God was calling you, but you weren't willing to listen. Now He has a special Gift of the Spirit for you, one that He wants you to use in a particular ministry for Him. If you're willing to get rid of the nicotine, He'll reveal more to you of what this is all about.'

Then the evangelist told Pat how to get free. 'If you will resist the nicotine for three days, the Lord will do the rest. At the end of that time, He promises to reveal something of the particular kind of work He's calling you to.'

As she drove home that night Pat thought, 'Well, I suppose I can do anything for three days.' But she was to find even three days so much more difficult than it had been the first time. Now it was a moment-by-moment battle.

On the third day, a friend whose marriage was in trouble came to thank Pat for helping her find her way out of darkness several weeks before. Immediately, Pat realised that she had allowed her bondage to cigarettes to interfere even with helping other people. She had been so preoccupied with herself and her hang-ups like smoking that there had been no time or mind space for anyone else. The impact of her friend's gratitude brought Pat tears of remorse followed by a surge of joy and a strong resolve that bolstered her resistance.

From that point, Pat found herself free of the desire to smoke — when she was awake! But strangely, she began to dream of smoking.

The dreams were so vivid! She could taste the cigarettes and smell the smoke, and would wake up with the knowledge that she had been fighting the desire to smoke on unconscious levels. Out of this experience Pat learned that we have to be of one piece — not divided between the conscious and the unconscious — before a prayer can be finally answered. In her case, Pat had been delivered from smoking on the surface; now a deeper work was going on in her unconscious.

Dreams by night and insights by day revealed to her what the evangelist had suggested; the smoking had started through insecurity during her courtship days. Now she was able to remember what had goaded her to start smoking — nothing more than several paragraphs in one of Dick's letters. He was then at the University of Florida, and to tease her, he had written glowingly about another girl.

Pat had over-reacted with anger and jealousy. Wanting to rebel against Dick and her whole life, she chose cigarettes as the best symbol of rebellion. Hadn't her mother always made *not* smoking a symbol of virtue? Before she and Dick could resolve the quarrel, Pat had started smoking.

The battle of the cigarettes is four years behind Pat now. Depending on the Lord (instead of cigarettes) in moments of friction and stress has brought Pat not only joy, but a steady stream of deepening insights to help other people with their problems.

When Jesus says, 'Follow Me', not one of us is going to drop his fishing nets to leave all and go after Him — unless he feels he can trust Him. One memorable sentence quoted by the Quakeress Hannah Smith sums it up, 'Perfect obedience would be perfect happiness if only we had perfect confidence in the power we were obeying.'[23]

So we're back full circle to the only basis there is for obedience — love and trust. It may seem hard to be asked to have this kind of confidence before we have had personal experiences of

God. But He also helps us out of that dilemma. The moment we 'purpose in our heart' to obey Him, at that instant He comes to help us. His incomparable gift is the ability to obey, to move out into what usually looks like uncharted and dangerous country.

That's the way it was for Abraham long ago. The Lord had told him to uproot himself and his family: 'Get thee out of thy country and from thy kindred . . . unto a land that I will show thee . . . and I will bless thee . . . and thou shalt be a blessing.'[24]

There was the word of command. There was the promise of blessing. There was no option to ask 'Why?' or 'Please explain everything to me.' Always and always the understanding comes after the obedience.

So Abraham obeyed. 'He went out, not knowing whither he went.' He did not need to know because God knew. And the result of this 'blind' obedience has blessed uncounted millions down all the generations.

CHAPTER SIX

'TO SLEEP! PERCHANCE TO DREAM...'

I dreamed last night . . .

> *In a living-room I saw a pedestal-stand about two feet tall. On it had been placed the head of a woman. From a distance it looked like one of those marble busts that one sees in palaces or museums.*
>
> *But this bust was different. It had been severed from the body of a living woman and placed atop the pedestal.*
>
> *In my dream as I looked on, a female figure appeared in the room. She looked at the bust as she passed within a few feet of it. Then she uttered just two words. 'It stinks.'*

I keep wondering, what is the dream trying to tell me?

Seemingly gruesome in imagery, I was to learn later that it held a potent spiritual message.

Few of us attached importance to dreams until the rising influence of psychiatry began to pique interest in the subject. Even those who have never been near a psychiatrist's office now know that patients are asked to take their dreams seriously enough to capture them on paper and consider them.

Even so, the average person wonders from time to time if dreams have anything rational and constructive to say to us? Or are they the result simply of eating too much pizza or from something one saw on the Late Late Show?

On the other side, I have heard of instances where scientists or inventors unable to finish an experiment or a project because of something eluding them, decided to 'sleep on it'. And some-how as they slept, the unconscious served up the solution needed — sometimes directly upon awakening, sometimes in a dream.

Yet most of us have regarded these experiences as flukes. What about the bulk of dream material? Isn't it mostly just garbage-pail residue of daytime experiences?

Clearly, psychoanalysts do not think so. It was in 1900 that Sigmund Freud published his book *The Interpretation of Dreams*, for the first time connecting dreams with the uncon-scious in an empirical study. Among physicians and the public in general, Freud's book met with contempt: it took eight years to sell the 600 copies of the first edition.

As time went on, dream interpretation came to be an ac-cepted part of psychotherapy. Even so, I could uncover little on the subject in Christian literature. The Church for the most part was ignoring the subject. This was strange when we con-sider the thread of dream material all through the Bible. I had no sooner become interested in the subject than I realised that the Bible is a veritable storehouse of dreams. How had I pre-viously overlooked this! Jacob dreamed of a ladder from earth to heaven; another time of spotted he-goats mating with the flock. Joseph dreamed of his brothers' sheaves bowing down and worshipping his sheaf; later, he interpreted the Pharaoh's dreams. The child Samuel's dream; Amos' dream of a plumb line; Isaiah's of his lips touched with the live coal from the altar; Ezekiel's dream of the valley of dry bones. The book of Daniel — full of dreams. Such an amazing amount of material!

The gist of the Bible's message is that God frequently uses dreams as a medium of revelation.

If there is a prophet among you, I the Lord make myself known to him in a vision, I speak with him in a dream ... in dark speech.[1]

Nor is there any diminution of this emphasis on dreams in the New Testament. We see the Wise Men being warned in a dream not to go back to Herod but to return to their country another way; Joseph told in a dream to take the young child and his mother and flee to Egypt. We see Pilate's wife frantically sending her husband the message, 'I have suffered many things this day in a dream because of him (Jesus).'[2] A major tenet of the early Church was turned on its head by the Apostle Peter's dream picture of the sheet let down from heaven with all manner of birds, reptiles, animals — clean and unclean — in it. And the last book of the Bible, Revelation, is almost entirely dream and vision material of John, then an old man.

Why does the Church in our time pay so little attention to dreams? For a number of years, Freud's viewpoint that the unconscious was concerned mainly with sexuality dominated the field. Perhaps the trouble was that blinded by Freud's emphasis, the Church could not find a connection between the Scriptural emphasis placed on dreams as the vehicle for all manner of messages — dreams thus being one way of God speaking to man — and the Freudian doctrine of sexuality.

As the years have gone on and Freud's dream theories have been amended and enriched by the works of Alfred Adler and Carl Jung and others, as well as a decade of work in sleep laboratories,[3] I discovered that a few men here and there in the Church have been constrained to take another look at the Biblical emphasis on dreams. Two of them, Morton T. Kelsey,[4] and John A. Sanford,[5] both Episcopal priests, have experimented, often successfully, in helping troubled people make use of dream material. (At the time I discovered this, little did I realise how much this was shortly going to mean to me personally.)

It's a big subject and generalisations are dangerous. Those who work in this field warn that we must not try to work out pat formulae to help us interpret our dreams. The point is that the psyche, the total mental and psychological structure of a person, is not just the repository for dead memories but is living and fluid; it will not be pigeonholed any more than the Spirit of God acting upon the psyche can be pigeonholed.

Having warned us, they nevertheless come to our aid with some helpful suggestions ... The unconscious usually 'thinks' or translates thoughts into pictures. These pictures usually take the form of either parables or cartoon-like story material. The parables are in many respects reminiscent of the stories and symbols Jesus used in His parable-stories; in other dreams they are akin to the kinds of stories in the folklore of all peoples. Often our dream cartoons or parables are woven into a story or play acted out on an inner stage while we sleep.

The unconscious mind does not think analytically, but symbolically or pictorially. Dream symbols are provocative in their wide variety and above all, in their originality.

We've only to take note of a few of our dreams to know that with our conscious mind we never could have put together such highly original imagery. In some images there is a great simplicity, but the originality is in the way the dream uses them. Here are some symbols from my own dreams and those of others close to me:

> The dreamer is in a rose garden eating rose petals, but carefully; eating the petals will make him intoxicated.

> A child's wicker toy basket is turned upside down over a flame to quench it.

> A flight of newly-constructed stairs has no place for one's feet because all the treads are missing.

> My house is burning, but is not consumed.

> A snowstorm of small squares of fresh white paper falls from the sky.

> A toilet is made of several huge shells.

A large pair of scissors is used as a murder weapon.

I see a baby in a tiny boat on a rushing stream.

We wonder where such highly original imagery comes from. In part, the experts say, from conscious sights, impressions, and thoughts passed on into the 90 per cent of the psyche below the level of consciousness, then screened, condensed, and translated into dream images.

But beyond this personal area, Freud, Jung, and others believed that the unconscious draws its material from the race mind — what Jung called 'the collective unconscious'. It is at this point that many dream figures and images connect us with the symbolism used by Jesus, the folk stories of all peoples, and the world's fairy tales.

It reminds us of that memorable little statement inserted in the Gospel of John. 'He (Jesus) knew what was in man.'[6] Therefore, it shouldn't surprise us that He deliberately chose to use symbolism which would speak to both the conscious and unconscious levels of men of all nations in every century. Notice how Jesus used objects in the external world to teach us truth about the internal world even as our dreams do:

A candle covered by a bushel basket.

A plank sticking out of a man's eyes.

Pearls being thrown before hogs.

Digging up a treasure in a field.

A minuscule seed growing into an immense tree.

A woman hiding starter-dough in a barrel of flour.

Fishermen with a drag-net pulling in unimaginable varieties of fish.

A serpent lifted high on a stick.

Though some dream symbols come out of this collective unconscious like visions replete with sights and sounds wafting out of some far country where we were once at home, our dreams are often intensely personal and self-reflective. Something deep within seeks to give us a message. Different characters in our dreams are usually parts of our own being.

Aspects of our personality we have ignored or even cast out of our consciousness now seek to be heard. This is so even when the dream figure is of the opposite sex from the dreamer. Psychology teaches us that every man carries within his dominant masculine psyche some largely unconscious feminine traits, what Jung chooses to call 'the anima' just as every woman possesses some masculine traits, 'the animus'. Thus a feminine figure in a man's dream may be trying to point him to 'anima' qualities of sensitivity, of the emotional life, of the willingness to love and be loved.

The kind of help our dreams can give us is as varied as people's temperaments and needs. Pat Baker[7] fighting her cigarette problem, for example, found that dreams helped her become a believer in a personal God who could comfort and guide her. Married at eighteen, Pat had become pregnant almost immediately. Throughout her pregnancy, she had been deeply troubled, feeling in no way ready for the responsibilities of motherhood. She had a hunger for faith, yet doubts about a personal God. During all those months, the cry of her deep spirit had been, 'How can I rear a child when I myself have no answers to what life is all about?'

During childbirth while Pat was under anaesthesia, she had a strange dream. She was sitting in the audience in a theatre with a large stage before her. The figures who appeared on the stage looked like cartoon characters come to life. Mrs. Baker describes every vivid detail of this dream ...

On stage-right appeared a woman slowly pushing a baby carriage across the stage. The baby, a girl, was sitting up in the carriage with knitting needles and a ball of yarn trying to figure out a knitting pattern. The baby's face was tense and worried trying to understand the pattern.

As the mother pushed the carriage on, the baby was making progress: another part of the pattern would be finished. The scene before me was so huge that I could clearly see the knitting in the baby's hands. By the time the carriage was almost across the stage, all the pattern was figured out except one stitch. Then the whole tableau — mother, carriage, baby and all, fell off the end of the stage.

Watching, I could feel the drop — kerplunk! in the pit of my stomach. I heard myself saying, 'Oh no! God, You can't let that happen. You can't let that poor baby die without figuring that pattern out.'

Then I heard a male voice offstage chuckling reassuringly, as if to say, 'Don't worry about it. I've got it all figured out.'

I then also understood that the baby would know that she wasn't going to be left with that one stitch of the pattern missing. I felt inside myself a relieved, 'Oh! Thank God!' as a great peace swept over me.

Then as though to dramatise before my eyes the truth of the reassurance, almost immediately the stage came back into view. There was another mother, another carriage, another baby like the first scene, only this time the baby was peaceful. No strain on her face.

I saw the same knitting in the baby's hands, but now with the missing part of the pattern figured out and an additional one added. This time the mother and baby did not fall off the stage.

Before this, it had never occurred to Pat Baker to take dreams seriously. As if to make certain that she would not discount her dream because of the anaesthesia, she was given a detail-by-detail repeat of this dream two more times — once while still in the maternity ward, and then again after she returned home from the hospital. This was the confirmation she needed.

The dream's first gift to Pat was peace of mind. It also helped her to believe in the existence of God in a way she never had before. At a deeper level and after meditating on the dreams prayerfully, Pat realised that the baby in the carriage was a part of her being: *she* was the one who in the first dream couldn't figure out the complicated 'knitting' of life; she was the one afraid she would fall off the stage of life.

The second time across the stage, she had figured out life's pattern and she did not fall off. Thus the new mother was given total assurance that the One whom she could not see but had heard as the Voice offstage, knew what was going on in her life and had everything under control. With His help, she and her husband would be able to rear their daughter.

In those rare instances when dreams do warn of a coming event, the purpose is never to frighten or discourage us. The Creator's work through the unconscious, as elsewhere, is affirmative, directed towards a constructive end. Therefore, the dream warnings present possibilities we are meant to avoid, seldom actualities.

Dr. Glen Clark told of how Stella Holbrook, a Minneapolis woman,[8] dreamed that she saw her best friend, a Mrs. Simpson, walking back and forth in a room holding her head between her hands. She had gone insane. Horrified by the dream, Stella was unable to sleep for the remainder of the night. Early the next morning, she telephoned the friend saying that she had to see her. When they met, Stella told her, 'You are in deadly peril. You must see a doctor immediately.'

'But I've never felt better in my life,' the friend, Mrs. Simpson, remonstrated.

'No matter. I plead with you to see a doctor. I've never had a dream so real.'

As much for her distraught friend's peace of mind as anything, Mrs. Simpson made an appointment with her doctor. He found a brain tumour located where it would probably cause insanity without prompt surgery. Mrs. Simpson was stunned. Her friend had dreamed the truth after all. But it was the rest of the dream that made her recoil in horror. In Stella's dream, Mrs. Simpson was stark raving mad. So wouldn't it turn out that way — surgery or no surgery?

With this double burden of fear upon her, Mrs. Simpson stopped off to see Dr. Clark on her way to the Mayo Clinic. His advice to her was first, to clear out superstition. 'There's no power,' he told her, 'in the psychic realm of foretelling the future that can stand against God's power. You must vigorously reject any form of superstitious attachment to this dream.'

Then he added that *the dream warning had been given so that the event foreseen would not have to come to pass.* 'To foresee a thing in time,' he suggested, 'is just like foreseeing a thing in space. You would not run head-on into it, would you? You'd make a detour around it.'

Having agreed between them how to make a detour by means of prayer, Mrs. Simpson went on to Mayo's. The earlier diagnosis was confirmed. They were preparing for the operation when it was decided to ask both Dr. Judd and Dr. Will Mayo to examine the patient. Dr. Will was one of those doctors who studied the person along with his symptoms. In conversation with Mrs. Simpson, he discovered the quality of her faith.

The great surgeon seemed to withdraw into his own thoughts. After a moment of silence, he spoke slowly, thoughtfully. 'Any brain surgery is drastic, carries its own risk. There's one other way to proceed. You're the sort of person who may be capable of this other way. The human body is a marvellous creation. When helped by faith and prayer, sometimes it can take care of its own problems. I wonder?' He paused and looked at her long and hard. Mrs. Simpson almost had the impression that he was listening.

'Yes, I believe this is the way. My advice is, let's not operate right away. Mrs. Simpson, I want you to go away for three months. Live quietly, in as healthful a manner as you know. Apply all the faith you have during this time. Then let us here at Mayo's see you at the end of three months.'

So Mrs. Simpson went to a mountain cabin and devoted herself to a three-months' prayer journey towards health. Day by day she sought on the one hand, to close every separation between her and God; on the other, to open every facet of her being to healing.

In September she returned to the Mayo Clinic. New X-rays plus carotid angiograms left the specialists puzzled; the tumour was no longer there. Yet in June it had been as big as a hen's egg.

Other doctors were called in including first, Dr. Judd, and then Dr. Will Mayo. After Dr. Judd had studied the X-rays and exhaustively examined the patient, he seized Mrs. Simpson's hands in excitement. 'This,' he exclaimed, 'is a great miracle.' Dr. Will was equally joyous. 'I think this calls for a celebration,' he said.

About the time I was realising how pinpointed dreams can be, I met the Reverend Morton Kelsey, Episcopal priest and Notre Dame professor. I then read some of his books and asked if he would be so gracious as to give me help in learning to interpret my dreams.

He replied that he would be happy not only to give me his thoughts on specific dreams, but also some general principles of interpretation. I was to send him eight or ten dreams written out. We would then agree on a date for a long telephone conversation.

The telephone conference was eventually set up for three o'clock on the afternoon of July 18th, 1973. With Professor Kelsey's permission, I recorded our forty-five minute conversation. Morton Kelsey was speaking from South Bend, Indiana.

'First,' he commented, 'let's put any work with dreams in this framework ... The only way anyone should go into the unconscious is first, to ask Jesus Christ for His power and direction and protection. Personally, I find that without Him I'm in danger even going to the grocery store without His direction, let alone trying to teach a college class.

'Then some general guide lines ...

Ninety-five per cent of dream material refers to the dreamer rather than to the one being dreamed about.

Realise that the process of dreaming is, in itself, therapeutic.

One of the greatest dangers in dream interpretation is thinking that you're getting guidance for other people. Almost always it's about *you*.

When one dreams of a husband or wife, it may not necessarily refer to the mate, rather what one is 'married to' emotionally and spiritually.

An often helpful procedure is:

Write down your dream immediately upon awakening; if necessary, interrupt your sleep to write it down. Keep a pencil, pad, and flashlight by your bed for this purpose.

Later, write down the main events happening in your life just then and any major fears or worries. You will need this framework for interpretation of your dream.

As your will consents to taking dreams seriously, you'll be able to remember more and more of them. The more dreams we write down immediately upon awakening, the more the unconscious will serve up.

After writing your dream down, talk it out with some

trusted person. Let his reflection add wisdom to interpreting your dream.

Third, turn your attention to a study of symbolism, analogies, and images. A good place to begin is to review (perhaps with notebook in hand) the Bible's rich symbolism.

Most of us soon find that our thinking and training has not been in such directions: when we were young, we probably read too many Dick-and-Jane-type stories about going to the supermarket, the dentist, or helping the nice teacher change her flat tyre, so now our imaginations need reawakening and nourishment. A deliberate return to the reading of the mythology and fairy tales of all nations and of books like *Hiawatha, Gulliver's Travels, Alice in Wonderland,* C. S. Lewis' novels[9] will help to reconnect us with an important part of ourselves and also assist us in interpreting our dreams. Take the significant insights or questions into your prayer life. This will provide material for meditation.

> During meditation it is helpful to confront the other person or persons in your dream (almost always part of you) and enter into imaginative dialogue with 'them'. Then invite Christ into this three-way dialogue for His thoughts and directives.

Following these general guide lines, I was eager for Morton Kelsey's observations about my dreams of rejection and danger during the sleeping pill crisis. 'Your dream of September 23rd and the one following[10] are both classics,' the voice on the phone had a quality of joy, even laughter. 'The first one involved an elaborate wedding. How often Jesus spoke of weddings! A wedding is the union of opposites. Nothing about a real mating of opposites was possible for you until after the pill-dumping.

'Your dream wedding included a fashion show. It is reminiscent of the prodigal son on whom the father placed the "best robe". The wedding, you wrote, was "more gala than solemn",

God is not dour or grim-visaged about His religion; His grace takes from us the burden of "oughtness" and duty, and releases us to worship Him joyfully as at a feast, a banquet, a celebration. When He has a wedding feast, He does it in top style!

'You were "incorrectly dressed" . . . you didn't have on the right wedding garment. Remember that on September 23rd you were still working through the aftermath of the pill-dumping. You were not quite ready for the celebration. So the dream ended without your knowing whether you were admitted to the wedding scene.'

Then Professor Kelsey went on to discuss the dream involving physical danger.

' "We had to walk a long way," you wrote. In late September with acute insomnia still with you, the road was seeming very long indeed.

'The rifle on the porch is a reference to the sleeping pills, I feel sure. The dream's gun booby-trap was meant to be a warning. Your victory was not yet complete. By returning to the pills you could fall back again. "Look out; Watch it! This is a life and death matter," the dream was saying . . .

'By September 30th,[11] you had won your victory, so this is a dream of promise. The house is a typical dream symbol representing one's total being.

'The dining-room is for feeding people. What have you done in your writing except to feed people! You wrote, "a carved table" on a "beautiful rug" . . . "portraits on the wall". You are going to feed people beautifully.

' "The tall cupboards . . . filled with china and glassware" unused for a long time. The years of the sleeping pills had cut you off from part of your own being. Now you can use a lot of content and rich creativity in your psyche you had even forgotten you have.

'I'll made a prediction, Catherine . . . What you write in the future may have more significance than what you've written in the past.'

'Morton,' I answered, 'I hope you're right!'

A little later I switched the conversation to the Head-on-the-Pedestal dream. 'I have some ideas about it,' I said, 'but I'm very curious about yours.'

'All right,' came the voice over the telephone. 'First, a random comment. The female figure's. "It stinks" reminds me of Martha's almost identical statement at the tomb of her brother Lazarus.

'Also, do you know C. S. Lewis' *That Hideous Strength?*'

'I have a copy,' I replied, 'but haven't read it yet.'

'You'd better!' Again the chuckle came over the phone. 'In the first chapter an Englishwoman dreams of a French prisoner visited in his cell by a rather coldly cynical man. The visitor unscrews the man's head and carries it away.'

'I'll start the book tonight.'

'All right. Now first, most dreams want us to look inward. Therefore, the head on the pedestal is your head. And the female figure is probably also another part of you.

'Now one or two questions to you, Catherine. Have you had trouble with always wanting to *understand* before you step out in simple obedience?'

'Always. Most definitely. In relation to healing and lots of things about the Holy Spirit, thinking I need to understand has been a real stumbling block.'

'Second question, which do you value most, the intellectual process or the emotions?'

'The mind — far and away. I think the emotions can really lead us astray.'

'True in part,' Morton Kelsey retorted, 'Well, I think the dream was issuing you a stern warning. It was saying, "The head needs a body to be whole — not just the emotions, but the *entire* person." You see, Christianity is the world's earthiest religion. Centuries ago even very spiritual monks knew that working with their hands — gardening or erecting buildings, working vineyards or even wine-making, copying manuscripts — whatever — was as much a part of true worship as prayer. The use of the whole person, you see.'

'Then the dream was saying that I am wrong to place the head, the intellect, on such a pedestal?'

'Correct,' came the voice over the phone.

'And that when we sever the mind from the rest of us, the end result is that we die — even intellectually and so begin to decay? And' — I paused — 'stink.'

'Right. Your prayer-meditation on this dream could include at least two questions: first, at what points are you resisting the real thrust of the Holy Spirit in your life because of an over-emphasis on the mind?'

'Ouch! Now you've put your finger on one of my hang-ups with some aspects of the Holy Spirit Movement.'

'A lot of us have the same difficulty . . . Now, ask yourself the second question: 'Lord, what must I do to get my head back on my body, to begin functioning as a whole person? What is my first step in that direction?'

I was beginning to see what he meant. 'My dreams are providing lots of material for meditation.'

'Not just for you personally either,' Professor Kelsey replied. 'Hasn't the twentieth century created a society where the head rules — education, science, and technology supreme? We thought we could cleave the head from the body — divorce, "put away" the spirit, the conscience, the imagination, and emotional life and get a Utopia. Maybe instead we have a civilisation that could be summarised with a quite inelegant "It stinks."'

Dream therapy of a poignant nature was given to Tom Dowling, whom I met in 1967 at the first *Guideposts* magazine

Writers Workshop. As the background for Tom's dream, it is necessary to fill in certain details of his life ...

The Dowlings lived in California. In September, 1958 Tom had taken his wife Babs to Hawaii on a vacation trip to help her recovery from a spinal fusion operation. The young couple had left their four children in the care of Tom's father. On the fourth day tragedy suddenly struck: Babs suffered a severe cerebral haemorrhage and after the necessary brain surgery was unconscious for thirty-five days. After consciousness slowly returned, it became apparent that the young woman was paralysed. Sight and hearing were left to her and she could on occasion speak a word or two. That was all. In the agony and shock of what had happened to her, Babs was in such desperate need of love and reassurance that Tom stayed by her bedside for the first fifty days, even sleeping there in a chair at night. Often, so often, he would reach for her hand or pat her cheek, and the gratitude in her eyes spoke volumes.

In November the paralysed woman was flown back to a hospital in San Mateo County. Babs lived for just over two years, never recovering from the paralysis. Part of the agony was that her mind was so sharp. She knew what was going on around her. Yet since she couldn't even move a finger, existence became a living death, like being buried inside one's mind. Bab's dark brown hair turned to white.

During the two years there were three major operations and twelve minor ones. Shouldering all home responsibilities and the care and rearing of their four children along with his job, Tom managed to spend forty hours a week at his wife's side. Sometimes he would lift Babs into a wheelchair, and take her to the hospital roof so that she could feel the sunshine on her face. Occasionally of a Sunday afternoon he would take her home for a few hours to be with her children and to see that home was being kept ready for her.

When death came to Babs, Tom was holding her hand,

whispering a prayer of benediction into her ear. It seemed a merciful release for her and him.

But Tom soon discovered that he had no release. He was tormented by a dream that kept repeating itself. Though Tom remarried in 1961 and was happy with his new wife Ginny, the dream recurred sometimes twice a week. Soon he developed serious insomnia. Here is Tom's version of the dream that refused to be turned off...

> I am hurrying to the hospital. When I get there I cannot find Babs' room. Frantically, I go from floor to floor, room to room, calling her name. My panic and frustration grow by the minute because I know how much she needs me.
>
> Finally I stumble into the right room. There she is as always, unable to move, sobbing my name.
>
> Then I awaken in a cold sweat, tears on my face. The nightmare had drained so much emotional energy I can hardly get out of bed and go to work.

Then came the 1967 Guideposts Workshop. Tom Dowling was one of twenty-four writers out of 1,200 applicants chosen for the week at a country estate on Long Island Sound, a scene of many religious gatherings. In this relaxed setting, companionship and a deep level of communication grew among the five Guideposts staff members and the writers from all over the country.

Although most of the time was spent on developing writing skills, there was an early morning prayer time for those interested. Each participant was asked to pick two people from the group to pray for. They could keep the names secret if they wished. Later on, Tom found that a writer from Texas, Dot Main, had chosen him because she sensed that he had pressing needs, though she had no idea what they were. Tom never told anyone at Rye about his nightmare problem.

Looking back, I see the hand of God in almost everything that happened that week. One of the Workshoppers' big discoveries was that writing grows out of life: get the life set right and enriched and creative production rises to new heights. Beyond that, how better to summarise what happened than to say that the Holy Spirit was there that week in fullness and power? Prayers were answered, problems resolved, lives changed.

At the end of the Workshop, Tom left for California feeling that this had been the greatest week of his life. When his wife Ginny met him at the San Francisco airport, she took one look at him, saw a new calmness on his face, and exclaimed, 'Tom, something wonderful must have happened to you!'

A few nights later Tom dreamed again . . .

As so often before, I am hurrying to the hospital. (Strange! I always know I am dreaming, but can do nothing about it.) *Oh God! Not again — please. Don't let it begin all over again.*

But this time when I reach the hospital there is none of the usual frantic searching. I go directly to Babs' room. She smiles up from the bed and oh, joy! extends her arms to me! She is no longer paralysed!

She takes my face in her hands and calls my name and great waves of joy, unimaginable joy, rise up in me.

She asks me to put her in the wheelchair as I'd done so often before. I start pushing her towards the elevator to the roof thinking she'd like to soak up some sunshine, but she says, 'No, not the roof. Take me in *there*.'

I turn in the direction she is pointing and find a room full of people. It's the library at the retreat house on the Sound where my little Workshop group had met each day.

As I wheel Babs into the room, the people come to greet her. Great rays of light, love-light, radiate from her as she holds out her hands to each of them!

My happiness is beyond belief. There are tears of happiness in my eyes. Yet there's much more joy to come ... When Babs has greeted each workshopper, she says, 'I want to stand.' And suddenly she's on her feet!

Then the scene shifts to Oakland, where Babs was born. We're walking beside Lake Merritt as we used to long ago. She's laughing and twirling like a girl full of life and happiness. Then she puts her head caressingly on my shoulder — and the dream ends.

Tom Dowling added, 'When I awoke, I bolted straight upright in bed. My usually heavy heart felt feather-light, gay. There was the unmistakable feeling of having been in God's presence. The messages of the dream were so plain:

Babs was no longer paralysed and was extremely happy.

God had let me know that He loves me.

There is an assurance — a knowing — that I'll never have the nightmare again.

And Tom never has, from that time to the present. The deep wounds to his emotional life and his psyche reaching into the unconscious that Tom sustained from Babs' terrible illness, had been healed — permanently.

Let's suppose the Church and its leaders want to return to the Scriptural view of the importance of dreams. How could we of the laity play a part?

One experience from a Fellowship-Prayer Group in Chappaqua, New York provides some hints. One of the members, Jean Nardozzi shared with the others her desperate feelings of exhaustion and her difficulty with sleeping. Because she is a kindergarten teacher with two separate groups of thirty five-year-olds each morning and thirty each afternoon, Jean called herself 'a walking disaster area'.

For two Wednesday nights the group prayed for Jean. On the third Wednesday, Jean told her friends, 'I had a strange dream last night. I'd like to know what you make of it . . .

Some people were holding a baby and indicating that it was mine. In the dream I acted astonished because I didn't know I *had* a baby. The child had been totally neglected, was pitifully thin and under-nourished.

Then the dream gave me a message over and over, "The poor thing needs milk." '

Two people present gasped simultaneously and both started to speak. Then it came out that in prayer during the interim week (with no communication between the two), each had been given identical guidance for Jean: 'She needs milk.'

In addition, one of the two, Elizabeth Sherrill, recalled that the morning she had been given this message, she had also been pointed back to Numbers 12: 1–10, the story of Aaron and Miriam's criticalness of Moses, particularly to Verse 6:

Hear now my words: If there be a prophet among you, I the Lord will make myself known unto him in a vision, and will speak unto him in a dream.

As events turned out, Jean was led to travel to Boston for an appointment with a specialist, a Nutritionist. Amongst other findings the Nutritionist discovered a serious calcium deficiency in Jean's system. In passing, the doctor remarked that calcium is one of nature's best soporifics, adding, 'The old folk remedy of warm milk at bedtime has that basis in fact.' The patient left with diet lists along with necessary supplements.

Within a short time Jean felt like a new person with her sleep improving night by night.

An incident like this reveals that we don't need to be sleep-laboratory researchers or trained analysts to get on with letting God show us how to use our dreams. It is encouraging to recall that our lives are set in the era prophesied by the Old Testament prophet Joel:

> And it shall come to pass in the last days, saith God, I will pour out my spirit upon all flesh . . . and your young men shall see visions and your old men shall dream dreams.[12]

'*All flesh* . . .' It had not always been so. In Old Testament times only the privileged few ever had the gift of the Spirit — only certain prophets, priests, and kings. From this *élite* group the only true dream interpretations had come. So the Bible's message for our time seems to be: not only will the Spirit of Truth use dreams and help us to understand them, but He is the Interpreter *par excellence*. And His help is available to every one of us.

At first we may be able to interpret only a fraction of the dream material that comes to us. But if we persist in taking our dreams into our prayer life and acting upon what we understand, we will experience an unfolding progression. In the years ahead I believe there will be exciting experimentation on this subject among Christians. God will lead us through our dreams to all sorts of provocative discoveries about our hidden selves in His plan to re-fashion us into whole people.

CHAPTER SEVEN

THE FALLEN ANGEL

Is Satan alive and well on Earth? You be the judge.

It happened a few years ago ... In the space of a few weeks incidents of striking similarity were related to me separately by two close friends. One came unexpectedly from Lamar, a man in his early thirties; the other I heard from Jennie, a young housewife, in the middle of a tape-recorded interview with her on another subject altogether. At the time, I could never have guessed that this was a door opening, urging me on to investigate a subject about which I had been largely ignorant.

The first incident was in a letter from Lamar:

... On this particular Saturday, an acquaintance afflicted with a creeping paralysis so that he was mobile only in his wheelchair, had been visiting in our home.

Dick attended services in our church and had been prayed for often at his own request at healing services — with no apparent results.

Dinner time approached and my wife asked him to stay to dinner. Ten o'clock came, ten-thirty. Still our guest made no move to leave. By then I had shared everything I knew to share with him.

'Dick,' I told him, 'tomorrow's another day.' Reluctantly, our guest left and my wife and I went to bed.

During the night I dreamed that I was still talking to Dick. This was one of those crystal-clear things; even the words I spoke to Dick. 'Have you ever heard a word, Dick, that comes down to us in many churches — exorcism? Do you know what it means?'

I woke up with a start and my voice not only had awakened my wife, but she actually jumped about a foot off the bed.

As I opened my eyes, my attention was drawn to a figure standing in the opening of the closet, the door having been left widely ajar. He was tall and lean with the statuesque, stately figure of a young man. His silhouette was sharp because he seemed to be dressed all in black.

But it was his face to which my attention was drawn. He had cropped black hair, high cheek bones, a pointed chin — clean shaven — piercing eyes that were glowering at me with rage. It was a face full of evil. Instantly, I knew this was Satan.

I was chilled and frightened. All I wanted was to get him out of that room. From somewhere deep inside me came the words, 'In the name of Jesus Christ! Satan, go!'

Even as I stared, within a few seconds he disappeared.

Later on, I went to see Dick and found out that he had been deeply involved in the world of the occult. He even had two spirits whom he called by name and who were now so familiar that they would wait upon him in various ways. When Dick flatly refused to submit to exorcism, I began to see why no amount of prayer effort or caring had worked for him: while he wanted to be healed physically, he did not want to let go his love affair with the occult. The last I heard of Dick, he had stopped coming to church.

You know me so well you'll realise that I'm not the type given to visions. But this experience has done one thing, since then I've never had any slight doubt about the existence of Satan.

My instant reaction was 'How wild!' The experience may have settled the matter of Satan as an incarnate spirit for Lamar, but for me it raised a lot of questions. Was Lamar telling me that he had actually seen a creature — Satan? If I hadn't known Lamar for some years and eaten many a meal in his home, I might have written his 'vision' off as the hallucination of a disturbed person. But this particular friend's level-headedness and love for life were in total contrast to the strange, dark, and unappealing world of his nocturnal experience. I wanted nothing so much as to slam the door on that world.

But the very next week while in the midst of a long recorded interview with Jennie (whom I have known well for five years or so) came another story. I took it from the tape:

On a particular night I went to bed, then later was awakened by a light coming in my room. At the foot of my bed stood this man about six feet two. He had a black Butch haircut and dark features and eyes. He just stood there looking at me.

Now since I came to know Jesus eight years ago, I've had many problems, yet I've never known such an out-and-out fear as I knew it at that moment. Through my mind went the thought, 'Oh my God, who is that?'

The thought had no sooner crossed my mind than I knew that Jesus Himself was standing beside me protectively on the right-hand side of my bed. And strange thing, He had His staff in His hand. As if in direct answer to the question in my mind, He explained the dark man standing at the foot of the bed. 'He is the personification of Man.'

Well, I'd never heard that word before, but I knew what it meant. My immediate reaction was 'I've got to get up out of bed and call someone to pray for me.'

That too, brought a response. It was like the Lord saying, 'No, you've got to face him sooner or later.' Only please understand that this was not in external words — it was all interior.

So I stayed in bed and screwed up my courage to look at the dark man again. He stood there unmoving, radiating — what

shall I call it? — the personification of evil. I couldn't have been
more grateful for the feeling of Jesus' presence and the security of that staff in His hand. Then Jesus said, 'He has to
appear to you personally so that you can learn that everything
that the devil and man can do to you are not going to harm
you as long as you stay close to Me. *Don't ever again let any of
his life in you or have any power over you.*'

As I began letting my mind roam over all the wonderful
changes that had come to me in the last eight years and the
fullness of my life in Christ, that personification of evil standing at the foot of the bed was instantly gone. Then I went to
sleep, peacefully and lovingly.

Two details of my friend Jennie's description struck me especially: the phrase 'the personification of Man' and her insistence that in her vision Jesus was holding a staff. I wondered
if a staff in His hand had significance in connection with
moments when we face evil?

Beyond that, my emotional reaction to Jennie's confrontation
with Satan was the same resistance I had felt to Lamar's experience. Yet — here were two friends whom I knew to be wise
and solid persons. I trusted them completely, yet they had presented me with what I regarded as 'far-out' stories.

I had also been noticing that every time I read a book review
page or saw the ads, more and more titles of the type of *Rose-
mary's Baby* were being published. Publishing houses had
whole lists of titles on Satan and the occult. Entire stories were
being given not only to occult books but to hundreds of items,
trappings of the occult such as masks, candles, incense, charms,
games, Zodiacal highball glasses, napkins, Tarot cards, and
witches' hats.

'Just a fad,' I thought. All of it went so directly against my
experience of God as being all-love and goodness that I had
decided to keep my eyes solely on Him as my personal answer
to the rise of the Satan cults. But when first, one close friend

thrust the distasteful Satan subject on me, then the other, I saw that I couldn't continue to duck it. Having a new respect for the importance of obedience, I realised that I was being asked personally to take a look at the kingdom of evil and become knowledgeable about it.

'All right, God,' was my response. 'If you're telling me that Satan is real and on the march and attacking today, and that You want me to look at him and hear what You have to say about all this, I'll do it. But please be with me every minute because I'm not looking forward to this.'

Up to this time, I had read little about Satan except in the writings of the late C. S. Lewis, eminent Cambridge scholar and convert to Christianity from atheism. In *The Case for Christianity*, Mr. Lewis had hit the Satan subject head on:

> I know someone will ask me, 'Do you really mean, at this time of day, to re-introduce our old friend the devil — hoofs and horns and all?' Well, what the time of day had to do with it, I don't know. And I'm not particular about the hoofs and the horns. But in other respects my answer is, 'Yes, I do' . . . If anybody really wants to know him better, I'd say to that person, 'Don't worry. If you really want to, you will. Whether you'll like it when you do is another question.'[1]

Neither of my friends, Jennie nor Lamar, had in any way sought an experience of Satan. And C. S. Lewis was right, they didn't enjoy Satan one bit. Still, questions had been raised and would not be put down. Given a devil at all, I realised that he must be spirit. Therefore, I resisted the idea of external manifestations, like horns and a tail and being dressed in a ludicrous red suit. Satan's appearance would be of less importance than his character. How was I to research Satan's character?

The obvious place to begin was to see what God had Himself chosen to reveal to us in Scripture about Satan and the problem of evil. I set myself to spend thirty minutes on this study early each morning before breakfast. Propped up in bed with a cup of coffee, a clean notebook, a chain reference Bible and full concordance, I began.

Right away I was surprised. The first reference I turned to described Satan as a beautiful creature, once a magnificent archangel called Lucifer, 'the shining one', or 'the son of the morning'. Some Bible scholars surmise that Lucifer was the greatest of the heavenly creatures who led all the rest in glorifying God. But the time came when Lucifer began to covet this worship for himself:

> How are thou fallen from heaven, O Lucifer, son of the morning ...! For thou hast said in thine heart, I will ascend into heaven, I will exalt my throne above the stars of God ... I will ascend above the heights of the clouds; I will be like the most High.[2]

When this shining angel broke his relationship with the Father, he led a revolt in heaven. The Book of Revelation hints[3] that Lucifer may have enticed one third of the heavenly hosts to revolt with him. After all, their angelic leader still had his superior intelligence, his attractive persuasiveness, and his power.

At that time Lucifer's name was changed to Satan — 'adversary' or 'resister'. I wrote down some of the other names I found for Satan. The names tell us a great deal about the ex-Lucifer's character:

    The Enemy
    The Tempter
    Destroyer
    Liar
    Unclean spirit
    Foul spirit

Accuser of the brethren
God of this World

As I thought about it, I realised that God must have known that this awful perversion of His beautiful creation had been possible. Ironically, it was because God had lavished so much on Lucifer that the tragic reversal came about.

But the Lucifer disaster did not dissuade the Creator from His eternal intention to create truly free man. For man He made a special place, the garden-planet Earth set like a blue and green jewel in the grey cosmos.

Man would be perfect physically, equipped with a body exquisitely formed, from the chromosome pattern of each cell, to the human eye with its retina composed of seven delicate layers of molecular and nuclear tissue, ganglion cells, and nerve fibres; from the chemical complexity of the blood with its own transport system for bathing and nourishing every cell; to the brain marvellously constructed of some 100 billion neurons and and at least twice that many glia. Neuroscientists like Dr. Francis Otto Schmitt have shown the human brain to be so complex that it makes a sophisticated electronic computer look like a child's toy.[4]

But more important than man's incredible body was God's plan that his judgments would partake of the Creator's own goodness and love, so that human beings would know unimaginable happiness and fulfilment.

So God looked on His creation — man — and pronounced that creation 'very good'. Yet by giving us the attributes of personality, especially a will with which to choose, He deliberately ran the risk that men or angels might reject His plan.

That is exactly what happened. By the time planet Earth had been formed, the archangel Lucifer had already become heaven's rebel. Our little planet became the stage for the fight to the death between Satan and his cohorts and God the Father.

The conflict began in Earth's springtime. God had warned Adam and Eve that if they ate of the fruit of the Tree of Knowledge, they would surely die. Even as Satan had wanted to be like God, so now he sought to transfer the same rebellion to the mind and will of Eve first and then, Adam . . . God didn't tell you the truth, the serpent suggested, 'for God doth know that in the day ye eat thereof, then your eyes shall be opened, and ye shall be as gods . . .'[5]

Man decided to take his chances on Satan. The result was tragedy for that man and woman and for every descendant down the long ages since. For man's decision to eat the fruit of the Tree of Knowledge was to set his will against God's to enthrone himself 'as a god' independent of his Creator.

It was as if my right arm 'decided' that it no longer needed the rest of the body, so it would separate itself and take up life on its own. The severed arm would die.

But physical death was only part of it. It was man's spirit that made him the crowning accomplishment of creation. *That* was why man was told that he had dominion over the animals, 'over every living thing that moveth upon the earth.'[6] It was because Jehovah had 'created man in his own image' that the writer of Hebrews echoing the Psalmist, could say lyrically:

> Thou madest him (man) a little lower than the angels; thou crownedst him with glory and honour . . .
>
> Thou hast put all things in subjection under his feet . . .[7]

That same spirit that enabled man to worship, to make decisions and moral choices, to plan, to remember, to assimilate ideas and store up knowledge, to reason — not only meant that there was a great gulf fixed between man and the rest of the animal kingdom; it also meant that man's spirit would be dependent for its real life on the Spirit of which it was a part. To the Tempter Jesus said, 'Man shall not live by bread alone.'[8]

As a result of man's disobedience, death entered life, precisely as God had said it would. Not just the cessation of the heartbeat and the decay of the flesh that marks the end of every man, but all the interim ills that lead up to death — sickness, disease, pain, weakness, accidents, famine, pestilence, plague, fear, loneliness, hatred, jealousy, hurt, cruelty, torture, murder, suicide. Now began the long history of man's inhumanity to man — man now bound tightly, stultified by the fallen divided nature which he himself had chosen. And because God had given man true freedom of choice, He could not and would not forcibly overrule that.

Man might have been left there. The story could have ended as the poet Edna St. Vincent Millay has it in her heart-breakingly beautiful sonnet sequence *Epitaph for the Race of Man* . .

> Here lies, and none to mourn him but the sea,
> That falls incessant on the empty shore,
> Most various Man, cut down to spring no more;
> Before his prime, even in his infancy
> Cut down, and all the clamour that was he
> Silenced; and all the riveted pride he wore
> A rusted iron column whose tall core
> The rains have tunnelled like an aspen tree . . .
> Whence, whence the broadside, whose the heavy blade . . . ?
> Strive not to speak, poor scattered mouth; I know.[9]

But it did not end that way. God's love yearned over His deluded creatures. 'God's impossible Love' as C. S. Lewis called it in one of the most brilliant, witty, and penetrating books on Satan ever written, *The Screwtape Letters*. He puts these words into the mouth of the influential demon Screwtape, as he instructs the underling tempter Wormwood:

'. . . He really loves the human vermin and really desires their freedom and continued existence . . .' Then, catching himself and realising that this is heresy in the underworld's theology . . . 'The reason one comes to talk as if he really had this impossible Love is our utter failure to find out that real motive. What does He stand to make out of them? That is the insoluble question . . .'[10]

Out of God's 'impossible Love' a rescue plan was evolved, surely one that only the three Persons of the Godhead together — Father, Son, and Holy Spirit — could have conceived: Jesus would leave for a time that perfection of communion and communication that He had always enjoyed with the Father and the Holy Spirit, and come to earth clothed in flesh, born of a woman like all the sons of Adam. Jesus would be God revealed, the God-man walking the earth demonstrating what the Father is like — His love and compassion, His reverence for all life, His power to unbind, to set free, to remake.

The plan became fact at a specific moment in time, thus dividing all history into two parts — B.C., 'Before Christ' and Anno Domini, 'In the Year of our Lord'. The God-man's teaching was incredibly impressive, had the sure touch of One who spoke 'with authority'. His miracles, even His enemies grumbled, had the world following after him.[11] It is at that point that people reading the Bible for the first time are in for a surprise. The writers of Scripture insist that the real point of Jesus breaking into human history was neither His teaching nor His miracles; rather, that Jesus came to earth for the purpose of dying and being resurrected to life on the third day.

Thus His death and resurrection was the Master Plan to win back for man all that he had lost in Eden. As the last Adam, Jesus would mount His cross taking all of us, Adam's heirs, with Him into the death of the old, now-spoiled creation. Thus He would accomplish a perfect exchange. As Derek Prince, British-born Greek scholar and author, has summarised it in a single memorable sentence, 'Jesus took the evil that was due to us and the entire Adamic race that we, in return, might receive the good that was due to Him by eternal right.'[12]

Jesus went to His cross as the willing agent of the divine plan. Nevertheless, His agony in Gethsemane shows us that humanly He shrank from the tortuous hours ahead. All His growing-up years in Nazareth He had seen crucifixions. When Jesus was about twelve, He could scarcely have helped seeing the crucifixion by Varrus, Prefect of Syria, of 2,000 rioters after the death of Herod the Great. The field full of 2,000 crosses would have made an indelible impression on any sensitive boy. How well He knew that the nails used in crucifixion (square, one-third inch on each side) were real enough, as real as the pain and the agonising thirst, the cramps, and the ultimate asphyxiation. Even so He considered that 'to this end was I born, and for this cause came I into the world.'[13] Therefore, He was 'obedient unto death'.

The victory was God's, for on the third day Life poured back into the dead and mutilated body of Jesus. The crucifixion and resurrection are history's watershed. Those who speak of some sort of 'spiritual resurrection' are missing the point. For the first Adam or the Last Adam or for any of us sons and daughters of Adam still in the flesh, nothing short of the resurrection of the flesh would have been any victory at all. Satan would not have been deceived; Jesus' surprised, incredulous disciples would not, and neither would we.

Satan knew defeat now. Henceforward any man or woman could look at the Tempter unflinchingly and say, 'You're a liar, a defeated foe, a bluffer, and a washout. I stand here in the name of Jesus — the Christus, the Victor — and on His finished work. Begone ...' There is nothing for the Tempter but to slink away.

Thus the Bible nowhere teaches us to believe in Dualism, the philosophic premise that two equal and independent powers — one of them good, the other bad — eternally vie for supremacy in the world. It is easy even for the Christian to attribute more power to Satan than he has and so fall into heresy. Rather we are told that our earth is enemy-occupied territory. The Rightful King has landed and has already won the decisive victory. But we are still living through the mopping-up stage of the battle. The time will come when Christus, the Lord Emmanuel, will finally ring down the curtain on all remaining pockets of rebellion and guerrilla warfare to establish His kingdom openly for all to see.

Satan still has one ace card to play. If he can keep any man from believing the truth about Jesus Christ — who He is, the Life He holds out for mankind, the fact of his (Satan's) defeat — Satan can then keep that man in bondage to his dark kingdom. For though I have a million pounds in a bank account in my name, if through some chicanery I am persuaded that I do not have it and make no overt move to use it, the money in the bank does me no good at all.

Thus the Accuser of men employs unbelievable craftiness and resourcefulness, artifice and deceit to keep mankind from knowing the truth and acting upon it. With him the technique of lying has been honed to a fine art. His ways of camouflage and duplicity are almost limitless. After all, this was Lucifer, the magnificent archangel, with his great intelligence, only now turned totally to negative designs.

Nor does Satan give up on us even after we become followers of Jesus. He never gives up so long as we inhabit these vulnerable bodies in this uncertain life. After we become Christians, his aim is to oppose and impede us so that our spirits will be stunted short of maturity. He also wants to keep us ineffective so far as spreading to others the good news of freedom in Christ Jesus.

Satan has not and cannot create anything new, cannot create

anything at all. He must steal what God has created. Thus he twists love and God's wonderful gift of sex into lust and sadism and myriad perversions. He disfigures the heart's deep desire to worship God and persuades us to bow before lesser gods of lust or money or power.

'But,' the protest rises within us, 'if Christ won the victory, then why isn't the war with Satan over? Why doesn't God simply wipe Satan out?'

It's a valid question. God's luminous answer was given me one morning, 'Because the Father is determined that all the sons of Adam will for as long as possible, have a second chance to reverse that decision made in Eden.' Jesus bought this second chance for us. The Father is determined that His Son's tremendous sacrifice will not go for nothing.

C. S. Lewis in his book *The Case For Christianity* expresses the same thought in different words:

> ... Christians think He (God) is going to land in force; we don't know when. But we can guess why He's delaying. He wants to give us the chance of joining His side freely ... I wonder whether people who ask God to interfere openly and directly in our world quite realise what it will be like when He does. When that happens, it's the end of the world. When the author walks on to the stage the play's over ...[14]

So it is as if nothing had changed since that moment aeons ago when man was presented with his stark choice: would he believe God or Satan ...? Which one had his happiness at heart ...? Would he let go his connection to Life in God and set up on his own? Time is still holding its breath for our answer now. Which way will each man, each woman decide now?

'But,' some may protest, 'I never consciously made any such decision.' We do not need to. That is the state we are all in just by being born of the flesh into the race of man and inheriting our father Adam's nature just as surely as we inherited the colour of some ancestor's eyes. And it would be just as useless to protest that inheriting a sin-disposed nature seems scarcely fair, as to protest about the colour of our eyes or the race that dictated the skin's colour.

The truth is that whether we are millionaires directing a financial kingdom or youthful idealists in revolt against a materialistic world, or quite ordinary citizens content to live self-centred lives of quiet mediocrity, until such time as we grasp our second chance, reverse the fiasco-decision made in Eden and get reconnected to Life, we remain vulnerable to Satan's cunning approach and to his designs. When I understood that, then I could see why the phrase which had been given to my friend Jennie, 'the personification of Man' was so appropriate. Satan remains the personification of adamic Man even as Jesus is the Personification of the new Man. Each of us can escape the bondage of Satan's kingdom for the freedom of Christ's Kingdom only when he resolutely sets the rudder of his will so to do.

That's why the moment of decision for Christ is so vital. That's why the angels themselves rejoice when even one lost lamb is brought back on the shoulder of the Good Shepherd.

As my morning study progressed, I began to see why God had insisted on this distasteful chore. A good hard look at evil as it is presented in the Bible and an obedient following-through of the whole story left me with one overwhelming impression — a great feeling of confidence and victory. The Bible story of the conflict between good and evil is not downbeat at all, but upbeat; it is the story of the total defeat of evil because of the absolute power of Christ.

But God had wanted me to study this subject for myself until I was not only aware, but fully persuaded of the reality of the kingdom of evil. Sooner or later a lot of tough experiences, doubts and temptations were going to be thrown at me (and at other people close to me) and it would be essential that we know how to fight them.

An additional reason why we dare not pretend that Satan does not exist is that God has deliberately placed Himself in the position of depending upon us human beings to tell His good news and to spread His kingdom on earth. We cannot get on with this task without being hindered by Satan at every step of the way. Satan's tactics fall into many categories, among them higher spiritual temptations, sexual temptations, and what we might call his harassment techniques.

An endlessly-used Satanic weapon in his spiritual arsenal is that of discouragement, often interlocked with a degree of self-pity and depression. During our early years in Washington when Peter Marshall often battled discouragement, I remember our quoting at one another one of Hannah Smith's favourite maxims, 'All discouragement is of the devil.' Of course the remedy is to realise the source of the depression and to remind oneself that spiritual reality can never be gauged by feelings.

Other strategies of the devil include presenting sin as a virtue; the old ruse of exhibiting the bait and concealing the hook; suggesting 'you aren't accepted by God, else you wouldn't continue to be tempted'; keeping Christians musing on their hang-ups and sins; using the seduction technique — good to bad in tiny steps.

Satan sometimes lays the groundwork for sexual sins by encouraging self-pride in a leader and in his achievements. This then is followed by the leader being flattered by 'opportunities for service' and over-extending himself. Family relationships suffer in the wake of too much travel for meetings and speaking engagements. As the home life deteriorates, then the Tempter at times arranges 'a plant' such as an immensely attractive married woman in deep distress who comes seeking the leader's help. When a liaison follows and becomes public news, the disastrous side effects of this situation always cause great rejoicing in hell. Among them, groups of disillusioned people who leave the church — 'If that's Christianity, I want no part of it' — as they judge the church by the fallen leader rather than by Christ and His perfection.

The third category of Satan's stratagem dips into the realm of the bizarre. For instance, on a day when a well-known evangelist was preparing to preach one of his rare sermons on Satan, he was dictating notes into a recording device when suddenly, the machine caught on fire. We might be inclined to think, 'Wouldn't the machine have caught on fire if the minister had been dictating on say, "God's love"?' Perhaps — except it gives us pause as we go on to experience this sort of harassment over and over whenever we are about to unmask Satan by writing or teaching or preaching.

The following list is taken from the experiences of Christian leaders, all of whom I know:

> The living-room chimney of a house catches on fire the last day before a book manuscript on Satan is to be delivered to the publisher.
>
> *En route* to a Christian meeting there is trouble with impossibly bad traffic and with the car. In addition to time delays, the leader loses his peace of mind, becomes irritated, and loses effectiveness. Mechanical difficulties are notorious. Tape recorders and amplifying systems often go wild or cease to function.
>
> As the time for an important talk or service approaches, the minister's family grows irritated and edgy. A spirit of contention enters the home. There are minor accidents.

Usually, these vexations are not serious trouble, more like a sort of nasty bullying. Even a few experiences with such obstructionist tactics, however, and we begin to see that the warfare spoken of in the Bible is absolutely real:

For we are not fighting against people made of flesh and blood, but against persons without bodies — the evil rulers of the unseen world, those mighty satanic beings and great evil princes of darkness who rule this world; and against huge numbers of wicked spirits in the spirit world.

So use every piece of God's armour to resist the enemy whenever he attacks ...[15]

In the thick of battle a soldier needs to be able to identify the enemy. In the old days warriors were identified by their uniforms or by a standard held aloft. So how can we Christian soldiers learn to identify the enemy Satan? From my study, I was able to draw the following antithetical lists to help us know what God wants for us against Satan's aims. Lining it up like this enables us to see it more readily ...

Satan	*Jesus*
Seeks to do his own will.	Always obeys the Father's will.
Aims to bind and blind men.	Yearns to free men and open our eyes to see.
Lies interminably.	Is the Truth.
Takes himself very seriously, cannot bear taunting or levity.	Often uses the light touch.
Wants us to live in darkness and hide portions of our life from others.	Wants us to live in the light.
Wants us to doubt and disbelieve God's word.	Longs for us to have faith that He always keeps His word.
Works to make us ignore, disbelieve or choose for ourselves what to believe in the Scripture.	Steadily assures us that the Scripture is the Word of God.

Satan	Jesus
Pushes us to disobey God.	Says, 'If you love me, you will obey my commandments.'
Urges us to use God for selfish purposes.	Longs for us to be used by God to help others.
Tells us, 'My body belongs to me.'	Tells us, 'The body is the temple of the Holy Spirit.'
Wants sickness and disease.	Wants wholeness of body, mind, and spirit.
Spares no effort to bring us sorrow and grief.	Wants our joy.
Desires our death.	Eagerly bestows life stretching on into eternity.
Condemns and accuses us.	Assures us, 'I came not to judge the world, but to save the world.'[15]
Pushes us towards self-contempt.	Assures us that each man is of infinite worth to Him.
Fosters discontent and grumbling.	Urges contentment and praise in all situations.
Urges us to think that we can get virtue in one big slug for life.	Desires that we depend on Him minute by minute for what we need and claim our 'daily bread.'
Urges us to concentrate on the sins of others.	Tells us to look at the beam in our own eyes and remove that first.
Wants us to hang on to resentment and bitterness.	Tells us to forgive others in the same way God forgives us.
Urges us to have our fun now, try to forget about paying for it.	Influences us to pay now in time or effort, then fun later is assured.

Satan	Jesus
Attempts to get us to hide our sins and make excuses for them, thus encouraging their festering within.	Wishes us to run to Him, bring our sins into the light and have them forgiven, cleansed, and forgotten.
Labours to have us believe that temptation *is* sin.	Assures us that temptations rightly handled strengthen us.
Wants us when we fail, to wallow in discouragement or despair.	Encourages us in failure to ask forgiveness, accept it, rise, and go on.
Aims for us always to wear a mask and act a part; be all things to all people.	Plants in us the desire to be true to ourselves; to let others know where we stand.
Wants our faith always to be for the future.	Wants us to cultivate a present-moment faith.
Seeks steady procrastination.	Teaches us that '*Now* is the moment of salvation.'
Strives to have us preoccupied with 'what ifs?' (what might happen); to be hag-ridden by the future.	Is concerned with what we do in the present; wants us to offer up the *present* moment to God.
Urges us towards a false, lofty super-spirituality.	Wants us to live out daily 'Without Me ye can do nothing.'
Delights in a moderate religion with no extremes.	Wants the total man — 'Thou shalt love the Lord thy God with *all* thy heart and with *all* thy soul and with *all* thy mind.'
Works for churches to be divided into 'clubs' or factions with 'party spirit.'	Leads us towards unity amid diversity of gifts of the Spirit amongst the people in the Church.

Satan	*Jesus*
Wants us to see all morality as relative, no final truth or falsehood.	Insists that He *is* the Way, the Truth and the Life; God's laws are absolute.
Labours to destroy all law, God's and man's.	Fulfils the law and the prophets and adds righteousness to it.
Labours for war.	Desires peace, the fruit of righteousness.

I was soon to find out that this period of instruction was not going to be limited to quiet bookwork. Lessons from life were just around the corner.

CHAPTER EIGHT

THE UNHOLY SPIRIT

It was from a pair of hippies, Carrie and Jeff Buddington, that I first heard the term 'the unholy spirit'. I met Jeff and Carrie in September, 1969 in the small Cape Cod church where my son Peter is pastor. It was a surprise to hear Peter welcoming to the platform to receive into the church such a young couple, 'swinging' in appearance, rather than the typical older retired couple of that Cape Cod community.

After the formal part of the ceremony was completed, Peter turned to the congregation, 'Because Jeff and Carrie have travelled such an extraordinary route to arrive at this point of commitment, I've asked them to share a little of their story with all of us.'

Jeff, tall and broad-shouldered, spoke of how long he had run back and forth across the United States, seeking the answer to what life was all about. Carrie, hair flowing to her shoulders, spoke softly of how she had come out of the jungle of drugs to find the reality of God. As they talked, people were leaning forward with interest.[1] I was so intrigued that after the service I asked for an interview. Our two-hour talk later that week proved to be memorable and revealing.

As I replay today the tape I made of that two-hour conversation, I can still see the scene in Edith and Peter's living-room: the warm afternoon sun streaming through the windows reflecting back from the silver-grey shingles outside; Carrie, hair swinging, sitting on the davenport with legs tucked under her like a little girl: both Jeff and Carrie refreshingly articulate.

The first part of Carrie and Jeff's story parallels the experiences of thousands of today's youth . . . They had met in 1968 at a California commune. Jeff was from Massachusetts. After one semester of college, he had restlessly ricocheted from job to job — selling insurance, building pipe organs, designing stagesets, even a circus big-top stint. Carrie was a Californian who had got hooked on drugs — marijuana, acid,[2] speed,[3] in that order — during her senior year in high school.

At the time the two met, each was on speed. 'I found out in a hurry,' Carrie explained to me, 'that speed makes you paranoid. All of life becomes one big fear trip. It also gives you this delusion of grandeur.

'But where I got hooked was, coming off it, crashing, is so awful you keep staying up because you can't bear to come down. If you ever do, you ache inside. Your guts get really uptight. Your nerves are on end. You get cramps. You can feel the heat coming off your head — "bzzy-bzzy" — like being plugged into a high tension wire.'

'Drugs do one good thing for kids, though,' Jeff added. 'They show that there's a world other than the material one. Maybe that's part of the reason so many kids these days have finally let go of two hang-ups of the older generation. First, the kids see no point in trying to accumulate things. Second, they know now that science doesn't have the answers to life they once thought it did. So science can never again be their god.

'Carrie and I had more in common than just thrill-seeking. We were on this big search for some meaning in life. We still thought,' Jeff's Massachusetts accent came from the tape recorder, 'that happiness meant the way you lived externally, that if things around you were the way you liked them, then you would be happy.'

They found very few answers to their big questions in the commune. The forty members (eleven children among them) had erected a large hexagonal lodge of logs on the 240 acres of

Oregon woodland[4] where the commune hoped to escape civilization and the Establishment. Meant for a central meeting place as well as sleeping and eating quarters, the lodge had homemade furniture, a cast iron stove for cooking, even a library of some 500 books. There was no electricity or running water — only the streams in which to bathe and wash clothes. The men dug a well. All possessions were shared.

Carrie added, 'It wasn't long until we discovered that we weren't going to eat if we didn't work. And the work wasn't going to get done without a routine.' The rule was made that everyone had to work at least four hours a day. They planted a vegetable garden, fished in the river, kept chickens and goats. Since the winters were severe, trees had to be cut and the wood sawed and split for firewood.

Carrie and Jeff started living together in a teepee they had built. 'But something was still missing,' Jeff explained. 'Carrie and I spent hours in that teepee huddled beside a little fire, watching shadows on the slanting walls, trying to figure out what it was that still eluded us. We were like people stumbling around in the Los Angeles smog.

'The reality we continued to seek in the LSD visions, was increasingly hideous. Eventually we got tired of seeing ourselves as we were — like people with naked bodies covered with warts and souls all deformed — and we knew it. But we couldn't find any way to change ourselves.

'Then we began having bad acid trips. I remember the first. It was a foggy day. Carrie and I were walking down this hillside, and the big old oak trees were dripping — one of those spooky days. I began to feel something evil reaching out to possess me.

'Crazy thoughts appeared in my mind. I kept seeing a kind of crude black basalt male figure with a hawk's head and a male phallus, a coiled snake on his arm, strange hieroglyphics all over him — and I kept having this urge to get down on my knees in front of it. It was as though I was being asked to take part in some ceremony that I knew nothing about. It seemed to be like something very very ancient. I could feel the control over myself slipping away. Something was eroding my will. Carrie felt the same thing.'

Carrie interrupted, 'It's like this evil power had been there all along, only he hadn't shown himself at first. He waits until you're well hooked; only then does he reveal himself. And he wants you to think that it's O.K. to play childish games with the drug-taking, that it's spiritual and beautiful — the lovely psychodelic colours, all that.

'But it's counterfeit spirituality, and believe me, it isn't beautiful. It's more hideous than anyone can imagine.'

Jeff grimaced in remembrance. 'The second of the bad trips was at Thanksgiving. The entire commune was crowded into the lodge taking acid together. That day we were acting out being "married" into the brotherhood of man. Outside it was raining steadily. There was a fire going, and the rhythm of drums.

'Suddenly Carrie and I had a loathsome feeling about the whole thing. So did one other couple. The four of us left the lodge and went to the teepee. We sat there huddling together, cold, miserable, too drugged even to build a fire.

'That night we knew that the answer we'd seen in drugs was really a mirage, just wasn't there. We knew then why so many kids commit suicide.'

The Oregon winter was severe that year and there was sickness. So few could work that firewood almost disappeared. Their chain saw was broken too. The situation was desperate.

Then came the miracle. One morning out of nowhere several strange men appeared with saws and axes. 'We've come to cut wood for you,' they said. The visitors worked all day until they had a big pile of firewood.

'Who are you?' commune members kept asking. 'Why are you doing this for us?'

'We're Christians,' was the answer. 'We have our own little community about fifteen miles up the road. We came because the Lord Jesus told us that your firewood was almost gone.'

'But why?' they persisted. 'How could God care about us and our commune?'

'Because He loves you.'

The experience rocked the hippies as nothing else had. Jeff and Carrie and a few others went up the road to find out more about this brand of Christianity.

'It was in this Christian community that we began at last to find answers,' Jeff told me. 'The key was the Holy Spirit. We'd had some experience of spirits, you see, we'd encountered the *unholy* spirit . . .'

'Holy Spirit — unholy spirit,' I interrupted, fascinated. 'I've never heard it put quite that way.' I said the phrases again, listening to the sound of them. 'How would you explain the difference between the two spirits?' my voice on the tape recorder asked Jeff.

'Well, we found that the unholy spirit does have power in the world, only it's a power each individual has to allow him. Once a person decides to play around with him and opens the door, the unholy spirit can be overpowering. He can perform "miracles" and has a lot of tricks: power over nature, power over the elements. But it's a power without any love. It wants just one thing, just one — to destroy.'

Carrie spoke up. 'The Holy Spirit has power, too, greater power than the unholy spirit. He, too, waits on our wanting Him. But He's different. He's all love — real love. And He's — *for* us.'

'What's the basis,' I asked, 'of your being so sure that the Holy Spirit has more power than the unholy spirit?'

'Because,' Carrie promptly answered, 'He enabled us to kick

drugs when we'd been on them for so many years. That's a *real* miracle!'

Jeff continued, 'Next, He took away the old haunted, fear-ridden "me". Inside each of us was born this new being, what the Bible calls "a new creature in Christ Jesus".'

'It's not a case of trying to be like Christ, to imitate Him,' Carrie went on. 'Who has the strength to do that? Through the Holy Spirit, Jesus comes to live in us and to do His own work.'

'The next step,' Jeff went on, 'was to find a church. We remembered one that had occasionally come to our rescue with a friendly meal or a warm bed. So we went barrelling there pretty eager, I guess. To our astonishment we found no sense of life or power there. More than that, they seemed almost scared of the change in us. They wanted to help us when we were on drugs and out of work, sure. A change of clothes, a hot meal, good advice, concern. But real change? Real power? God really doing what He said? Wow! They backed off like crazy.'

'Tell me about the change,' I said. 'How did it start?'

'Well,' Jeff said, 'one day all by ourselves, we had our own Pentecost and accepted Jesus. Later we were both baptised in the creek and also legally married. People came from everywhere for the wedding — hippies still on acid and straight people. We spent the whole day telling them all, "Jesus is the One you're searching for." '

The Buddingtons spent four months in the Christian community, learning. 'That new person born in us had to start from scratch and go to school,' Jeff said. 'But it was so great! When you go up on acid, there's always that terrible coming down again. With Jesus, you just keep going up, gradually and surely. You keep growing and learning step-by-step how to meet and overcome your difficulties. There are problems with self-discipline, of course, but joy all the way. It's that "living water" for sure.

'Other hippies followed us to the Christian community. The big difference between the two groups is this: in the hippy commune, they're still doing their own thing; in the Christian community, they're doing His thing.'

This was not the end of the story. Christ as the new life within them led Carrie and Jeff to Cape Cod to teach for a time in a home for retarded children, then on to become part of another Christian community whose calling is teaching, retreats, help, counselling. They've been there ever since — learning, growing, giving.

On July 9th, 1970, Catherine Heidi Buddington was born, by the grace of God, a healthy, normal baby. Then on June 5th, 1972, Daniel Jeffrey was born; in November, 1973, Ruth Anne, also strong and normal. And still Jeff and Carrie go on from strength to strength as they dig deeper into Christian disciplines and learn to show others the way.

The childish games with which Jeff and Carrie started out to explore evil's terrain are being played by millions of people today. Witchcraft, the occult, Satan worship, sorcery, spiritualism, Tarot cards, horoscopes are currently big business over most of the world. Among the more popular courses currently offered in many high schools and universities are telepathy, precognition, clairvoyance, and other aspects of scientology; spiritism, I Chang, and witchcraft.

There are now an estimated 10,000 full-time and 175,000 part-time astrologers in the United States. Horoscope readings are computerised. Almost every newspaper and periodical in the nation now regularly prints them. In France 60,000 sorcerers are said to be taking in $200,000,000 a year. A national magazine estimated that in 1970 there were then 500 witches in Manhattan alone.

This fascination with the occult climaxed in the early months of 1974 when Warner Brothers released the film *The*

Exorcist producing what *Time* magazine called *Exorcist* fever. All over the United States serpentine lines waited for hours outside theatres to see the horrifying movie about a little girl possessed by the devil. Once inside, audience reaction repeatedly included screams, hysteria (some requiring hospitalisation), blackouts, heart attacks, vomiting, at least one miscarriage, and speedy exits. In New York City, a boy ran from the theatre towards a nearby church, tearing off his clothes and shouting, 'Exorcise me! Exorcise me.' Longer-range effects included people believing themselves possessed, acute insomnia, nightmares.

Exorcist fever uncovered an American public with such a morbid fascination with despair, pain, and gore. William Blatty's book from which the film was taken sold almost four million copies (in addition to the five million previously sold) in five weeks immediately after the movie was released; the motion picture is, reputedly, going to be the top moneymaker of all time, exceeding *The Sound of Music* and *The Godfather*.

Most of this upsurge has come since 1967. A brilliant young Englishman, Os Guiness, whom I met at L'Abri, Switzerland in the summer of 1972, had researched the new interest in witchcraft, the occult, Satan, and kindred subjects. He could find almost no major works on these subjects for the last two hundred years. History books treated black magic and the occult as curious extinct phenomena: the enlightenment following the Renaissance, together with the rise of modern scientific knowledge had effectively silenced witches and laid the ghosts.

Then in 1967, like the cap blown off a volcano after centuries of molten churning underground, there erupted into the open a torrent of publications on Satan, Satanism and all kindred subjects. The underworld's debris has been spewing up ever since.

'Why 1967?' I asked Os Guiness.

'I don't know,' was his cautious reply. 'Except perhaps that year was, in some strange way, evil's "fullness of time". Between June 5th and 10th occurred an event clearly foretold in Scripture — Israel's six-day war when Old Jerusalem and sacred sites such as the wailing wall were repossessed.'

'But what connection . . .? I don't see . . .'

'Scripture prophesied that event as the beginning of the end times — an accelerating warfare period between good and evil, God and Satan.'

This conversation later gave me much food for thought. We are living in a period when evil is getting more evil while good is no longer satisfied with pallid goodness. In the last ten years a movement of the Holy Spirit has swept through the Catholic church and most branches and denominations of the Protestant church. It may well be that the rising popularity of Satanic activities is the unholy spirit's terrified counter attack against the moves of the Spirit.

Be that as it may, I marvel that so many moderns, particularly the young, can be taking witchcraft and devil worship seriously. As Andrew Greeley, a Roman Catholic priest teaching sociology at the University of Chicago wrote: 'What the hell is going on? God is dead but the Devil lives.'[6] One answer must be that this generation has revolted against positivism. They no longer believe in religion, humanism, or even the imperialism of science that claims to be the only valid form of knowledge. In the words of one graduate student,

> Let's face it, science is dead. While the newspapers and magazines were giving all the attention to the death of God, science was really the one that was dying.[7]

The second reason why so many moderns now 'believe in' Satan may be that large numbers of people have been simply bored with life, seeking a costless thrill, and unsuspecting that there was any real world of evil or of good either. Having been taught the doctrine of relativism (that is, that there is no real or final good or no real evil) they expected their exploration to end in fantasy. It came as a shock but also a strange relief, to discover that evil is real. A relief in the sense that people in this machine age were beginning to wonder if anything was real except our machines. One student expressed it in this question, 'Is there anything so powerful that it can even make us real? I mean *really real*.'[8]

Professor Mircea Eliade of the University of Chicago defines the sacred almost in the precise words of the student: 'That is exactly what the sacred is, the really real.'[9]

It should come as no surprise that the modern existentialist is not interested in second-hand philosophy or theology. To him, the 'really real' is what he or another person experiences first-hand. Thus if some come to a belief in the reality of the world of the spirit via the negative underside (as the Buddingtons did in order to get to the Godward side), at least we can be grateful that they *are* finding reality.

History proves that there are two tests of experiences which will flush out the power of evil and make Satan surface — one is to reconnoitre deeply in evil's territory; the other is to become a follower of Jesus.

So long as we remain secularists — whether just conventionally good members of society, or even church members who deny the supernatural aspect of religion — then probably we shall give no particular thought to Satan. If we consider the devil at all, we are likely to dismiss him as an outmoded, non-sensical symbol. Incidentally, Satan, like any other saboteur, would prefer to keep it that way. Disbelief in his existence is the best camouflage. If I have a mortal enemy who is intent on destroying me, my ignorance of such an enemy only makes my danger greater.

But I had learned Scripture's observation that Satan is not

only real, but that each human life is in dire danger from the unholy spirit.

Be sober, be watchful: your adversary, the devil, prowls around like as a roaring lion, walketh about, seeking someone to devour . . .[10]

And Jesus speaking to the Pharisees:

Ye are of your father the devil, and the lusts of your father ye will do: he was a murderer from the beginning . . .[11]

Moreover, our danger from Satan is to our physical bodies,[12] our families,[13] our possessions,[14] along with the eternal part of us — our spirits.

Meanwhile, my eyes were progressively being opened to substantiation of these Scriptural lessons by events all around me in contemporary life. Occasionally we can catch the Destroyer in the very act of trying to destroy.

Derek Prince, whom I know well, recently related such an incident.[15] At a preaching mission in Chicago, Mr. Prince had emphasised the dangers in playing around with the Destroyer's toys — ouija boards, Tarot cards, going to fortune tellers or mediums — even when we tell ourselves that we are taking none of this seriously.

He had commented that something like going to a fortune teller just for a 'joke' is quite like entering a lion's cage to count the lion's teeth for fun. Where there has been such dabbling, the speaker urged repudiation with a prayer for cleansing and if necessary, the Church's ancient rite of exorcism.

After one of the services, a woman approached Derek Prince, confessing that she had been a medium, and asked him to pray with her. As he looked into her eyes, he sensed duplicity. Knowing that his prayer for her would do no good unless she was ready to make a clean break with Satan, Derek suggested that she was not yet ready.

A day later she came again asking for prayer, this time insisting that she had changed her mind about spiritualism and had repented. Though Derek found himself nagged with doubts about her sincerity, finally he agreed to pray with her. But he found it hard going, like a series of obstacle courses all the way. After a few moments, he told the woman that he wanted to take a little rest, so he withdrew a few steps away and was leaning against the altar rail, thinking and asking for God's direction.

Suddenly he was jerked out of his reverie. A loud, clear voice of a different timbre from the one the woman had been using made him whirl around. He saw her pointing a finger at him. 'I see you in a car and it's wrecked against a tree.'

Derek Prince's reaction was trigger-quick. Recognising now what he was really up against, with great firmness of voice he said, 'You spirit of divination, I refuse to accept that from you. That's Satan's lie. I will *not* be in any car that's wrecked against any tree.'

Later, telling of this incident, he concluded by saying, 'Had I not been on my guard, had I begun to believe this woman, I would have been in real trouble. The woman was seeing and describing Satan's destiny for me. By admitting this idea into my mind, I would have submitted myself to Satan's plan.'

The Bible not only spells out the peril of Satan's life plan for us, but goes on to give us a plan of defence. For our reassurance, God has made us sure promises of help and deliverance . . .

Submit yourselves therefore to God. Resist the devil, and he will flee from you.[16]

. . . God is faithful who will not suffer you to be tempted above that ye are able but will with the temptation also make a way of escape, that ye may be able to bear it.[17]

And Jesus ... spake unto them, saying, All power is given unto me in heaven and in earth.[18]

Thus reassured that God has made us 'a way of escape', what are those defence tactics?

First, it's a blessed relief to learn, as Carrie and Jeff Buddington discovered through hard experience, that while 'the unholy spirit does have power, it is a power each individual has to allow him'. That freedom of choice God gave man is so real that the unholy spirit cannot violate it. He must therefore persuade or deceive us.

Satan can call God a liar, he can flash before our dazzled eyes all the supposed sin-fun imaginable, but if we do not agree to his blandishments, give him the nod, he remains helpless. Although the divine part of man — the inner core of him, his spirit — is sacred, nevertheless God has made each man the keeper of his inner castle. We do not therefore have a built-in protection against evil. But we have been given truly free wills. That is why it is possible to hand over so much to Satan and why to do so places us in such jeopardy.

When we understand the factuality of this free will, then we'll be more likely to perceive why it's so dangerous to hand over to Satan any ground in our life on which he can stand. What I have come to call 'the beachhead trick' is a favourite one of the enemy.

During World War II the term 'beachhead' came into popular usage. A beachhead is that first landing on an island or a shore on which the whole battle may depend. Once that toehold on land is secured, it is usually only a matter of time until the rest of the island or country or even empire will fall.

Just so — my life, my body, my affairs are as an island-empire that the unholy spirit hopes to win *en route* to his ultimate objective of my eternal soul. To do that, he too must first gain a beachhead in my life. With that toehold, then he can take his time about gaining control of the rest of me and my affairs — yard by yard, decision by decision. But the analogy breaks down at one important point. In war, through physical overpowering, the victor can force his opponent to bend to his will, whereas God has kept from the unholy spirit the ability to force any human being against his will. Either Satan has to be granted permission by God (as in Job's case), or we have to give Satan the beachhead voluntarily, else he can't have it.

But who in warfare would be foolish enough voluntarily to give a beachhead? We do. We're foolish enough. How often we fall for the Destroyer's beachhead arguments, finding them amazingly appealing . . .

A little sinning is a good thing, the father of liars suggests to us. Not enough to sink us, of course. Just enough to be easier to live with and more socially acceptable. Anyway, who wants to be Mr. Goody-Two-Shoes?

Another day, another approach. Don't we realise that a civilised person doesn't want to be 'narrow' in morals, ethics, or religious belief? True, we agree, it is a sunny day on the beach, sparkling sand, fluffy clouds floating in a blue sky. Spiritual warfare? What made us even think about such a thing?

Then comes the whispered argument, 'All of life has to be compromise.' We can even take it from there for Satan. Of *course* a little ground here and there, not be rigid about everything. How else would conflicting points of view ever reach agreement on anything?

Then there's always 'moderation' and 'normal' — such reassuring words when compared to 'fanaticism' and 'extremist'. Above all, who wants to be tagged 'religious fanatic!'

Thus we succumb to Satan's beachhead strategies. Once he has this bit of ground, then he uses it to stand on for further assaults. I have received tremendous help by keeping this picture of the tempter's beachhead strategy in my mind's eye. It reminds me how dangerous is the initial bit of sinning on any given front.

We are creatures of habit patterns for good or ill. In other words, we do not make a series of equal and independent decisions, rather one decision leads to another. Unfortunately, the natural inclination which we have inherited from our father Adam towards making the wrong choice means that this phenomenon works more easily downward than upward. Any parent or teacher concerned with children knows this well. For instance, it is easier to let a child be sloppy and to allow careless habits to develop than it is to fight uphill towards his becoming an ordered, neat person.

Moreover, each repetition of a downbeat choice makes the next one easier and bothers us less as sin's inevitable deadening process sets in. Even after collaborating with the enemy by handing over the beachhead, we think ourselves still in control, able to call a halt to the enemy's advance any time we choose. Instead, Jesus warns us that 'whosoever commiteth sin is the servant (or slave) of sin.'[19]

Notice how clear-cut Jesus was about His own total refusal so to collaborate with Satan: (Jesus is speaking here to His apostles at the Last Supper):

> Hereafter I will not talk much with you: for the prince of this world cometh, *and hath nothing in me.*[20]

Jesus had given no ground because He knew how deadly playing with Satan is. Just as a physician would not dare ignore or underestimate the malignancy of a few cancer cells, even so in God's eyes there is no harmless little 'white' evil.

The second defence God has provided for us is what Scripture calls 'the armour of light'.[21] So long as we stay in the light we're safe because Satan cannot endure light and will not come near it.

A true incident has become an unforgettable symbol of this for me. Some years ago *Guideposts* magazine editors received a short manuscript in the mail. The writer, whom I'll call Mary, was married to Bill W., a travelling salesman, and was the mother of three children, the youngest a baby girl. She and her husband were both active in their local church where the couple had met and grown fond of an attractive young man, John Ames.

On those Sundays when Mary's husband would be out of town on one of his frequent business trips, John would give her and her children a ride to church.

Nothing was wrong with that, except that soon it was becoming a habit. Mary found herself looking forward to seeing John and thinking of him often.

An inner warning signal went up for her as she remembered Jesus' words about lust beginning inside us — in the thoughts and the will. 'I'll duck this,' she decided. She and the children went early to Sunday School to get there ahead of John's proffered ride.

The strategy worked the first Sunday. But on the next one when Bill was out of town, John started early for Sunday School too — and picked them up.

On both sides the attraction was intensifying. Even sitting across the room from one another in a group of people, Mary was acutely conscious of John and of his eyes often on her. An electric sexual attraction was developing between them, no question about it.

One night Mary forced herself to face the issue. 'I made myself think through the end results if John and I kept on the road we were going. A romantic interlude, nothing more? To think so would be kidding myself. Rather, probably a broken home. My husband's life cruelly hurt and twisted. Worse still for our children. And tawdriness as my reward. On the other side was the frightening intensity of the electricity between John and me.

'In desperation, I dropped on my knees. "Oh God! This is too much for me." It was a cry wrung out of me. "I can't fight any more. I turn this battle over to You." That night I slept calmly.'

The next day with her husband still out of town, Mary spent the entire day cleaning — closets, drawers, cupboards, windows. In some way, it must have been symbolic.

That evening after the children were in bed, John Ames appeared at the front door. 'Bill's not home,' Mary told him. But he came in anyway.

Mary didn't ask her caller to sit down. She remained standing in the centre of the room bathed in a cone of light from the electrical fixture overhead. There was an awkward interlude during which John Ames made persistent small talk, his eyes fastened on Mary. As she concentrated on Jesus as represented by that light, she felt herself becoming less aware of John and more and more aware of the enveloping light of God all around her.

Finally her caller noticed the baby asleep on the sofa. 'Don't you want me to carry her to her crib?' he asked.

Mary nodded, but did not follow John into the darkness of the adjoining bedroom. Somehow she knew that she must not. There in the darkness John's arms would reach for her as inevitably as — No, *she must stay in the light.* As long as she stood in the light, the values she really cared about — her marriage, the home she and Bill had made together, their children — would be safe.

John remained in the bedroom for what seemed like an eternity, waiting for her, Mary thought. At last he emerged. For a long moment he stood looking at Mary, indecision written on his face. At last, reluctantly, he left.

'Then I understood,' the author wrote, 'the truth of the Scriptural teaching that there's nothing wrong with being tempted. It's what we *do* with the temptation that matters.

'My tumultuous feeling for John Ames did not disappear overnight. But as I prayed more about it, the entire episode just faded from my emotions, leaving no trauma, no scars, no regrets — just praise to God for delivering me from a serious temptation.'

Mary had found for herself the reality of 'the armour of light'. That protecting armour is, of course, Jesus Himself as prophesied in Isaiah's beautiful words:

> The people that walked in darkness have seen a great light: they that dwell in the land of the shadow of death, upon them hath the light shined.[22]

So as His disciples, we are urged:

> For ye were sometime darkness, but now are ye light in the Lord; walk as children of light.[23]

We walk as children of light when we insist upon transparent openness and honesty, no dark secrets, no duplicity, lies, or double-dealing. It was from my spiritual mentor, the Quaker Hannah Smith, that I learned the valuable lesson that hidden sin — no matter how carefully denied, glossed over and secreted away — will give Satan his beachhead and result in our inability to stand victoriously before the enemy or any of his cohorts.[24] The emphasis here is on any accursed thing being tucked back in our lives, hidden out of sight. We may have almost forgotten about it, but Satan never forgets. For us, the result will be failure every time. This is the reason that Jesus had so much to say about the necessity of light and our coming to the light. When men's deeds are evil, they love darkness rather than light.

> But he that doeth truth cometh to the light, that his deeds may be made manifest, that they are wrought in God.[25]

So it helps to stay aware of this principle: whenever we prefer to keep something secret or hidden, tucked away in the darkness, we do well to question our real motives.

Truth is the name of a third defence against the Destroyer pointed out by Scripture. The cynic would always echo Pilate's sarcastic question to Jesus, 'What is truth?' — the assumption there being that all truth is relative, so there is no final clear-cut truth. But this is Satan's position, not Christ's. Jesus' words echo down the centuries, '*I* am the way, the truth, and the life.'

Naturally, Satan could never agree to clarity. The saints of all ages are in agreement that the unholy spirit delights in fuzziness. He would have us believe that we are being properly humble when we intone, 'I hope my sins are forgiven' . . . 'Well, Y-yes, I think I'm a Christian. I try to be.' Jesus wants us to *know* that our sins are forgiven and that we *are* Christians.

Thus one of our greatest weapons is not just defensive, but offensive: the use of Scripture as truth hurled in Satan's teeth, wielded as the 'sword of the Spirit'. Jesus' repeated use of 'It is written' in His wilderness temptations is a vivid example. Of course, in order to use Scripture in this way, we have to get the habit of reading it so that the truth cast in the cadences of the great English of the Bible sinks deeply into heart and mind. I have found that when I do my part, then the Holy Spirit can do His. So often it has happened! It is as if the Helper searches through the library stacks of my unconscious where all manner of information has been filed away (much of it long since forgotten by the conscious mind) and produces the particular 'It is written' needed for the moment of battle. Always Satan flees before this. He flees because the unholy spirit has final respect for the authority of Scripture. Though the Destroyer loathes truth, he recognises it, thus tipping his hand about those aeons spent in the presence of God. Certainly this should give us pause at a time when the authority of the Bible has been so generally called into question.

Satan and his lackeys always recognise and must bow before Jesus, who is our Deliverer. Long before even Jesus' apostles recognised that He was more than an exciting Teacher and Healer, the unclean spirits (demons) who had taken up abode in human beings recognised Him as the Son of God. So over and over in the Gospels we hear an unclean spirit crying out, 'What have I to do with thee, Jesus, thou Son of the most high God? I adjure thee . . . that thou torment me not.'[26] Each time Christ was able to cast out the unclean spirit because He is the only One who has never given any ground to Satan.

Usually we think we deserve a 'little fun' by a fling into sinning when life has handed us some injustice or when we have stuck faithfully through some protracted trial. A degree of self-pity joins the blown-up pride of our self-congratulation at having been so patient and reliable. Many of us have found out to our sorrow what a deadly brew this is. Our eyes are completely off Christ and on ourselves. Out of this little mess Satan has worked some great triumphs.

But what if we are already in the middle of such a mess? What if one's life is snarled up by habit-pattern chains, bad human relationships, fears that one can't get rid of, debts, and illness? What then? Is there any hope?

There certainly is! That's precisely the good news Christ brings us . . .

So also the Lord can rescue you and me from the temptations that surround us . . .[27]

Behold, I give unto you power . . . over all the power of the enemy; and nothing shall by any means hurt you.[28]

Because thou hast kept the word of my patience, I also will keep thee from the hour of temptation . . .[29]

When we bring our misdeed into the light of Jesus' love and forgiveness and renounce it, we have taken the first step. The renouncing part is especially important when we have been toying with ouija boards, spiritualism, witchcraft, fortune telling, and the like, even though this be years behind us. In order to belong to Christ, we have to make a clean break with the accoutrements of Satan's kingdom by renouncing them. Once that break is made, then we are free to 'turn around' and accept Jesus' forgiveness.[30] Thereupon Satan loses his beachhead and we are again free.

But Satan, the liar, will throw everything into the fight to blind us to this final power before which he is helpless — the finished work of Jesus on His cross, the sacrificial Lamb, His blood being shed for us. God's wish is that no matter what we've done, we feel guilt only long enough to bring it to the Light of the World to be dealt with. Satan's aim is to bog us down through the emotion of guilt, somehow convince us that *our* sin is too rarefied to be forgiven (an odd form of inverted human ego!), thus making us feel estranged from God and inept in serving Him.

The opposite of Satan's lie is given us in a ringing declaration in Colossians:

> ... he (Christ) cancelled the regulations that stood against us ... when he nailed them to the cross, when he cut away the angelic Rulers and Powers from us, exposing them to all the world and triumphing over them in the cross.[31]

I remember how Peter Marshall once made this truth real and personal. One evening a friend had questioned him about God's judgment. Did he really think that there was going to have to be an accounting for each of us?

'Yes, I do think so,' Peter answered promptly. 'The Bible makes it quite clear. I think I may have to go through the agony of having Old Scratch, the accuser, recite my sins in the presence of God.

'But I believe it will be like this — Jesus, our High Priest, will come over and lay His hand across my shoulders and say to God, "Yes, all these things are true, but I'm here to cover up for Peter. He is sorry for all his sins, and by a transaction made between us, I am now solely responsible for them." '

Suddenly Peter smiled. 'And sister, if I'm wrong about that, *I'm sunk.*'[32]

But we're not sunk. Glory be to God!

CHAPTER NINE

THE ENIGMA OF HEALING

Most of us feel no need of facing the question 'Does God heal directly today?' until we are personally confronted with some physician's blunt finality: 'There's nothing more we can do.'

Those were the precise words my friend Sandra was hearing so incredulously that night — February 8th, 1966. I did not learn of this sequence of events until later when Sandra Ghost (now a close friend. Yes, her name really is Ghost) shared it with me. Arriving at the hospital room where her little son lay, Sandy had encountered Dr. Gallo.

'Mrs. Ghost, there's been no improvement in Kent's condition since this afternoon,' the distinguished-looking, dark-haired doctor told her. 'No question of the diagnosis — a cerebral haemorrhage. He's still in deep coma.'

Over his shoulder Sandra could see the slight form of her two-year-old son, usually unable to stay still for an instant. Now there wasn't a flicker of movement anywhere — from his toes to his blond head.

Dr. Gallo asked gently, 'You did call your husband in Louisville?'

'Yes, I did. Bill caught the first plane possible. He should be here at ten o'clock.'

'I must warn you ... Kent may not hold on until your husband gets here. Mrs. Ghost, you may go in now.' He paused. 'There's nothing more we can do.'

The words spoken so slowly for emphasis struck Sandra like a physical blow. Their impact detached some part of her mind and sent her thoughts spinning backwards to that first day when she and Kent, his hand clinging so tightly to hers, had walked through the front door of the National Institutes of Health on the outskirts of Washington, D.C. What relief she had felt! To think that this great research arm of the United States Government had been willing to take on their son's case of acute lymphocytic leukaemia. Why, this place was one of medicine's frontiers. In these vast government buildings they were finding answers. Surely, she told herself, only God could have made the connection between the Ghost family in Louisville, Kentucky and NIH. Therefore, the fine and compassionate doctors on Two-East (the Leukaemia unit) would discover the key to the healing of Kent's leukaemia.

And in the two months since, the doctors had indeed proved themselves compassionate. In fact, the warmth of everyone around NIH — laboratory technicians, housekeeping detail, clean-up crews, and Mr. Botts, the gentle black elevator operator who 'God-blessed' all his passengers — had steadily reassured her.

So how could Dr. Gallo be saying so seriously, 'There's nothing more we can do.'? For what he meant was, 'Kent is going to die and I can't prevent his death. Medicine, science, the best we know, has no further resources to give you.'

Her thoughts reeled and staggered. 'But that can't be! This is the twentieth century. I — Sandra Ghost — am a twentieth-century woman. I have relied on science. Science can do *anything*.'

But she only stared at the doctor, nodded her head, and murmured, 'Thank you, doctor.' For an instant she watched the physician's back retreating down the long corridor almost at a trot, as though eager to be away. Then she hurried into Kent's room.

This was Intensive Care with Di-Gi on duty, a nurse whom Sandra had learned to know well during the two months. Every ten minutes, Di-Gi was taking vital signs: would Kent respond to the beam of light flashed directly into his eyes? Any sign of consciousness by grip or response? Any change in temperature? Blood pressure?'

But there was no visible response — none at all. Her child was so still and so white, his legs so limp. Almost the smell of death was in this room. Was Sandra imagining it? No, this was no illusion; she saw it in the nurse's eyes.

Sandy kept a grip on her emotions through two of the ten-minute periods. Then she broke down, sobbing quietly.

Di-Gi understood. 'Some black coffee would help,' she suggested, 'help me too. Why don't you go down to the Snack Shop for two cups?'

The distraught mother realized the nurse was using psychology on her, but she also knew that some activity would help. 'Sure,' Sandra agreed, 'good idea.'

On Sandy's return from the Snack Shop, she was surprised to see Mr. Botts running the elevator; it was rare to see him on night duty, rarer still for her to be the only passenger. As the doors slid shut and the elevator mounted, Mr. Botts asked as he always did, 'And how's my little man?'

This time the question brought quick tears to Sandra's eyes. She shifted the tray with its two steaming cartons of coffee to her left hand in order to grope for her handkerchief. 'Mr. Botts, Kent's bad. He's — not expected to live.' Then from deep inside her came a request that she was surprised to hear herself making, 'Will you — would you pray for Kent?'

At that moment they arrived at the second floor and the elevator doors opened. Sandra was no more than three steps into the hallway when she heard Mr. Bott's voice behind her, 'Get back on the elevator, would you? Let's pray *now*. Please get back on.'

Wordlessly, Sandra obeyed. The elevator doors shut, only

this time Mr. Botts left the elevator stationary at the second floor.

'Lord Jesus,' he prayed, 'I ask you to heal this child as you healed me when the doctors told me I would never walk again. The Church prayed and You heard their prayers, and there's nothing wrong with me now. I ask You to do for this child what You did for me since the Good Book says, 'God is no respecter of persons.'

'Lord, enter this little boy's body. Heal Kent, Lord, and let him walk again. And Lord Jesus, give Kent's mother here Your strength. She needs it so much . . .'

Was there more of the prayer? Sandy could never remember, only that she was aware of God's love in that elevator as she had never before felt it. And wasn't it odd that during what had seemed to her a long stretch of time, no one had rung for the elevator? Fumbling for words, she tried to thank Mr. Botts. Then she ran left down the corridor and through the double swinging doors to Kent's room. As she went, she glanced at her wrist watch — six minutes before nine.

'Any change?' she asked the nurse.

Di-Gi shook her head. 'No change.'

As the two women sipped coffee, Di-Gi talked. Sandra discovered one reason for this nurse's special depth of compassion. She had been through trouble too: her mother and her younger sister had died in an automobile wreck just two months before. Sandra wondered why Di-Gi was not angry with God or bitter. She had the feeling that the nurse knew Him.

As they talked, two sets of vital signs were taken. At the third, Di-Gi seemed startled and made no attempt to hide it. 'His blood pressure! Coming down fast, toward normal.'

Almost immediately, Kent stirred in the bed. His eyes fluttered open. Recognising his mother, he turned towards her, 'Mommy, I'm thirsty.'

Di-Gi restrained her excitement long enough to finish taking all the vital signs and recheck them, then she ran for the doctor. He made the return journey in a hurry.

By the time Bill Ghost arrived from the airport, Kent was fully conscious, sitting up in bed, sipping a soft drink through a straw, anticipating his Daddy's coming.

During the night hours Kent continued to improve. The next day, February 9th, Dr. Robert Gallo appeared to be in sharp disagreement with a battery of neurologists at NIH. Though the parents at NIH are always considered a part of the 'medical team' for their own child, the Ghosts were surprised to hear the physicians openly discussing their differences: Dr. Gallo could not possibly have been correct in his diagnosis, the neurologists insisted; no patient could recover from a cerebral haemorrhage as quickly as Kent Ghost had.

Dr. Gallo stood his ground. Yes, he reiterated, his diagnosis had been correct. He had performed the requisite spinal tap. Nor had a vein been punctured during the tap, thus accounting for blood in the test tube.

Finally the neurologists would not be appeased unless they performed another spinal tap, so Kent was wheeled away to a treatment room. There Dr. Gallo was vindicated: yes, the little boy had had a brain haemorrhage.

Two days later, Kent was riding the rocking horse in the playroom at NIH, unaware of the doctors and nurses who kept drifting by the playroom door, staring at him ... 'Can you believe that's Kent Ghost?'[1] Between his turns on the rocking horse, he would ride Mr. Botts' elevator up and down, down and up, and each time a jubilant Mr. Botts would pat 'his little man's' head, make gleeful remarks or hum under his breath, all the time looking as though he possessed a secret too marvellous to contain.

My first reaction to Sandy's story was joy. My second was, then why doesn't God always come to our rescue as He did to

Kent Ghost's? Here is a query asked not so much by non-Christians nor even by the Christian who has never admitted healing into his understanding of the whole Gospel, but by those of us who have long struggled with this matter of healing through God's intervention.

I first asked the question in 1943 when because of a lung condition, I too heard the doctors say, 'Sorry! Nothing more we can do right now. Just lie in bed and rest.'

So I was bedridden during 1943, 1944 — winter ... spring ... summer ... into autumn. During the long, tedious days I was doing a lot of praying and thinking. Since the birth of modern scientific enquiry, men had come to rely on the order-liness of nature, what science calls 'the uniformity of natural causes'. I could see how Christians had picked up this concept and applied it to Christian thinking. An idea can often be as catching as a virus. Such was the case with an idea that surfaced in the late 'thirties and was verbalised from thousands of pulpits through the decade of the 'forties. It could be sum-marised like this ...

'We are accustomed to the fact of physical laws — dis-coverable, definite, immutable. When we drop an object from the top of a tall building the object always drops because the Law of Gravity always operates. In the spiritual realm too there are laws just as discoverable, just as precise, always operative.

'Therefore, the way to get on with spiritual research to find out how prayers are answered and healing effected is to discover these spiritual laws and apply them. The results will then be just as certain as in the realm of the physical laws.'

It was an exciting concept. Many of us had turned to it with relief. It had given us a way to go. It was like having in our hand the last AAA strip map for our spiritual journey. If we followed the directions carefully from point A to point B and then C and D, our destination was assured.

Lying in bed feeling half-alive, my need was great. I set out eagerly to find those spiritual laws governing healing. After studying the New Testament I would then delve into what I could uncover from human experience as recorded in books and in any sort of verbal contemporary sharing for which acceptable proof was offered.

So methodically, I started, searching out each of Jesus' healing miracles and analysing them. I was groping for some common denominator in these healings by which I could uncover the principles or secrets I could apply to my situation. Thirty-seven miracles are detailed in the gospels in addition to thirteen separately recorded times when Christ healed 'many' or 'multitudes' or 'great multitudes'.

In order to make a comparative study of Jesus' dealings with the sick and the afflicted, I ruled wide sheets of paper into seven divisions, like this:

The case of	The trouble	Means used	Time	Patient's part	Others' part	Christ's Instructions
The deaf man (Mark 7:32-38)	Deafness and severe speech impediment	Jesus' touch of afflicted part with saliva and His word of authority	Immediate cure	None	Friends brought man to Christ, begging that He lay hands on sufferer	Forbade man or his friends to tell others about it

My conclusion from this study could be summed up like this ⸳ . . Jesus came to earth to reveal His Father's nature and will for and to mankind.[2] Jesus saw sickness and disease as intruders in His Father's world, part of Satan's work,[3] therefore evil all the way. Consistently, He fought disease just as any dedicated physician fights it.[4]

I could find no Gospel record that the Master ever refused anyone who came to Him and asked for healing, though He did, upon occasion, select one to be healed out of a group — such as the man at the Pool of Bethesda[5] — thus obviously leaving other sufferers around that Pool unhealed.

He did not once say in regard to health, 'If it is God's will.'[6] There is no beatitude for the sick as there is for others like the bereaved, those who suffer persecution, the peacemakers.[7] Nor did there ever fall from Jesus' lips any statements that ill health would further our spiritual growth or benefit the Kingdom of God. Rather, He not only wants to heal our diseases, He also wants us to stay healthy.[8]

So I asked myself the question, 'Then did Jesus intend for these healings to go on after His ascension — even into our own time?' According to the New Testament, He certainly did! How else could we interpret His words, 'Verily, verily I say unto you, he that believeth on me, the works that I do shall he do also; and greater works than these shall he do because I go unto my Father.'[9]

All of this added up to what seemed an unassailable 'yes' on the side of healing through the direct action of God today.

Yet this study, including that wistfully well-ordered chart of Jesus' healing was disappointingly frustrating in uncovering any rules or methodology for healing through prayer. At first glance, faith on the part of the sick one or his relatives or friends (such as Mr. Botts for Kent Ghost) seemed to be necessary. But closer scrutiny told me that while sometimes Jesus placed great emphasis on faith, at other times faith was never mentioned. For instance, what about those crowds whom Jesus healed?[10] Did every person in those crowds have faith? It isn't likely.

Perhaps going to Jesus and *asking* for healing could be put forward as a rule. No, because many were healed who never asked, like the man with the withered hand[11] or the sufferer at the Pool of Bethesda.[12]

Well then surely, I thought, some degree of goodness must

be necessary. Not a bit of it! Here Scripture's message is re-soundingly clear: all humankind is born into this earth life with the same stain. 'All have sinned and come short of the glory of God.'[13]

And this 'coming short' is such a great gap that it can never be filled by human effort: 'Not for thy righteousness or for the uprightness of thine heart, dost thou go to possess their land . . .'[14]

'Not by works of righteousness which we have done, but according to his mercy he saved us . . .'[15]

Jesus healed out of pure compassion because He was ever — and always will be 'The Father's Restorer'. True, after Jesus healed the man at the Pool of Bethesda, He told him that now he would be wise to repent and change 'or something even worse may happen to you'.[16] But the healing came before the man's change and in no way seemed dependent on it.

Though I was learning, I could find no uniform dependable act or attitude on the part of the sick person that would provide certain healing. At that point I began wondering if things of the spirit could really be pigeonholed and categorised in the way that has been such universal procedure in the physical world? I was beginning to doubt it.

Even so, my search went on into the second phase, the area of human experience since New Testament times. Of several such areas I investigated, I'll mention only one — the healings at Lourdes in south-west France. This has been a healing shrine since a fourteen-year-old peasant girl, Bernadette Soubirous, had a vision of Mary, the mother of Jesus, on February 11th, 1858. The girl was told to dig in the earth at a certain place where she would find a spring. She was instructed to ask that a healing shrine be built over the spring.

Bernadette obeyed. Digging in the dry earth, she was aston-ished to find a trickle of water appear, no bigger than a finger. But over the days, the spring grew larger and larger until today it pours out thirty-thousand gallons of water every twenty-four hours. More than forty-five thousand sick people go to Lourdes each year, most of these as a last hope.

Investigation convinced me that there have been healings so remarkable as to fall clearly into the category of 'miracle'. The first one in 1858 was that of the eighteen-month-old boy Louis-Justin Bouhohartz, a neighbour of Bernadette. Dying from a disease that Dr. Dozous, the local physician, had said 'hesitates between meningitis and poliomyelitis', the little boy had intermittent convulsions with high fever, was unable to sit up, walk or stand. Feeling that she had nothing to lose, the child's mother plunged him into the icy spring for fifteen minutes and took him home with his little body stiff and blue. The next day Louis-Justin was walking and eating normally.

Dr. Dozous who had attended the boy and given him over to death watched the icy bath and its results and this convinced the physician. Incidentally Louis-Justin lived to be a very old man.

Over the years other miracles have followed, stories that fascinated me as I read of them.[17] The distinguished scientist Dr. Alexis Carrel has left us with an impressive eye-witness report, his observation of the healing of the eighteen-year-old Marie Ferrand from advanced tubercular peritonitis between two-forty and three o'clock on a July afternoon in 1903.

At the time Carrel was on the faculty of the Medical School of the University of Lyons. Born into a Catholic family, he had become first a Stoic, then a disciple of Kant, then sceptical of any belief in a supreme being. All religious concepts had been ground down and finally destroyed by intellectualism, especially the rigorous German system of higher criticism. Any attempt to discuss primary causes seemed useless to Carrel; rationalism satisfied his mind all the way.

Out of this background, having heard so many rumours of cures at Lourdes, the young doctor decided to accompany a trainload of pilgrims in order to observe, analyse, examine, and discredit these vaunted cures. On the train he was summoned to see Marie Ferrand, who was apparently dying. He learned that there was a history of tuberculosis on both sides of Marie's family. After examining the girl, Dr. Carrel concurred in the diagnosis of her home town doctor — tubercular peritonitis too far advanced to risk surgery.

Dr. Carrel examined Marie again after she got to Lourdes and before she was taken to the Grotto. He found her with an emaciated white face, a pulse racing at 150 beats a minute, an abdomen markedly distended with viscera and fluid, ears and nails of a pale greenish hue, her nose and hands cold. He scarcely expected the patient to live long enough to be carried from the Lourdes hospital to the Shrine.

Later on at the Grotto Shrine, Dr. Carrel stayed close by the girl thinking that she might need medical help. As he watched, astounding changes took place; the lines and shadows on her face began disappearing as colour returned; the blanket over her distended abdomen was flattening out while her heartbeat was slowing down to a regular pace. One of the nurses offered her a cup of milk which she drank eagerly. Then she began moving her legs without any discomfort.

Still incredulous, Dr. Carrel re-examined Marie that same evening. She was sitting up in bed. Her pulse was now a steady eighty beats per minute. All traces of distension, hard masses, and fluid had disappeared from her abdomen; hers was the flat, slightly concave stomach of an undernourished girl. [18, 19]

Witnessing this case changed Alexis Carrel's life in several respects. Upon his return to the University of Lyons, he decided that he could no longer call himself truly scientific if he failed to speak out about what he had observed at Lourdes. He was promptly summoned into the office of the Dean of the Medical School. 'With such views, sir,' he was told, 'you can hardly expect to stay on as a member of our faculty.'

'In that case,' Carrel replied, 'I must look elsewhere.'

That was why Alexis Carrel left France to come to the United States, first, to the University of Chicago, then to New York as a member of the Rockefeller Institute for Medical Research. There in 1912, he received the Nobel Prize in physiology and medicine for his contribution to the surgery of blood vessels.

The Catholic Church — at first as sceptical about Lourdes as was the medical profession — had finally seen the point of detailed medical substantiation. Thus, in 1885 a Medical Bureau had been established for professional examination and verification of alleged healings. Later an International Medical Association (nicknamed AMIL) with five thousand doctors from thirty countries was added to support the Medical Bureau and the scientific study of Lourdes cures.

Of the many apparent healings at Lourdes, only 1,200 in eighty-nine years have passed the Medical Bureau's rigid standards, with probably an additional 4,000 genuine cures not finally substantiated because of incomplete data in the Bureau's files. Out of the total, only sixty-two have been submitted to the Catholic Church's Canonical Commission, finally to be pronounced 'miraculous'.

This rigorous medical substantiation gave me in Lourdes an ideal modern showcase to set alongside the New Testament in searching for that common denominator or set of spiritual laws in healings. Yet a careful scrutiny of the Lourdes healings left me with the same confusion as had the Gospel search. Try as I might, the why or the how of the Lourdes' healings could not be pigeonholed or categorised any more than the New Testament ones. For among those gloriously healed at Lourdes have been some roust-about sinners all but dragged to the healing grotto, while others who apparently fulfilled every prayer condition departed with their physical infirmities unchanged.

Some of the ill suffered severe pain at the time of healing; others were healed with no physical sensation.

While persistence on the part of the sufferer often appeared to be a factor, some have been cured at the Lourdes Grotto at their first bath in the springs.

The conclusion from all of this was clear: there was no neat set of spiritual laws, no cut-and-dried pattern I could follow to ensure the return of the health I so desperately wanted. But back in 1944 I was not yet ready to admit to such a conclusion. I tried every way I knew: confession and spiritual house-cleaning, asking for the gifts of faith followed by collecting faith passages of Scripture, memorising affirmations, practising positive thinking — and so on.

Finally, having prepared myself in every way I knew, with all the faith I had, I asked Christ to heal me. Then I waited impatiently for the next physical check-up and set of X-rays, certain that a loving Lord had observed my stupendous efforts, and would respond.

The blood tests and X-rays were taken. Receiving the report two days later was always a traumatic experience for me ... a racing heart, a pulse I could feel in my dry throat as I picked up the phone and dialled the number.

The doctor's voice revealed no such excitement. 'No change in the X-rays; markings just the same. Sedimentation rate, ah — the same. Just carry on!' And he hung up.

No change — after all that! Incredulously, I sank back on the pillows. I had come to the end of self-effort and the sign before my face read DEAD END.

I hit bottom, and there I met God at the place where He had been waiting for me all along: where I knew that I wanted Christ's presence in my life more than I wanted health. Never mind healing, I wanted to be certain that God wasn't dead, that Jesus Christ lived, that He was real, and that I had been received by Him.

I poured all this out before Him, 'God, I don't understand
You at all. I've tried. You know I have. You told us that "Your
ways are not our ways." That's certainly the understatement of
the ages! Even so, I don't understand why You're so hard to
find. But here I am. I want You to take me over and do what
You like with me. I'm no good as I am, so I'm not giving You
much of a gift. But if You want me to lie here on and on, like a
vegetable — all right, that's up to You.'

There was no fine theological language in this prayer and
certainly, no graciousness in the gift of myself. But it was
honest, probably the most straightforward prayer I had ever
made. Finally, I meant business with God. In the years since,
I've learned that our Lord waits patiently until we stop playing
games with Him. The instant we leave off our childish fooling
around, He knows it and responds. It had taken me eighteen
months of trying everything else, but at last I wanted the Giver
more than His gifts.

That did it! The connection was made. At 3 a.m. the
next morning, I awakened suddenly to a feeling of crackling
electric power in the darkness. There followed an experience
of the Risen Christ. Since I've described this elsewhere,[20] I
shall not repeat the details here except to say that I saw
and heard Christ with the eyes and ears of the spirit. And my
observation of His personality, of what He said, and of
my replies and reactions, was even more specific than most
of my contacts ever are with my fellow human beings in the
flesh.

The results in my body were observable too. The next set of
chest X-rays revealed healing. Every X-ray thereafter showed
more healthy lung tissue until finally the healing was complete.
Nor has there ever been any relapse.

Surely there is no joy like that first rush of discovery in
experiencing for oneself that the Lord is alive, so much more
alive and real than any of us. And I had stumbled into that

revelation in the last way I would have thought logical — through the relinquishment of myself to Him.

At that point I caught a glimpse of God's sense of humour — His revelation of Himself had outmanoeuvred logic.

CHAPTER TEN

THE ROOF ON THE HOUSE

When one touches a live electric wire, there's no mistaking the instantaneous power that jolts the body. In the same way, when through relinquishment, I had touched the power of the Risen Christ in my quiet bedroom in the middle of the night, it had been as startlingly obvious.

We have Jesus' promise from his own lips that the Holy Spirit will lead us into all truth,[1] including all puzzling questions we need answered about healing. My problem was that often I was not content to have the Good Shepherd lead me into truth; like a rambunctious sheep, I kept running on ahead, nosing around the pastureland, always thinking that the truth I sought must surely lie immediately on the other side of the nearest hill.

That is how I acted back in 1944 after my return to health. In no time, I had all but forgotten about the necessity for relinquishment. Then, in my joy over experiencing the presence of the risen Lord, I rushed to pray for all manner of neighbours and friends who were ill. These included Kenneth Grey, a neighbour on Cathedral Avenue in Washington who was dying of a brain tumour; an appealing small boy in the last stages of leukaemia; a friend in our church with cancer.

I hope that my prayers brought comfort to the ill and to those around them. But they had no appreciable effect on the disease of the sufferers. In each case the illness took its course and the sick ones died.

That was deeply discouraging. Once again I had to go to

God to ask Him my mistake. 'Go back and look carefully at the way I've led you,' I was told.

So I studied all the efforts in 1943–44 that had failed to bring results:

My effort	*God's response*
Tried to find blanket laws.	No methodology; He deals with each one of us as His child, and each case individually.
Tried to make myself worthy.	'All your righteousness is as filthy rags to me.'[2]
Tried to have faith in faith, and to work up faith by positive thinking, affirmations, and picturing.	He showed me that this is putting faith in a technique rather than in a Person — Jesus.
Demanded healing as my 'right' as a child of God who thought she had met the conditions.	'You have no rights or righteousness in yourself, only in Christ Jesus.'[3]

I saw that my demanding spirit, with self-will as its rudder had blocked the answer to prayer.

'Now take a close look,' I was told, 'at how Jesus Himself handled the problem of will.'

I was startled to find that Jesus (before His resurrection and glorification) insisted upon His helplessness:

> The Son can do nothing of himself, but what he seeth the Father do . . .[4]

> . . . I can do nothing of myself; but as my Father has taught me, I speak . . .'[5]

Thus Jesus' helplessness meant a total dependence upon His Father for everything.

But His *will*, what of that? Since Jesus' perfect humanity was as real as His divinity, His would have been a strong human will, stronger than any of ours. Over and over He reiterated that He had handed over that will:

'For I have come down from heaven not to carry out my own will, but the will of him who sent me . . .'[6]

And to His disciples He said:

'My meat is to do the will of him that sent me . . .'[7]

And at the end, He was 'obedient even unto death'.

Given Jesus' dependence on the Father together with His laying down of self-will, then I asked myself, 'Why didn't Jesus have to go through the process of relinquishment (for most of us a lengthy and agonising process) each time He wanted to stretch out His hand and heal some sufferer?' Reading between the lines of the gospel records, I believe He *did* relinquish His will each time, then immediately looked to the Father for what to do. But for Him it was neither an agonising nor a lengthy process because He was altogether clear of our sticking points: does God really love the individual as we understand love; does He really have final power to break or overrule so-called 'natural law'? Most of us have never settled these basic dilemmas. Jesus had.

So persuaded was He of His Father's complete love, trustworthiness, and Omnipotent power over all evil that He could make these relinquishments quickly. And just as quickly there flowed back from the Father to Jesus the particular Word to give the sinner or the sufferer along with the necessary faith.

Thus occurred the resultant miracle healings. With us it takes longer — hours, weeks, sometimes years of trying everything else.

Meanwhile, as though to keep me seeking in the direction of relinquishment and to let me know that this had not been just one woman's isolated experience, instance after instance kept coming to my attention in literature and history, in journals and letters and by word of mouth. One of the most convincing and dramatic was Maude Blanford's remarkable recovery from what was diagnosed as terminal cancer fourteen years ago. A friend in Louisville, Kentucky first put me in touch with Mrs. Blanford.

Attached to a brief typed outline of her story was an impressive statement signed by Mrs. Blanford's physician, Dr. Oscar J. Hayes, making it all but impossible to dismiss the patient's recovery as one of those occasional 'remissions' as medical men usually speak of them. I was excited enough to fly to Louisville to get the details from the woman herself, now gloriously restored to health.

In the dining-room of our mutual friend, we three women sat around the table sipping coffee as I questioned Maude Blanford. There was no trace of grey in her reddish hair, though she is middle-aged now, a motherly type, comfortable to be with. 'How did your trouble begin?' I asked.

'In my left leg,' was her prompt reply. 'The leg had been hurting me for two years. I thought it was because I was on my feet eight or ten hours a day. Finally, when I couldn't stand it any longer, my husband and I decided that I should see a doctor.'

As the Blanford's family doctor examined her, he became increasingly sober. Her leg was not her only problem. On the patient's left lower abdomen there were lumps — large, firm tumour masses.

'I'm going to have to send you to a specialist immediately,' he told Mrs. Blanford. The unspoken word hung in the air between them, 'malignancy'.

The specialist to whom Mrs. Blanford was sent discovered uterine haemorrhaging. Mrs. Blanford read in his eyes the poor prognosis. 'I must warn you,' he told her, 'I suspect that this is extremely advanced.'

'But doctor,' the patient pleaded, 'there must be some way you can stop it. I'll go through *anything* — radium, surgery . . .'

'Mrs. Blanford, I promise you I'll do everything I can.'

On July 7th, 1959, the patient was admitted to the hospital for seventy-two hours of radium treatment in an effort to stop the haemorrhaging — without success. So in August she was given an additional seventy-two hours of this treatment. 'The effect of the radium was total misery,' she told me, 'like having a hot oven inside me.'

On September 29th she underwent surgery. Three days later, as she pleaded with the surgeon, Dr. Hayes, for the truth, he admitted. 'The malignancy is extensive and we removed as much as we could. Lymph nodes are affected — that's why the pain in your left leg. One kidney is non-functioning because of blockage of the ureter. There is an area of metastasis in the liver. I am sorry. I am so sorry.'

Maude Blanford was sent home, apparently to die. She was put on strong narcotics and tranquillisers to control the pain, and she was supposed to come back into the hospital for radium at regular intervals. Over a six-month period, she consumed $1,000 worth of pain-relieving drugs — Zactirin, sometimes Thorazine, and morphine.

Meanwhile, the sick woman began reviewing her spiritual resources, not to make her peace with God before death but for His help to continue battling for life. Mrs. Blanford had no church affiliation and no knowledge of the Bible. She did discover within herself a childlike (though untested) belief in the Person of Jesus Christ.

On the first Saturday of January, 1960, she suffered a cerebral haemorrhage and remained unconscious for twelve days. Afterwards, she related a vivid image that had come to her. She saw a house with no top on it. The partitions between the rooms were there, the furniture in place, but there was no roof. She remembered thinking, 'Oh, we must put a roof on the house. If it rains, all the furniture will be spoiled.'

When she came out of the coma, Mrs. Blanford was bewildered. Instinctively, she turned to the Lord to ask Him in prayer what the vivid image had meant. 'Christ showed me,' she explained almost matter-of-factly, 'that without Him as my covering, my body had no protection. Therefore, my life was in danger. But at that time I didn't know how to get the roof back on the house.'

But Maude Blanford's fallacy, as mine had been, was that all her attention was focused on her danger, her roofless house. So despite all her prayers between then and July, 1960, day by day her condition worsened. Breathing became so laboured that she was reduced to speaking in whispers.

Still she kept struggling back and back for the radiation treatments. Then came Friday, July 1st, 1960; she remembers it well. As the radiologist examined her, she asked anxiously, 'Is it getting any better?'

'No, as a matter of fact . . .' his voice trailed off. Mrs. Blanford could read pessimism in his eyes. 'I dare not give you any encouragement.'

A few minutes later as Maude Blanford's son-in-law helped her into the car and she lifted her bad leg on to the seat, she broke down and wept. 'For the first time, death looked good to me. May be I couldn't fight any more. I just hoped the Lord would take me quickly.' It was a complete handing over of herself for God to do with as He pleased.

As He pleased . . . a bell of remembrance rang in my mind. My thoughts went spinning back to that September night in

1944 when I had ceased my frantic human striving and laid down my will almost in the same words she had. Only my situation had not been as stark as Maude Blanford's. For me, the alternative to healing was just having to lie in bed year after year; for her, it was death.

I leaned forward, eager to learn the result of this Prayer of Relinquishment. Had she made contact with the Source of power?

'That last visit to the radiologist and my turning myself over to God,' she continued, 'had been on Friday, July 1st. Well, I didn't have long to wait.'

Monday, July 4th dawned beautiful but hot. That afternoon Joe Blanford made a bed for his wife outdoors with chairs and cushions. As the ill woman rested, hoping for the relief of a breeze, into her mind came some Scripture which she was not aware of ever having read . . .

Is not this the fast that I have chosen? To loose the bands of wickedness, to undo the heavy burdens, and to let the oppressed go free, and that ye break every yoke . . .? Then shall thy light break forth as the morning and thine health shall spring forth speedily . . . Here I am . . .

As Maude Blanford quoted this, I found myself looking at her in astonishment over the rim of my coffee cup. 'But I thought you didn't know the Bible that well?'

'I didn't. I'd never read the Bible and I didn't even know that verse was there. When I was given those verses in my mind, I was also told, "Isaiah 58". My husband had to hunt up a Bible that had gathered dust on a spare-room shelf for years. Then I had to search and search to find the part called "Isaiah". But when I found the great verses just as I had heard them, even that "Here I am" on down in the ninth verse, I knew the Lord Himself had spoken to me.'

In the next few days the ill woman felt an intense desire like an authoritative inner summons to get outdoors and absorb the beauty of the good earth. She found a way to express this to her husband, 'Joe, I want to go fishing.'

That made no sense to him. Suppose his wife died on the way to the lake? The back road was rough. His wife would have to be carried down the steep hill to the lake.

Finally Maude Blanford's insistence that God had told her to do this won her husband over. He allowed some neighbours to take her to the lake. That first day she stayed at the lakeside all day until 6.30 p.m. Just watching a breeze ripple the water, looking at the clouds and the wheeling birds and the distant hills brought a refreshment of spirit. That night she was relaxed for the first time in many months and slept soundly.

After that, the lake trip became routine. In three months' time, Maude Blanford was climbing up the hill to the road by herself. Then that inner Voice told her to begin walking upstairs slowly, praising God on every step. Still lifting her left leg with difficulty, at each step she would murmur fervently, 'Thank You, Jesus.'

Following that came the insistent instruction to undertake a few household chores. So she would sit in a chair and dust a mahogany table top saying, 'Thank You, Jesus. Isn't that wood beautiful! Thank You for giving me the strength to lift my arm.'

Then she tried putting a small amount of water in a pail. Sitting in a light chair, she would mop the floor in the area immediately around her, then inch the chair along and mop another spot. 'Thank You, Jesus. I praise You for helping me do this. Is this the way we get the roof back on my house?'

Not that all pain or difficulties were over. She was still on heavy narcotics, still experiencing much nausea as the aftermath of the radium.

About this point she commented to me, 'I learned a lot about the difference between self effort which is the result of our human will to live and the self effort that's obedience to what God tells us to do. We have to co-operate with *what we see God doing*, as Jesus put it.'

She was so right. After our relinquishment when the initiative passes to God, we need to follow willingly, obediently, trustingly. There must be no running out ahead of Him, but also no lying back limp or passive either. Instead we learn to listen and we follow.

About this time Mrs. Blanford was led to another type of nourishment. The doctor had ordered vitamin therapy and iron sulphate. Iron, she learned, is one of the best oxygen carriers to body tissues. After one of her conversations with Jesus, the insistent direction came: to slough off disease, your body's cells need all the oxygen they can get. He directed how much to increase the dose of iron sulphate.

The next morning as she was preparing breakfast for her husband, she said to him, 'Honey, I've been healed.' He lowered the morning paper and looked at her quizzically as she told him what had happened. His silence told her that he didn't believe her; so far as Joe Blanford could see, his wife looked exactly as before — except happier.

Mrs. Blanford knew that she was being ordered to share this faith with others, rather like those lepers whom Jesus had healed being told to go and show themselves to the priests. To obey, she had to relinquish false pride and risk a degree of embarrassment. Though not a churchgoer, Maude Blanford went to a small Baptist church near her home. The minister allowed her to stand in the service and tell her story. 'I have no idea how long I talked,' she reminisced. 'I do remember seeing tears on different faces in the congregation.'

Even so, it took time to rebuild her body-house — nine months for her bad leg to be near normal, three years for evidence of the cancer to leave her. As her body created new cells, the vicious malignant ones were sloughed off as waste. The 'football' in her side disappeared. Vitality returned.

One problem remained, however. She still had so much pain. In April she went to her family doctor. 'Is there anything more you can do for me to kill this pain?'

To her surprise, she saw tears in the doctor's eyes. 'No,' he had answered slowly, 'there's nothing more I can do except give you the drug by hypodermic.'

Suddenly she knew ... After all her other relinquishments, the one she faced now was the toughest of all: could she let go the drug crutch? Did she have the courage to say to God, 'Okay, I'll even take the pain, if that's what You want for me?'

It was going to take a year of struggle to make that decision. On April 27th, 1961, Mrs. Blanford was returning on a long bus trip from a visit to her son in West Virginia. At a five o'clock rest stop, as she popped the pain-killing pill into her mouth, she knew that at last she could say, 'Yes, Lord,' even to this: it would be her last narcotic pill.

So it turned out. Not that all pain left immediately. But what remained was bearable and gradually it faded away.

Two years passed during which Maude Blanford had no contact with any doctor. Then when she called Dr. Hayes again over some small unrelated matter, the surgeon shouted in astonishment, 'Mrs. Blanford! What's happened to you? I thought you were ...'

'You thought I was long since gone,' she laughed.

'Will you get in here to my office and let me examine you?'

'Look,' she retorted, 'why should I spend a lot of money for a complete examination when I'm a perfectly well woman?'

But Dr. Hayes insisted. 'Mrs. Blanford, I promise you that if you will make an appointment and let me examine you, this one will be on me.'

What the doctor found can best be stated in his own words:

I had lost contact with Mrs. Blanford and had assumed that this patient had expired. In May of 1962 she appeared in my office. That was 2½ years following her operation and her last X-ray had been in July 1960. She had had approximately one-half of the X-ray treatment usually given, which certainly was well below what would be required for any effect.

The swelling of her leg was gone. She had full use of her leg; she had no symptoms whatsoever ... Her examination was completely negative and no evidence of cancerous disease could be found ...

She had been seen periodically since that time for routine examinations ... She is absolutely asymptomatic ... This case is most unusual in that this woman had a proven, far-advanced, metastic cancer of the cervix (epidermoid carcinoma) and there should have been no hope whatsoever for her survival.

(Signed) O. J. Hayes, M.D.

A follow-up examination nine years later by Dr. Hayes in January, 1972 was followed by the same conclusion ... 'absolutely no evidence of any cancerous tissue.'

Dr. Hayes, Mrs. Blanford, and the Record Librarian of St. Joseph's Hospital in Louisville were kind enough to allow me access to the medical data on her case. We lay people with meagre medical knowledge little realise the extent to which we are shielded from abhorrent details. I've no desire to expose them further. It is enough to say that the greater part of this patient's body was in a pre-death, putrescent state, riddled all through with metastic cancer.

When I expressed appreciation to Dr. Hayes, the surgeon reiterated, 'I'm only stating the facts. Truth must be served. Not that I understand it. I've no medical explanation to offer for Mrs. Blanford's return from certain death.'

The puzzle in a case like Maude Blanford's is why relinquishment? Why does God insist on our laying down our wills even when what we are clamouring for also happens to be His will for us?

I believe that the answer lies in this direction ... God is interested in more than our recovery from a specific illness; He is intent on our learning how to obey Him in the totality of life. Back in 1943–44 my personal desire for health was the focal point of reality for me. Perhaps so much of me had been packed into that eager longing that there was no room for God to enter and do anything at all so long as my myopic thinking was equating 'life' with the health I wanted.

Everything turns here on what constitutes life. In the end God's answer was infinitely more inclusive and richer than mine. So long as I was assuming that fullness of life corresponded to what I was striving for, I was actually defying my own goal. And 'Thou shalt have no other gods before Me' had to apply to my personal desire-world. There was nothing for it but to 'put away' that most beloved of all idols inscribed 'What I want.' And the scrapping of a treasure is always painful.

Our struggle with giving up self-will goes right back to the beginning of man's history on earth. It is significant that the fruit of the tree that Adam and Eve insisted on eating at all costs was the Tree of the *Knowledge* of Good and Evil.

The temptation to hang on to self-will is tagged 'man's autonomy' and the bait is our covetousness for understanding. It is a temptation to which I, for one, have succumbed as often as most people by always wanting to know 'Why?' I've even handed myself accolades for that. Doesn't that show that I'm a seeker, even a spiritual researcher? Didn't even Solomon ask for the gift of wisdom?

No, it doesn't prove much of anything except that I'm like my Mother Eve. She could have offered up the same rationalisations ... 'And when the woman saw that it was a tree to be desired to make one *wise* ... she ... did eat.'

Wisdom ... understanding — all tempting bait. Except for the thoughts God chooses to share with us, it's still forbidden fruit. So long as we wear the garment of flesh, we can never understand the mind of our Creator.

At the time of the Protestant Reformation, men like Luther, Zwingli, Calvin, Farrel and others kept insisting that the Biblical view of Man's Fall was that every part of Man fell, including his mind. Indeed, once we admit the Fall at all, what other view makes any sense?

Yet the western world's humanism rests upon the opposite view. Our virtual deification of human intellect goes straight back to Thomas Aquinas (1226–74), the intellectual and spiritual father of the western nations who taught that while man's will fell from grace, his intellect did not. This is the same teaching that reached its height in the eighteenth-century Age of Reason.

When we realise that it was the eighteenth century which gave America her legal and constitutional documents, we can see why the Aquinas views are so deeply imbedded in our thought. His dogma was even accepted almost completely by the Church. Along with the United States, Britain and other western nations have inherited from Aquinas a mind set driven to such depth that we are all but unaware of it.

Whenever anyone sets up his reasoning against God's, he is going the Aquinas way of humanistic autonomy ... even though he may piously call it faith. The only true wisdom is facing up to what we actually are — creatures — and then yielding ourselves to the love and wisdom of our Creator. This yielding is relinquishment. And as we relinquish our own defective, incomplete human judgment, it feels like death because it *is* death — the beginning of the end of the old Adam in us.

The psychologist Fritz Kunkel has called this 'The Crisis' — the major crisis of egocentricity. For many years prior to the crisis the basis of life has been — openly or secretly,

'My will be done.' The result has been increasing rigidity, an inability to change ideas or life-patterns, and a decreasing ability to handle life's burdens. The ego becomes a hard shell around the person, layer by layer, deed by deed. Now there remains but one way to crack the shell — exterior circumstances. To the person hiding within, these appear to be tragic: surely the end of everything.

A marriage is in difficulty. Health or financial resources are lost. There are misunderstandings between friends. Somone is taken by death. Then

> he comes to realise the deeper meaning of the great paradox, 'He that would save his life must lose it' ... It seems to him to be a real death ... for the Self, the only form of life that he knows, must disappear, and therefore, he believes its collapse is death. Thus he believes he faces the end of his life ... It is true, indeed, that one must lose that which *seems* to be one's life — the system of mistaken ideas and values which are embodied in one's Ego — in order really to live, to release into life the creative, enriching, productive powers of the true Self ...[9]

Yet ... doesn't this complete laying down of one's life seem to be a denial of the need for faith? After my book *Beyond Our Selves* was published, I began receiving letters like this:

> ... you mentioned in your book that we must give in to God's will. I am confused ... Does relinquishment mean that we can never be sure about praying for any definite thing? If so — how can that be faith ...?

Indeed, many stories of healing in the Bible seem to indicate that just the opposite of relinquishment — an insistence on life — was the key to Christ being able to heal. In the cases of the woman with an issue of blood[10] and the palsied man carried by four friends and let down through the roof,[11] healing apparently had nothing to do with relinquishment; rather there was an intensity of desire in both cases.

Though the importunate widow in Jesus' parable on prayer[12] was not seeking healing, she was trying to make contact with the Source of help. Clearly, Jesus was here praising the strength of the widow's determination.

And in the instance of Marie Ferrand on the train to Lourdes? The girl was too ill to be struggling with relinquishment or anything else except her next breath.

These people were not 'relinquishing' in the usual sense. They were instead, going to incredible lengths to insist on healing, letting nothing discourage them.

It was the extraordinary experience of our friend Virginia Lively that shed great light on this seeming contradiction.

I've know Virginia for nine years. She's a housewife (now a widow) in Belle Glade, Florida who does her own cooking and cleaning, saves grocery stamps, and has to watch her weight. She and I have had dozens of meals together, visited back and forth, gone on retreats and prayed together often. Virginia has a homespun quality including a sense of humour that bubbles up in an infectious laugh. She is about the last person I would expect to have any far-out spiritual experience.

It happened in 1950 after her father Roy Wolff had been in the Tampa Tuberculosis Sanatorium for seven months. The sixty-three-year old man's illness had been discovered almost by accident. A casual visit to the T.B. truck going the rounds had revealed three cavities about the size of silver dollars in the top of his left lung.

That was bad enough. But Mr. Wolff's condition did not respond to treatment and he was losing ground. The crisis came in October. Mr. Wolff's latest X-rays gave a grim prognosis. INH (Isoniazid), almost a miracle drug for many tuberculosis patients, had effected no change in the patient's diseased left lung. The three cavities had enlarged into what looked like a figure eight. The physicians at the sanatorium dared give the drug for only six more weeks. The patient was too old to undergo surgery; they could hold out little hope.

Virginia and her mother and sister were together when they got the news. At that time not a one of them knew how to pray. Roy himself had little use for religion. He had not attended a church service all his married life because as a boy he had been 'churched to death'.

True, Virginia and her husband were church members, active at fund raising, church committees and bazaars. Civic-minded church activists, neither husband nor wife had ever taken subjects like prayer or healing into serious consideration. It would never have occurred to Virginia or her mother or her sister Doris to ask God to step into Roy's case and change medical facts.

One night soon after this discouraging hospital visit, Virginia was driving home from a P.T.A. meeting when suddenly, she began to cry. She realised that she was under pressure as head of the Hallowe'en Carnival that year, but it wasn't really the Carnival. She knew that. A deep intuition told her that the tears were for something much deeper.

Tears, more tears, floods of tears started over again that night and then the next morning. The crying lasted for four days and three nights. Virginia was convinced it was the start of a nervous breakdown.

But on the morning of the fourth day, after her husband Ed had left for the bank and the two children for school, all at once she felt power in the air around her. The atmosphere in the quiet living-room seemed to hum and crackle as though she was standing in the centre of an electric storm.

As she sat in a high-backed chair, through the window she saw a ball of light on the eastern horizon. The light was moving, travelling towards her with incredible speed. It appeared white, yet from it poured all the colours Virginia had ever seen.

Then it was beside her. Although it seemed impossible that anything with such energy could hold still, it took a position at her right shoulder and stayed there. As she stared, she started to smile. She smiled because He was smiling at her. For she now saw that it was not light, but a face.

Even now Virginia finds it hard to put into words a description of that beautiful countenance. His forehead was high. His eyes exceptionally large. But she could never fix the colour of His eyes any more than she could have the colour of the sea.

More than individual features was the overwhelming impression of life — unhampered life, life so brimming over with power and freedom that all living things she had seen seemed lumps of clay by comparison.

Not for a moment did Virginia hesitate to call this Life at her side Jesus. And two things about Him struck her most. The first was His humour. She was astonished to see Him often break into outright laughter. And the second was His utter lack of condemnation. That He knew her down to her very marrow — knew all the stupid, cruel, silly things she had ever done. But she saw that none of these things, or anything she would ever do, could alter the absolute caring, the unconditional love that she saw in those eyes.

It was too immense a fact to grasp. Virginia felt that if she gazed at Him for a thousand years, she could not realise it all.

She did not have a thousand years. She had three months. For as long as that, the face of Jesus stayed before her, never fading, never withdrawing.

For the first two weeks of this great experience, Virginia had given little thought to her father. She felt so joyous and free that there was no way she could have recaptured the previous mood of fretful grief.

Just after lunch one day she was lying on her bed reading the

Bible. Growing drowsy, Virginia turned on her side, intending to take a nap. She was looking at a patch of sunlight on the wall thinking of Him, of how wonderful He is. That crackling vitality! 'When He'd said that He was Life,' she smiled to herself, thinking, 'Is that ever the understatement of the ages!'

Suddenly her train of thought was interrupted as an X-ray picture of lungs three times larger than life appeared in the middle of the sunlight. Unmistakably, her father's X-ray; she would have recognised it anywhere. There was the unusual figure-eight cavity and the single dollar-sized one at the top of the left lung. There were the same shadows and areas of scar tissue she had seen so often on the hospital X-rays.

Could this be an odd quirk of tree or cloud shadows? Virginia turned to look out of the window. No, nothing.

As she turned back to puzzle over the picture on the wall, a white line about three-inches wide moved slowly up the wall. As the white line passed the lower lobes of the lungs, it left behind healthy lungs with the scar tissue gone. As it travelled upward over the diseased portion, it left behind healthy tissue — no cavities.

Virginia stared incredulously. What was going on anyway? She hadn't even been thinking about her father, much less praying for him. As if in answer to her perplexity, the entire episode began again. A second time there was the enlarged picture of Roy Wolff's X-ray on the wall, all the familiar distinctive markings. Once more the same white line appeared at the bottom and travelled slowly up, leaving behind it the shadow print of two perfect lungs.

'Then Dad's well!' Virginia whispered.

In the Face at her side she was suddenly aware of a new dimension of joy. He threw back His head and laughed and the laughter filled the room.

Virginia found herself crying again, only this time it was for gratitude. She wanted to fling herself on her knees to thank

Him. For some reason it was in the kitchen where she knelt as the torrent of praise poured from her.

She never knew how long she spent there, the linoleum cold against her bare knees, but she does remember that as she got up, she looked at the kitchen clock. Twenty minutes after two.

From the wall-phone in the kitchen she spoke to her mother. 'Mother, this is Virginia. Daddy's *well*!'

'Yes, honey, his spirit's been wonderful.'

'Mother, not like *that*. Really well. Daddy's healed.'

'Yes, dear.' Her mother's voice sounded flat and tired. 'We mustn't let ourselves be discouraged.'

Virginia stifled her exasperation. 'Mother, when are the next X-rays?'

'Next Wednesday.'

'Then I'll call you Wednesday evening,' she said. 'But remember I told you, Daddy's *well*.' And she hung up.

The minute Virginia heard her mother's voice on Wednesday night, she knew that the truth had begun to surface. 'Virginia, the most annoying thing. They got the plates mixed up! Poor Dad's got to go back for more X-rays tomorrow. Why, they sent down pictures of someone who never even had T.B. . . .'

Virginia almost laughed. 'Mother, Dad's O.K. No matter how many X-rays they take, they're not going to find anything wrong.'

And of course the next set of X-rays showed no sign of disease either. The sputum tests were negative; the culture test was negative.

By then the doctors were puzzled. Perhaps they had X-rayed from the wrong angle. More chest studies were made, this time from every conceivable angle. No sign of disease in the lungs.

A week or so later Virginia and her sister Doris stood beside a doctor at the sanatorium looking at the latest set of X-rays. 'Where are the cavities?' Doris asked in pretended innocence.

A frown creased the doctor's forehead. 'Well, I'll tell you — Hmmm . . . Well, there aren't any cavities.'

'How do you explain that?'

'I haven't any explanation,' the physician admitted. 'There are times — Well, what can I say?'

The sisters left the doctor's office for a long visit with their father, who was still being kept in bed because the hospital couldn't quite credit their own tests. That day the sisters heard the patient's side of the story . . . 'It happened one day at my nap time . . .'

Virginia remembered the kitchen clock. 'Excuse me, Dad. When do you take your nap?'

'About two — few minutes before, few minutes after . . .'

Then that was about the same time I was lying in bed, Virginia's thoughts went. *Because twenty minutes later I was in the kitchen . . .*

'Well,' her father continued, 'I was just lying here when all at once there was the strangest feeling — like something draining from my body out of my feet. As first it frightened me.

'But there wasn't much time to be scared because the draining sensation was followed by a swoosh of well-being that filled up my whole body. I felt warm and cared-for. Loved — that's it. Loved. Never felt so well in my life. No reason to be here now. I'm going home.'

It was soon apparent that Roy Wolff's healing was not just physical. His attitude about Christianity was totally changed. For the rest of his life he was a happy man in love with His Lord. Almost every time the church doors were open, he would be there. He started a Sunday School class to share his growing faith with other men. He was always seeking people out to talk about Jesus. Moreover, many chores he had always before disliked — like mowing the lawn or gardening — were now a delight to the new creature Roy was.

The tuberculosis never returned, and Roy lived out his life in thanksgiving to God.

After that Virginia has gone on to a remarkable healing ministry. It is quiet but well-grounded. The healing always includes any sickness of the spirit and the deep mind along with the body. Virginia is given such amazing insights into the depths of human personality that recently professional men — doctors and psychiatrists — have been consulting with her about specific patients.

'And every time,' Virginia told me, 'I learned the same thing I'd learned with my father — that when healing comes, it's because our eyes have been on Jesus one hundred per cent. We can get our attention so firmly fixed on the problem or even on the general topic of healing that we get our eyes off the Healer.'

This was where Virginia's story showed me that what I had thought was a contradiction between relinquishment and faith was no contradiction at all. In each of the cases mentioned earlier the sufferer was rushing to Jesus as the Source of help. Each one had faith in *Him*. It was His robe they wanted to touch.

Yet Virginia, like the rest of us, is still groping her way with many questions about healing unresolved. If in our early Christian search, we pour forth glib and ready answers, in later years we dare not do so. With the earthly loss of two grandchildren still vivid to me, I know there are no easy, simple answers as to why some are healed in this life and some are not.

But we have learned that God's objective is whole men, wholly dependent on Him. So His Spirit will counteract each time we try to tag, categorise, and pigeonhole Him — for instance, in the direction of rules for healing. Obviously, we are to worship Him rather than a set of spiritual laws.

We resist that because laws are pat and predictable whereas people are not. Since this is true with human persons, then how much more so with God!

Even as Jesus advised us to begin by taking the lowest seat at banquets, so with healing we are well advised to begin with the lowest place . . . 'Lord, what would You like to tell me about this situation? How do You want me to pray? What do You want me to do?'

Relinquishment and such a seeking prayer will always bring His response. Often it is a surprising response that we could not possibly have anticipated.

The twenty-three-year-old daughter of a close friend of mine had been treated for years for attacks which the doctor tentatively diagnosed as myoclonic seizures (often linked to petit mal, a form of epilepsy). The girl's mother was told by the Spirit, 'Ask the doctor for a blood sugar test.' It turned out that extremely low blood sugar (hypoglycaemia) had been responsible for the trouble.

In another less serious case, a woman's leg and back pains were submitted to Jesus. 'Your white sandals, look at them,' she was told. The left sandal had a strap across the instep so tight that it was interfering with circulation. 'Throw the sandals away,' came the simple, practical order. She obeyed and the pains were gone by the next day.

Does this seem too simple, too obvious even to mention? Not when we understand that our Lord was a carpenter who wore sandals and who knows all about the mundane details of our lives. Often we miss the wisdom He seeks to give us because we are so intent on the high-flown super-spirituality of our preconceived image of Christ.

Through all of this we need to be careful not to confuse what the old egocentric self wants — to succeed, to get well, to be loved — with that positive, trusting, obedient attitude that wants only God's will for us . . .

Self will turns the eyes on self and what
self strongly wants.

> Faith turns the eyes on Christ to ask Him
>   what He wants.
> Self will worries about the results.
> Faith worries only about obedience, then
>   leaves the result to Jesus.

Until we have heard His directives regarding a given situation, we would do well not to assume healing 'on general principles' and run out ahead of the Lord trying to claim healing anyway. If we do, we'll be guilty of the sin of presumption, and not even Jesus — the Son of God — ever dared presume on the Father.[18]

Then how can we tell the difference between presumption and faith? Presumption assumes something to be true in the absence of God's proof to the contrary. Faith hears and receives God's word first-hand via the Spirit speaking to our spirit, and moves forward only on that word.

Jesus meant it when He said, 'The Son ... does only what He sees the Father doing.'[14] Notice the word 'only' in Jesus' statement. That's altogether different from doing something because God hasn't said not to do it. The latter road is a tangled maze of errors, mapped out by Satan. When we run out ahead of God, an element of daring God and of boldness bordering on impertinence, even unbelief, enters the situation.

But then when we *have* got His directives and obeyed them, we no longer have to carry the responsibility for the results. Jesus is the Healer. The results are His.

There will be times when the results are not what we yearn for: not all for whom we pray are restored to health. Honesty and honest sharing is necessary here. The sceptic has a point when he accuses some Christians of sweeping negative experiences under the rug. True, but I have never known a hospital to shut down because it lost some patients. Despite disappointments, the Christian is obligated to pray for the sick because we are bidden to do so[15] and because the crumb of our caring is but a morsel broken from the whole loaf of the Father's infinite and tender love.

With our eyes fixed on Jesus we go forward, knowing that the time will come when the whole person — body and spirit and mind — will be presented unto Him faultless, without spot or blemish.

CHAPTER ELEVEN

THE KING'S TREASURY

Some years ago a physician's wife took issue with something I had written about daring to trust God for material and physical needs. 'That's being selfish,' she remonstrated, 'and self-centred prayers just aren't answered. I don't think we have any right to pray about anything but *spiritual* things. Besides, the Bible says that God knows what we need before we ask Him, so why should we ask?'

The God I know does not want us to divide life up into compartments — 'This part is spiritual, so this is God's province, but that part over there is physical, so I'll have to handle that myself.' If we are to believe Jesus, His Father and our Father is the God of all life and His caring and provision include a sheep herder's lost lamb, a falling sparrow, a sick child, the hunger pangs of a crowd of four thousand, the need for wine at a wedding feast, and the plight of professional fishermen who toiled all night and caught nothing. These vignettes, scattered through the Gospels like little patches of gold dust, say to us, 'No creaturely need is outside the scope or range of prayer.'

The experience of Edith and Francis Schaeffer beautifully illustrates how material, physical, and spiritual needs are all part of a whole. I first became aware of this couple through reading Francis Schaeffer's *The God Who Is There* in 1971, followed by Edith Schaeffer's *L'Abri*.

In 1945 Dr. Schaeffer, theologian and philosopher, was a pastor in Grove City, Pennsylvania when he was asked to go to

Europe to make a study of the condition of Protestant Christianity. He visited thirteen countries in thirteen weeks, encountering such need as he had never seen and finding this a searing spiritual and emotional experience. Dr. Schaeffer was more deeply stirred by Europe's post-war spiritual devastation than by the shell-holes and bombed-out buildings.

Then in August 1953, he became convinced that God was calling him and his family to a higher level of giving, working and sacrifice; to give up the security of a fixed income for an uncertain non-structured work in Europe, possibly with a Swiss base.

After reading Edith Schaeffer's account of all this and pondering it, what interested me was that as the Schaeffers moved on to that higher level of obedience and commitment, God's supply started to work in their lives in a different way, what I choose to call supernaturally. I wondered if I wasn't glimpsing an important principle here.

With a wife and four children to provide for, Dr. Schaeffer knew that this had to be a family decision and a family commitment. As the spiritual head of his home, Francis Schaeffer laid out before his wife Edith and their children all the alternatives. The decision was unanimous — they would say 'Yes' to God's call and depend on Him to supply the $1,800 the six of them needed for the boat fare to Europe. However, circumstances had created a deadline; if the Schaeffers were to go, they would have to have all the $1,800 in just three weeks, by September 9th when the boat sailed.

Their daughter Priscilla painted a big thermometer on a poster. Within a few days the poster was beginning to show a red line depicting the money received. Opening the mail became the most exciting event of each day. Cheques began arriving from the most unexpected sources, most of them for small amounts. The red line on Priscilla's thermometer kept rising. God was giving the Schaeffers a foretaste of what was to become a way of life for this family — trusting the 'God who is there' to supply whatever they needed.

Years afterwards, Edith Schaeffer would explain this more fully: 'What happens when you pray? God is all-powerful in every realm . . . One way in which He works is to "move" in the realm of men's minds . . . God can cause someone to feel a strong "urge" or "conviction" to do something. So when we pray for a certain amount of money, God can cause one person to reach for a cheque-book and send that amount, or He can cause a dozen people to send odd fractions of that amount, causing the total to be exact . . . When that kind of thing happens, you know that you have contacted a *Person* who has replied.'[1]

In those days of late August and early September, 1953 God the Person replied. During the three weeks, all of the $1,800 arrived. It was the opening door to the work that became L'Abri (meaning 'shelter'), a Christian evangelical community in the tiny village of Huémoz high in the Swiss Alps.

In reading *The God Who Is There*[2] I had been intrigued by two strong features of Dr. Schaeffer's approach not usually found in the same person: he is a conservative committed evangelical who stands upon all the major tenets of the Christian faith, yet his appeal is to the intellect rather than to the emotions.

The notion that we must throw away human reason for leaps of faith in the dark is anathema to Francis Schaeffer. Did not the God who is there create man's intellectual equipment — the ability to think, to reason, to plan, to will? If this seems a flouting of the danger of going the Thomas Aquinas route of deifying reason, Dr. Schaeffer's answer is that when Christ redeems us, He redeems the mind along with the rest of us. We have exchanged our fallen intellect for that mind 'which was also in Christ Jesus'.[3] After that, we are not to belittle or throw away the intellect but keep it subject to Christ who nourishes and upbuilds it through His Spirit and the truth revealed in Scripture.

Extremely knowledgeable about the world's major figures who have moulded philosophic thought-forms — such as Aquinas, Calvin, Kant, Rousseau, Hegel, Kierkegaard, Barth, Jaspers, Sartre, Heidegger — Doctor Schaeffer speaks especially to the young who so often these days are not aware that any intelligent educated person can believe the Bible to be true. Emphasising 'content' (one of his favourite words) he is fond of saying that 'honest questions deserve honest answers' rather than the usual dodge, 'Don't question, just believe.'

I kept hearing that the L'Abri community had become one of the favourite haunts for agnostics, atheists, scientists and intellectuals, seekers of all nationalities and types — especially the young. But in just fifteen years how had it grown from this one family with no material resources into such a world-renowned community? In the summer of 1972 my husband Len and I decided to find out for ourselves.

That August we flew from New York to Geneva, planning to go on to see the Schaeffers the next day. But even before we got to L'Abri, we had a foolish little experience that pointed up in a ludicrous way a larger truth we would learn later on.

We started out from Geneva for L'Abri in a rented Fiat on a very warm afternoon. All along the road we passed bicyclists and back-packers. I wondered how many of them were also going to L'Abri? If so, how had the Schaeffers handled and supplied so many transients all those years?

With Geneva an hour behind us, Len, quite thirsty, spotted a filling station with a row of refreshment machines and turned confidently into it.

'Swiss francs?' He held out his hand and I dutifully supplied several coins from the envelope marked 'Switzerland' out of the packets of foreign change we had purchased before leaving New York.

Len put in a coin in the dispenser, then looked puzzled when no drink appeared. He pushed levers, fished around in the coin return, pounded the machine with his fist. Nothing. He shrugged, put in another coin, and tried again. Still nothing. Glowering now at the bright-red machine, he gave up and walked over to seek out the station attendant.

Len said a few words in English, gesturing towards the offending machine. The attendant first shrugged, then scowled and began whipping the air with his hands as words in French poured from him. 'Voilà — mais Monsieur, naturellement cette machine marche . . .'

'Marche? Not on your life! That machine isn't marching. It's not going anywhere or doing anything. It's broken.'

'Brok-en? Ah, non, Monsieur. L'inspecteur l'a vérifié hier. Vous vous êtes trompé.'

'Trompé? That's what I feel like — tromping on it.' Then taking a new grip on his patience, Len said slowly, 'Now look, I put in a franc just like it said.'

'Montrez-moi les francs dans votre main . . .'

Len held out the Swiss coins. The man took one look. 'Mon dieu!' He raised his arms heavenwards. 'Monsieur, c'est la France. Vous — êtes — en *France*.'

'France!' Len looked incredulous. 'I thought this was Switzerland. How can we be in France? We weren't stopped at any border.'

The man merely grinned as he turned the palms of his hands outward. 'Oui, Monsieur, France. La machine ne prend que de francs français.'

Len grinned too — weakly — and we drove off, two thoroughly cowed and still thirsty Americans. Sure enough, there on the map I saw that a corridor of France ran for forty-five miles along the southern shores of Lake Geneva. French officials simply didn't bother to check passports in and out of this small section of their country.

The absurd experience of the Drink Machine that Wouldn't

kept nagging at my mind. Then in simplest terms I saw it: thirsty, we had needed a drink. Not realising what country we were in, we had sought to buy what we needed in the coin of another realm.

Just so, many of us — even Christians — not realising that we are living in the kingdom of God on earth, try to buy the fulfilment of our needs with the coin of another realm — earth's coinage, not God's. It doesn't work, any more than the stubborn red drink machine would work.

The Schaeffers seemed to be living in God's kingdom using the coin of that realm. I was eager to see with my own eyes what the coin was and how it worked.

By the time we reached Ollon, now back in Switzerland, the road had begun to climb. Suddenly we were in the tiny remote village of Huémoz. All around us was sparkling sunshine and brilliant flowers cascading from balconies and windows of Alpine chalets. A sharp turn up a steep driveway and we were at Chalet les Mélèzes.

It was a surprise to see that Dr. Schaeffer, born an American, had become so European in appearance, rather like some philosopher-hermit out of the Middle Ages. Not a tall man, his grey hair was casually cut and he wore a trim grey goatee. Kindly, intelligent brown eyes dominated his face. He was fond of wearing baggy Swiss tweed knickerbockers, long woollen socks, and brogue-type shoes that should by all rights have been ornamented by a silver buckle.

Edith Schaeffer was a more vivacious, gregarious version of her philosopher-husband. Her mind, her speech and her body seemed ceaselessly active. As individualistic as her husband, she wore her long dark hair combed straight back, loosely twisted into a chignon. More often than not she was a study in browns — her deep brown eyes set off by one of the brown dresses she was fond of wearing.

Their community consisted of one small church and a series

of chalets scattered throughout the village. When Len and I attended the Sunday morning service we saw first-hand what a world crossroads L'Abri really is.

To the pealing of myriad church bells across the valley, we arrived at the church thirty-five minutes early. Even so, we were fortunate to get a seat. The interior was panelled with honey-coloured wood; there was a large stone fireplace and a Flentrop organ. Wide windows opened inward to reveal a panoramic view of the Rhône Valley with the peaks of the Dents du Midi in the distance.

When all seats were taken, worshippers sat on the floor before the platform. There were boys and girls in dungarees with knapsacks beside them, together with little girls in fluffy white dresses. A man from India cast off his sandals before he sat on the floor cross-legged alongside a woman garbed in an expensive green trouser suit.

With seemingly every inch of the floor covered with bodies, I sat there wondering how the preacher would ever make it to his pulpit. By then the balcony was filled with those who would listen through the open windows. People were even sitting on the platform floor.

Dr. Schaeffer entered and began carefully threading his way between the people, pausing to pat the heads of children, beaming on the hippies and jet-set types, obviously delighted with what he saw. The service was simple, joyful; the message, a penetrating look at Christian commitment.

Our first few hours at L'Abri provided the initial clue as to how God provides material resources for those living in His kingdom on earth: the Schaeffers' part was a total self-giving with every inch of space, every scrap of food, every last franc, every quarter-hour and vestige of strength. Dr. Schaeffer still had no office, nowhere to work privately except the bedroom.[4] It is a rare night one finds no youngsters sleeping on Mrs. Schaeffer's kitchen floor.

That Sunday, as usual, Edith Schaeffer herself cooked a three-course meal for forty-five people. We were seated at tables so crowded that the plates of food had to be passed overhead, then from hand to hand.

During that Sunday meal we heard incredible human interest stories of how so many different individuals had got to L'Abri. This is a working-out of the second of four prayer principles on which L'Abri is grounded: that God will bring the people of His choice to the community. This too depends on prayer alone; L'Abri has never put out any advertising leaflets.

The four principles are:

(1) Financial and material needs will be made known to God alone, in prayer, in lieu of sending out any pleas for money.

(2) That God will send the people of His choice to L'Abri for work and study.

(3) That God will plan the work and unfold His plan day by day. (This is in place of planning for the future in the usual 'efficient way', such as committee meetings.)

(4) That God will send the staff and workers of His choice for the community rather than L'Abri seeking them through the usual channels of solicitation or pleading.

Here then, was a most important coin of the kingdom — giving God and His ongoing work priority in one's life. Jesus stated it like this, giving us a command followed by a promise:

Seek ye first the kingdom of God and his righteousness; and all these *things* shall be added unto you.[5]

An example of how magnificently God fulfilled His promise by handling the Schaeffer family's needs is the story of their acquiring the Chalet les Mélèzes. In 1955 they needed $7,366 by May 30th for the final payment on the chalet. Eight days before the deadline they had exactly $4,915.69. Once again Priscilla had made one of her thermometers. The family felt that God had led them to this particular chalet, though speaking humanly (in dollars and cents) purchasing it seemed impossible. Yet each mail brought them unsolicited cheques so that the red line on the thermometer kept rising.

There were times when it seemed that the suspense would be more than they could bear. Many a man who has lived by faith has testified that though God moves slowly, He never moves too late. Nevertheless, by breakfast on May 30th, the day the payment was due, the family still lacked over 800 Swiss francs. The last mail was due at eleven o'clock in the morning. Dr. Schaeffer would need to take the two o'clock bus in order to make the required payment. In that last mail there arrived fifteen gifts. When the letters were opened, the total filled in the gap on Priscilla's thermometer — exactly $7,366. God had done it again! Jubilantly, the family went to their makeshift living-room to pray their thanksgiving.

When Dr. Schaeffer caught the yellow bus for Aigle that afternoon, he was lacking only the notary's fee, and he did not know how much that would be. As he arrived at the Notary's office, he found a special delivery letter awaiting him. Thinking how extraordinary it was for a letter to be sent there, he tore it open to find a letter of encouragement from Mr. X — along with the last cheque: 'Enclosed is something that will give me a small share in the purchase of the house today.' That gift was the precise amount of the notary's fee — 300 Swiss francs.

In Edith Schaeffer's own words to me, 'The miracle was the exactness and the timing and God's arithmetic.'

After the family was settled in the Chalet les Mélèzes and had time to appraise what had happened, the totality of it seemed even more remarkable. Over a two-month period, 157 gifts had been sent from all over the world. No giver had any way of knowing how the amount of his gift would fit into the total needed. The smallest gift had been one dollar; the largest, $225, with the exception of a single cheque for $1,000. Yet the total was so exact and the timing so perfect even though many of the gifts had come from far-flung places. Not only that, but after May 30th the gifts stopped as miraculously as they had started. Not another gift came for the house.

Francis Schaeffer would be the last one to say that he and his family are living by faith in order to prove something to the world about God. The God who is there has no need of vindication by His creatures. Rather, for the Schaeffers it has been a matter of obedience: this the way God has called them to live.

Why had God chosen to ask this of the Schaeffers — and then proceeded to supply their every need? Here is the heart of their prayer-miracle of supply: they could ask and confidently expect *because they had given everything in advance.* After a few hours at L'Abri, one realises that Edith and Francis Schaeffer have long since laid everything on the altar, even their privacy.

Why? In Dr. Schaeffer's words, 'What we seek supremely here in the L'Abri community is to exhibit in some poor fashion the love of God and the holiness of God simultaneously in the whole spectrum of life.'

Even in our short visit Len and I felt God's love as all feel it at L'Abri. We sensed Edith and Francis Schaeffer's deep concern and interest in the young people, especially the hippies and the floaters. They care passionately, totally, with utter self-giving about those who don't know what to believe, who have lost their way in life. That there is truth to be found in the Scripture, that God will see to it that we have that truth — that is the fire in their souls, the light in their eyes, the ring in their voices.

As Len and I were leaving, we witnessed a little scene that

remains in my memory as a miniature parable of L'Abri. Walking along with Dr. Schaeffer as he waxed eloquent on some point of homilectics, we were stopped by a little boy outside one of the chalets. He was crying over his tricycle; a wheel had come off. Instantly, the child had Francis Schaeffer's full attention.

First, some comfort tendered by one obviously on the child's wave-length. Then a careful examination of the wheel. 'Matthew, come here and let's talk about it,' Dr. Schaeffer said, drawing the boy into his arms. 'Now, I want to show you. I've put the wheel back on, but see this end here? — It's not going to stay on. See, you've lost a part — right here. Understand that?'

The child nodded gravely.

'Now, Matthew, the minute your father comes home this afternoon, you show him what you and I did and ask him please, to fix the wheel so it will stay. Will you do that?'

'Oh *yes*!'

'So, Matthew, ride very carefully now.'

Exhibiting the love of God in the whole spectrum of life.

As we take our first timid steps in God's kingdom, we will begin to find the principle of God's supply working for us too.

'But,' most of us think, 'I'm not as committed as the Schaeffers.' True, but we have to begin where we are.

As long as we have a low threshold of expectation limited to our needs and those of our immediate family, we probably won't turn to God for help in this area; our own efforts will handle it. But when we, in obedience to God, decide to be totally His person at His disposal and take on some enormous task He requires of us, then we are going to find ourselves thrown upon His unlimited supply.

Negative situations throw us upon God's supply when we have made a mess of our emotional or financial or material situations. Perhaps we have abused our body or our relationships; perhaps we have family problems, are in debt or some other sorry predicament. In this plight we long to know how God's unlimited supply can start flowing in our direction.

How God supplies is spelled out for us in Scripture. Beyond that, we have the accumulated wisdom of men and women who have tested out those Scriptural principles and promises over the centuries and can provide us with so many illustrations of how faithful God is.

The first step is to get our eyes off our own need, to look instead at God's unlimited supply. One of Christ's fundamental premises was that God the Father controls all of earth's material resources. Simple words, but what a tremendous assertion! Most of us do not really believe this at all. Yet the Bible emphatically declares it:

> The earth is the Lord's and the fullness thereof . . .[6]

Secondly, we are assured that we are beloved children of this King:

> Behold, what manner of love the Father hath bestowed upon us, that we should be called the sons of God . . .[7]

Then since we are His children and all the world's riches belong to the King, it follows that He can and will take care of our physical needs:

> But by God shall supply all your needs according to His riches.[8]

So if we really believe that we are children of the King and that we can trust Him to supply all our needs out of His unlimited supply, there would be no reason for a greedy storing up of things. There would be no fear about inflation or money shortages, for fearing would be a sure sign that we do not believe God's ownership of earth's resources. It would be wrong to have a 'poverty complex' because to think ourselves paupers is to deny either the King's riches or to impugn our being a child of that King.

To call our Father in heaven a King, in my opinion, is to understate the truth. Consider the prodigality of the Father's world. He did not create a single kind of fern, but some 10,000 kinds; not one type of palm tree, but 1,500 different palms. Not one insect, but 625,000 and more that scientists have not yet named. Thus far astronomers have been able to photograph thirty billion stars; we have no idea how many there actually are. No poverty complex in this Creator!

The magnificence of His handiwork is seen in the tumbling seas, in a sunset slashing the Grand Canyon of the Colorado. Ride to the top of the mountain at St. Moritz, gasp with awe at the snow-covered panorama of rugged peaks spread out at one's feet. Or see the turquoises and blues in the waters around Moorea and Bora-Bora in the South Seas, colours so intense that no painter could capture them on canvas.

How much of this beauty we bring into our homes and our lives is limited only by our appreciation and desire for it and our faith in the King's ability to supply us. Yet always, this must be a personal discovery. The second step in discovering how to become a good receiver of the King's bounty is to invite Jesus into our need. As we see our situation through His eyes we begin to understand how intensely practical God is in dealing with us, His carnate creatures.

Reflecting that practicality, Jesus' directives to us are always specific, never vague and generalised. He would not allow those who came running after Him wailing, 'Lord, have mercy,' to stop there; He was for ever forcing them out of this 'general blessing' area by asking questions like 'What do you want Me to do for you?'[9] In other words, 'Use your mind, my son. Make up your heart. God is not the Father of sloppy thinking. Nor is He the Lord of generalising.'

With Jesus' help we can separate our true needs from false ones and be specific and whole-hearted about our deepest desires. Then we are ready to begin using the coin of God's kingdom. He told us what another important coin is: *to receive, one must give, even out of poverty.*

> Give, and it shall be given unto you: good measure, pressed down, and shaken together and running over, shall men give into your bosom. For with the same measure that ye mete withal, it shall be measured to you again.[10]

This is not only a promise, but a fact of the Father's world, part of the rhythm of the universe. In the last century every farmer knew it as he primed the pump by pouring a dipper of water in to start the water flowing. We feel it each time we stand on an ocean beach and feel the tugging rhythm of the tide washing the sand beneath our feet. We experience it when we step out on God's promise and to our astonishment discover that our Father will never allow Himself to be in debt to any child of His.

Here is an exciting principle for all those in life's holes. Of what do we have a shortage? Money? Household possessions? Ideas? Friends? Love? Prayer-power? Creativity? Strength? Health? Whatever it is, when we, under God's direction, give away out of our shortage, like the tide returning we get back abundance — 'good measure, pressed down, running over'.

There was a time back in 1964 when Ellie Armstrong would have said she had nothing to give — least of all money. With faith and almost no cash, she had attempted to buy a $64,000 motel on U.S. Route 6 in the rolling hills of western Pennsylvania.

Ellie knew the truth, that when we set our eyes on Jesus and in obedience attempt a big task for Him, we can trust Him for supply. It was in that framework that she was praying for this motel.

The dream she was given was a motel where Jesus would be the Host. There weary travellers could find a spiritual oasis in their travels. More importantly, people who might not have heard about Him and would not go near a church could meet Him there.

I have visited the Port Allegheny Motel, read the inspirational literature Ellie puts in the rooms, and heard story after story of travellers helped and healed of problems and hang-ups and physical ailments as incredible dividends to their good night's sleep. Each of the fourteen motel units has been dedicated to God for a specific purpose, such as a room for healing, a special room for honeymooners, one for alcoholics, another for the mending of broken relationships, the happiness room. When each traveller checks in, Ellie asks the Host which room He wants them in, then asks Him to be present in that room to meet the guest at his point of need.

But for Eleanor Armstrong, it took many a time of testing, many a crisis-situation before her dream about the motel could be fulfilled. She had to learn to live in a state of financial dependence as constant as that of the Schaeffers. When Ellie had acquired the motel, one of her prayer-requests had been that she would never fail to meet a mortgage payment on time. One mid-winter a $300 mortgage payment was due in a few days and she had only fifty dollars to her name. To make it worse, this was off-season and for five consecutive nights not a single car had stopped at the motel.

Ellie began to pray. At last an inner voice seemed to tell her: 'Send the fifty dollars to Dave Wilkerson in New York for his work with young drug addicts.' Ellie was as startled as any of us would have been. Surely this was not the time to give away money! But the inner Voice had been very clear. She mailed off the fifty dollars that afternoon to Mr. Wilkerson. That same night nine cars came in, one right after another. As she stood behind the hotel register, she shook her head wonderingly as she remembered Jesus' words, 'Give, and it shall be given unto you.'

The rest of the week the motel was filled to capacity. The mortgage money was paid on time. Ten years of blessings have followed for the Port Motel as a business venture and as a ministry to wayfarers.

Knowing about this second coin of the kingdom, that to receive we must give, helps us to understand the Scriptural admonition to tithe. Tithing was a practice God asked of the Jewish people back in Old Testament times. It means giving to God through giving to others a minimum of one-tenth of one's gross income or harvest or cattle production or whatever. 'Minimum' because even as Christ upholds tithing, He also strengthens it by often asking that we give away more than the base 10 per cent.

In teaching the practice of tithing to the Jews, God was seeing to it that they would have an unending demonstration of how sound the coin of His kingdom is. To buttress this further He gave them — and us — that magnificent promise:

> Bring ye all the tithes into the storehouse, that there may be meat in mine house, and prove me now herewith, saith the Lord of hosts, if I will not open you the windows of heaven, and pour you out a blessing, that there shall not be room enough to receive it.[11]

Notice God's invitation and challenge to each of us to prove Him, to try out tithing. That when we put Him first, we won't have to worry about our supply.

I remember how pointed a challenge this was to me back in

early February, 1949. In those early weeks after Peter Marshall's sudden death on January 25th, I was still groping to find what God intended the new basis of my life to be. There was that crucial evening when three men had come out to the manse to discuss business matters with me.

'I've worked it all out,' the young insurance salesman said, showing me impressive-looking graphs. 'From Dr. Marshall's insurance and the Presbyterian Church's pension fund, you'll have a total of $171 a month for the first eight years, then it will drop.'

The men were good friends and were trying to be helpful. Yet all that they said that evening added up to a gloomy prognosis indeed. $171 per month wasn't enough to live on in Washington. I had no specific vocational training and uncertain health. They recommended that I sell our car and the Cape Cod cottage. At the end of the evening the men left troubled because they felt I was not worried enough.

They were right. I had heard their words and seen the neat columns of figures and the graphs. Figures didn't lie. Or did they? Deep, deep inside I felt that these three kind men were reckoning without God.

Looking back, I know it was no spiritual strength or virtue of mine that kept me from accepting gloom and doom and sinking into fear. From a few hours before Peter's homegoing to several weeks afterwards, heaven had opened wide and was carrying me over and above all circumstances. From that brief experience I know what it is like to live in the Kingdom of God on earth: it is glory and joy even in pain, and crystal-clear guidance, and oneness with other people, and a giving and receiving of incredible love.

So my guidance was clear, I was to pick up my pen and edit and write. I was to trust God to provide for me and Peter John so completely that yes, we would tithe even the inadequate $171 a month.

We obeyed, and God provided all right. I did not sell the car or the Cape Cod cottage. Every need was met on time. There were no debts. For Peter John and me it happened precisely as God had promised, the windows of heaven opened and poured out so many blessings that there was scarcely room to receive them.

There is endless fascination in seeing what has happened to individuals who have picked up God's challenge to tithe. A correspondent-friend, Barbara Reynolds, had spent nearly eighteen years in Hiroshima, Japan, as a part of the Quaker World Friendship Centre ministering to atom bomb survivors and crusading for peace. Eventually the Japanese themselves were handling more of the affairs of the Centre. Meanwhile, Mrs. Reynolds had been offered a scholarship to Pendle Hill, the famous study centre near Philadelphia. It seemed right to accept. There was only one difficulty: she did not have money for the trip home.

It was at this point, she wrote me, that I read Peter Marshall's sermon, *Research Unlimited*.[12] I will never forget the challenge that started me on one of the most exciting adventures of my life:

'Suppose, for example that a group of Christians decided to experiment with the Lord's exhortation to tithe for one year. What do you suppose the results would be?'

I had never tithed. Quakers don't even pass the collection plate ... Nevertheless, when I finished reading that particular sermon, I felt moved to try.

I began by adding up all the money I had in the world; a few thousand yen in a Hiroshima Bank, a couple of hundred dollars in the United States, and some small change in my purse. I resolved to set aside a tenth in a special purse and the next day, withdrew enough from my bank account to start my Fund for the Lord. I also began to keep a special record of my experiment.

And would you believe it! On January 26th when I began to tithe, I had less than three hundred dollars. By the time I left Japan two months later (on March 23rd) I was able to turn over, in tithes, more than I had to begin with!

Now, a year later, I can report that the experiment which I began without any particular expectations has developed into a way of life which has opened up amazing and undreamed-of potential. I'm sure you know that I am *not* speaking of tithing as a way to get rich quick! No, the amazing effect of my tithing experiment has been twofold: (1) It has completely freed me of the panic fear that used to grip me about being penniless. Now I *know* that my needs will always be supplied. And (2) it has helped me to know the job of being a channel through which blessings can flow to those around me. The Lord's purse is never empty!

When we give God our unlimited 'Yes,' then we find in our hands yet a third coin of His realm: *each of us has within himself, the clue, the secret, and the potential for everything he will ever need.*

The essence of creativity is to seek His first, making full use of whatever master coin is yours — to give priority to the kingdom of God and His righteousness. Then as we begin living in the kingdom of God on earth, He will show us how to make the best use of our talents. We begin with a seed idea or a seed talent and create something that other people need or enjoy. That plunges us directly into the stream of the Creator's unending creativity and generosity.

This was the truth God was teaching me. When as a widow I was facing what looked like financial extremity, He told me to begin what I had never done before — editing and writing.

The Schaeffers put God's kingdom and His righteousness first by laying lives, time, energy, privacy on the altar to establish L'Abri Community. For over twenty years God has seen to it that all necessary 'things' were added unto them.

Ellie Armstrong was giving God's kingdom and His righteousness priority when by faith, she undertook the motel on Route 6 to minister to wayfarers. For over ten years God has provided the mortgage payments and running expenses and all other 'things'.

When Barbara Reynolds decided to obey God by tithing, she was taking a first big step towards putting God's kingdom and His ways first. And she has been blessed accordingly.

So I would have to say to that physician's wife who so strenuously objected to any prayer for personal or material needs and to all those who are afraid to pray about money and those other 'petty' things — nowhere in Scripture or Christian experience can I find any justification for the idea that prayer should be limited to spiritual needs. So far as I can understand, Jesus taught us quite the opposite.

It is as if God, knowing full well that while we are in these bodies of flesh and blood, we are going to be physical creatures of this earth, earthy, says to us, 'There's only one place and one way you can learn of Me, that's just as you are in your present circumstances. Let's deal with your obvious needs and lacks by looking at your assets — no matter how small. I'll show you step by step how to approach Me, how the coinage of My kingdom is put into circulation, how to hand Me your lack and get back My adequacy. What better demonstration of My reality and My love and caring for you could you have? Come, try it.

'Taste and see that the Lord is good. Prove Me!'

CHAPTER TWELVE

THE DILEMMA OF OUR REBELLION

There they were, six little words, staring up at me from the page of the New Testament: 'So do not criticise at all . . .'[1]

But isn't that a little too easy? my thoughts went. That would knock out all judgments, all sifting, all screening. 'Do not criticise at all . . .'? *I don't get it.*

What I really meant was 'I resist it.' I have always prided myself on my critical ability, enjoying the sizing up and analysing of people and situations. I did it almost in spite of myself, whether I enjoyed it in a particular instance or not. I identified with the eighteen-year-old-girl who recently wrote of her parents and home-life:

> We could be called opinionated. Certainly we are a hyper-critical family — we don't lavish superlatives on things and places and people. I was raised to look closely, not to accept easily . . . I couldn't suspend judgment even when I wanted to: it was if I went through life with X-ray glasses on, seeing through not just the things I wanted to see through but the things I'd just as soon have believed in too. I was old before my time . . .

> The criticism we applied to everything we encountered we applied to ourselves as well. Never 'You are bad', but 'You could do better . . .'

> The critical faculties my parents gave me made me more demanding than I should be, gave me standards that the real, flawed world can't live up to . . .[2]

But isn't it good to be observing and analytical, to discuss how things can be improved? I can speak from experience here because I might almost have been this girl. My home training was surprisingly like hers, and for much of it I am grateful. But I have lived a number of years on the other side of eighteen. From my vantage point, I can see the underside — or backlash — of such sharpened critical awareness.

In every situation, this girl and I have fallen into the habit of seeing what's wrong with it, not what's right with it. The good qualities, those things well done, are passed over quickly — in time, scarcely noticed — in order to get on with the critique. All encounters in life, every personality, every institution and relationship is a mixture of the good and the bad. When we habitually focus on the bad, we are training ourselves in negativism.

We call it by other names. Looking with such analytical eyes must surely be constructive, we tell ourselves, because what we're really asking is, 'How can such-and-such be improved?'

But there is a secret cost in such an outlook to one's spiritual and mental health. In my case, I woke up twenty years into adulthood to find myself deeply schooled in serious negativism. That, in turn, can bathe all of life in emotional gloom. When the habit continues into mid-life or later, the dark glasses of criticalness can lead to long periods of melancholy and even to serious depression.

Exactly this happened to a long-time friend, the author Agnes Sanford. In her case, the depression led to emotional disturbance and thoughts of suicide. In writing of this in her recent autobiography, Mrs. Sanford refers to her escape from this pit of chronic depression as the major healing of her life. But what first caught my attention was her account of how the seeds of the near-disastrous negativism were planted. The setting was Yansheng in Northern China where the young Agnes' parents were Presbyterian missionaries. On any given Sunday, there would be worship at the Union Church . . .

But on the long homeward drag, my heart would sink, for I dreaded the Sunday dinner . . . The grown people's Sunday sport was the tearing apart of the sermon phrase by phrase and argument by argument. Dr. Harry Emerson Fosdick once preached at our church, and fragments of his sermon were scattered over every course . . .

Dr. Fosdick preached in Christian love, but he was not *sound* because he did not mention the Blood of the Lamb in about every third sentence. This went on and on until finally I burst into tears and left the table, to the utter consternation of my parents . . .

What was the trouble? I could not tell them. I did not know. They were good, they were completely Christ-centred . . . but something was wrong.[3]

In Agnes Sanford's words, 'super-criticalness was a breaking of the bonds of love'. By her teen years, she was beginning to experience the consequences:

The deep dissatisfaction with life and with God that had begun in me at age eleven was growing. Something was lacking, not only in life, but in me . . . I remembered the days when I had come home by the high-road, literally dancing, my feet hardly touching the ground for joy. And thought, 'That was the joy of childhood. Grown people never feel like that.' Thank God I was wrong!

Yet it was to be many years before Agnes Sanford would be healed of depression and would finally rediscover joy.

The insistence upon picking apart, upon pronouncing judgment, which Agnes recalls from her childhood, is by no means unusual in missionaries' and ministers' families. We Protestants especially belong to a tradition which imposes on every

Christian not only the right but the duty to judge every word spoken from the pulpit or printed between the pages of a book. Doubtless this has served as a necessary corrective in the long history of the Church. But the effect of this constant vigilance upon individuals — and whole denominations — can also be a deficiency of love and a lack of joy.

And it is not only Christians who almost from the cradle are taught to be criticisers. It is not only the spirit of the Renaissance and the Reformation in our religion, but the spirit of eighteenth-century rationalism in our politics which encourages every American to be judge of the men and events around him. Our national heroes, the founders of our country, were precisely those men who refused to accept unquestioningly the world as they found it.

The two hundred years since then have trained us that an uncritical populace is a populace in peril. As in religion, so in the secular world: 'eternal vigilance' is the price of what we hold dear. From school days on, each citizen must be responsible, must inform himself, must stay on top of issues.

I wonder if we who form judgments of people and issues over our morning coffee realise how unique in the experience of the world is our concept of good citizenship. In most places on the globe even today people are trained in a kind of docile numb acceptance which is the very opposite of the critical spirit.

During a trip to the Middle East, our party of four took a three-and-a-half-hour drive in Jordan, with a guide — clearly an intelligent, well-informed man. In the course of the long trip, we asked him a single political question, something about King Hussein and an important meeting to be held that week.

The guide's face went as blank as though a sponge had gone across it. 'Oh,' he said with finality, 'I don't think about those things.'

He didn't sound like someone who'd been intimidated into silence. His attitude seemed merely to reflect that of the society in which he had grown up. 'These are not my affairs.'

The opposite, democracy's insistence on each citizen's responsibility to be informed and to judge, is accepted throughout Western Europe and North America as a positive thing. Yet judging can also have a negative side. Just as the missionary groups in China (which Agnes Sanford knew so well) regarded themselves as knowledgeable 'sermon tasters' and experts in theology, so most of us consider ourselves expert armchair politicians. The result is that any man in public office gets sniped at continually by the public and the press. All of us can be grateful for a free press made operative by reporters like the two *Washington Post* newsmen who, in the face of incredible pressure to 'let sleeping dogs lie', brought the Watergate offences to the attention of the nation.

And yet I recall during the years I lived in Washington, especially during the McCarthy era, more than one man's career was ruined by innuendo, character assassination, and black-listing. Sometimes the news media seemed to thrive on it — not a needed exposé of wrong-doing, but criticism because criticism is one of our national sports. It can be a dangerous sport.

Critics and protestors insist that dissent is for some good end — 'for the exploited' — 'for peace' — 'for liberalising university rules'. Behind that insistence is the conviction, blown up into a philosophy, that insubordination — mild to violent — is the best technique for reform, a healthy process for necessary change. How often I have felt that way as I have agonised over child labour, the living conditions of migrant workers, our inhuman treatment of the insane, the slum conditions of our inner cities.

Sunday afternoons during college days I used to go with a group who visited in the tenements (since torn down) around the State Capitol building in Atlanta, Georgia. My journal reflects my shock and dismay:

> I had dimly realised that places like that existed, but had never seen any before — squalid, miserable, dirty, ill-ventilated. The broken windowpanes stuffed with paper; the sick child doubled up on the dirty bed; the absurdly young mother wearing red ankle socks of which she was so proud, nursing her baby before us; the drunk woman; the crying children ...

If protest rallies and sit-ins at legislators' offices had been the style among college students then, I would have been part of them.

Years afterwards our family ran head-on into one of those injustices in our society that scream for reform. In 1956 soon after my mother and father retired to Evergreen Farm in Loudoun County, Virginia, Earl Cook, our black tenant-farmer, was caught in a classic loan-shark trap. The manager of the loan company telephoned saying that they would repossess the Cooks' household goods unless their debt was paid up within twenty-four hours.

We managed to postpone the immediate crisis, then dug in to appraise the situation. The original loan taken out two and a half years before, had not been large; incredibly, the loan company claimed Earl now owed twice that much. The apparent interest rate was only $3\frac{1}{2}$ per cent, but a clause hidden in fine print enabled the loan company to calculate the interest charge each month. That made the real annual percentage rate 36 per cent. If Earl defaulted a month's payment, the interest for that month was added to the principal and future interest calculated on the total. He could never get out of debt.

What was wrong with our laws, I raged, that exempted dishonest outfits of this type from the Small Loan Act and the strict supervision of bank inspectors? Regularly I drove past a

cluster of them with flashing neon signs just across the Key
Bridge into Arlington. 'Quick cash' ... 'Get your bills paid.'
The bait dangled hiding the hook.

Earl's plight turned into a family crusade. We made the loan
company a proposition: we would pay the total (then take it
gradually out of Earl's wages) provided that total was reduced
to a fair figure. They refused. We peppered them with letters
and phone calls. One morning I was astonished to hear my
gentle mother scornfully telling the head of the loan company,
'I marvel that you can hold up your head in public, preying on
the poor and those who don't know better. You're no gentleman, you're a — a — ' Here her vocabulary failed. 'Horse-
whipping would be too good for you.'

Finally the man buckled. We paid, demanding a receipt
declaring Earl completely free of debt.

And yet there they were, each time I drove into Washington,
those neon signs challenging me, what are you doing to root out
this evil from your community? One family had slipped
through the net so cunningly laid; how many thousands were
trapped for the duration of their working lives unless people
with typewriters, and education, with acquaintances in the
government — mounted some form of protest? How else, my
conscience asked me?

'So do not criticise at all.' How are we to understand these
words? Criticism, protest, even open rebellion, sometimes seem
the only ways that essential change can come about. What
about the American Revolution — surely there is an example of
great good coming out of revolt?

Or ... is it? I remember my first dispassionate look at this
touchstone of the American experience. It came during college
days when I earned part of my tuition by doing clerical tasks
for Dr. Philip Davidson, head of the History Department as he
prepared his book *Propagandists of the American Revolution.* I
remember my surprise at the irrefutable evidence of the extent

to which propagandists aided by the Liberty Boys deliberately whipped up the inflamed feelings that led to war with England.

No doubt the American colonies should have received more understanding and eventual independence. The question is, were war, revolution, hatred, and bloodshed the best way to achieve needed goals?

Two hundred years later, may we not still be suffering the results in the American temperament? Perhaps the 'good' revolution was not as harmless as we like to think. During the last six years when violent crimes in the United States have increased more than 90 per cent, many sociologists and historians have been telling us that the seeds of that violence may well have been planted during the very founding of our country. The National Commission on the Causes and Prevention of Violence asserted:

> Our nation was conceived and born in violence — in the violence of the sons of liberty and the patriots of the American port cities of the 1760s and 1770s . . .

These analysts then went on to point out what a large part violence played not only in the launching but in the expansion of the young Republic westward, in our violent and dishonest ways of dealing with the Indians, in the vigilante groups of frontier society. They cite evidence that America's long training in insubordination of the heart is resulting today in a schism-ridden, polarised society with cracks and rifts all through.

Whether analysing the steps that lead to the break-up of a marriage, or of the high-school student who joins a violent revolutionary group, or even what caused the American Revolution — the process goes something like this ... Criticalness leads to discontent. Discontent expels appreciation and gratitude. Self-pity moves in and turns the attention inward; surely self deserves something better, we tell ourselves, such as happiness, prosperity, that its ideas and demands be heard and implemented. If what self wants will hurt others — spouse, children, parents, store-proprietors, educational institutions, by-standers — well, they asked for it in one way or another. Anyhow, the end justifies the means.

But if rebellion has such built-in dangers, how can necessary change come about?

It is at this point that we can see a clear parting of the ways between the philosophy of dissent and the wisdom of Jesus of Nazareth. How else could we view statement after statement of Christ's?

'Thou shalt not kill.'[4]

Then said Jesus unto him, 'Put up again thy sword into his place; for all they that take the sword shall perish with the sword.'[5]

'Whosoever is angry with his brother shall be in danger of the judgment ... whosoever shall say, Thou fool, shall be in danger of hell fire.'[6]

'Agree with thine adversary quickly, while thou art in the way with him...'[7]

'If ye forgive not men their trespass, neither will your Father forgive your trespasses.'[8]

'Try to show as much compassion as your Father does. Never criticise or condemn — or it will all come back on you.'[9]

Yet no one accuses Jesus of a Pollyanna attitude towards the evil and injustice of His time. His fury at the perfidious money changers was a form of violent protest, no question about it.

Studying Jesus' response to evil I began to see three guidelines. Firstly, is the question of motivation. We see into the heart of Jesus' motive in one of the most beautiful verses in the New Testament:

Thou (Christ) hast loved righteousness, and hated iniquity: therefore God, even thy God, hath anointed thee with the oil of gladness above thy fellows.[10]

'Loving righteousness', in His case came before 'hating iniquity'. Does it, I wondered, in our crusades and causes? When we go forth to stamp out sin, disease, poverty, oppression — as He did — do we keep uppermost in our minds the heart-stirring vision of the world as God intended it to be? Or does hatred of the enemy we are opposing gradually fill our horizon? —

Then secondly, He gave us the love test:

'Listen all of you. Love your enemies. Do good to those who hate you . . .'[11]

Here Christ was making a clear distinction between the iniquity which He hated and the sinner, who, even though his own will was responsible for his sin, was nevertheless now the victim of it, bound by it. I saw only too clearly why I could never, relying on my own strength, launch a 'just' campaign against the loan shark industry: my reaction to these businessmen falls so far short of love. Indeed, this command to love our enemies is often not possible for us worldlings; it is a miracle God Himself has to work in the human heart.

Therefore, the third guideline follows inevitably. In the end Jesus chose God's way, not man's, to deal with the iniquity He loathed. Judas Iscariot wanted his Master to use the world's technique by rebelling against Rome. Judas, the classic revolutionary, wanted armed political rebellion against the godless forces of Rome. Jesus deliberately refused, thereby telling us for all time, 'No, the end does *not* justify the means.' He chose instead God's way of changing men's hearts and minds and lives via the Cross.

Certainly we cannot 'love righteousness' and 'hate iniquity', then use any of iniquity's techniques. Those who recognise in Jesus of Nazareth the First Rebel, see equally that His weapons were never those of unrighteousness. He will never allow us to do evil with the claim that it's to achieve justice or right.

Part of the problem here may be that we have not understood Jesus' way. When I realised that He was standing against my critical spirit, I felt the need to dig into the Bible to get its teaching as to what's wrong with grumbling and revolt. Right away I found the answer to my questions about that verse which had so startled me, 'Do not criticise at all.' I saw too why God regards even the lowest rung of protest — complaining and grumbling — not as a petty personality flaw or even as an offence against another person, but as serious sin against Him directly. The Apostle Paul wrote stringent words on this . . ;

And don't murmur against God and His dealings with you, as some of them (the Jewish people) did, for that is why God sent His angel to destroy them. All these things happened. . .as object lessons to us — to warn us against doing the same things; they were written down so that we could read about them and learn from them . . .[12]

I found that 'all these things' in this passage referred back to the Books of Exodus and Numbers. We read there how God had tapped the reluctant Moses on the shoulder, directing him to lead the Jewish people out of bondage in Egypt to the Promised Land.

As Moses obeyed, remarkable proof of Jehovah's presence and protection was given to the children of Israel time after time . . . the rolling back of the Red Sea so that they could cross it; a pillar of cloud by day and fire by night to guide them; the provision of food and water in the desert. God made them the solemn pledge that if they would trust Him, He would supply their every need from the smallest to the greatest.

The Israelites had less than two hundred miles between them and their goal. That distance could be covered in weeks. But they did not trust God. From Exodus 14 when they fled slavery in Egypt, to Numbers 14 in the midst of their desert trek, there is the record of a series of 'murmurings' against circumstances, against their leaders Moses and Aaron, against the lack of water, the hardships of the journey, the strength of their enemies. They were dissatisfied with the food God provided and longed for the dainty fare of Egypt. Each time the complaints reached the level of mutiny, Moses would intercede with God on behalf of the people. Each time Jehovah would humour His fussing children and stoop to meet their demands. Miracle followed miracle. But rather than being grateful and praising Jehovah for these mighty acts, the people would soon begin complaining again, offering back to God discontented hearts and yet more grievances.

The murmurings reached a climax as recorded in the fourteenth chapter of Numbers. This time the murmurings went too far. The congregation wallowed in self-pity, lamenting and weeping through the night, 'Would God that we had died in the land of Egypt!'

By then the Israelites had finally traversed the two hundred miles and were virtually on the doorstep of the Promised Land. In fact, it had already been spied out by a group led by Caleb, who had pronounced it a good land ready to be taken with the Lord's help.

Wearily, Moses once again entreated God with long and eloquent pleading. But this time, though God agreed to pardon, a price had to be paid: a generation had lost the Promised Land by making grumbling and rebellion their way of life. In doing so, they had been steadily acting out a spurning of God and of His promise for them. Therefore they were told, 'Tomorrow turn you, and get you into the wilderness by the way of the Red Sea ... All ... from twenty years old and upward, which have murmured against me ... shall fall in this wilderness.'[18]

Thus sadly, on the threshold of achieving their destination, the Israelites were turned back to wander in the desert for forty years. Their children would enter the Promised Land — but not those who had started out in such high hopes, those to whom God's glorious promises had first been made.

By this story, my eyes were opened to several truths. From the time the Chosen People first left Egypt, God had been trying to teach them some facts about Himself: first, He was (and is) a personal God. 'I will walk in and with and among you, and will be your God, and you shall be My people.'[14] Thus as a Father, no detail of His children's lives was beneath His notice — from the dimensions of the wilderness tabernacle or the tassels on the hem of the priests' robes, to the adjudication of the minutest quarrel between neighbours.

It follows that when the Israelites or any of us have really accepted God as our Father in the personal way He means it, then we are going to trust the circumstances He permits us to have. That is why our grumbling about God's provision is at the least attributing more power to circumstances and to evil than to God. And murmuring and rebellion can lose us our personal Promised Land. Our Promised Land means God's will perfectly done in our life and affairs. It means the supplying of every provision — spiritual and physical — for our every need. We can miss all of it through complaining.

On a larger scale the same principle applies to modern nations just as much as to the Israelites. Greed and lack of gratitude stemming from the grumbling spirit, could eventually cost us or any nation the blessings of God.

What the Israelites needed — and what I believe we who build our lives around criticalness need today — is to see that the antidote to negativism is the power of God. It is a transforming power in and over the world He has made. On the reality of that power Scripture never backs down or gives ground. From the time God called Moses to lead His people, through the plagues visited on the Egyptians, through the parting of the Red Sea, through many miracles in the desert, God was saying, 'I do have power. I am the God of the supernatural. You are to trust Me for more than you would expect through "natural" law or "natural" causation.'

Power over what? Precisely those factors about which the Israelites were murmuring — the harsh desert, the difficulties of their trek, physical ailments and illnesses, and the hostility of their enemies. In other words, over the external conditions of life.

Rebellion of a far different sort — against dishonest United States government inspectors — turned into a surprisingly positive experience for two Florida businessmen several years ago. At that time the Meloon family boat business, Correct Craft, Inc., owed $500,000 to 228 creditors and faced financial disaster.[16] The trouble had begun when Walter Meloon and his brother Ralph had been awarded a government contract to build 3,000 assault boats.

Shortly afterwards they were called upon by a member of the three-man team who would inspect the boats. 'Did you know,' the inspector asked Walter, 'that you are one of only two companies in the south-east that does not have someone on their payroll who takes care of their inspectors' expenses?'

Walter shook his head, knowing that the government paid all the inspectors' expenses.

The two brothers talked it over and decided to dismiss the overture as an ill-considered remark rather than as a request.

Soon, they learned differently.

Correct Craft, founded in 1925, had always been proud of producing quality boats. But now, as the sleek 18-foot fibre glass boats began coming down the assembly line, great numbers were being rejected by the government inspectors. Many for tiny flaws allowable under the contract.

One day the brothers quietly took one of the rejects, cleaned off the inspector's chalk marks and sent it back through the line. It was passed.

It was now clear what they faced. In desperation they went to the inspectors' superiors, but to no avail. As the silent war continued, they foresaw financial disaster for Correct Craft and for over 100 employees and their families.

Temptation whispered to Walter one night, 'Why not pay those men off? It really isn't much compared to what the company stands to lose.'

No, it wasn't the money, Ralph knew. Something far deeper. At night he would wrestle with the problem. Trying not to disturb his wife Anne, he would slip out of bed to think and pray.

'Lead me, Lord. Tell me what to do.' By the little bedroom lamp, words glowed on the printed page open on the table. 'Trust in the Lord with all thine heart; and lean not to thine own understanding. In all thy ways acknowledge Him, and He shall direct thy paths.'

To pay off the men would not be trusting the Lord.

Ralph crawled back into bed. 'All right, Lord. We'll just try harder to build perfect boats.'

Then one grey afternoon came the final blow. A flat truck had just been loaded with forty boats, each stamped 'approved' by the inspectors. As Ralph watched the shunt engine back up to it, the chief inspector came out.

'I don't like their looks,' he said flatly. 'They've got to be unloaded and refinished.' Ralph waved the engine away and turned wearily to his car.

The brothers had reached the end of their rope. The contract had already cost them one million dollars. They had delivered 2,200 boats with 600 rejects stacked in their storage yard.

Ralph found himself battling his bitter animosity against the chief inspector. He knew that Christ has told us to forgive our enemies. He tried his best to forgive the man, only to stay awake for hours with his mind seething with fury.

Then one night the Lord spoke. 'I love that man too. I died for him as well as for you.' The words were like a cooling hand on Ralph's brow. After that, he was able truly to forgive the inspector.

Then what seemed like a wild thought came to Ralph . . . *God has allowed the inspectors to reject all those boats. Then God has something that He wants us to learn out of this. We will learn it only when we stop rebelling against all this and begin to look to Him in thanksgiving.*

As the Meloon brothers accepted this concept and acted on it, God answered with an explosion of miracles. First, a loan came unexpectedly from business friends in Norway. The second miracle came from Pakistan. The minister of defence ordered six boats for $139,000. With the first shipment Correct Craft sent along one of their 'rejected' assault boats, explaining they had more. Back came an order for 239.

The third miracle came in the form of an idea which God put into Ralph's mind. The brothers were led to set up five factory warehouse distribution centres in different parts of the country. Each would operate as an autonomous company selling Correct Craft boats to dealers in their area. A boating industry innovation, those centres proved successful in tapping new markets. In effect, the five satellite companies acted as flotation barges around a sinking ship, lifting the company to the surface.

God was not only teaching the Meloon brothers how to handle temptation and adversity constructively, He was giving them a basic business lesson: no company can exist on a solid foundation with only one big customer. The government might have stopped buying their boats for a perfectly legitimate reason . . . Indeed, His ways are wondrous.

Today the business is a healthy and growing Orlando

concern. Ralph can say, 'As I look back, I praise the Lord for those dark days. They helped us become a much stronger company. More important, our faith has been greatly strengthened to the point where I will confidently walk with Him anywhere.'

With an approach like Ralph's and Walter's, we are at the opposite of the critical spirit. Here we have trust and praise as the antithesis of complaint and rebellion.

We have seen this in so many situations . . . When Ellie Armstrong faced the crisis of the $300 mortgage payment due with only $50 in the bank and no motel guests for five consecutive nights, she might have felt justified in rebelling against such a predicament. Instead, she acted out her praise of God for His provision by giving away the $50 as He had told her to. That same night the motel filled up, stayed filled, and the payment was made on time.

In my battle of the sleeping pills, when I stopped rebelling and sought God even at the point of sleeplessness, then I was given the praise-filled message of the old hymn:

> Blessed assurance, Jesus is mine . . . !
> This is my story, this is my song,
> Praising my Saviour all the day long.

In retrospect I can see the steps — from rebellion, to acceptance, to praise, to God changing the situation. I began to see more clearly too why God sets Himself so seriously against a disobedient or rebellious or judgmental spirit: this is the precise frame of heart and mind which blocks His loving intervention on our behalf.

The wisdom of Solomon tells us, 'Out of it (the heart) are the issues of life.'[16] Jesus enlarged on this: the human heart and will are the main problem, He kept explaining. Every true reform in civilisation involves a change of heart followed by a change of mind of human beings. So how can we get our hearts set right?

Traditionally men have tried to change the minds of other men in two ways — neither of them Jesus' way. The basest effort is the use of physical force to compel another person or an entire nation to do what the opponent wants. The trouble with this method is that the 'victory' usually left untouched and unchanged the hearts and minds of the vanquished. No military victory could have been more complete than the Roman legions' over tiny defenceless Palestine in Jesus' day. Yet the Jewish fractiousness and insurgentism was worse than ever.

The second, more civilised technique is to use words and the power of personality to try to change the other person's mind and heart. Governments employ many tools to this end: controlled news media, education biased until it is a mere political tool; every imaginable form of pressure and propaganda, every skill of the advertising profession in what amounts to buying a change of mind.

In our times the art of persuasion has been developed to an all-time high, but there has been a curious result. Though a veritable frenzy of words is being spoken over millions of television sets as well as pouring from the presses, modern men seem less trustful of words than ever. It would also appear that both the spoken and the written word are less effective. 'As a poet,' W. H. Auden once wrote, 'there is only one political duty, and that is to defend one's language from corruption. And that is particularly serious now. It's being so quickly corrupted. When it's corrupted, people lose faith in what they hear, and this leads to violence.'[17]

And to obscenity, Auden might have added. As the printed word along with movie and stage scripts are increasingly peppered with four-letter words, we can't help wondering: isn't the obscenity really our frustration at the poverty of language that no longer really communicates or works any changes in people's minds and hearts? Perhaps then, the unconscious reaction goes, people can be *shocked* into paying attention — and so the foul words pour out.

There are other signs of the increasing ineffectiveness of persuasion . . . In the last decade 'credibility gap' has become one of our favourite terms.

The lecture method of teaching is increasingly under suspicion.

The great issues before Congress are seldom debated any more on the floor of the House or the Senate.

Presidential speeches are similar casualties. For a quarter of a century television has provided the unprecedented advantage of intimate chats in every living-room. Yet these speeches, usually written by hired speech writers, tailored to computer determined political requirements, make us wonder, where have great speeches and speakers gone? What has happened to the passion of a Patrick Henry, the sober sincere honesty of a George Washington, the homespun grandeur of an Abraham Lincoln, the flaming oratory of a William Jennings Bryan or a William Gladstone, the persuasive logic of a Woodrow Wilson, the person-to-person warmth of Franklin D. Roosevelt, the rolling thunderous cadences of a Winston Churchill?

It would seem that the harder we have tried our 'modern' techniques of persuasion, the more break-downs in communication we have been experiencing on all fronts — between parents and children, between the races, between government and people, between nations. Our frustration then breeds more rebellion.

Psychologist Paul Tournier in his book *The Whole Person in a Broken World* diagnoses the prevalence of rebellion in our society not as a healthy sign of progress nor a means to needed reforms. Rather, Dr. Tournier sees rebellion as a neurosis of epidemic proportions startlingly comparable to adolescent neurosis.[18]

In normal adolescence, the storms and stresses — the negative self-assertion, the customary disparagement of established mores — are ultimately worked through to integration — adulthood. But in cases where this integration is unduly delayed, psychiatrists call the resulting illness the 'neurosis of defiance'. 'Something like this,' Dr. Tournier maintains, 'has taken place in the development of human history since the Renaissance . . .'

He cites the classic signs of neurosis in the individual. First, anxiety. We do not have to look far to see much anxiety today. Restlessness and dissatisfaction with oneself and others are epidemic. In society the flood of criticism may be in part an effort to hide a deep anxiety. Jean-Paul Sartre went so far as to say 'Man *is* anxiety.'[19]

The second sign of neurosis, individual or societal, is sterility. 'Big dreams do not produce the fruit . . . True values do not play an effective role in the destiny of society . . .'

The final characteristic of the neurotic is inner conflict — ambivalence; the classic adolescent's awkwardness when everything he tries gets botched, and more often than not he gets the opposite result from the one he sought.

Certainly there are marked signs of ambivalence in our society. We undertake the war in Vietnam to keep peace in Asia and to ensure the good life for the South Vietnamese; we end up with the longest war in American history and the devastation of the Vietnamese homeland.

Protestors of that war march for an end to violence, and clash violently with the police.

The present administration sees protestors as traitors to law and order. But the Watergate investigation ends up showing that same administration in flagrant violation of the law.

The government sets out to avoid inflation by controlling the economy; the result is runaway prices and a devalued dollar . . . The ambivalence and contradictions go on and on.

Since our ways are achieving the opposite of what we intend,

perhaps we are ready to ask what is Jesus' way? The first move,
He told His disciples who asked Him the same question, has to
be made on behalf of the inner man. You have problems in your
lives, problems in society, but you must see that

> '... from within, out of men's hearts, come evil thoughts of
> lust, theft, murder, adultery, wanting what belongs to others,
> wickedness, deceit, lewdness, envy, slander, pride, and all
> other folly; they are what pollute you and make you unfit for
> God.'[20]

Anger in the heart and the contempt of one human being for
another precedes the act of murder.[21] Lust in the heart precedes the act of adultery.

The last thing God wants for us men is conflicts and neuro-
ses that tear us apart. His primary concern is the healthy
integration of man's heart and will. This health He measures by
whether we are still running from Him in rebellion, or are re-
united with Him, having found our way back to our heart's
home.

The closer I looked into the dilemma of our rebellion, the
more this central truth stood out for me: underlying all cleavage amongst us, behind our broken human relationships, lies a
basic break — between God and us. We do not often recognise
this, being inclined to blame any dislocation in our lives on
other people, or on 'circumstances', and to look for the remedy
anywhere but in a reconciliation with God.

Since we human beings are rooted in God, rebellion against
Him is like revolting against part of ourselves. Of course we are
not able to 'find ourselves' when we are such divided beings!

That is precisely what our adversary Satan wants for us. He
was the original instigator of rebellion. Revolt was Satan's sin
too. In the Garden of Eden he succeeded in luring Adam and
Eve to join him in rebellion. And ever since Satan has whispered to us that the way to improve our lot is to rebel.

But if this is Satan's way, what is God's way? That was essentially the question the thoughtful scholar Nicodemus came asking Jesus during their quiet midnight talk. The Master's answer was, 'Those deep inner changes are never going to come about through men's efforts in trying to change the thinking or patch up the old person. There's only one way, Nicodemus: *"except a man be born again, he cannot see the kingdom of God".'*

And when Nicodemus probed and questioned, 'How *can* these things be?' Jesus pointed him to a cross. How well He knew that soon He would hang there suspended between earth and heaven. And there, if we will recognise it and allow it to be so, our old selves can die too so that the new person can be born.

Can the way of the Cross do in men's hearts what force and persuasion and all man's artifice fail to do? A few years ago during a trip to Austria I heard a true story which suggests that it can and does. A Lutheran pastor, a former Nazi storm-trooper, gave me this account of how he, trained in hatred and destruction, had been changed into a follower of Christ . . .

In December 1941 the trooper was with the German armies invading Russia. In the Crimea in heavily-wooded terrain, the battle began going against the Germans. As they had to fall back, the German found himself within the Russian lines separated from his regiment. Alone, he made his way through the forest, fearful at every minute of being captured. Suddenly, he saw a thin cloud of smoke coming from the chimney of a hut. Creeping up warily, gun in hand, he knocked on the door. It was answered by a tiny elderly Russian woman.

Shoving past her and searching the hut, he satisfied himself that the woman lived alone. Apparently, her menfolk were off fighting — perhaps had already been killed. To the German's surprise, the woman offered him food and drink. Neither spoke a word of the other's language, but in the end, the Russian woman hid the soldier, feeding him and caring for him for three days and nights. The German grew increasingly baffled. Certainly, no worse enemy than he, a Nazi, could have come to the door here in Russia, where Germans murdered more civilians than the total number of Jews killed in all Europe. The woods swarmed with Russian troops; surely she knew that if she were caught harbouring a German, she would be shot.

Out of his mounting desire to communicate, he managed through sign language and facial expressions to convey his question, 'Why have you risked your life to hide and befriend me?'

The old woman looked at him for a long moment in silence, then turned and pointed to a crucifix on the wall above her bed.

Telling me the incident, the Lutheran pastor added, 'After I escaped back to the German lines, try as I would I couldn't forget what had happened. I hadn't known love like that was possible. In the end, I was drawn irresistibly to the One who enabled the little Russian lady to prefer another to herself — even when that other was a cruel and deadly enemy. I wanted to know the power of the cross in my life too. That's why I'm a Christian today.'

The way of the Cross, Jesus' way. The way that puts others ahead of self. What would be the difference in our world today if we began to let the Cross work its change in our hearts?

Ezekiel's prophecy could come true for us individually and collectively as a society,

> A new heart also will I give you, and a new spirit will I put within you: and I will take away the stony heart out of your flesh, and I will give you an heart of flesh.
> And I will put my spirit within you ... and ye shall be my people, and I will be your God.[22]

Rebellion and mutiny would be seen as a paltry playing at life as we enter into the glorious liberty of the children of God.

What that liberty could mean for us was spelled out long ago at the beginning of God's dealings with the Israelites. It is a vision that has haunted us ever since . . .

The good earth, its seas, lakes, rivers, and streams, the air, the trees, the animals will no longer be ravaged by man.

Crops would be blessed and be sufficient to end hunger for all mankind. The nation that produces plenty would rush its aid and know-how to those countries with less.

Happiness would reign in homes across the world. Marriage and family life would thrive and be blessed. Once again babies would be wanted and cherished.

In the words of Isaiah, 'Violence shall no more be heard in thy land, wasting nor destruction within thy borders.'[23] Wars will end.

In real and practical ways, men will recognise that this really is one world. With an effective world-organisation, destructive and fear-motivated nationalism will disappear. As the nations no longer need to spend most of their substance on armaments, creative research will burgeon. The cure will be discovered for cancer, for rheumatoid arthritis, for multiple sclerosis, arteriosclerosis, heart disease, emphysema and the myriad of other diseases that have defeated research and plagued mankind.

In all branches of the arts, the new creativity will bring a renaissance — music, art, writing, the theatre, crafts.

Mourning shall be ended as men everywhere begin to understand that because ours is a God of love, submission and obedience to Him is not only our greatest good, but the way 'to enjoy Him for ever'.

CHAPTER THIRTEEN

RUN FOR THE STRONG TOWER

Recently I opened the newspaper to read headlines on a major article:

VIOLENCE

As Crime Soars, a Puzzled Nation Asks, 'Why, Why?'

The first paragraph read:

> It is an age of fear — a stark, pervasive, gnawing, mind-numbing, gut-wrenching fear.[1]

Fear and anger are universally recognized as the two most destructive emotions in man. Yet it seems that year by year fears are growing and striking deeper as we — individually and collectively — are increasingly frustrated in our efforts to deal with our problems. In our newspapers we read of events like a grocer murdered for $20; rapes and killings of young girls in the Boston area; stabbings and hold-ups in Washington and in London; a grandmother stamped to death by two youngsters, kidnappings and skyjackings.

Long articles are written suggesting ways the average citizen can protect himself: replace spring-type door locks with dead-bolts; put chains and peepholes on doors; have keys made by licensed locksmiths recommended by a city Burglary Squad; install bars or ornamental metal grillework on windows; buy one of the many burglar alarm systems now on the market; bring into the family unit a trained police dog; keep lights burning in stores, warehouses, and homes throughout the night.

Common-sense precautions are certainly necessary. But there come times when all the safeguards man has devised can't stand between us and the raw evil loose in this world. It is then that we discover a surer protection, the only final protection there is. This was dramatised for me by what happened not long ago to a neighbour in Delray Beach, Florida . . .[2]

It was a beautiful sunshiny June morning. Jean Klinger started out in her car for Delray Beach to take her final teacher's examination. As she turned from Military Trail down Fourth Street, she noted the time on her watch. It was 8:50. Good! She'd be at school by nine.

Fourth Street near Military Trail is a lonely stretch of road until it runs into the residential area. Just ahead of Jean was a light-coloured pick-up truck. It slowed down, then pulled over to the side of the road. An arm out of the car window signalled to Mrs. Klinger to pull over too. She did so instinctively, wondering if the other driver had noticed a flat coming on in that left rear tyre she'd been worried about.

A big burly man wearing a sports shirt open at the neck strode up to her window. 'Lady, can you tell me how to get to Dixie Highway?'

Mrs. Klinger was unsuspecting. After all, it was broad daylight. 'I'm so sorry. I don't live in Delray. I'm just on my way to school here. Afraid I can't give you directions.'

The man was looking at her intently. Suddenly the expression on his face changed. Jerking open the car door, he pressed a hard metal object into Jean's back. When she sat there paralysed, he shoved her to the other side of the seat and climbed in beside her. Instinctively, she screamed, then reached over and pressed hard on the horn. But there was not a car or pedestrian around.

He pressed the object harder into her back. 'Don't try that again or I'll kill you,' the man growled. Fear, panic, terror washed in waves over her.

Jean admits that she has always had many fears. Sensitive, intense, vivacious, she feels deeply. Long ago she determined to face up to her fears and to search for ways to eradicate them. Her search led her to seek God for His help in freeing her from these shackles. She had asked that in certain circumstances He'd help her do the things she feared or found difficult. This led her to apply for teacher training at the Montessori School.

During an early session there she confided to her instructor that she had not yet learned how to deal with her fears. The instructor gave her a copy of a printed prayer that has been widely circulated. The words soon became part of the fabric of Jean Klinger's life . . .

> The Light of God surrounds me.
> The Love of God enfolds me.
> The Power of God protects me.
> The Presence of God watches over me.
> Wherever I am, God is.

Upon arising that June morning, as every morning, she had prayed that prayer of affirmation. Thus at the crisis moment, sitting beside the threatening man in the car, when panic and terror almost overcame her, she discovered in herself this mighty prayer resource. Jean cannot remember the exact words she used, but she knows their essence.

'How can you force yourself on me this way?' she cried. 'You are a child of God. God's love is in you. He cares about you. And I am His child too, and completely under His protection. His love and protection surround me . . .'

As she spoke the words, she felt warmed. 'There was a kind

of aura around me,' she said later. 'I could see it, feel it. It was like a soft light.

'Then a strange thing happened,' she recalled. 'Into my mind there came the clear picture of the face of the janitor at my school, one of the kindest, most gentle men I'd ever known, beloved by everyone. It was as if God was saying, "You told the man sitting beside you that he is a child of Mine. To help you feel that as well as know it, superimpose the janitor's face and image on this other man."

'I followed directions and, sure enough, after that, I could actually sense God's love flowing to my abductor.'

The result was immediate. The man suddenly appeared confused. Lust seemed to leave him. He removed the metal object from Jean's back. Then she saw that it was a key case.

He started Jean's car, drove on in silence for a while, little trickles of perspiration running down his face as his confusion increased. Then he drew over to the side of the road and stopped. 'Get out,' he ordered. Quickly Jean opened the door and jumped out. The man turned the car around and went careering down the road.

He was no sooner out of sight than the police car she had so desperately longed for pulled up. 'Something the matter lady?'

She and the officer found her car abandoned further down the road and the pick-up truck gone. At the police station she was shown a group of photographs. With a start she recognised one of them as the very man who had halted her. As she opened her mouth to identify him, something on the inside of her would not let her say anything except, 'I'm not sure.' The man had no police record except a series of traffic violations. 'I know it seemed weak, unco-operative with the police,' she said later. 'I only know something stopped me from identifying him.'

Despite the ordeal Jean Klinger continued on to the school, took her examination, passed it. She was glad to share her experience because she believes it may point to the most important protection for all of us.

'I am the light of the world,' Jesus told us. In the past, we have usually considered this symbolic, even exaggerated imagery. Now I wonder!

In this era of artificial light and of increasing energy shortage we are very aware of the merit of lighted areas for protection. Banks and business establishments are now commonly lighted throughout the night. A group of women in Indianapolis, crusading for years to make their streets safe again, has discovered that crime goes down as much as 85 per cent when street lighting standards go up.

Was Jesus speaking figuratively only when He said

> For everyone that doeth evil hateth the light, neither cometh to the light, lest his deeds should be reproved.[3]

I wonder if Christ means for us to take His 'I am the light of the world' more literally than we do. Of course, the statement also points to a theological truth. But He who created the atom and the sun[4] remains the power-centre, the dynamo of the physical universe. As such, He is as distinctly light as any Edison bulb. And as Light, He is also Protection — largely unrealised, untapped, unresearched.

An increasing number of people are experiencing Jesus' contemporary Presence in this way. To me it is significant that Jean Klinger felt 'a soft light' around her and that her attacker either could not or would not penetrate it.

> Let us therefore cast off the works of darkness and let us put on the armour of light.[5]

Could the apostle Paul, so often the target of hostile crowds, have experienced the Light of Christ as actual armour?

In promise after promise, the Bible seeks to teach us that in God and in His resources there is physical protection surer than any weapon or defence known to man. Other descriptions of this protection are given in addition to light, such as this one from the days of walled cities . . .

> The name of the Lord is a strong tower: the righteous runneth into it, and is safe.[6]

Short of magic or hocus-pocus, the question is, how could there be enough power (as the world understands power) in the invoking of a mere name to be a genuine safety-factor to anyone?

All through Scripture there is the insistence that a man's name is never just a casual handle for identification purposes. Rather, concentrated in a man's name is the essence and character of the person. Thus when God was allowed to enter a man's life and control it, more often than not the man's name had to be changed because the character-focus of the man was then different. So Abram became Abraham; Jacob became Israel; Simon became Peter; Saul became Paul. Frequently the Bible tells us the meaning of names. Seth, for instance, means 'granted'; Noah means 'relief'; Isaac denotes 'laughter'; Moses means 'to draw out (of the water)'.

There is great significance in the many names Scripture gives to Jesus Christ, among them:

The Last Adam	Light of the World
Saviour	Bread of Life
The Good Shepherd	Cornerstone
The Door	Counsellor
King of Kings	The Prince of Peace
The Lamb of God	Great High Priest

When we think of Jesus' ringing statement after His resurrection, 'All power is given unto me in heaven and in earth . . .',[7] we see why many descriptive words are needed to cover 'all power'. But all of them are caught up and comprehended in the name of Jesus. Again and again we are assured that the power to save, to redeem, to heal, to guide, to give wisdom, to protect is wrapped up and focused like a laser beam in this 'Name'.

> And whatsoever ye ask in my name, that will I do, that the Father may be glorified in the Son.[8]

When we pray 'in Jesus' Name', we are not simply verbalising a word or phrase; rather, our petition is to the complete character of the Lord and all of the power implicit in His Name. The Scripture abounds in 'holy mysteries' and the full meaning of praying in the Name of Jesus is one of those mysteries. In heaven, the mystery is understood; on earth, we shall probably never know it fully. Yet as we step out in faith using that Name, we do learn bit by bit. Even some of Christ's first followers, the seventy whom He sent out two-by-two during His earthly ministry, discovered early that His Name had power indeed:

> And the seventy returned again with joy, saying, Lord, even the devils are subject unto us through thy name.[9]

Surely here is the real reason that men with evil in their hearts back off so quickly when confronted by this Name: evil has always recognised and reacted against the power of this word, often more incisively than 'religious people'.

A short time after my friend Jean Klinger's experience, I came upon a similar incident. Roberta Lashley,[10] a young girl of Mt. Savage, Maryland, was fortunate enough to have learned about the power of Jesus' Name prior to a desperate crisis-moment. One night she had stayed later than she had realised at an interesting church meeting. When the bus let her out on a lonely country road, there was still a twenty-minute walk to the Lashley home.

She thought with distaste of the steep climb to her house on Bald Knob Road. It was not until a car drew up beside her on the dark road that she realised how tired she was. 'How about a lift?' a man's voice asked from the car.

In the dim light Roberta assumed that this was a neighbour. She climbed into the car gratefully, then realised she had been mistaken: the driver was a stranger. Even so, in that rural community sharing rides was such an accepted practice that the seventeen-year-old girl felt no alarm. She thanked the driver, but noticed that he made no reply.

They drove in silence until Roberta pointed out her house. Still the man said nothing and there was no decrease in speed.

'That's my house,' the girl repeated, small prickles of alarm alerting her.

Was it her imagination or were they actually going faster? 'There's a lane ahead where we can turn around,' she told the driver, trying to keep panic from her voice.

The car was gaining speed, careering up the twisting mountain road. The last house was behind them now.

'Stop the car!' Roberta cried. 'Let me out!'

Without slowing, the car swerved up a bumpy side road that led to an abandoned coal mine high on the mountain.

The girl looked wildly at the trees whizzing past them. A person could be killed and hidden for ever in one of those deserted shafts. Her hand closed on the door handle.

But as her fingers gripped the handle, suddenly she remembered something she had heard at the church service several weeks before. A missionary to the Philippines had said that Jesus Christ has dominion over the evil in man, but that we have to call upon that dominion. *We must ask.*

Shutting her eyes, Roberta tried to remember the exact words the missionary had used. Then very slowly and clearly, addressing the evil intent within the man, she said in a firm and clear voice, 'I rebuke you in the Name of Jesus Christ.'

For the first time the man looked at his passenger. 'What do you mean?' he asked. 'What's "rebuke"?'

'I mean,' she replied, 'that Jesus Christ has absolute authority on this earth and that I am under His protection. He's protecting me this very minute.'

They had reached the abandoned mine shaft. The car stopped. Time stopped too as Roberta felt her pulse pounding in her temples. The driver remained motionless, hands still on the wheel.

'I didn't know,' he said at last. The force that had gripped him was gone. He started backing up, then turned down the steep mine road to the main highway. The crisis was past; waves of relief washed over Roberta.

'I'm not really so bad,' the man went on as he headed the car down the mountain. His voice sounded almost pleading. 'I've been to church some. It just never made any sense to me.'

The girl beside him was never sure afterwards that all she said to the man in the next five minutes made sense either. But in the time it took to reach her house she poured out her heartfelt conviction of Christ's love for each of us, how much He loved the bewildered man beside her, and of the need for Him in every life.

The car stopped at the Lashley's driveway. With relief Roberta got out, then ran trembling into the house to find her mother waiting up for her.

'God took care of me,' was all she could say. 'God took care of me,' over and over again like a child waking up from a nightmare.

The words Roberta Lashley spoke to her mother stirred a slumbering childhood memory in me. As a little girl, I had suffered what seems now like a long period of fear of the dark. Night after anguished night, I would lie rigidly in bed, eyelids screwed shut, afraid to breathe for fear of what lurked in the dark corners.

Looking back I am surprised that I didn't share it with my mother. Pride was fierce in me. And I was much too young to reason out that faith was the opposite of fear. As I tried to handle the fears myself, what helped me most was the chorus of a hymn I had learned in Sunday School:

> God will take care of you
> Thro' every day, in all the way:
> He will take care of you,
> God will take care of you.[11]

As I would lie there singing this softly over and over to myself, an ease would flow into me, assurance and confidence that nothing else supplied. For one little girl the childlike words of the hymn became at once both an affirmation of faith and also her response to Him — her prayer.

When I mentioned this childhood experience and the 'God Will Take Care of You' hymn in a recent article, to my astonishment letters came flooding in from readers. Most wanted to share a similar experience. My words had apparently evoked half-forgotten scenes and impressions, childhood experiences still charged with so much emotion. Clear impressions rising again to the surface — the panic we felt as children followed by the relief of the particular word of consolation.

Sometimes we like to think of fear as an emotion that belongs to the childhood of the race, or perhaps to the child who still lives in every adult. Yet fear resides in the strongest, the most resourceful of men. They learn to handle fear not by hiding it, but through learning an important fact about evil: it has a cowardly side. I find a striking example of this in the life of David Livingstone, the Scottish missionary–explorer who opened up and mapped so much of Africa.

In 1856 Livingstone was facing one of the gravest perils of his sixteen years in the Dark Continent. He had to pass through the wild country of the local chief Mburuma. The chief was not only hostile himself, but was seeking to rouse the whole countryside against the white man's expedition. Warning after warning had been given to Livingstone by runners going ahead of the expedition. There were reports that warriors were in the jungle creeping towards his camp.

Alone in his tent, Livingstone opened his Bible at the promise on which he had staked his life so often. Then he wrote with such stirring eloquence in his journal:

> January 14th, 1856. Evening. Felt much turmoil of spirit in view of having all my plans for the welfare of this great region knocked on the head by savages tomorrow. But Jesus said, 'All Power is given unto Me in heaven and in earth. Go ye therefore, and teach all nations ... and lo, I am with you always, even unto the end of the world.'
>
> It's the word of a Gentleman of the most sacred and strictest honour, and there's an end on it! I will not cross furtively by night as intended. Nay, verily, I shall take observations for latitude and longitude tonight, though they may be the last. I feel quite calm now, thank God![12]

During the hours of darkness nothing happened. The next morning Livingstone, still calm, directed the crossing of the river for his 114 men and their oxen while Mburuma and his tribesmen watched from the jungle's edge.

Deliberately, the missionary reserved for himself the last place in the last canoe. One of the party, fond of Livingstone and fearful of treachery, pleaded with him not to give the chief a chance to shoot him in the back.

'Tell him to observe that I am not afraid,' Livingstone replied. Then with dignity he thanked the astonished tribesmen, wished them God's peace and walked very slowly to the canoe, never looking back. No shot was fired, no hand raised against him.

For me the incident has great personal significance. About two years before Peter Marshall's death, one day I noticed a strange inscription carefully written on the flyleaf of his favourite Bible...

> It's the word of a Gentleman of the most sacred and strictest honour, and there's an end on it!
>
> David Livingstone

Then underneath Livingstone's name, Peter had signed his own.

When I asked Peter about the inscription, he told me of the incident in Livingstone's life. It meant much to Peter not only because this giant of the nineteenth century was born in the village of Blantyre not far from Peter's home in Scotland, but also because he too had often staked so much on the trustworthiness of the promises in this Book.

Occasionally God can provide the necessary confident poise to overcome evil with such an overflow of good that it takes on a sort of gay exuberance. That's the way it was for Brother Bryan of Birmingham, Alabama, a man whose memory is almost legend to many Southerners. His real name was James Alexander Bryan, and for more than forty years he was the pastor of the Third Presbyterian Church of Birmingham, located at 22nd Street and Avenue G. in a downtown section of the industrial city.

Citizens of all sorts — policemen, firemen, the ill in hospitals, those in jail, the hungry and the poor, the black people, businessmen — had long since stopped caring what denomination the preacher was, what colour, what social class, just that he was 'Brother Bryan', chaplain to the entire city. Since 1934 there has been at the heart of Five Points in downtown Birmingham with traffic flowing on every side of it, a white marble larger-than-life statue of Brother Bryan. He is kneeling in prayer, wearing a baggy old overcoat with a scarf half sliding off his neck, just as the sculptor Georges Bridges had seen him so often.

For Brother Bryan had a way of praying in most unlikely places at most unlikely times. Many a Birmingham citizen had heard his 'Brother, let us pray' and couldn't wait to relate the latest Brother Bryan story . . .[13]

One Thursday night he had been detained late after a Prayer Meeting at the church and had to walk home alone. As he was crossing a dark narrow alley between business buildings, a man slipped out, stuck a gun in Brother Bryan's face and ordered, 'Hands up.' Obediently, his hands went up.

The thief methodically went through the preacher's pockets, extracted all the money he found, and removed his watch. Then he almost dropped the watch when his victim said calmly, 'Brother, you and I are going to pray about this right now.' Then the pastor lifted up his face and said, 'Lord, here's a man who needs Your help in the worst way. I ask You to show him a better way to live, help him make a new start. Lord, You love this man, make him feel Your love right now.'

Slowly the gun lowered. The thief thrust the money and the watch back into Brother Bryan's hands. 'Go on home,' he said. 'The likes of you is not for me.'

We might wonder where the Brother Bryan[15] kind of cool-headedness comes from? I know only one possible source — an utter trust in God that turns into a total form of protection.

'Fear not' is one of the most reiterated exhortations in Scripture. The Bible denounces fear over and over and describes this deadly brew as one of humanity's major ills . . .

For God hath not given us the spirit of fear; but of power, and of love, and of a sound mind.[14]

For ye have not received the spirit of bondage again to fear; but ye have received the Spirit of adoption, whereby we cry, Abba, Father.[15]

It is helpful to understand the basis on which the Bible regards fear as a sin of disbelief in God. Most of us moderns are resistant to the term 'sin' since it implies condemnation. Yet Jesus stated categorically that He did not come into the world ever to condemn men and women but to save us.[16] Therefore, if we have God's view of sin, it is 'missing the mark', missing out on the good things He wants us to have and experience.

Thus any emotion or attitude that disorients or disintegrates human personality so that we 'miss the mark' is certainly therefore a sin — a negative to be expelled. Whether at its simplest level when fear 'roots us to the spot' or causes our knees to buckle, or a more sophisticated form of jealousy-fear, or the fear of hardship or disaster in times of economic depression, it destroys co-ordination, riddles personality, blocks logical thinking, and makes creative solutions to problems impossible.

When we see fear through Jesus' eyes, it is the acting out of our disbelief in the loving Fatherliness of God. By worrying and fretting, we are really saying, 'I don't believe in any God who can help me, and I do not trust Him.' Thereby we are sinning against God by impugning His character and calling Him a liar.

At that point there is only one way to get rid of fear; like any sin, we must recognise it, confess it in true repentance, claim God's sure promise of forgiveness, cleansing and renewal, accept these gifts, rise and get on with life.

As Jesus walked the earth and so frequently felt fear in men around Him, again and again we hear that cry of His, 'O men, how little you trust Him!'[17] In the cry there was more than a little rebuke and sorrow along with a sort of marvelling astonishment that men could be so blind: 'Why are you afraid? How little you trust God!'[18]

Behind Jesus' sharp reaction to our faithless fears lay His consistent viewpoint that this is our Father's world still in His control. Nor did Jesus ever use the word 'Father' lightly out of slick sentimentality. He taught that God deals with each of us personally in the way the best of fathers would. Therefore, the kind of love necessary to bring in the kingdom on earth is not brotherly love, but fatherly love. When we take Jesus' teachings (for example, the last four Beatitudes) in the light of this fatherly love, what has before seemed hopelessly idealistic becomes altogether possible.

Our Father never forgets the way we humans really are. He knows well that we, His children, are beset with fears. Therefore, in almost every example of God breaking into life on earth, the opening words are, 'Fear not' ... 'Fear not, the Lord will go before thee' ...'Have no fear, I am with thee' ... 'Fear not, nor be dismayed' ... and a hundred variations. Our Father knows that like small children, we need constant reassurance.

Whether small children or grown-up children, we need to develop a sense of dependence on the Fatherliness of God. It may seem to us at first thought that any dependence is the opposite of strength or a mature personality. But when we look closely at Jesus, we see that this is not so. Always the Master gave the impression of a moment-by-moment companionship and dialogue with the Father, yet here was a Man afraid of nothing. Not fearing men's opinions of Him, He spoke the truth bluntly. He was not afraid of unpopularity because He knew that when we are true to our real self, it is impossible to please everyone. He did not cringe when He walked through the mob at Nazareth. Here was a truly dangerous mob-lynching scene. Yet with Jesus' faith in the Father, He strode through the midst of them with such assurance that the crowd simply faded before Him.

When we look at His constant dependence on God alone, we begin to suspect that we may be teaching our sons a false basis for manliness. So long as we are in these bodies, we are going to be subject to the limitations of flesh and we shall always know a degree of loneliness. To ignore these facts of life is not to nurture independent manliness, but to suppress fears and cram them into the unconscious where they do further harm.

The Nazarene asks for strong men — the tensile strength of the inner spirit. He would seem to be telling us that much of our bravado is artificial. He is for ever calling us to a simpler, sturdier faith.

Faithlessness makes us suffer multitudinous troubles that we never do, in fact, face. Not many of us are actually going to be called on to face the spears of African tribesmen or look down the barrel of a gun or confront a would-be rapist. But untold thousands suffer diminished lives through the fear of all the things that might happen.

'I have known many troubles,' the humorist Mark Twain wrote when he was an old man, 'but most of them never happened.'[19]

Peter Marshall was fond of telling a fairy tale to illustrate how fears have a way of growing smaller and then evaporating when we resolutely face up to what we fear most. It is the story of Miobi, the boy who lived far to the south beyond the Third Cataract, and how he went on his journeys to overcome his fears . . .[20]

> Miobi had come to a village where the people were doing nothing else but moan and wail. The fires were not lit, the goats were not milked because all the villagers were expecting to be eaten shortly by the Monster on the Top of the Mountain.
>
> This monster had the head of a crocodile and the body of a

hippopotamus and a tail like a very fat snake, and smoke came from his fiery breath.

But Miobi said, 'I will go up the mountain and challenge the monster.'

There he was, sure enough. But as the boy climbed and came nearer, the monster looked definitely smaller.

'This is very curious indeed,' he said. 'The farther I run away from the monster, the larger it seems, and the nearer I am to it, the smaller it seems.'

When the boy reached the cave, he found no monster — but a quiet little thing as small as a frog, which purred; and he brought it home as a pet.

When the villagers saw him return, they wanted to make a hero of him for killing the monster, but he explained just what had happened and how he had brought the monster home as a pet.

What was its name?

The monster answered, 'I have many names. Some call me famine, and some pestilence; but the most pitiable of humans give me their own names.'

It yawned and added, 'But most people call me What-Might-Happen.'

Is Jesus a tower-light of protection against this kind of fear? Yes, because Jesus is Light and that Light can melt and dispel these submerged incapacitating fantasies.

Sometimes it helps to write down one's fears, then hold them up one by one to the light of Christ's clear understanding. Never is Jesus as the Light of the World more clear than in these murky areas of our semi-conscious fears, most of them unreal and psychotic. The trouble with the imaginary fears is that they can, if allowed to go on and on unchallenged, really destroy. As we talk over each fear on the list with Christ, He will illuminate for us some steps to expose them for what they really are...

For a woman with husband and children away from home who has always been afraid of spending even one night alone, God may simply tell her to try it for one night and trust Him.

He may provide a man who is terrified of public speaking with an opportunity, directing, 'Don't duck it. Step out on faith and make that talk. Trust Me to help you with the flow of ideas and words.'

A person who has some physical discomfort and is reluctant to go for a medical examination, fearful of fatal disease, may be told to pick up the phone immediately for an appointment with the doctor. This is the objective attitude, the opposite of that preoccupation with self that is one of the fear-dragon's breeding grounds.

He may simply direct the one who is frightened of flying to make reservations and board a plane.

Not only new confidence but real growth in character follows this facing up to what we fear, provided we are acting under God's direction.

Scripture tells us that the real enemies we should fear are not what or whom they seem to be...

> For we are not fighting against people made of flesh and blood, but against ... the evil rulers of the unseen world ... and against huge numbers of wicked spirits in the spirit world.[21]

The question here is, were Jean Klinger's and Roberta Lashley's real antagonists the men who wanted to harm them? Or were these men merely being used by 'the evil rulers of the unseen world'? Were Livingstone's real enemies a group of

African tribesmen, or were they spiritual forces using the ignorance of the natives as their tools for evil?

Our spiritual enemies take a variety of forms and use many devices. In our family we experienced a curious example of this in 1968 at Evergreen Farm in Virginia, my mother's and father's home for their retirement years.[22]

During the first years at the farm we had happy times with Flossie and Earl Cook who lived in the tenant house. In the years since they left, the little house on the hill seemed to fall on evil times. It was almost as if the house was drawing people of unhappy, violent temperament to it ... There was Mr. K., who turned out to have a vicious temper. It erupted with frightening intensity at anyone not white and Anglo-Saxon.

Then Mr. K. left and Mr. and Mrs. W. came. Soon there was trouble in their marriage. One day Mr. W. came home from his job as manager of a grocery store and found his wife and children gone with their clothes and most of the family furniture. Several months later a man entered the grocery store and shot Mr. W. dead. The police never discovered the murderer or the motive.

Three other couples followed, all of whom had financial and marital troubles. A stretch of ten years of acute unhappiness plagued the Little House.

In the living-room at Evergreen the family prayed about it. Part of the prayer book took the form of questions. 'How can we break the chain of gloomy and tragic events? Is some sort of cleansing needed here?'

We had to wait several months for the answer. Eventually it came in two parts: first, we were sent an unusual couple, named Rodriguez. They had emigrated from Spain several years before. People with a great spirit, they love family life and love the land. Of course, Isabel and Jacinto knew nothing of the history of the Little House.

Certain that God had sent them to us, we began cleaning the house, repainting and furnishing it for its new tenants. As we scrubbed and painted, our conviction grew that the house had suffered a kind of pollution that oceans of soap and gallons of paint couldn't remove. And we could not bear the thought of the delightful Spanish couple moving in to face any such threats.

'Are we imagining this or being superstitious?' we asked ourselves. How is it that buildings can take on the aura and character of the persons and events that their walls have held? Who can tell! But here is something that most of us have experienced: we step into certain church buildings and are immediately warmed and blessed; going into others we are chilled and no inspiration flows to us, only sterility.

We walk through the door of some homes even when the occupants are away, and know instantly that love is in this place. On the other hand, I've been in beautiful homes from which I wanted to turn and flee, later to find out that discord, strife, or tragedy of some sort had occurred there.

It must be then that the living patterns of those who dwell in these houses are being affected by those 'evil rulers of the unseen world' Scripture warns us about.

We knew well that Jesus' authority is the only one which evil must finally obey. It happened that Edith and Peter John Marshall were at Evergreen at the time, so Peter led our assault on the Little House. Len and I, Peter and Edith paused for our first prayer at the doorway of the house. There Peter, using the Apostle John's great words,[23] asked that every sin ever committed within the house to violate the peace and purity and sanctity of a real home, be cleansed 'through the blood of Jesus who cleanses us from all sin'.

Walking through and around the scrub buckets and paint pails, we went from room to room, in each one pausing for a prayer for cleansing, followed by thanksgiving that all darkness and evil would from henceforward pass over the house. Finally, we asked the Lord to bless the house and its occupants.

All of us felt a strange power in this procedure. We left that day knowing that something important had happened: all would be well. And events since then have borne this out. Light entered that home and abides there still. Jacinto and Isabel and their little daughter Maria Delores love their home and have known a lot of happiness there. When Mary Elizabeth Marshall, age five, comes to Evergreen, she and Maria spend hours together happily playing 'house' there with their tiny china dishes and their dolls.

Faith is the Strong Tower into which we can run for protection today. It isn't a physical place but the Light of a protecting Presence. It makes the unreal fears vanish and gives us literal protection against the real ones.

But something is required of *us*:

Let us therefore cast off the works of darkness and let us put on the armour of light.[24]

In other places in the Bible the pieces of our armour are described. Integrity is our coat of mail, truth is our belt, salvation is our helmet. Our shoes are the stability of the gospel of peace. And above all, faith is our shield.[23] This kind of armour suggests that every hour of every day we are in the thick of battle. Not only must we put on that armour of light, but we must practise walking in it on ordinary days when we think we feel no danger. Jean Klinger was doing exactly that as she daily saturated her mind and heart with the words about the light of God. We are putting on the coat of mail when we resolutely expel dishonesty from our lives. We are sharpening our spiritual sword as we memorise some of the great passages of Scripture and seek out the life-giving promises.

But when evil pursues, challenges, persists — at those crisis-moments we need to seek that cleansing of 'the blood of Christ' as well as His light, and to speak out His Name in ringing tones.

There in the Strong Tower we shall be safe. 'It is the word of a Gentleman of the most sacred and strictest honour.'

CHAPTER FOURTEEN

THE HELPER

That night at the dinner table our son was almost too busy talking to eat. He had flown in from Taylor University that afternoon having just finished his freshman year.

'Pops,' Chester's voice was excited, 'you wouldn't have believed the scene in the Notre Dame football stadium last weekend.'

'Football in June?' his father asked quizzically.

'No — lots of singing and prayer and praising the Lord . . . 25,000 people. It was fantastic!'

'What was the occasion?'

'A big meeting of the Catholic Jesus People. A bunch of us students drove up from Taylor. Six hundred priests came pouring on to the field from where the players enter, singing, carrying banners. The whole place was clapping and singing. I've never seen people so excited.'

Later that week, we read *Time* magazine's coverage of the event . . . First, men in business suits or sports coats carrying banners aloft: THE SPIRIT OF JESUS AMONG US emerging from the football team's tunnel on to the Notre Dame field; then the double moving line of priests in white robes and clerical stoles singing; their arms raised heavenward, hands open, palms up. The excitement of the crowd built, erupting into applause. Then as eight Roman Catholic bishops followed by Leo-Jozey, Cardinal Suenens of Belgium resplendent in brilliant red chasubles came into view, the clapping exploded

into a mighty roar. From 25,000 voices 'Alleluia! Alleluia!'
rocked the stadium.

Commented *Time*:

> The ceremonies at Notre Dame last week made it clear that
> the fastest-growing force within the church is that of the Pen-
> tecostals — or as many prefer to be called, Charismatics. Orig-
> inating as an off-campus prayer group at Pittsburg's
> Duquesne University in 1967, Catholic Charismatics form the
> third major group of Pentecostal believers ... There are prob-
> ably more than 200,000 of them in the U.S. today, organised in
> more than 1,100 prayer groups. The movement has taken root
> in foreign countries more recently and is growing even
> faster ...
>
> To the crowd of 25,000 in the stadium Cardinal Suenens
> said, 'The Pentecostal renewal is not a movement. It is a cur-
> rent of grace ... growing fast everywhere in the world. I feel it
> coming. I see it coming.'[1]

One portion of a sentence in that report leapt out at me:
'Originating as an off-campus prayer group at Pittsburg's
Duquesne University in 1967 ...' Yes, I remembered about
that. I had heard the story from Kevin Ranaghan, at that time,
a Catholic layman.

The seed bed of the Catholic Pentecostal movement was a
group of four or five laymen (all members of Duquesne's faculty) who had begun meeting together in the fall of 1966. A
book that fell into their hands led them to ask for the gift of the
Holy Spirit for themselves: David Wilkerson's *The Cross and
the Switchblade*, written by John and Elizabeth Sherrill. The
story concerned David Wilkerson and his street ministry to
gangs and dope addicts in the New York Bedford–Stuyvesant
area.

'By February of 1967,' Kevin Ranaghan told me, 'the four
Catholics from Pittsburg had received a release of the great gift

of the Holy Spirit. They began to witness quietly among close friends.' Some of these friends were at Notre Dame University. Beginning with small informal groups there on whom the joy of the Holy Spirit has fallen, the movement has gathered momentum like a prairie fire.

The Catholic Holy Spirit movement has the official sanction and approval of the Pope and church fathers. Their attitude is that the baptism of the Holy Spirit is completely scriptural and nothing new; it simply 'makes operative' the ancient sacraments of Baptism and Confirmation. This sanction has lent a freedom and an openness to Catholics in the Holy Spirit movement not always enjoyed by their fellow-Christians in Protestant churches.

In reporting the June mass meeting *Time* went on:

> Catholic Charismatics form the third major group of Pentecostal believers ... The 'classical' Pentecostal denominations ... grew up around the turn of the century and are by far the largest group — some 2.4 million in the U.S. alone.
>
> A 'Neo-Pentecostal' movement has developed over the past 20 years within mainstream Protestant churches — Episcopal, Presbyterian, Lutheran — and is still spreading.

'Spreading' is right!

It is difficult to estimate how far the Holy Spirit movement has spread. A conservative estimate would be that at least 300,000 members of main-line Protestant churches in the United States have found fresh springs of faith and vitality in the surge of the Spirit. By 1970 so many Presbyterian clergymen were caught up in the movement that the highest governing body of the church, the General Assembly of the United Presbyterian Church appointed a Special Committee to investigate. The gist of that report, as adopted by the 1970 Assembly was:

(1) 'We cannot follow the view ... that the purely super-natural gifts (of the Holy Spirit) cease with the death of the apostles ...

(2) '... know the misuse of mystical experience is an ever-present possibility, but ... (see) no reason to preclude its appropriate use ...

(3) '(believe that when such) experience clearly results in new dimensions of faith, joy, and blessings to others, we must conclude that this is "what the Lord hath done" and offer Him our praise.'

The Protestant movement has been quieter than its Catholic counterpart because there has been more resistance — even persecution, with some pastors asked to leave their churches in various parts of the country. One of the earliest (now classic) cases was that of the Episcopal priest, Father Dennis Bennett, asked to resign in 1960 from the 2,500-member St. Mark's Church of Van Nuy, California. He went on to a rundown mission church, St. Luke's in Seattle, now large and thriving.

Unprecedented growth has gone on anyway, in spite of such resistance. And perhaps it is time for the whole of this branch of Christendom to ask ourselves if this approach to the topic of the Holy Spirit is healthy and does honour to the Third Person of the Trinity.

Either the coming of the Holy Spirit into individual lives and upon the Church is Jesus' own teaching with His authority behind it, intended to result in sound and fruitful Christians — or else it is heresy that has no place in Christianity at all. I, for one, can see no middle ground.

What then did Jesus Himself tell us about the Holy Spirit?

Back in 1945, a personal health crisis led me to seek an answer to that question. Using a concordance and a notebook, I began methodically looking up references I could find on the Third Person of the Trinity. Gradually I worked the findings into a logical outline in the notebook. The part of it directly bearing on the question above could be summarised like this .．．

During the Last Supper conversation Jesus made it clear that the promises He was making that night were not meant just for the eleven men within the sound of His voice, but for 'future believers' as well.[2] And what He promised for the future could scarcely be more exciting:

It was 'expedient' that He 'go away'.[3]

When He went away, He would send the Holy Spirit to be 'poured out on all flesh.' (In contrast to the Old Testament way of a few chosen people — prophets, priests, kings.)[4]

He Himself would be the Giver (or Baptiser) of the Spirit.[5] His plan was that this Spirit would dwell (with our per- mission) in our bodies. This would be God the Father coming closer to man than He had ever been before.[6]

The apostles and all believers who would follow them down through the ages, were from the moment of Jesus' ascension, entering a new era — the era of the Holy Spirit. This would last until His second coming in physical Presence back to planet Earth.[7]

The Spirit would make Jesus' continuing Presence and His teachings real to us. He would always turn the spotlight on Jesus and glorify Him.[8]

The chief hallmark of the Holy Spirit would be *power* for service and ministry to others.[9]

The Spirit would be our Teacher; Guide; Comforter; Counsellor; Prayer-Intercessor; Giver of joy; of freedom; of many spiritual gifts; of eternal life.[10]

The Spirit would not ever be totally operative in an indi- vidual alone, but primarily in the fellowship of Christ's Body on earth — the Church.[11]

The apostles and those who would come after, must expect a degree of resistance, cleavage, even persecution and expulsion from their synagogues (or churches) because 'the world cannot receive Him — the Spirit of truth.'[12]

After His resurrection and ascension the apostles were 'to go into all the world and preach the above Good News to everyone, everywhere . . .[13]

They were not, however, to leave Jerusalem or start telling the Good News or attempt any ministry of any kind until *they had received the Holy Spirit.*[14]

Jesus promised, 'I will manifest myself to you.'[15]

And that He *would* 'lead you into further truth.'[16]

As I put all of this together back in 1945, it shed new light on the account of what happened next. That story is told in the Book of the Acts — really the Acts of the Holy Spirit. The Spirit's first great miracle was to transform the erstwhile timid, cowardly, and contentious disciples into bold men moving with power and authority. Thus the infant Church was born.

Jesus' explicit promises both to manifest Himself to us human beings and to lead us into further truth began to be fulfilled immediately. Old religious mores and set habit patterns had to be broken.

Virgin truth is always unexpected, often shocking. Though Jesus had spoken often of the Holy Spirit to the apostles, I could find no record that He had mentioned details of the Pentecost to come such as the sound of a roaring wind or flames of fire or the sudden speaking of languages they had never learned. Nor were these disciples prepared for the 'further truth' such as that Jewish food taboos were no longer necessary[17] or that the Gentiles were also beloved by the Father and chosen by Him to receive the Spirit.[18]

In fact, it seemed to me that Jesus' promise of 'further truth' gives us clear reason to believe that not all the truth and instruction Christ has to give us is contained in the canon of the Old and New Testaments. How could it be? He who *is* Truth will never find the people of any given century able to receive everything He wants to give. Because the Holy Spirit is a living, always-contemporary Personality, down all the centuries there must be an ever-unfolding manifestation of Jesus, His personality, His ways of dealing with us along with new, fresh disclosures of the mind of the Father. I found this concept endlessly provocative . . . and I still do.

At that point in my study some action on my part was clearly indicated. I had already summarised how we receive the Spirit.

(1) By going directly to Christ for Him.

(2) By asking for the gift of the Spirit.

(3) By receiving the Spirit by faith (the only way to receive any gift from God).

(4) By entering upon the discipline of hourly, daily obedience to Christ and the Spirit.

So very simply, I asked for the gift of the Helper, thanked Him for granting this, and entered upon that fourth step — the daily living out of this new relationship. I experienced no waves of emotion or ecstasy. Even when eighteen years later, I was given the gift of a heavenly language (glossolalia), it was with no particular fanfare; rather as a divine quartermaster might casually hand out a tool for a job; 'Here. You'll need this.'

When I had asked myself, 'Can we expect a manifestation of the Spirit?' I had little idea how to answer. Since the Helper is a Person, I reasoned, then of course He has personality traits, and presumably, these traits will show themselves. How or in what way, I could not guess.

Manifest Himself He did, though not in a way I could have guessed. As I stepped out in faith back in 1945, day by day listening to the inner voice for instructions, the first discipline He gave me was a leash for my tongue. For others the Spirit may give torrents of ecstatic speech; I needed the discipline of not speaking the careless or negative or discouraging word. For weeks I was put through the sharp training of opening my mouth to speak and hearing from the Teacher 'Stop! No, don't say it. Close the mouth.'

Many other experiences followed which I have described elsewhere[19] such as the joy of discovering the Helper's concern with guiding us in the details of everyday life; the reality of His guidance; the way He brings us to life at the emotional level. None of this I could have predicted. My experience was rather a solitary one. In 1945 I knew no one who was experimenting along the same line.

I realised that my husband Peter had already been given the Helper along with the unmistakable gift of preaching. Unlike me, he had not been seeking the Spirit *per se*, rather what God's specific will for his life was. Probably the Helper had come to Peter at the same time he was 'tapped on the shoulder by the Chief', as he liked to put it, and told to emigrate to America to enter the ministry. Having long known the Spirit's presence and help in so many ways, Peter did not feel the need for conscious search that I did.

Later, at the time of my husband's sudden death, I shall be forever grateful that I was able to know the Spirit as Comforter during those days. Without Him, I might have survived but only as a truncated person and without ever knowing the grace and splendour of the Comforter's presence on this, one of life's starkest frontiers. Not only did He comfort me but in one practical step after another, He showed me how to handle the devastation of widowhood.

By 1950 I was in need of another kind of help. I was under contract to deliver the manuscript of *A Man Called Peter* by May 1st, yet had never had a single course in the craft of writing and almost no practice except scribbling in personal diaries and journals. In that extremity, the Spirit became my Instructor in creative writing. For instance, He took me by the hand

and showed me that the opening pages must present Peter
Marshall in the framework in which the public knew
him — through his Senate chaplaincy. Only then could I flash
back (I did not even know the term 'flash-back') to Peter's early
life in Scotland and come forward.

I tried to outline the book and knew that it was not right.
When I asked my Teacher the right way of outlining the book,
I was told that Peter's biography would have no lasting
significance apart from what his life demonstrated about
God — His goodness, His revelation of truth, His ways of deal-
ing with men. 'Outline the book *that* way,' was the instruction.
I did and the material fell into place.

My Teacher showed me how to construct a book, what to
include out of the totality of one man's life, what to omit. All
the way through He kept insisting on the importance of the
light touch and humour as the way to emphasise greatness.

Now I experienced all the emotion I had *not* felt when I'd
first asked for His presence — plus much much more. 'No creative work,' He told me, 'has final impact unless it touches the
reader at the level of the emotions.' As I worked on the manuscript, He poured through me a stream of strong emotion, yet
permitted me none of the sentimentality into which I was
tempted to slip.

So functional and effectual was the Teacher's guidance that
I had fewer editorial suggestions, less outside help with *A Man
Called Peter* than with any book since, and I wrote it more
swiftly.

Little did I dream that some sixteen years later I would see
the rise of a major surge of the Spirit like a groundswell across
the world.

It came in 1966–67 when a rising tide of evil had plunged
our world into a mess. The young, already disillusioned with
war, were convinced that humanism had failed. High school

and college students were more clear-eyed about man's failure than were most liberal theologians. Liberal churches and seminarians who mostly told us what *not* to believe, were still teaching the sad doctrine that any reform — humanitarian, sociological, political, racial, or religious — must be made by human effort alone.

To which the younger generation's consistent reply was 'No way! Human effort alone hasn't worked, and never will.'

So out of the vacuum of churches 'holding the form of religion but denying the power of it'[20] the young groped their way — some of them through the jungle of drugs or the occult or Eastern religions they didn't really understand, to become 'Jesus' people'. They not only carried Bibles, they feverishly read them. They waded into the ocean or into backyard swimming pools to be baptised. All over the world they formed communes or 'communities'. And throughout the Jesus Revolution ran highly-charged emotionalism — hand-clapping, hugging, singing, religious rock music, filled with words like 'wow!' and 'far-out!'

Of course some of these youthful experimenters were not serious and soon drifted away. Yet many — like Carrie and Jeff Buddington — were permanently healed of long-standing hangups and had their lives turned right side up.

Like most adults I've had emotions ranging from delight — to wonder — to perplexity about all this. Yet surely these young people have been saying something important that the rest of us need to hear: we could use more joy and more love in our spiritual lives; perhaps we have become so occupied with worshipping God with our minds that we have forgotten that the rest of our beings, including the physical body, need to worship Him too.

Self-forgetfulness, a sort of joyous holy abandon is indeed one of the Helper's trademarks. An experience Len had in 1962 is still vividly present with me . . .

During our Chappaqua, New York years we were part of a group of six or eight couples who met once a week in one another's homes for sharing, Bible study, and prayer. I remember that Len came to a particular meeting that spring discouraged and frustrated. An individual with whom he worked professionally was being difficult. In addition, he and I were having problems with our teenagers.

That evening Len shared some of his problems and asked for prayer. Two members of the group especially seemed led to respond. With obvious concern, they stood by his chair, lightly rested their hands on his shoulders and head, and prayed. The particular request, as I recall, was that the power of the Holy Spirit would free Len of all resentments and antagonism. He told me later that he felt warmth coming from their hands. The prayer ended and he expressed gratitude. The meeting broke up.

Hours later after we were in bed, Len spoke softly, 'Catherine, I hate to wake you up, but I have the strangest feeling.'

A little alarmed, I asked, 'How do you mean?'

'There's this rushing, headlong joy inside me! It started in the pit of my stomach after I got in bed, then has kept bubbling up right into my head. I've been lying here thinking how silly it is to be so joyous when I should be asleep, but I can't control it. Catherine, I'd like to pray about it.'

'Well, fine,' I responded sleepily. 'Go ahead — pray.'

'But it isn't enough just to lie here. I'd like to kneel.' So both of us knelt beside the bed.

Len's prayer began quietly enough. First, he expressed gratitude for the friends who had cared enough to pray for him. Then he thanked God for our life together. After that he expressed love for each member of our family near and far. In between he kept telling the Lord how much he loved Him. Heartfelt love rose from the depths of his being for each person who had been a human thorn in Len's side. Afterwards he began God-blessing everyone he could think of, as if this love were so great it had to encompass the whole universe.

Always before Len's prayers had been short, even abrupt. Well thought out, words carefully chosen, but quite unemotional. In contrast, that night words poured from him lavishly, exuberantly repetitious, a geyser of deep emotion, unabashedly expressed. Like a bird uncaged, his emotions were darting, wheeling, soaring, wanting nothing so much as to keep on flying for ever.

Minutes passed — half an hour, an hour, as the love and joy kept pouring from Len. Finally, becoming aware of me kneeling there, too, Len interrupted himself long enough to say reluctantly, 'This isn't fair to you, Catherine. I'd like to go on and on, but you need some sleep.'

In the morning he reported, 'It was the most cleansing experience I've ever had. I got to thinking it was almost like a car engine being overhauled. It's as though negative emotions — my frustrations and anger had built up a residue in the body just like carbon deposits foul up spark plugs. That love and joy pouring through me was like fresh warm sudsy water washing away the bitterness. This morning I have — I don't know. A scrubbed feeling.'

In the years since on two other occasions Len has felt the same kind of rushing flowing love. In between times, he has tried seeking it on his own — to no avail. We know now — this kind of love is the Spirit's gracious gift, not something we humans can achieve on our own.

In 1970 I received as a gift a very old (1885) copy of *The Christian's Secret Of A Happy Life* by the Quaker, Hannah Smith, in whom I have been intensely interested for years. As I eagerly turned the yellowed old pages — but, what was this? A chapter on the Holy Spirit. I had many editions of *The*

Christian's Secret in my library, knew this book practically by heart, and there was no such chapter.

Why the deletion, I wondered?

I couldn't wait to read the chapter. As usual, Hannah Smith first turned to the Bible to summarise what it taught about the Spirit, then took a middle-of-the-road position liberally seasoned with common sense. The gist of her conclusion went something like this . . .

We make the mistake of looking upon the 'baptism of the Spirit' as a single experience rather than a life, as an arbitrary bestowment rather than a necessary vitality.

It's plain from Scripture that we can't possibly enter into a new life in Christ or be a child of God at all without knowing the Spirit.[21] However, there is a big difference between being indwelt by the Spirit and being 'filled' with His presence. For years (sometimes a lifetime) Christians can keep the Spirit at a sub-basement level by the insistence on running one's own life. Then through teaching or need — or both — the person consciously recognises his divine Guest's presence, opens the hitherto closed doors into certain rooms in his being so that the Spirit can enter there too. Thus the individual now deliberately abandons himself to the Helper's control.

'The result of this when done suddenly,' Mrs. Smith explained, 'is what many call "the baptism of the Holy Spirit".[22] It can be but isn't always, a very emotional and overwhelming sense of His presence.

'In seeking for the baptism therefore, it is not God's attitude towards us that needs to be changed, but our attitude towards Him. He will not give us anything new; rather we are to receive in a new and far fuller sense that which He has already given at Pentecost. The Holy Spirit is the world's sunlight, its energy and power. Sunlight can be kept out only by erecting barriers against it. All we need to do then, is to take down our shutters and barriers and walk out into the sunlight already given.'

But then Hannah Smith issues a strong word of warning. 'Baptism means,' she says, 'far more than emotion. It means to be immersed or dipped into the Spirit of God, into His character and nature. The real evidence of one's baptism is neither emotion nor any single gift such as tongues, rather that there *must* be Christ-likeness in life and character: by fruits in the life we shall know whether or not we have the Spirit.'

Nor does this mean instantaneous holiness. The disciples had to learn that right after Pentecost, and so do we. Ananias and Sapphira[23] could still lie and cheat, and so can we. In practical fact, our life with the Spirit is a walk, a growth, an unfolding as we learn to trust Him, and open more and more of our being to His presence and control.

To me this seemed such solid teaching that I wondered all the more why the chapter had been deleted from all more recent editions of the book. Intent upon unravelling the mystery, I sought the story behind this chapter. These are the facts as I dug them out of Hannah Smith's letters and writings and more recent books about the Smith family.[24]

Hannah was born in Philadelphia on February 7th, 1832 into a Quaker family who were eminently successful glass manufacturers. Though Hannah grew up a lively girl in a happy home, by age sixteen she was writing of 'the aching void in my heart'. This was in part adolescent drama, but the spiritual hunger was real enough, so much so that for the rest of her long life she was an eager, open-minded spiritual researcher. Like John Wesley in the century before her, she would listen to anybody with a religious experience to relate; she read constantly, investigated tirelessly.

Such eagerness might have led this Quaker girl straying down dead-ends and into paths of heresy. Fortunately, she possessed qualities to balance her insatiable zeal — a thorough knowledge of Scripture and a high degree of common sense.

Hannah had long since arrived at the conclusion that the only

solid ground of our faith is the character of God — who and
what He is. The only sure route for us humans to know Him
and experience His love and guidance resides 'not in the region
of the emotions, but in the region of the will — not "How do I
feel?" but always "What does God say?" ' Though initially she
had set out on 'a feverish search for emotional religion', she soon
grew mistrustful of emotionalism in religion.

In 1865 Hannah and her husband, Robert Pearsall Smith,
and their children moved to the village of Milltown, New
Jersey where Robert took charge of a branch of the family glass
business. There Hannah met a group called 'the Holiness
Methodists'.

Some of the most penetrating and valuable parts of *The
Christian's Secret*, a book helpful to generations of Christians,
was to come from what Hannah learned from this group. She
was able to translate their teaching from its in-language to fresh
everyday vernacular. No mean accomplishment!

Eventually Robert Smith was as caught up as his wife in all
this. One summer the Smiths went to a ten-day Holiness Camp
Meeting at a woodland camp-site along the New Jersey coast.
The purpose of these meetings, in Hannah's words, was 'to
open our hearts to the teachings of the Holy Spirit and His
coming into seekers' hearts'. But it was Robert rather than his
wife who received an extraordinary emotional experience. As
Hannah later reported it:[25]

> After the meeting my husband had gone alone into a spot in
> the woods to continue to pray by himself. Suddenly, from
> head to foot he was shaken with what seemed like a magnetic
> thrill of heavenly delight, and floods of glory seemed to pour
> through him, soul and body, with the inward assurance that
> this was the longed-for Baptism of the Holy Spirit.
>
> The whole world seemed transformed for him, every leaf
> and blade of grass quivered with exquisite colour ... Every-
> body looked beautiful to him, for he seemed to see the Divine

Spirit within each one ... This ecstasy lasted for several weeks, and was the beginning of a wonderful career of spiritual power and blessing.

Naturally, this made Hannah renew her efforts to receive similar joy. She described how she 'went forward' to the altar night after night in the meetings, then would go with a smaller group to one of the tents where they would spend hours kneeling in the dark, pleading and wrestling in prayer. For Mrs. Smith all this effort seemed of no avail. Not then or ever did she have an emotional experience of the type that had meant so much to her husband.

At first Hannah was disappointed. Then she realised that what *had* been given her was a 'real revelation of God that made life to me a different thing ever since'. She wanted emotions and was given conviction. She 'wanted a vision and got a fact'.

Later, Mrs. Smith came to feel the difference between what she and her husband experienced was largely a reflection of the difference in their natures: Robert was emotional, inclined to feel response in physical sensations; Hannah was a more reserved and analytical person.

In 1873 the Smiths emigrated to England to become one of America's most famous expatriate families with their lives intertwined by marriage or friendship with Bertrand Russell, Bernard Shaw, Beatrice and Sidney Webb, Bernard Berenson, the great art critic, and Henry James. For some years the Smiths carried on a remarkable joint lay ministry in England, especially in aristocratic circles. These meetings became known as the Higher Life Movement, and much of their teaching was carried on at house parties in some of England's great country places.

In the spring of 1875 Robert also travelled to Germany where he held highly successful evangelistic-teaching meetings

before large crowds — always in a highly-charged emotional
atmosphere. 'All Europe is at my feet,' exulted Robert in a
letter to his wife. When engraved pictures of him were offered
for sale, eight thousand sold immediately.

Then the blow fell. Gossip began about Pearsall Smith's
improper conduct with female admirers. No one then or now
knows the exact truth. The emotionalism so appealing to Smith
had apparently got out of hand. It seemed that Paul's instruction to 'salute one another with an holy kiss,' had spilled over
to the physical.

The rumours got into the press. Meetings scheduled in England were cancelled by their sponsors and for a time the Smiths
returned to New Jersey. Hannah quietly stood by her husband.
She wrote to a friend of their 'heart-scald' and of that 'crushing
blow' that had befallen Robert.

And crush him it did. He gave way to discouragement, disillusionment, and to a degree of cynicism. Robert sank into a
joy-less old age, while Hannah went on from strength to
strength, her quiet deep faith carrying her triumphantly over
all sorts of trials and difficulties.

With this story as background for the Smiths' experience of
the Helper, we begin to see the many forms and results His
coming into the life can have. Each opportunity for Christian
growth, each step forward brings new temptations and dangers.
In Robert Smith's case, tragedy resulted when he succumbed to
the temptation to idolise emotion instead of worshipping Jesus.
With Hannah Smith, no ecstasy was apparent but a quieter joy
from the fruitage of her convictions about God.

As for the missing chapter, clearly editors had been afraid of
the subject. It was fire. Hadn't Robert Smith been burned?
Safer to omit it, they must have concluded.

As Len and I pondered Hannah's story, we agreed that the
modern surge of the spirit may stand poised at the edge of this

same problem — too great a love affair with emotion, too little grounding in Scripture, too wanting in garden-variety discipline, too small an emphasis on purity, strict honesty, morality — Christ's own life living in us.

What is needed, of course, is balance: plenty of solid teaching — but plenty of joy as well. Let's admit that over-emotionalism is the last problem most of us face in our main-line denominational churches. We shall achieve a proper balance between the emotions and the mind when we are truly led by the Helper — 'always a Gentleman'.

It may well be that the missing element in Robert Pearsall Smith's experience was a small corrective fellowship of other Christians like that of the infant Church in Acts 5. What was still missing in the late nineteenth century was a body of wisdom concerning the Holy Spirit movement and the Scriptural teaching of group submission. Recent experience is teaching us that as we go adventuring in the Spirit, we must deliberately make ourselves subject one to the other, be willing to be checked and corrected as well as encouraged and strengthened.

Thinking back to his own bubbling joy that memorable night in Chappaqua, Leonard commented, 'It was heady stuff. No wonder people at Pentecost thought the disciples were full of new wine! No wonder Robert Pearsall Smith got himself in trouble! I have no intention of stopping at this point, just with waves of emotion, I mean. The emotion's great, but — well, a quiet day-by-day rooting and grounding in love and obedience is far more important.'

The excising of Hannah Smith's chapter on the Holy Spirit points up the real question, why are we afraid of the Helper?

Something that happened to Elizabeth and John Sherrill illustrates just how fearful our society can be. In 1962 the Sherrills published *The Cross And The Switchblade*, the previous mentioned story of David Wilkerson's work with New York drug addicts and warring gangs. For religious circles the book was clearly a departure necessarily depicting foul lives and some raw violence. The question in the Sherrills' minds was, would the public really be interested in reading about drug addiction in the big city? In those years it seemed like a remote sort of subject.

The publisher received a large order from one of the major denominational accounts. However, a condition was attached to the order: two chapters — 21 and 22 — which described the Baptism in the Holy Spirit, must be deleted 'because such material would not be acceptable to our readers'. The crime and violence the Sherrills had worried about was apparently perfectly permissible; it was the Spirit which was suspect!

The order was a temptation because the number of books in question was so large and the title was not expected to sell well. However, to Wilkerson and the Sherrills, these chapters on the Baptism contained the point of the book, the secret of the amazing success of Wilkerson's work. To hold out a promise of help and then not tell how to obtain it would have been cheating. They declined to make the deletions. As it turned out, *The Cross And The Switchblade*, with the 'unacceptable' chapters, became one of the best-selling religious books of the decade — including enormous sales to the denomination in question. To date *The Cross And The Switchblade* has sold a total of eleven million copies, domestic and foreign.

Some of us are afraid. Could we be terrified that if we invite the Holy Spirit into our hearts, we will lose control of our own emotions or the guidance of our individual life? Or are we afraid that the comfortable structures we have known may be altered or even blown to bits? Still others say they want to stay in safe areas that won't offend anybody, thus avoiding controversy and divisiveness.

There are dozens of theological dug-outs in which people hide, such as 'When I became a Christian I received everything there is to receive.' Or, 'All those experiences in the Book of the Acts were just for the first century. Our time is different. We don't have the same needs today.' Or again, one hears over and over, 'I want my faith to remain middle-of-the-road *orthodox* Christianity. That's good enough for me.'

The odd part of this latter statement is that I can think of nothing more central to Christianity or 'orthodox' than the doctrine of the Trinity: God, our Father; Jesus, our Saviour and Friend; the Holy Spirit — Comforter, Counsellor, and Helper who mediates the Father and our Lord to us. What Jesus Himself taught us must be central to 'Christianity'. Since He Himself bade us 'Be filled with the Spirit' and told us that He personally would be the Baptiser, we can't very well extirpate the Third Person of the Trinity and still be 'orthodox'.

Part of our fear may also be that instinctively we know that the Spirit means power, and power makes all of us acutely uneasy. We're like people who have always lived with candles and camp-fires. We've heard rumours of electricity, but because we've never seen electric lights and are not certain we would know how to handle electric power, we'd rather make do with candles all our days.

As for our churches, they must choose whether they wish to remain ecclesiastical monuments to Christ as just another historical figure — a great teacher whose brief life was cut short in 29 or 30 A.D. (Those churches would be limited to such things as liturgy, organisations, and a degree of social action.) Or the alternative is the church as the close fellowship of followers of the living Christ, the contemporary Lord, that fellowship made alive and operative by His Spirit and marching to His now-orders.

Until the surge of the Spirit began in the 1960s, far too many churches had chosen to be ecclesiastical monuments. A churchman like Dr. Carl Henry has warned about the danger of making the Holy Spirit 'a displaced person': 'Whenever the

Church makes the Spirit of God a refugee,' Dr. Henry wrote,
'the Church — not the Spirit — becomes the vagabond.'

Once we understand what Jesus told us would happen in the
Era of the Spirit, we next ask, are these miracles of grace,
restoration, guidance, new teaching, healing, rescuing, and all
the rest actually happening today?

The account of what took place in the life of someone like
Tay Thomas points up what a resounding 'Yes' can be
answered to this. Tay is Mrs. Lowell Thomas, Jr.; her husband
is the son of the famed radio and television commentator and
world traveller. The Thomases live in Alaska where Lowell is
one of Alaska's state senators.

Good Friday, 1964 began as such a happy day for the
Thomas family. The snow which had been coming down steadily for two days finally let up. Lowell could fly from Spenard to
a meeting in Fairbanks, and get back so that the family could
spend Easter together. David Thomas was then six; Anne,
eight. The story is best told in Tay's own words:[27]

'The children and I waved goodbye as Lowell drove off to
the airport, then shut the door quickly because it was still below
freezing outside. About five o'clock, feeling lonesome for him,
Anne, David, and I went upstairs to watch TV. We took off our
shoes so we could sit on the bed.

'It was half an hour later that I heard a rumbling sound.
Although we frequently hear a similar roaring — the firing of
guns at a near-by Army base — I knew instantly that these
were no guns.

'I leapt off the bed, yelling "Earthquake!" Grabbing Anne, I
called to David. We had got as far as the front hall when the
house began to shake. As we ran outside into the snow, David
was crying, "Mommy, I'm in bare feet!"

'We were about ten feet beyond the front door when we were
flung violently to the ground which was jolting back and forth

with unbelievable force. The hallway through which we had just run split in two. We heard the crashing of glass, the ear-rending sound of splintering wood. In front of us a great tree crashed full length. Our garage collapsed with a sharp report.

'Now the earth began breaking up and buckling all about us. Suddenly between Anne and me a great crack opened in the snow. I stared in disbelief as the trench widened, apparently bottomless, separating me from my child. I seized the hand she stretched out to me in time to pull her across the chasm.

'We were left on a wildly-bucking slab. Suddenly it tilted sharply, and we had to hang on to keep from slipping into a yawning crevasse. Now the earth seemed to be rising just ahead of us. I had the weird feeling that we were riding backwards on a monstrous Ferris wheel, going down, down towards the water (our house had stood on a high bluff overlooking Cook Inlet). The entire face of the bluff had fallen to sea level. A few feet away, at the water's edge, lay the roof of our house.

'All I could think of was that the water would rise as earth tumbled into it and we would be trapped. The cliffs above us were sheer, with great sections of sand and clay still falling.

'The children both were hysterical, crying over and over, "We'll die! We'll die!" I realised we'd have to find a way up that cliff, but the children were too frightened to walk.

'I looked up at the leaden grey sky, the bleak clouds, and silently cried out, "Jesus, where are You — I thought You'd be with us at the end." *Suddenly, I felt a sense of peace so intense that I knew beyond all doubt He was with me — not way up in the air, but right there inside me.* It was a revelation that gave me a tremendous courage.

'We clambered up and down the great slabs of earth and snow, our bare feet aching and raw in the cold. I found a large tree leaning against the cliff and thought for a few moments that we might be able to shinny up it, but we gained only a few feet.

'Suddenly a man appeared above us. "Help!" we called to him. He shouted down that he would hunt for a rope, then disappeared. As we waited we were aware for the first time that we were soaked to the skin, the children shaking and their lips blue.

'At last six or eight men appeared at the top of the cliff. One of them, a stranger to us, started down, finding one less steep spot. The children threw their arms around him as he reached us. He took off his black wool jacket, put it around Anne, then boosted David into his arms and led us all back up along the rope. At the top, when I turned to thank our rescuer, he had gone.'

Tay Thomas went on to describe the mounting suspense during the hours when Lowell and his family could not communicate; then the drama of their reunion. For so many hours Lowell had not known whether his family was dead or alive.

The earthquake experience bound families and neighbours together as never before. For Tay it was another in a series of spiritual adventures that have been part of her life's search.

In 1954 she and her husband had flown around the world together in a single-engine Cessna plane named 'Charlie'. They spent long days with bearded Afghan nomads and Pygmies of the Congo; they sailed in a primitive dhow on the Persian Gulf; they put in an appearance at the birthday ball of the Emperor of Abyssinia.

On the dashboard of the plane Tay had pasted this poem:

> Peace be in thy home
>   And in thy heart.
> Or if thou roam
>   Earth's highways wide,
> The Lord is at thy side,
>   To bless and guide.

In 1958 the Thomases had put three-year-old Anne in 'Charlie's' back seat and taken off on three months' work on a television film documentary on Alaska, the new 49th state. It was an area pulsing with vitality, full of the promise of the frontier and of undeveloped resources. Tay's book *Follow The North Star* is a vivid account of travelling in a small plane through wilderness areas with a small child.

Out of this trip had come the Thomases' decision in 1960 to make Alaska their home. Soon Lowell was elected a state senator, Tay to the Anchorage School Board, and to the important Land Use Planning Commission.

Tay's spiritual search had begun two years after the move to Alaska. In her own words . . .

'My family, the Sam Pryors, had been lifelong Episcopalians in the traditional manner. But intermittent years of roaming the world had deprived Lowell and me of a church home. Then I suddenly realised that the children were old enough for Sunday School and the time had come to find a church. Within a few weeks I found our second home — St. Mary's Episcopal Church, a small wooden structure sitting on a hilltop, with windows looking out over our magnificent mountains. But it wasn't the building that won us over — it was a warm, loving, informal congregation and pastor. To me, St. Mary's meant the finding of my "faith ladder".

'In 1963 I climbed up the first of two most important rungs. It happened the night I heard the visiting pastor, Dennis Bennett, talk in a crowded school auditorium. My whole life was changed that night.

'While driving home I realised that Christianity wasn't just going to church on Sunday and trying to follow the Ten Commandments — that I actually had to commit my life to Jesus, to give up all of my own personal ambitions and desires and let Him take over, using me in whatever way He saw fit. At first I was frightened, scared to death of letting go the "command" of my own life. But I did, talking to Him while driving, "I am Yours, Lord, do with me what You wish." My fear was suddenly replaced by such a joyful, peaceful feeling that I sang praises all the way home.

'Once I had climbed on to that first rung of my faith ladder, life changed in many ways. I was happier, I prayed informally often, all during the day whenever I felt the need for support or guidance, and with missionary zeal I plunged headlong into a massive load of community social work.

'I'm so grateful that I had achieved that first rung of the ladder before the trauma of the earthquake. But it was traumatic, and while it taught me that God is a present power, I knew that I needed something more. That was when I embarked on my search for what step would take me up the second rung of my ladder. The second part of the search took almost five years.

'One day after many hours of reading and searching through the Bible, the answer came to me. The original apostles had Jesus as their constant companion and guide, but when He was about to leave them, He promised to send the Comforter, one who would continue to be with them in everything they did — the Holy Spirit. I had always considered the biblical story of the day of Pentecost as an historical happening, but now, as I read through the letters of St. Paul, I knew I was wrong — the Holy Spirit had been promised to all people for all time, bringing to all believers the same gifts and fruits of the Spirit as in those earliest Christian days.

'I longed to be filled with the Holy Spirit because I could see what His presence was doing for friends and for the many Spirit-filled people I was reading about. But who isn't afraid of the supernatural!

'As I prayed more and more about my dilemma, one Sunday our minister announced that there would be a Wednesday evening prayer meeting at the home of a parishioner and his wife whom I knew were having real experiences of the Spirit. I had the immediate realisation that here was my chance to step up on to that next rung of the faith ladder. I was so excited that by Wednesday I was ready for anything — all reticence gone. An uncanny coincidence of timing, perhaps, but I still think that Jesus has His eye on our movements up that ladder.

'That night I received the laying on of hands, felt the joyful inpouring of the Holy Spirit. Needless to say, my elation increased until I thought I'd burst with joy, a state of euphoria which lasted for several weeks. Once I had returned to a more normal emotional level, I realised that many startling changes in my life were coming one after another. I knew that Jesus was now a close personal Friend, that same closeness which I had experienced briefly during the earthquake. I felt a great strengthening of my private prayer life — I could now talk to and praise God in a way and a language I'd never known before. I am also learning to listen to that "still small voice" and discovering that prayers are being answered, but not always in the way I want or expect. I am seeing miraculous healing through prayer, and have experienced it myself. When I face up to my many former fears now, they vanish. And I feel a new relationship to other people, a deeper love and understanding which has helped immeasurably in my community work — the old anger, frustration and irritation are gone, leaving me more energy and enthusiasm.

'And one of the changes that startled me most had to do with my old reticent Episcopal solemnness towards worship in church. I had resisted the folk mass, the new liturgy, the general informality of worship. I wanted to go to the altar for Communion in reverent silence, to pray quietly by isolating myself in the pew. Now I am in the midst of the loudest singing during services, the words of the prayers, old and new, have taken on a deeper meaning, and I almost dance as I go up to the altar. I often hug my neighbours sitting around me and feel a togetherness in worship I'd never known before. I have laughed and cried as never before during folk masses and at retreats, and I feel, along with this great release of emotions, a readiness to share this new growth of my faith with others.'

Tay Thomas has been amazed at what has been happening in her state. 'In just the last five years,' she wrote us recently, 'the Holy Spirit has roared through Alaska from the Panhandle to the tiny Arctic villages. Many churches are open about the wonderful experiences felt by so many people of all denominations.

'I don't see how this tremendous and exciting Power can be stopped when it is so clearly supported by the Bible and so firmly supported by so many "conservative" people of traditional background. Anyway, as for me I feel strongly that it's time for me to speak up and be counted.

'We're told there was an earthquake on the First Good Friday too. But then dawned the calm and the victory of Resurrection morning. What happened on the first Easter morning made possible all the good that has come out of our Good Friday earthquake, for me perfectly captured in lines from an old hymn:

> Speak through the earthquake, wind and fire,
> O still, small voice of calm.

There is a sense in which every page of this book is about the Helper. Jesus told us He would send Him to us — and He has. As Comforter and Teacher He was with Edith and Peter John and me in that little Cessna 205, tenderly brooding over Peter Christopher's tiny white casket, saying to us, 'I have many things to teach you. Walk softly, with heads up. This too will teach you . . .'

Nancy De Moss's friend Ginny learned what Jesus meant when He promised, 'He — the Spirit — will tell you about the future.' The Helper knew about that fire. The baby Brandon must be saved. 'Go and get Brandon,' He directed Ginny.

'It's the risk in *not* obeying the Helper that gives me the shivers now,' Nancy De Moss reflects.

That day in the little church, the Spirit came to Pat Baker in His role as Counsellor. He spoke through the young preacher's lips, 'He's ready to deal with your problem of nicotine.'

How does he know that?

'It started when you were a teenager. The problem grew out of the soil of rebellion.'

So He does know! Wise Counsellor ...

That bitterly cold winter in Oregon it was the Helper who rescued Carrie and Jeff Buddington and their friends by alerting the men up the road in the Christian community, 'Go — and saw wood.'

'Saw wood, Lord?'

'Yes, saw wood. I was a carpenter, I know all about wood. Remember? But the woodpile will be only the beginning ...'

Or I think of Jean Klinger and Roberta Lashley who got an intimate look at how swiftly and ingeniously the Helper comes to protect from immediate danger those who ask Him, even as David Livingstone experienced the same protection a century ago in Africa.

And Maude Blanford, so grievously ill of cancer, knows now how surely Jesus fulfils His promises about the Helper. 'He, the Spirit of truth, is come, He will guide you into all truth.'

'The truth is,' the Helper told Maude, 'your life is in danger. See, your body-house has no roof. Without Jesus as your covering, you have no protection.'

'But how do I get the roof back on my body-house?'

'Here I am — I, the Lord thy God, to loose the bonds, to let the oppressed go free. I will lead you out step by step.'

'Yes, a healthy Maude Blanford knows that the Spirit is also this, the Great Physician, Lord of the body ...

You and I are living in rough times. We must make our way through minefields of evil, booby traps of deception, brush fires of sickness and disease, wastelands of economic disaster, burning deserts of disappointment. 'I won't take you out of this world,' Jesus told us. 'But don't be afraid because I've overcome that world of dangers. All power is Mine. I promise to be with you always.'

'How, Lord? How are you with us?'

'Through the Helper.'

It is true. He is here. We who in moments of desperation have asked, 'What can I do? What is there left?' have felt His answering presence and experienced His help ... We know now ... always He holds out to us the exciting promise of something more.

NOTES

Chapter 1   *Yes, God Is in Everything*

1. Acts 4: 20
2. Job 1: 21
3. Hannah W. Smith, *The Christian's Secret of a Happy Life* (Westwood, N. J.: Fleming H. Revell Company, 1962), pp. 148, 149
4. I Thessalonians 5: 18
5. Hannah W. Smith, *The Christian's Secret of a Happy Life*, pp. 144, 146, 147, 149
6. Romans 8: 28
7. Shakespeare, *Hamlet IV*. v. 78.
8. This story and other examples of relinquishment are included in Catherine Marshall's *Beyond Our Selves* (New York: McGraw-Hill Book Company, 1961), ch. 6, 'The Prayer of Relinquishment.'
9. Luke 18: 10–14
10. Matthew 10: 29–31
11. Matthew 25: 37–46
12. Acts 9: 4, 5
13. Matthew 18: 5
14. Frank C. Laubach, *You Are My Friends* (New York: Harper and Row, 1942), p. 22
15. Mark 1: 40, James Moffatt, *A New Translation of the Bible*, New York
16. Matthew 18: 12–14

Chapter 2   *The Golden Bridge of Praise*

1. Merlin R. Carothers, *Prison to Praise* (London: Hodder and Stoughton, 1971)
2. Psalm 22: 3
3. I Thessalonians 5: 16–18
4. Colossians 4: 2
5. See also I Peter 2: 9; Philippians 4: 4–6; Romans 1: 21
6. Hebrews 13: 15
7. *Random House Dictionary of the English Language* (New York: Random House, 1966, 1967)
8. Habakkuk 3: 17, 18
9. II Chronicles 20: 21, 22
10. The Acts 16: 19–40
11. Luke 10: 20
12. Isaiah 12: 2, 3
13. Philippians 4: 11 (Revised Standard Version)
14. Philippians 4: 4–6
15. II Corinthians 11: 23–30
16. Ephesians 5: 20
17. This incident has also been told in Corrie Ten Boom's *The Hiding Place* (London: Hodder and Stoughton, 1971) pp. 180–81
18. Though the material here (and at several other places) is set in much the same style as Peter Marshall's sermons, I have borrowed the style but not the material

Chapter 3   *Forgiveness: The Aughts and the Anys*

1. Mark 11: 25
2. John 16: 8
3. Catherine Marshall, *Beyond Our Selves*, pp. 47–48
4. Matthew 18: 18
5. Matthew 22: 37, 38 *The Living Bible* (Wheaton, Illinois: Tyndale House Publishers, 1971)

6. Luke 15: 25–32
7. Matthew 17: 20

Chapter 4   *The Law of the Generations*

1. Deuteronomy 28: 41
2. Biblical scholars agree that Moses' towering spirit, along with his remembered and recorded words, were the inspiration for Deuteronomy. As usual, there is disagreement about the actual date of the book. Some would place it as late as Josiah's reign, about 638 B.C. Others offer evidence that the book discovered in the Temple and read to the people as told in II Kings 22, 23 was the book of Deuteronomy
3. Deuteronomy 30: 15, 19 *The Amplified Bible* (Grand Rapids: Zondervan Publishing House, 1965)
4. Romans 12: 5
5. Exodus 20: 5
6. Malachi 4: 6
7. Ephesians 6: 17, 18
8. Hebrews 4: 12
9. Luke 4: 18
10. II Corinthians 3: 17
11. Romans 8: 21
12. Starr Daily, *God's Answer to Juvenile Delinquency* (St. Paul, Minnesota: Macalester Park Publishing Company, 1953), pp. 43–51; 132–142
13. Matthew 18: 19
14. Matthew 6: 4
15. Starr Daily, *Love Can Open Prison Doors* (Worcester, England, Arthur James, 1943), *Release* (New York, Harper and Row, 1942), *Faith, Hope, and Love* (St. Paul, Minnesota, Macalester Park)
16. Matthew 6: 33
17. Acts 10: 28
18. This and the material that follows is taken from Elisabeth D. Dodds' *Marriage to a Difficult Man* (Philadelphia: The Westminster Press, 1971)

19. Exodus 20: 6
20. Acts 2: 39

Chapter 5   *The Joy of Obedience*

1. Art De Moss is founder of National Liberty Corporation, a life insurance company
2. Matthew 7: 24, 25
3. John 14: 21-23
4. Hebrews 5: 9
5. John 7: 17
6. Matthew 12: 50
7. John 14: 23
8. John 14: 21
9. Acts 5: 32
10. James 1: 25; I John 3: 22
11. John 14: 21
12. Titus 3: 1; I Peter 2: 13-17; Romans 13: 1, 2; John 19: 11
13. I Peter 5: 5
14. Hebrews 13: 17; I Peter 5: 1-5
15. I Corinthians 11: 3
16. Ephesians 5: 21-24; I Peter 3: 7; I Samuel 3: 13
17. Ephesians 5: 25-33; I Peter 3: 1-7
18. Colossians 3: 20
19. C. S. Lewis, *The Screwtape Letters* (London: Geoffrey Bles)
20. The existence of both a sleep system and a wakefulness (activating) system in the brain is now generally acknowledged. The sleep inducing mechanisms have been experimentally demonstrated in the lower brain stem, the descending limbic hypnogenic circuit, and the neo-cortex; the reticular arousal system is thought to be in the brain stem. For more on this, see J. Edward Murray, *Sleep, Dreams and Arousal* (New York: Appleton-Century-Crofts, 1965)
21. Such as the sleep experiments of the Sleep Research and Treatment Facility of the Milton S. Hershey Medical Center, Hershey, Pennsylvania

22. Hymn 'Blessed Assurance' by Fanny J. Crosby
23. Hannah W. Smith, *The Christian's Secret of a Happy life,* p. 208
24. Genesis 12: 1, 2

Chapter 6   *'To Sleep! Perchance to Dream ...'*

1. Numbers 12: 6, 8 (Revised Standard Version)
2. Matthew 27: 19
3. Research typical of sleep laboratories is the research of Dr. Charles Fisher as summarised in 'Psychoanalytic Implications of Recent Research on Sleep,' *Journal of the American Psychoanalytic Association,* Vol. 13, p. 20 (April 1965)
4. Morton Kelsey, *God, Dreams and Revelation, A Christian Interpretation of Dreams* (Minneapolis: Augsburg Publishing House, 1968, 1974)
5. John A. Sanford, *Dreams: God's Forgotten Language* (Philadelphia: J. B. Lippincott Company, 1968)
6. John 2: 25
7. See pp. 101–106
8. Glenn Clark, *How to Find Health through Prayer* (New York: Harper and Row, 1940), pp. 105–108
9. Lewis' fiction works (New York: Macmillan) include *Out of the Silent Planet; Perelandra; That Hideous Strength; Till We Have Faces*
10. See p. 99
11. See pp. 100–101
12. Joel 2: 28; Acts 2: 17

Chapter 7   *The Fallen Angel*

1. C. S. Lewis, *The Case for Christianity* (New York: The Macmillan Company, 1943), p. 40
2. Isaiah 14: 12–14

3. Revelation 12: 4
4. For a summary of current research in an effort to solve the mysteries of memory, learning, and consciousness, see 'Exploring the Frontiers of the Mind,' *Time* (January 14th, 1974)
5. Genesis 3: 5
6. Genesis 1: 28
7. Hebrews 2: 7, 8 is quoted from Psalm 8: 5, 6
8. Matthew 4: 4
9. Edna St. Vincent Millay, *Wine from These Grapes* (New York: Harper and Row, 1934), p. 91
10. C. S. Lewis, *The Screwtape Letters* (London: Geoffrey Bles, 1942)
11. John 12: 19
12. Derek Prince, 'Spiritual Conflict' (from the Cassette Teaching Series, Derek Prince Publications, Fort Lauderdale, Florida)
13. John 18: 37
14. C. S. Lewis, *The Case for Christianity*, pp. 55, 56
15. Ephesians 6: 12, 13, *The Living Bible* (London: Coverdale House Publishers, 1971)

Chapter 8   *The Unholy Spirit*

1. Out of this interview also came Catherine Marshall's 'An Answer to Drugs,' *Guideposts* (May 1970)
2. Lysergic-Diethylamide (LSD)
3. The Amphetamine drugs
4. *Life* (July 18th, 1969)
5. *Time* (February 11th, 1974) and *Newsweek* (February 11th, 1974)
6. Zechariah 12–14
7–9. This and the quotation from the graduate student and from Professor Eliade are from Andrew M. Greeley, 'There's A New-Time Religion on Campus,' *New York Times* (June 1st, 1969)

10. I Peter 5: 8
11. John 8: 44
12. Luke 13: 16; Mark 9: 25, 26
13. Job 1: 2, 5, 18, 19
14. Job 1: 9–11
15. Derek Prince, 'Deliverance and Demonology' from the Cassette Teaching Series, Derek Prince Publications, Fort Lauderdale, Florida
16. James 4: 7
17. I Corinthians 10: 13
18. Matthew 28: 18
19. John 8: 34
20. John 14: 30
21. Romans 13: 12
22. Isaiah 9: 2
23. Ephesians 5: 8
24. Joshua 7: 11–13
25. John 3: 20, 21
26. Luke 8: 28
27. II Peter 2: 9 (*The Living Bible*)
28. Luke 10: 19
29. Revelation 3: 10
30. I John 1: 7–9
31. Colossians 2: 14, 15 (Moffatt)
32. Catherine Marshall, *A Man Called Peter* (London: Peter Davies, 1951), pp. 120, 121

Chapter 9   *The Enigma of Healing*

1. As this book goes to press, Kent Ghost is still an out-patient at NIH at Bethesda, Maryland, U.S.A. The happy ending of the February, 1966 crisis was but one of many episodes in an eight-year battle with leukaemia. The end of the story is not yet. C.M.
2. John 6: 38; 14: 9
3. Acts 10: 38

4. Luke 4: 18; Matthew 4: 23; Matthew 12: 15
5. John 5: 1–14
6. Luke 5: 12, 13; Mark 9: 22–24
7. Matthew 5: 3–11
8. III John 2
9. John 14: 12. See also Mark 16: 15–18; Hebrews 13: 8
10. Matthew 8: 16–17; Mark 3: 7–11; 6: 53–56; Luke 6: 17–19
11. Mark 3: 1–5
12. John 5: 1–14
13. Romans 3: 23
14. Deuteronomy 9: 5
15. Titus 3: 5
16. John 5: 14 (*The Living Bible*)
17–18. One compilation of these case histories: Ruth Cranston, *The Miracle of Lourdes* (New York: McGraw-Hill Book Company, 1955)
19. Dr. Carrel's own account of this is: Alexis Carrel, *The Voyage to Lourdes* (New York: Harper and Row, 1950)
20. Catherine Marshall, *A Man Called Peter*, pp. 175–77

Chapter 10   *The Roof on the House*

1. John 16: 13
2. Isaiah 64: 6
3. Romans 3: 20; Philippians 3: 8, 9
4. John 5: 19
5. John 8: 29; 15: 30
6. John 6: 38 (Moffatt)
7. John 4: 34
8. For other instances of relinquishment, see Catherine Marshall, *Beyond Our Selves*, chapter 6
9. Fritz Kunkel and Roye E. Dickerson, *How Character Develops* (New York: Charles Scribner's Sons, 1944), pp. 116, 120
10. Luke 8: 43–48
11. Mark 2: 1–12

12. Luke 18: 1–8
13. Matthew 4: 4; 6, 7
14. John 5: 19 (*The Living Bible*)
15. Luke 10: 9

Chapter 11   *The King's Treasury*

1. Edith Schaeffer, *L'Abri* (London: Norfolk Press, 1969). Other books by Mrs. Schaeffer describing the L'Abri community are *Hidden Art* and *Everybody Can Know*

2. Francis Schaeffer, *The God Who Is There* (London: Hodder and Stoughton, 1968). Dr. Schaeffer is also the author of thirteen other books including *Escape from Reason, Death in the City, True Spirituality, The Church at the End of the 20th Century, He Is There and He Is Not Silent, Pollution and the Death of Man*

3. Philippians 2: 5

4. In late 1973 after nineteen years of living with almost no privacy in the Chalet les Mélèzes, the Schaeffers now have a private home. Yet typically they wrote me, 'At last we have the space to share in a new way with endless teas, meals, conversations, meetings, Bible studies, discussion'.

5. Matthew 6: 33

6. Psalm 24: 1

7. I John 3: 1

8. Philippians 4: 19

9. Matthew 20: 30–32

10. Luke 6: 38

11. Malachi 3: 10

12. Peter Marshall, *Mr. Jones, Meet the Master* (London: Peter Davies, 1950)

Chapter 12   *The Dilemma of Our Rebellion*

1. I Corinthians 4: 5
2. Joyce Maynard, 'My Parents Are My Friends,' *McCall's* (October 1972)
3. This and the quotation that follows are from Agnes Sanford, *Sealed Orders* (Plainfield, New Jersey: Logos International, 1972), pp. 51, 52
4. Matthew 5: 21
5. Matthew 26: 52
6. Matthew 5: 22
7. Matthew 5: 25
8. Matthew 6: 15
9. Luke 6: 36 (*The Living Bible*)
10. Hebrews 1: 9
11. Luke 6: 27 (*The Living Bible*)
12. I Corinthians 10: 10, 11 (*The Living Bible*)
13. Numbers 14: 23, 25, 29, 32
14. Leviticus 26: 12 (*The Amplified Bible*)
15. *Guideposts* (November, 1973)
16. Proverbs 4: 23
17. W. H. Auden
18. Paul Tournier, *The Whole Person in a Broken World*
19. Walter Kaufmann, *Existentialism from Dostoevsky to Sartre* (New York: The World Publishing Company, 1956)
20. Mark 7: 14–23 (*The Living Bible*)
21. Matthew 5: 22
22. Ezekiel 36: 26, 27
23. Isaiah 60: 18

Chapter 13   *Run for the Strong Tower*

1. David Shaw and Bill Hazlett, *The Miami Herald* (January 7th, 1973)
2. *Guideposts* (November, 1966)

3. John 3: 20
4. Colossians 1: 16; John 1: 3
5. Romans 13: 12
6. Proverbs 18: 10
7. Matthew 28: 18
8. John 14: 13
9. Luke 10: 17
10. *Guideposts* (December, 1965)
11. Lyric by C. D. Martin, Hymn *God Will Take Care of You*
12. Schapera, ed., *Livingstone's African Journal*, 1853–1856, 2 vols., (London: Chatto and Windus) 1963, vol. II, p. 374
13. Hunter B. Blakely, *Religion in Shoes* (Richmond, Virginia: John Knox Press, 1953), pp. 89, 90
14. II Timothy 1: 7
15. Romans 8: 15
16. John 3: 17
17. Matthew 6: 30 (Moffatt)
18. Matthew 8: 26 (Moffatt)
19. Ralph I. Woods, *The Modern Handbook of Humor* (New York: McGraw-Hill, 1967, p. 471)
20. *The Scarlet Fish and Other Stories* (Author unknown)
21. Ephesians 6: 12 (*The Living Bible*)
22. Catherine Marshall, *To Live Again* (New York: McGraw-Hill, 1957), pp. 299–325, and *Beyond Our Selves*, pp. 247–256
23. I John 1: 7–9 (*The Living Bible*)
24. Romans 13: 12
25. Ephesians 6: 16

Chapter 14 *The Helper*

1. *Time* (June 18th, 1973), p. 91
2. John 17: 20
3. John 16: 7
4. Acts 1: 4, 5; 2: 17
5. John 1: 33b; Mark 1: 8; Matthew 3: 11

6. John 14: 17; Galatians 2: 20; I Corinthians 6: 19; John 15: 18–26

7. John 7: 39; 16: 7; Matthew 24: 14, 30, 31

8. John 15: 26; 16: 13, 14

9. Mark 16: 15 (*The Living Bible*) John 14: 12

10. *Teacher:* John 14: 26; Luke 12: 12; I Corinthians 2: 13
    Guide: Romans 8: 14
    Comforter: John 14: 16, 26
    Counsellor: Matthew 10: 19, 20
    Prayer-Intercessor: Romans 8: 26, 27
    Giver of Joy: Romans 14: 17; I Thessalonians 1: 6
    Giver of Freedom: Romans 8: 2
    Giver of Spiritual Gifts: I Corinthians 12: 4–11; 27, 28; Hebrews 2: 4
    Giver of Eternal Life: Ephesians 1: 13, 14; Galatians 6: 8

11. Ephesians 1: 22, 23; Romans 12: 4, 5

12. John 14: 17; 15: 20

13. Mark 16: 15 (*The Living Bible*)

14. Acts 1: 4

15. John 14: 21

16. John 16: 13

17. Acts 11: 1–10

18. Acts 11: 11–18

19. Catherine Marshall, *Beyond Our Selves*, chapter 14, 'Journey into Joy,' pp. 227–46

20. II Timothy 3: 5

21. John 3: 5, 6; Romans 8: 9; Galatians 4: 6

22. Hannah W. Smith, *The Christian's Secret of a Happy Life* (Boston: Willard Tract Repository, 1885), p. 249.

23. Acts 5: 1–11

24. *Philadelphia Quaker, The Letters of Hannah Whitehall Smith* (New York: Harcourt, Brace and Company, 1950)
    Logan Pearsall Smith, *Unforgotten Years* (Boston: Little, Brown and Company, 1939), pp. 29, 30
    Ray Strachey, *Group Movements of the Past and Experiments in Guidance* (London: Faber and Faber, Limited, 1928)

Robert Allerton Parkes, *The Transatlantic Smiths* (New York: Random House, 1959)

25. This summary of the Smiths' experience together with the exact quotations are taken from Hannah W. Smith, *My Spiritual Autobiography or How I Discovered the Unselfishness of God* (New York: Fleming H. Revell Company, 1903), pp. 288–96

26. Letter to Mrs. Henry Ford Barclay, June 3rd, 1876, Hannah W. Smith, *Letters*, pp. 29, 30

27. This portion of Tay Thomas' story was written originally for *Guideposts* (April 1965). Used by permission

28. 'Dear Lord and Father of Mankind,' lyric by John Greenleaf Whittier